READING with PICTURES

COMICS THAT MAKE KIDS SMARTER!

READING with PICTURES

COMICS THAT MAKE KIDS SMARTER!

READING with PICTURES

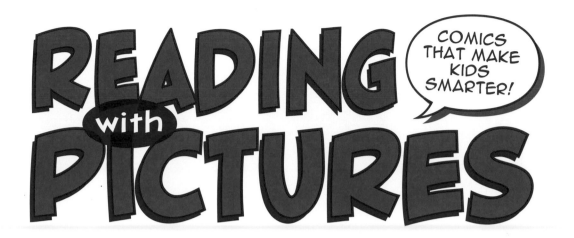

Josh Elder
Founder, Reading With Pictures

Andrews McMeel Publishing

Kansas City • Sydney • London

CONTENTS

LANGUAGE ARTS

SCIENCE

VIII

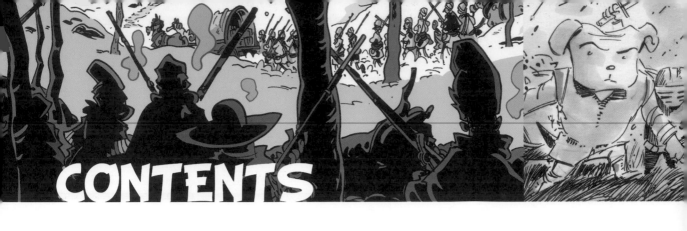

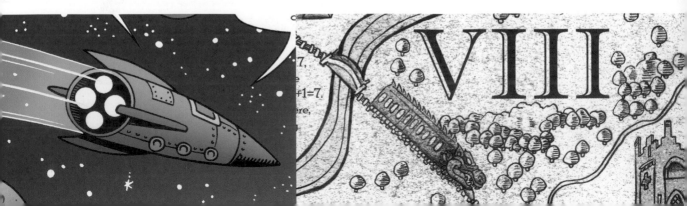

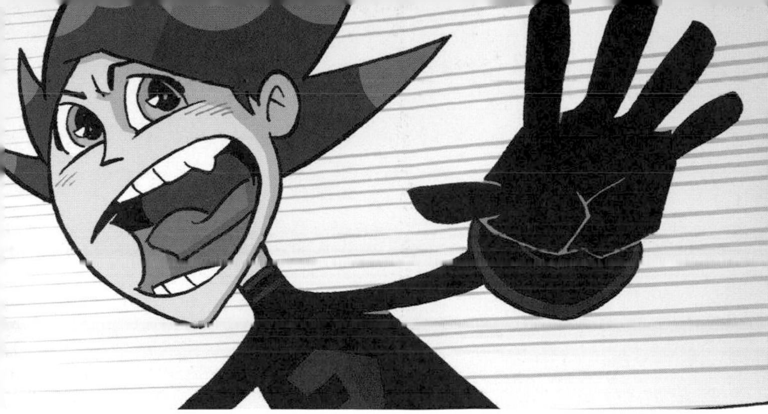
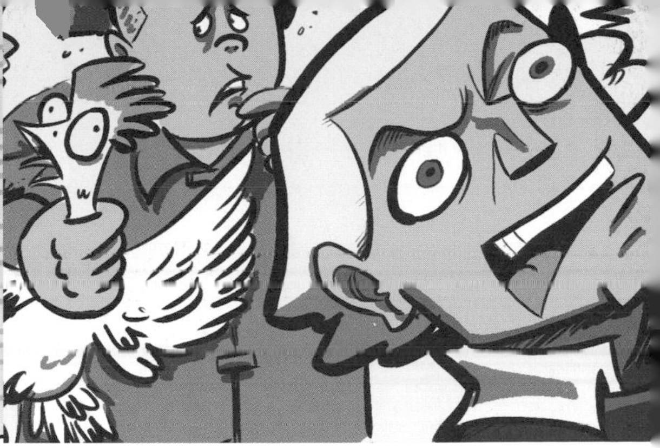

MATHEMATICS

SOCIAL STUDIES

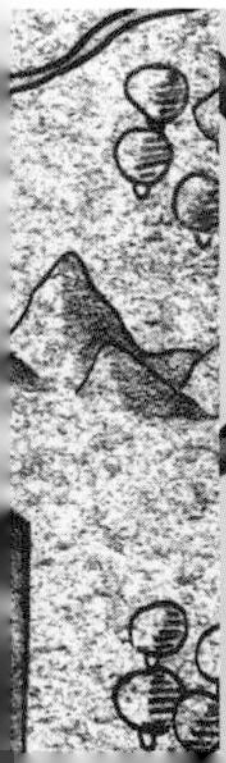
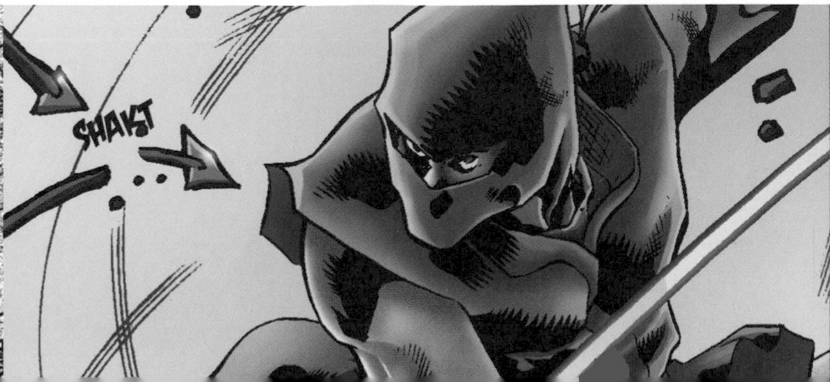

SHAKT

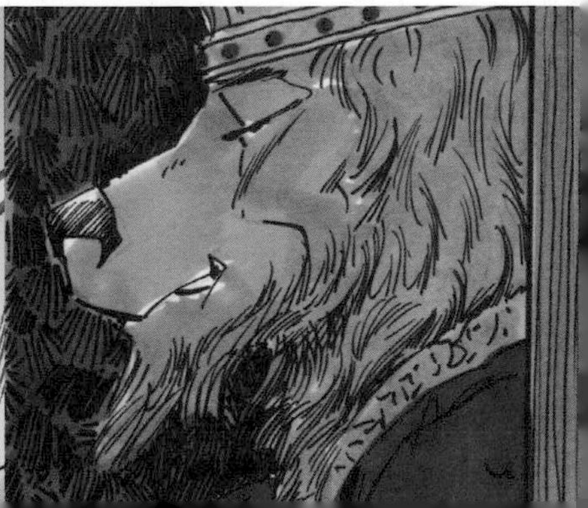

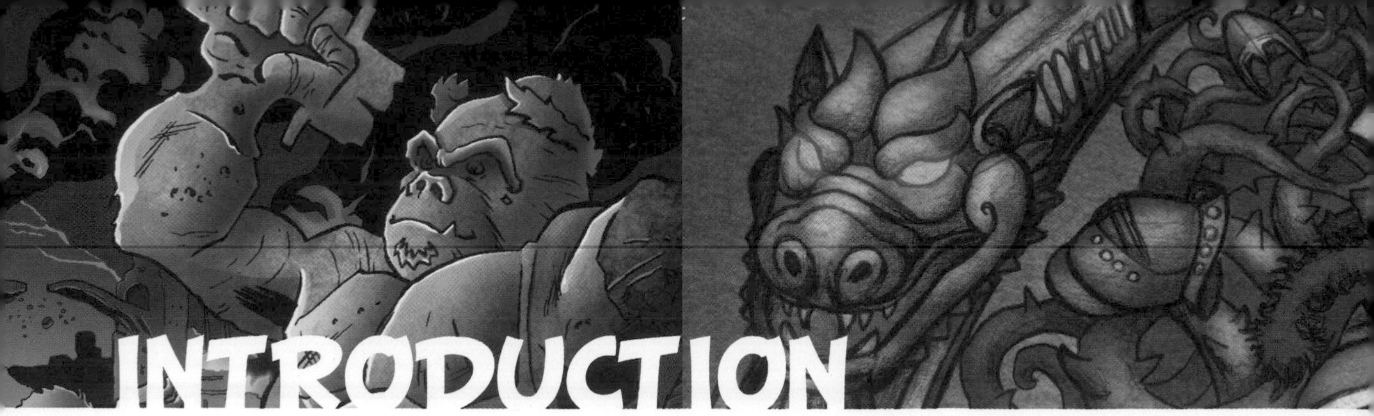

INTRODUCTION

THE SECRET ORIGIN OF THIS BOOK

I first learned to read—and more important, to *love* reading—because of comics. Comics made reading easy, and they made reading fun. So much so that by the fifth grade, I was reading at a college level. By the seventh grade, I was taking college courses on nights and weekends. I attended Northwestern University on a National Merit Scholarship and went on to a successful media career working in comics, prose, video games, and journalism.

In summation: Hooked on comics worked for me! And if comics worked for me, then they can work for everyone.

So I founded Reading With Pictures in 2009 in order to "get comics into schools and get schools into comics." In the years since, I've become a sort of "comics ambassador," traveling across the United States and around the world to speak in schools, libraries, and universities about the revolutionary potential of comics in the classroom. And while I may have been brought in as a speaker, I also made it a point to listen.

I listened when parents said they needed research to prove the educational value of comics. I listened when teachers said they needed lesson plans to make the most out of the comics in their classrooms. I listened when administrators said they needed high-quality content that *also* met state and national curriculum standards if they were going to justify the use of comics.

I listened, and Reading With Pictures listened. This book is our reply. I mean, it's right there in our mission statement:

WE COLLABORATE WITH CARTOONISTS TO PRODUCE EXCEPTIONAL GRAPHIC NOVEL CONTENT FOR SCHOLASTIC USE.

To that end, *Reading With Pictures: Comics That Make Kids Smarter* unites some of the finest creative talents in the comics industry with the nation's leading experts in visual literacy to create a book that is overflowing with awesomeness while also meeting the criteria necessary to be accepted as classroom curriculum. *Reading With Pictures* uses a comics format to make traditional educational content more engaging (especially to struggling readers), more efficient (for more advanced readers) and more effective (for all readers).

Aimed at grades three through six, *Reading With Pictures* features more than a dozen short stories (both fiction and nonfiction) that address topics in a variety of subject matter areas (Social Studies, Math, Language Arts, and Science) in concordance with a variety of educational standards. The accompanying Teachers' Guide (available to download for free at www.ampkids.com) includes standards-correlated lesson plans customized to each story, research-based justifications for using comics in the classroom, and a comprehensive guide to establishing best classroom practices.

Now you know what Reading With Pictures is and how it came to be. It's been an incredible journey thus far. We hope that you'll all join us for what comes next.

JOSH ELDER

FOREWORD

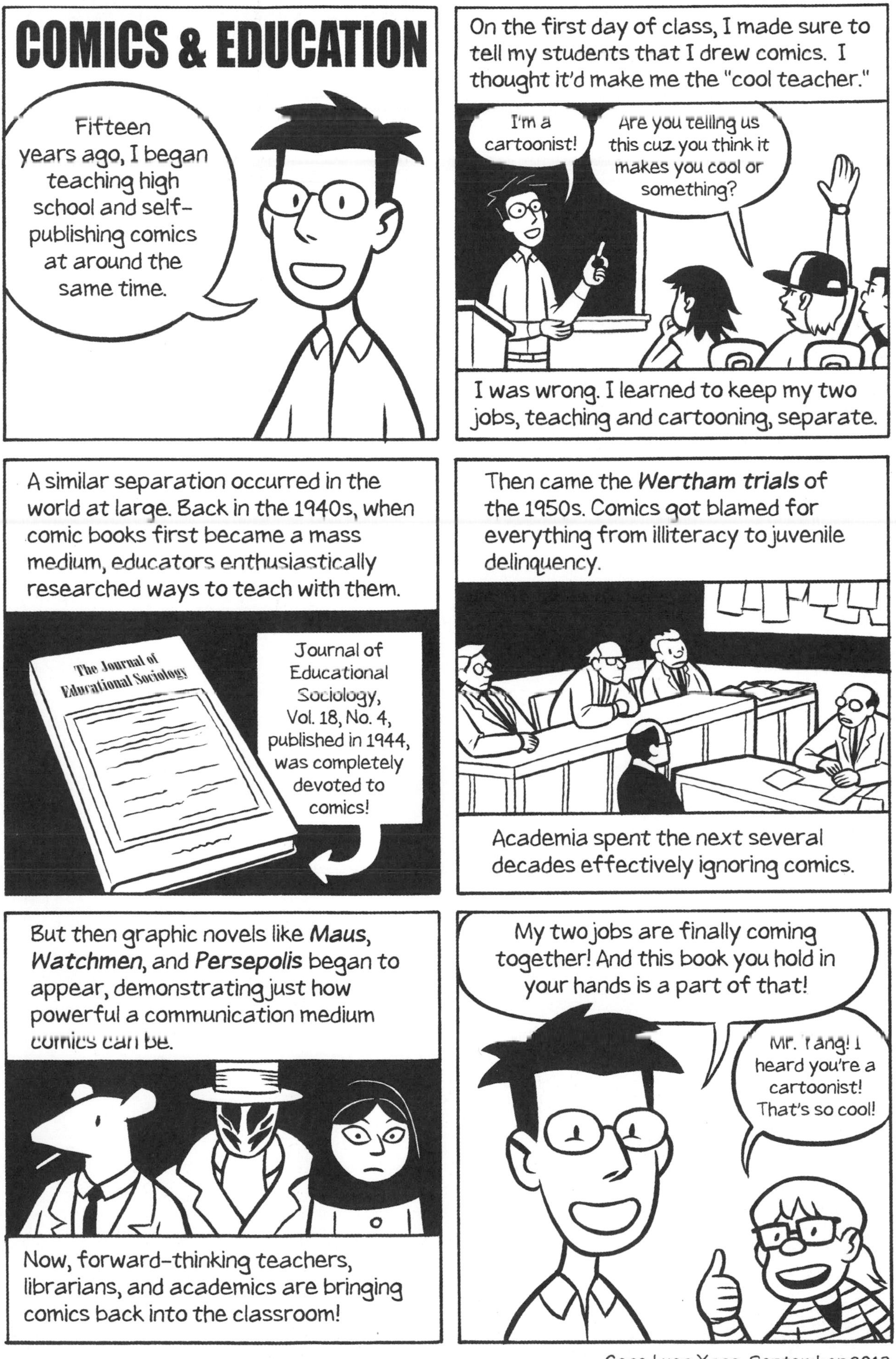
COMICS & EDUCATION
Fifteen years ago, I began teaching high school and self-publishing comics at around the same time.
On the first day of class, I made sure to tell my students that I drew comics. I thought it'd make me the "cool teacher."
I'm a cartoonist!
Are you telling us this cuz you think it makes you cool or something?
I was wrong. I learned to keep my two jobs, teaching and cartooning, separate.
A similar separation occurred in the world at large. Back in the 1940s, when comic books first became a mass medium, educators enthusiastically researched ways to teach with them.
The Journal of Educational Sociology
Journal of Educational Sociology, Vol. 18, No. 4, published in 1944, was completely devoted to comics!
Then came the *Wertham trials* of the 1950s. Comics got blamed for everything from illiteracy to juvenile delinquency.
Academia spent the next several decades effectively ignoring comics.
But then graphic novels like *Maus*, *Watchmen*, and *Persepolis* began to appear, demonstrating just how powerful a communication medium comics can be.
Now, forward-thinking teachers, librarians, and academics are bringing comics back into the classroom!
My two jobs are finally coming together! And this book you hold in your hands is a part of that!
Mr. Yang! I heard you're a cartoonist! That's so cool!

Gene Luen Yang, September 2013

HOW TO READ A COMIC

by Tracy Edmunds, M.A. Ed.

Panels are frames that each contain one segment of the action. Panels can be any shape or size. Read the panels from left to right, top to bottom.

Gutters are the spaces between panels. This is where the reader must imagine the action from panel to panel.

Slow down! Read both the text and the pictures. Think about what is happening between the panels.

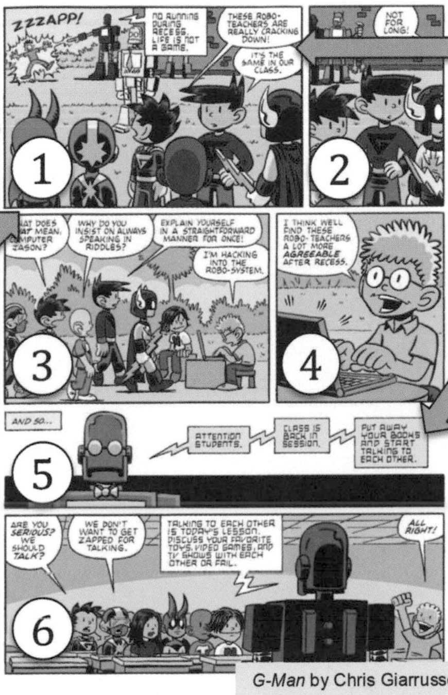

ZZZAPP!
NO RUNNING DURING RECESS. LIFE IS NOT A GAME.
THESE ROBO-TEACHERS ARE REALLY CRACKING DOWN!
IT'S THE SAME IN OUR CLASS.
1
NOT FOR LONG!
2
WHY DO YOU INSIST ON ALWAYS SPEAKING IN RIDDLES?
EXPLAIN YOURSELF IN A STRAIGHTFORWARD MANNER FOR ONCE!
I'M HACKING INTO THE ROBO-SYSTEM.
3
I THINK WE'LL FIND THESE ROBO-TEACHERS A LOT MORE AGREEABLE AFTER RECESS.
4
AND SO...
ATTENTION STUDENTS.
CLASS IS BACK IN SESSION.
PUT AWAY YOUR BOOKS AND START TALKING TO EACH OTHER.
5
ARE YOU SERIOUS? WE SHOULD TALK?
WE DON'T WANT TO GET ZAPPED FOR TALKING.
TALKING TO EACH OTHER IS TODAY'S LESSON. DISCUSS YOUR FAVORITE TOYS, VIDEO GAMES, AND TV SHOWS WITH EACH OTHER OR FAIL.
ALL RIGHT!
6

G-Man by Chris Giarrusso

Word balloons contain character dialogue. The tail of the bubble points to the speaker. Sometimes different colors, shapes, or fonts are used to show the personality of a character.

A cloud-like thought bubble means a character is thinking, not speaking.

Captions usually contain narration but sometimes dialogue or other text information.

Doctor Sputnik: Man of Science by Roger Langridge

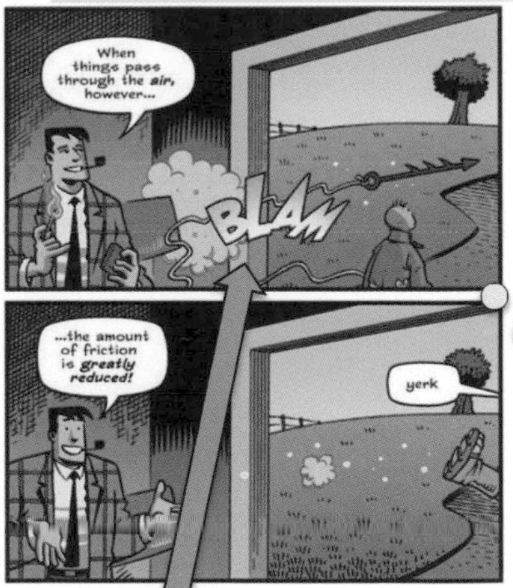

When things pass through the air, however...
BLAM
...the amount of friction is greatly reduced!
yerk

Sound effects are usually drawn to visually represent the volume and feeling of the sound.

Splash panels are large images that take up most or all of a page. They are often used to establish location or mood.

Bleed is when an image goes all the way to the edge of a page.

What action takes place between these panels?

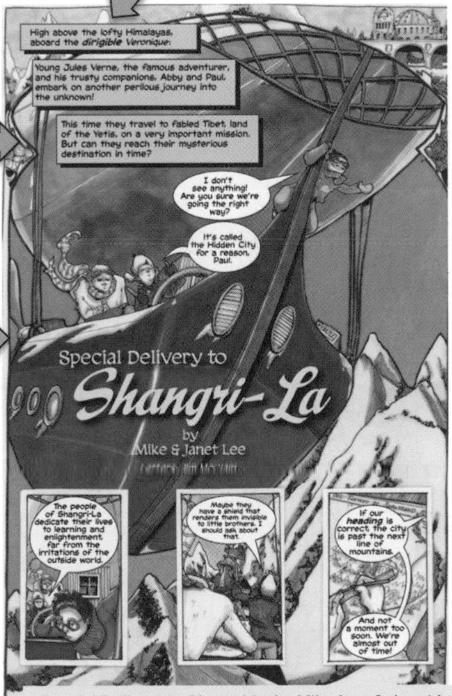

High above the lofty Himalayas, aboard the dirigible Veronique:
Young Jules Verne, the famous adventurer, and his trusty companions, Abby and Paul, embark on another perilous journey into the unknown!
This time they travel to fabled Tibet, land of the Yetis, on a very important mission. But can they reach their mysterious destination in time?
I don't see anything! Are you sure we're going the right way?
It's called the Hidden City for a reason, Paul.
Special Delivery to
Shangri-La
by
Mike & Janet Lee
The people of Shangri-La dedicate their lives to learning and enlightenment, far from the irritations of the outside world.
Maybe they have a shield that renders them invisible to little brothers. I should ask about that.
If our heading is correct, the city is past the next line of mountains.
And not a moment too soon. We're almost out of time!

Special Delivery to Shangri-La by Mike Lee & Janet Lee

LANGUAGE ARTS

G-MAN™

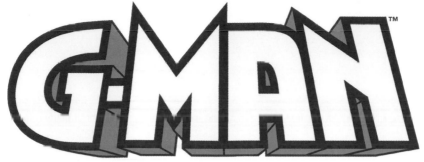

Reign of the Robo-Teachers

story and art by Chris Giarrusso

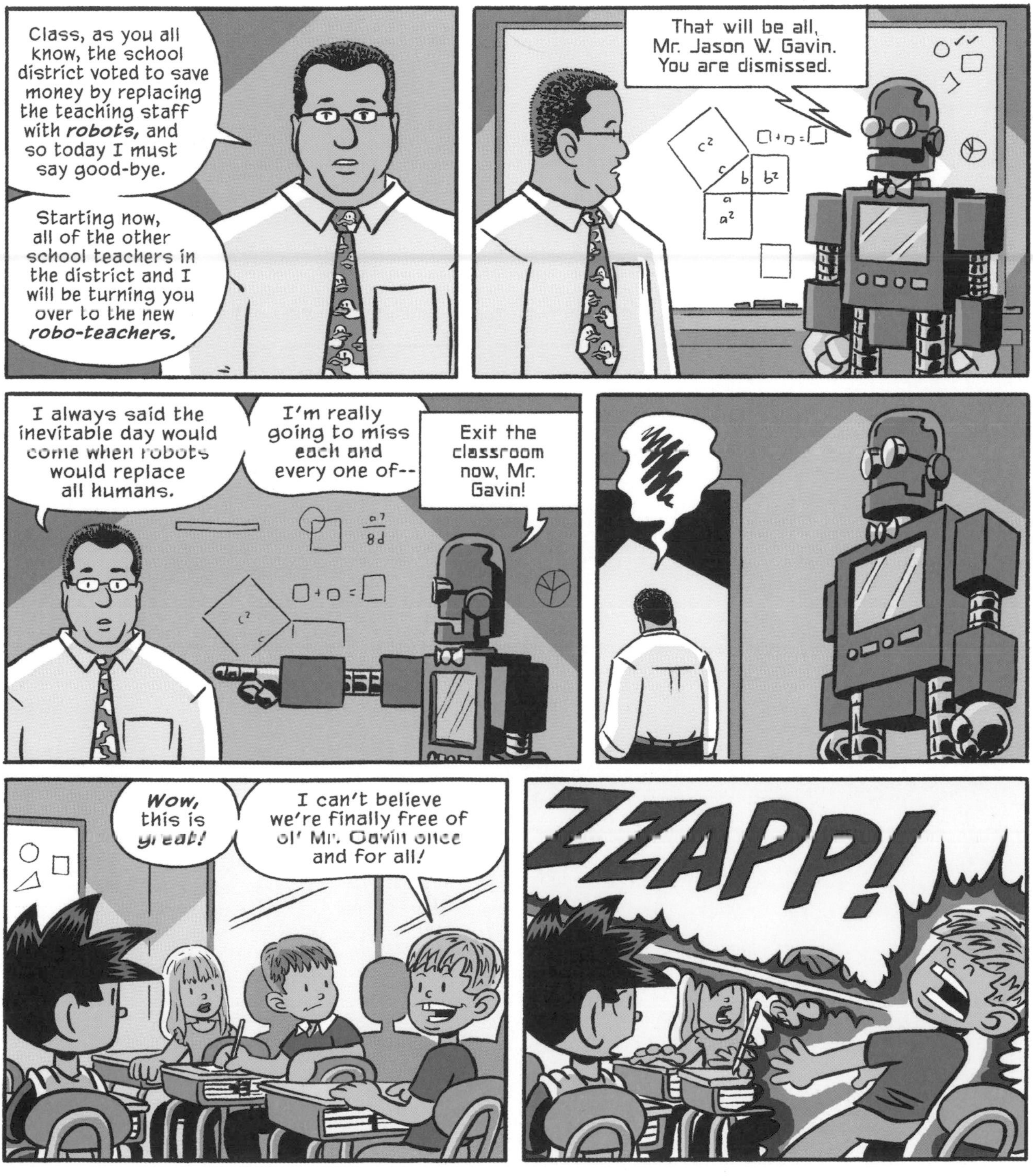
Class, as you all know, the school district voted to save money by replacing the teaching staff with *robots,* and so today I must say good-bye.
Starting now, all of the other school teachers in the district and I will be turning you over to the new *robo-teachers.*
That will be all, Mr. Jason W. Gavin. You are dismissed.
I always said the inevitable day would come when robots would replace all humans.
I'm really going to miss each and every one of--
Exit the classroom now, Mr. Gavin!
Wow, this is *great!*
I can't believe we're finally free of ol' Mr. Gavin once and for all!
ZZAPP!

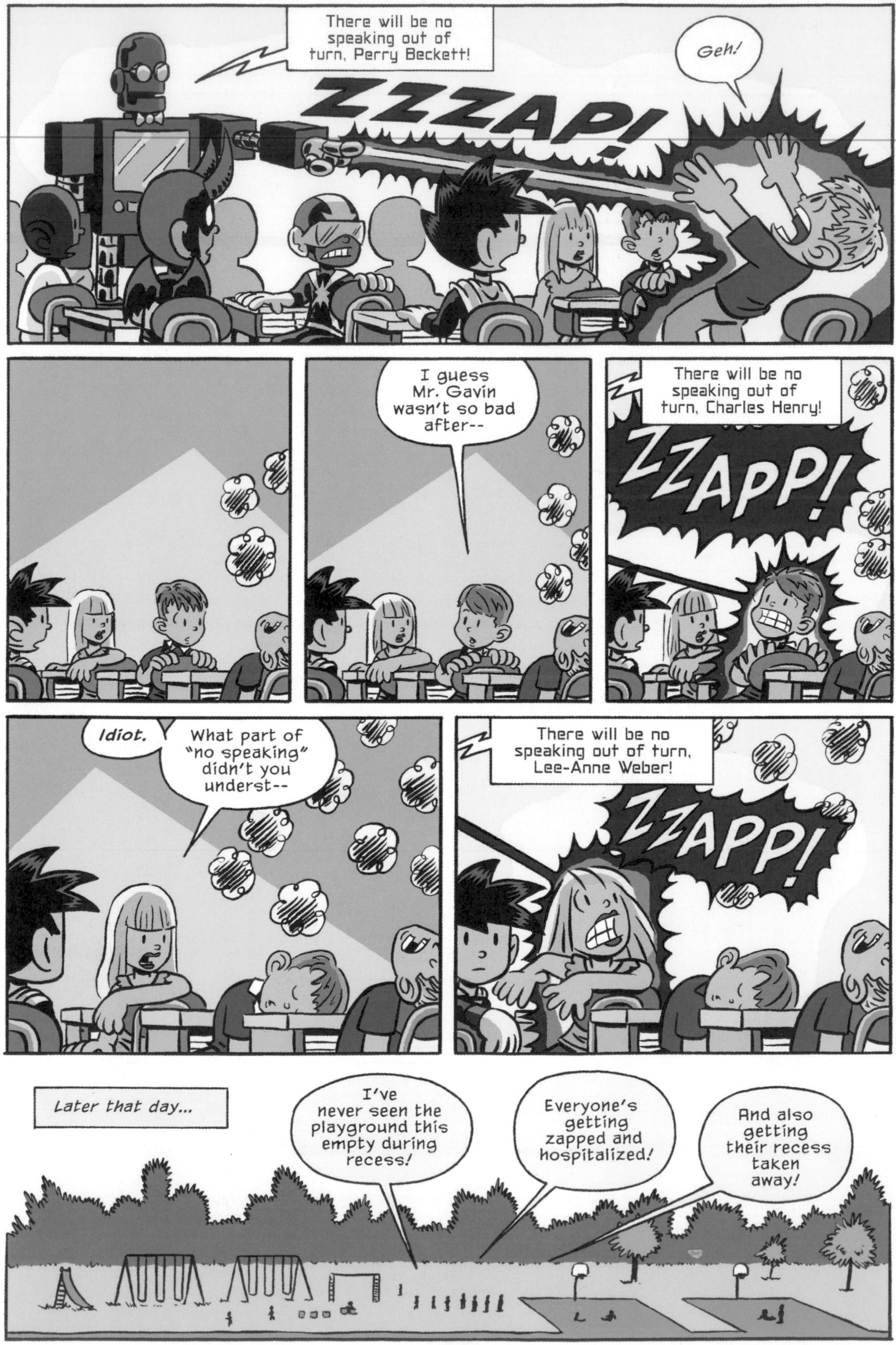
There will be no speaking out of turn, Perry Beckett!
ZZZAP!
Geh!
I guess Mr. Gavin wasn't so bad after--
There will be no speaking out of turn, Charles Henry!
ZZAPP!
Idiot.
What part of "no speaking" didn't you underst--
There will be no speaking out of turn, Lee-Anne Weber!
ZZAPP!
Later that day...
I've never seen the playground this empty during recess!
Everyone's getting zapped and hospitalized!
And also getting their recess taken away!

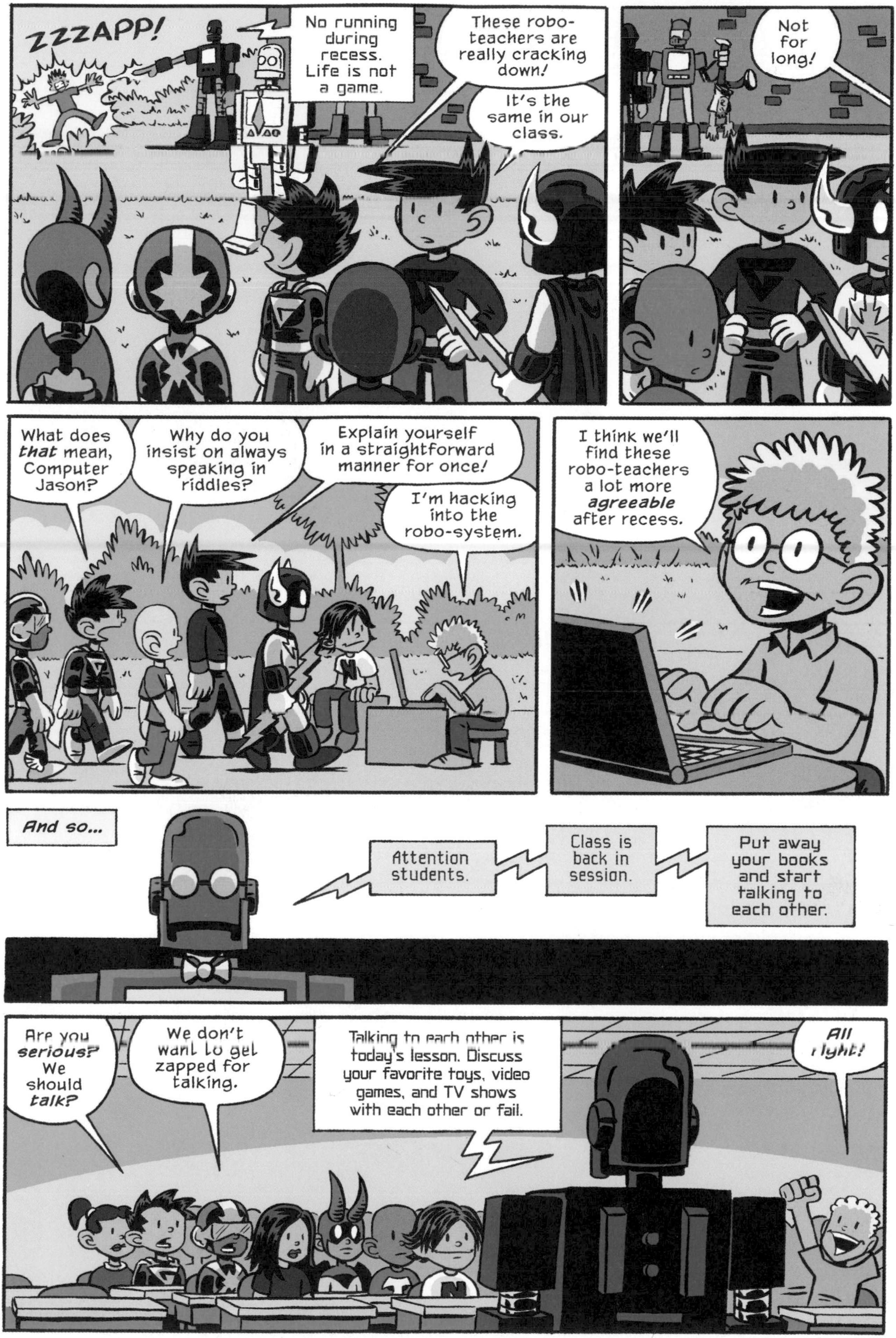
ZZZAPP!
No running during recess. Life is not a game.
These robo-teachers are really cracking down!
It's the same in our class.
Not for long!
What does *that* mean, Computer Jason?
Why do you insist on always speaking in riddles?
Explain yourself in a straightforward manner for once!
I'm hacking into the robo-system.
I think we'll find these robo-teachers a lot more *agreeable* after recess.
And so...
Attention students.
Class is back in session.
Put away your books and start talking to each other.
Are you *serious?* We should *talk?*
We don't want to get zapped for talking.
Talking to each other is today's lesson. Discuss your favorite toys, video games, and TV shows with each other or fail.
All right!

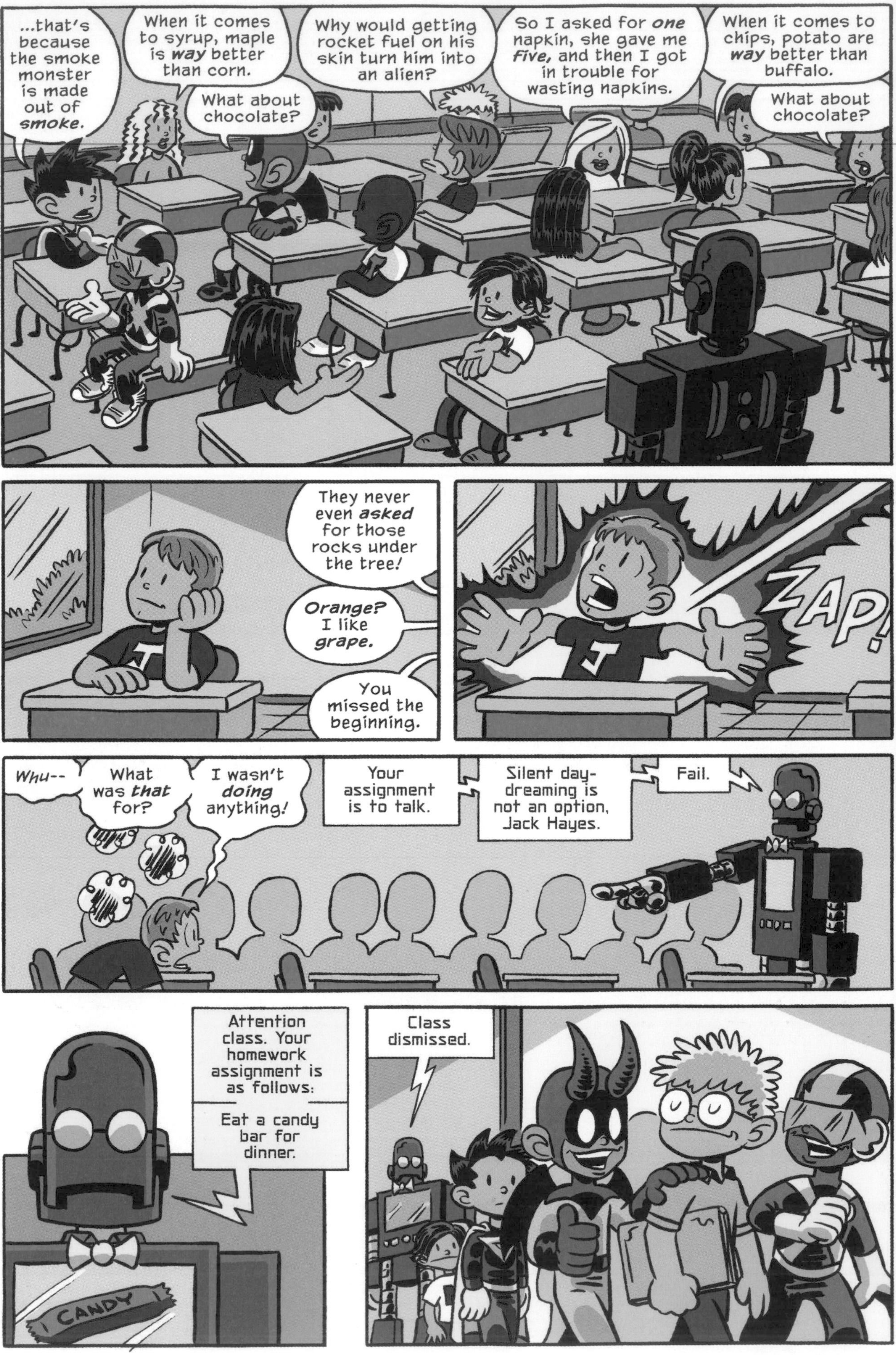

...that's because the smoke monster is made out of *smoke*.
When it comes to syrup, maple is *way* better than corn.
What about chocolate?
Why would getting rocket fuel on his skin turn him into an alien?
So I asked for *one* napkin, she gave me *five,* and then I got in trouble for wasting napkins.
When it comes to chips, potato are *way* better than buffalo.
What about chocolate?
They never even *asked* for those rocks under the tree!
Orange? I like *grape.*
You missed the beginning.
ZAP!
Whu--
What was *that* for?
I wasn't *doing* anything!
Your assignment is to talk.
Silent day-dreaming is not an option, Jack Hayes.
Fail.
Attention class. Your homework assignment is as follows:
Eat a candy bar for dinner.
CANDY
Class dismissed.

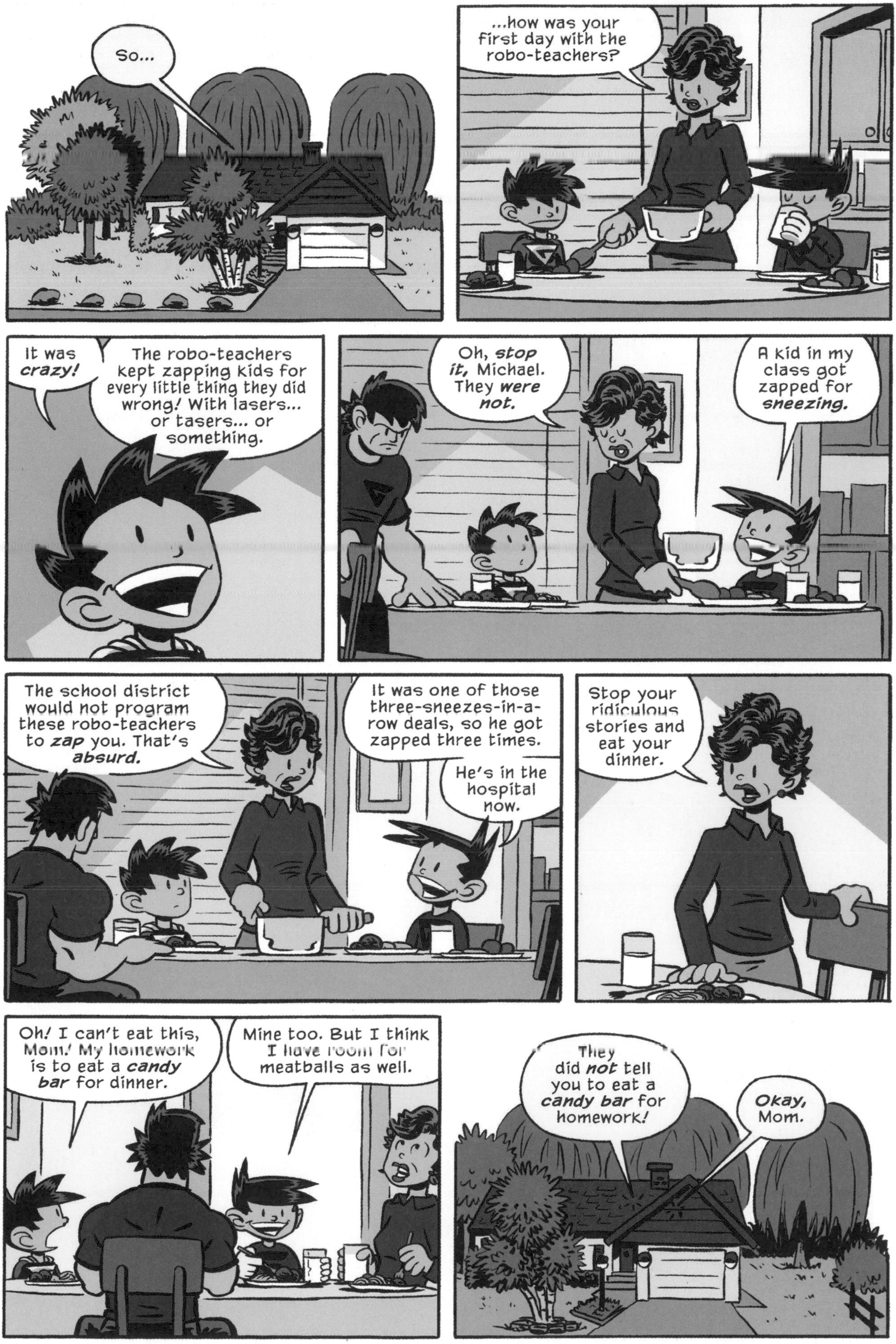
So...
...how was your first day with the robo-teachers?
It was *crazy!*
The robo-teachers kept zapping kids for every little thing they did wrong! With lasers... or tasers... or something.
Oh, *stop it,* Michael. They *were not.*
A kid in my class got zapped for *sneezing.*
The school district would not program these robo-teachers to *zap* you. That's *absurd.*
It was one of those three-sneezes-in-a-row deals, so he got zapped three times.
He's in the hospital now.
Stop your ridiculous stories and eat your dinner.
Oh! I can't eat this, Mom! My homework is to eat a *candy bar* for dinner.
Mine too. But I think I have room for meatballs as well.
They did *not* tell you to eat a *candy bar* for homework!
Okay, Mom.

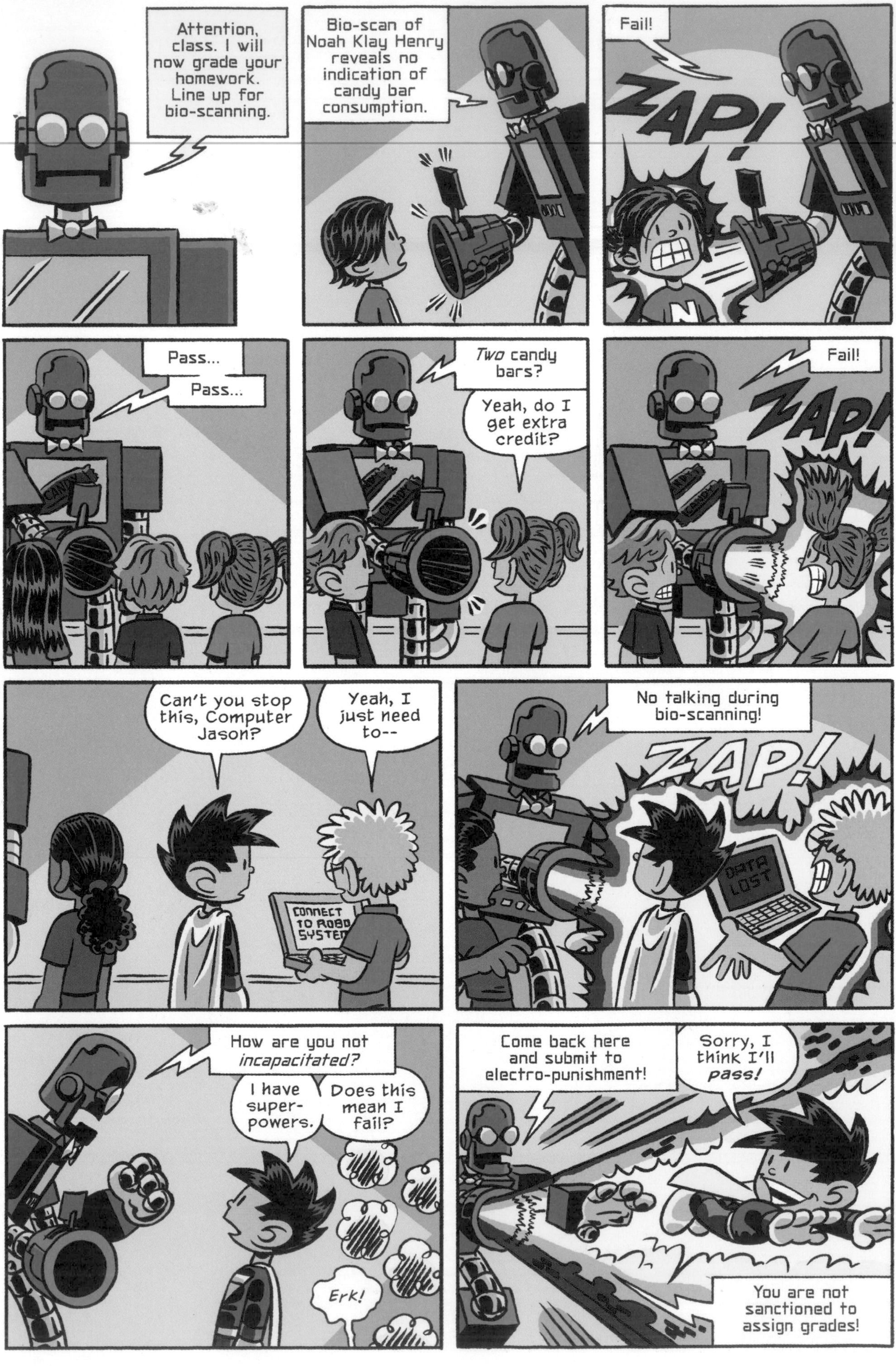
Attention, class. I will now grade your homework. Line up for bio-scanning.
Bio-scan of Noah Klay Henry reveals no indication of candy bar consumption.
Fail!
ZAP!
N
Pass...
Pass...
CANDY
Two candy bars?
Yeah, do I get extra credit?
Fail!
ZAP!
Can't you stop this, Computer Jason?
Yeah, I just need to--
CONNECT TO ROBO SYSTEM
No talking during bio-scanning!
ZAP!
DATA LOST
How are you not *incapacitated?*
I have super-powers.
Does this mean I fail?
Erk!
Come back here and submit to electro-punishment!
Sorry, I think I'll *pass!*
You are not sanctioned to assign grades!

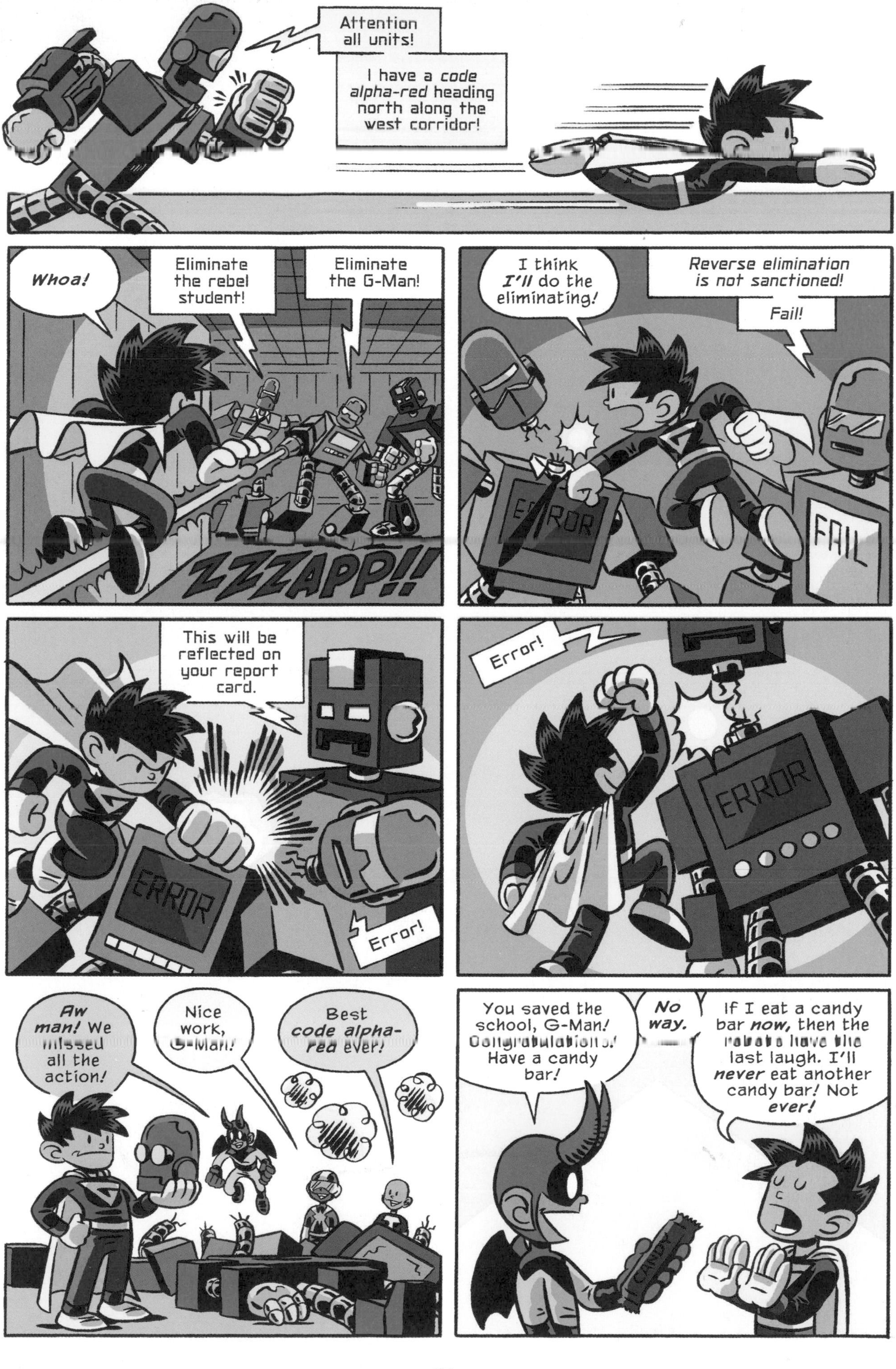
Attention all units!
I have a *code alpha-red* heading north along the west corridor!
Whoa!
Eliminate the rebel student!
Eliminate the G-Man!
ZZZAPP!!
I think *I'll* do the eliminating!
Reverse elimination is not sanctioned!
Fail!
ERROR
FAIL
This will be reflected on your report card.
ERROR
Error!
Error!
ERROR
Aw man! We missed all the action!
Nice work, G-Man!
Best *code alpha-red* ever!
You saved the school, G-Man! Congratulations! Have a candy bar!
No way.
If I eat a candy bar *now,* then the robots have the last laugh. I'll *never* eat another candy bar! Not *ever!*
CANDY

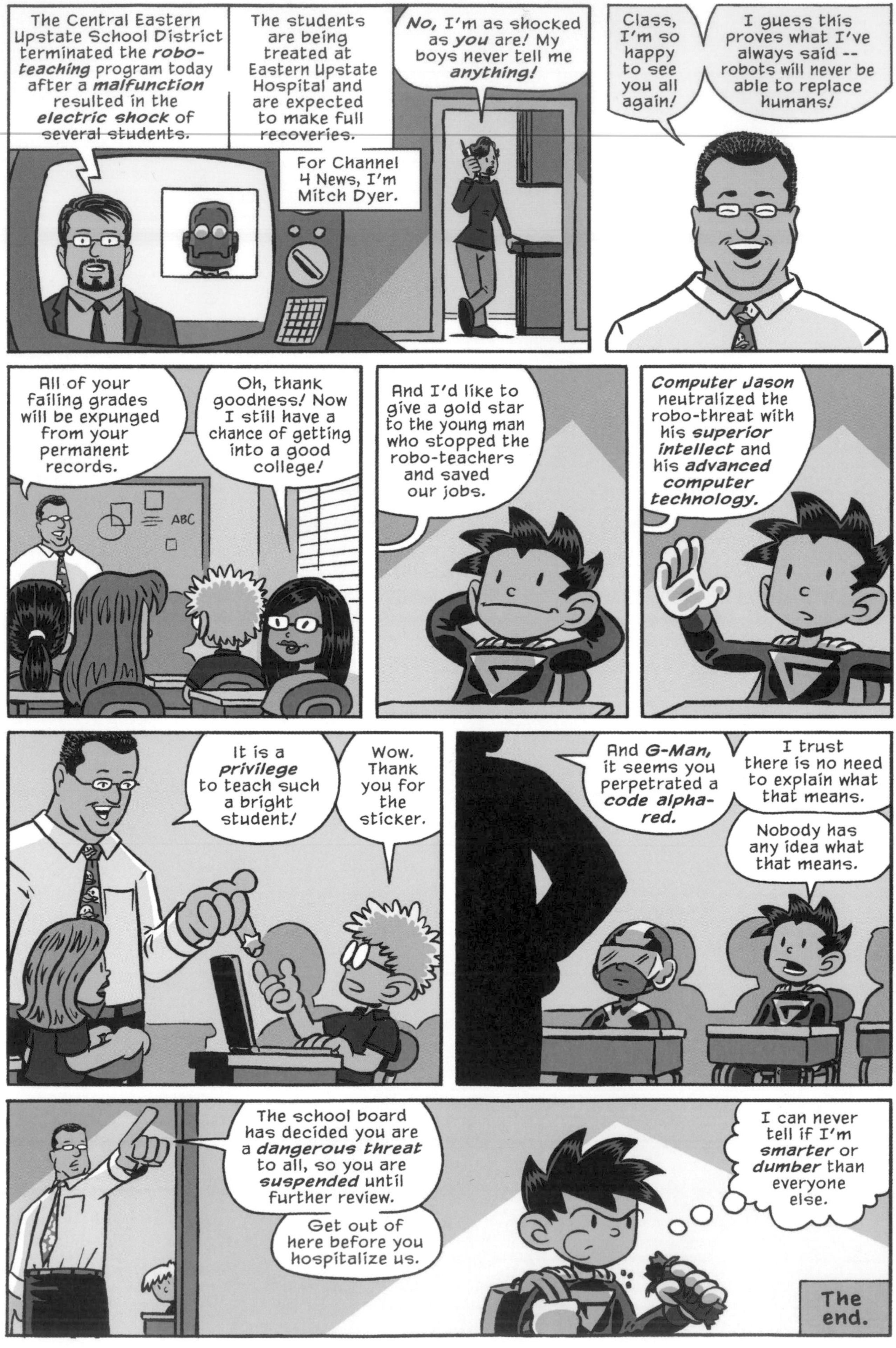
The Central Eastern Upstate School District terminated the robo-teaching program today after a malfunction resulted in the electric shock of several students.
The students are being treated at Eastern Upstate Hospital and are expected to make full recoveries.
For Channel 4 News, I'm Mitch Dyer.
No, I'm as shocked as you are! My boys never tell me anything!
Class, I'm so happy to see you all again!
I guess this proves what I've always said -- robots will never be able to replace humans!
All of your failing grades will be expunged from your permanent records.
Oh, thank goodness! Now I still have a chance of getting into a good college!
ABC
And I'd like to give a gold star to the young man who stopped the robo-teachers and saved our jobs.
Computer Jason neutralized the robo-threat with his superior intellect and his advanced computer technology.
It is a privilege to teach such a bright student!
Wow. Thank you for the sticker.
And G-Man, it seems you perpetrated a code alpha-red.
I trust there is no need to explain what that means.
Nobody has any idea what that means.
The school board has decided you are a dangerous threat to all, so you are suspended until further review.
Get out of here before you hospitalize us.
I can never tell if I'm smarter or dumber than everyone else.
The end.

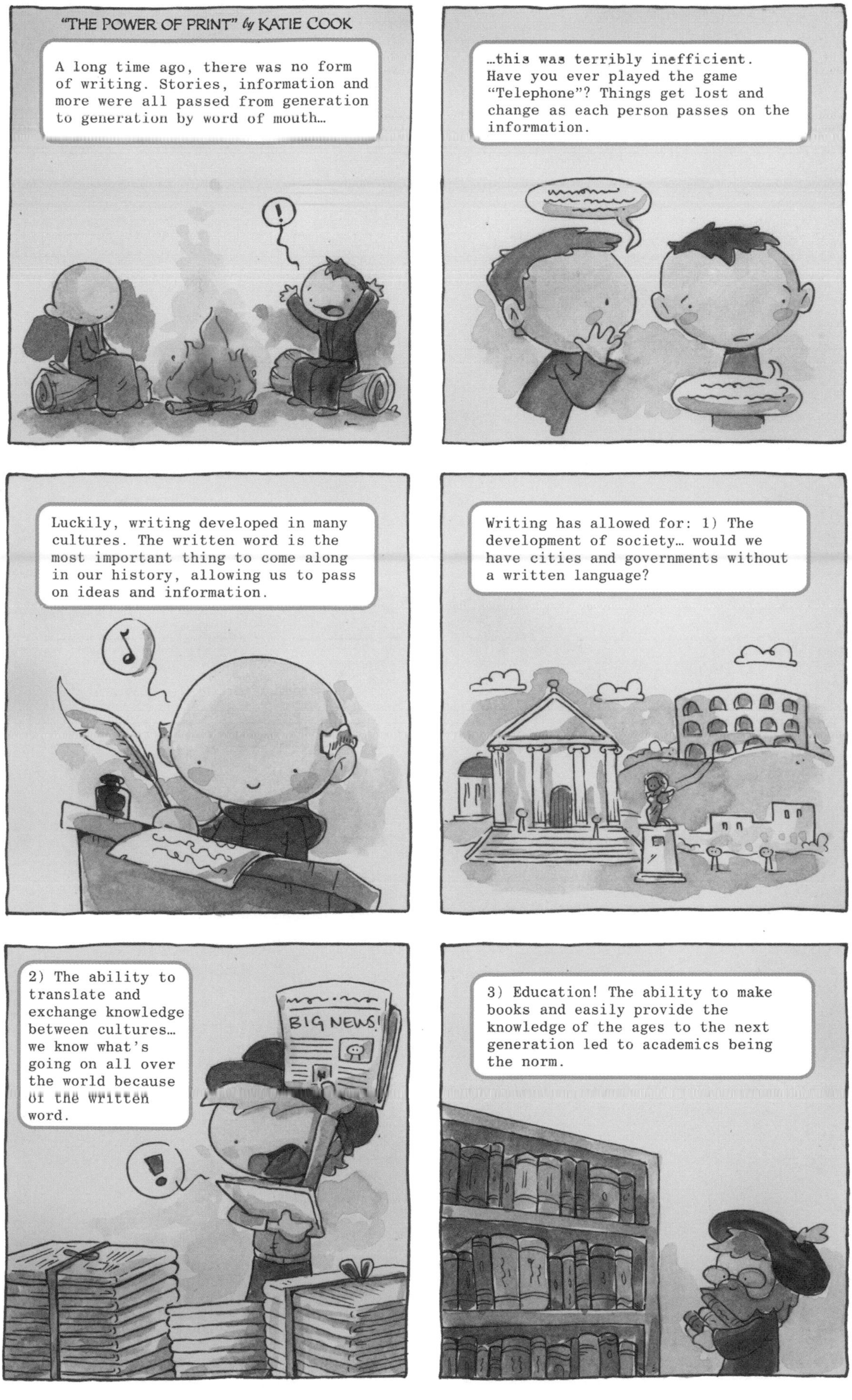
"THE POWER OF PRINT" by KATIE COOK
A long time ago, there was no form of writing. Stories, information and more were all passed from generation to generation by word of mouth...
!
...this was terribly inefficient. Have you ever played the game "Telephone"? Things get lost and change as each person passes on the information.
Luckily, writing developed in many cultures. The written word is the most important thing to come along in our history, allowing us to pass on ideas and information.
Writing has allowed for: 1) The development of society... would we have cities and governments without a written language?
2) The ability to translate and exchange knowledge between cultures... we know what's going on all over the world because of the written word.
BIG NEWS!
!
3) Education! The ability to make books and easily provide the knowledge of the ages to the next generation led to academics being the norm.

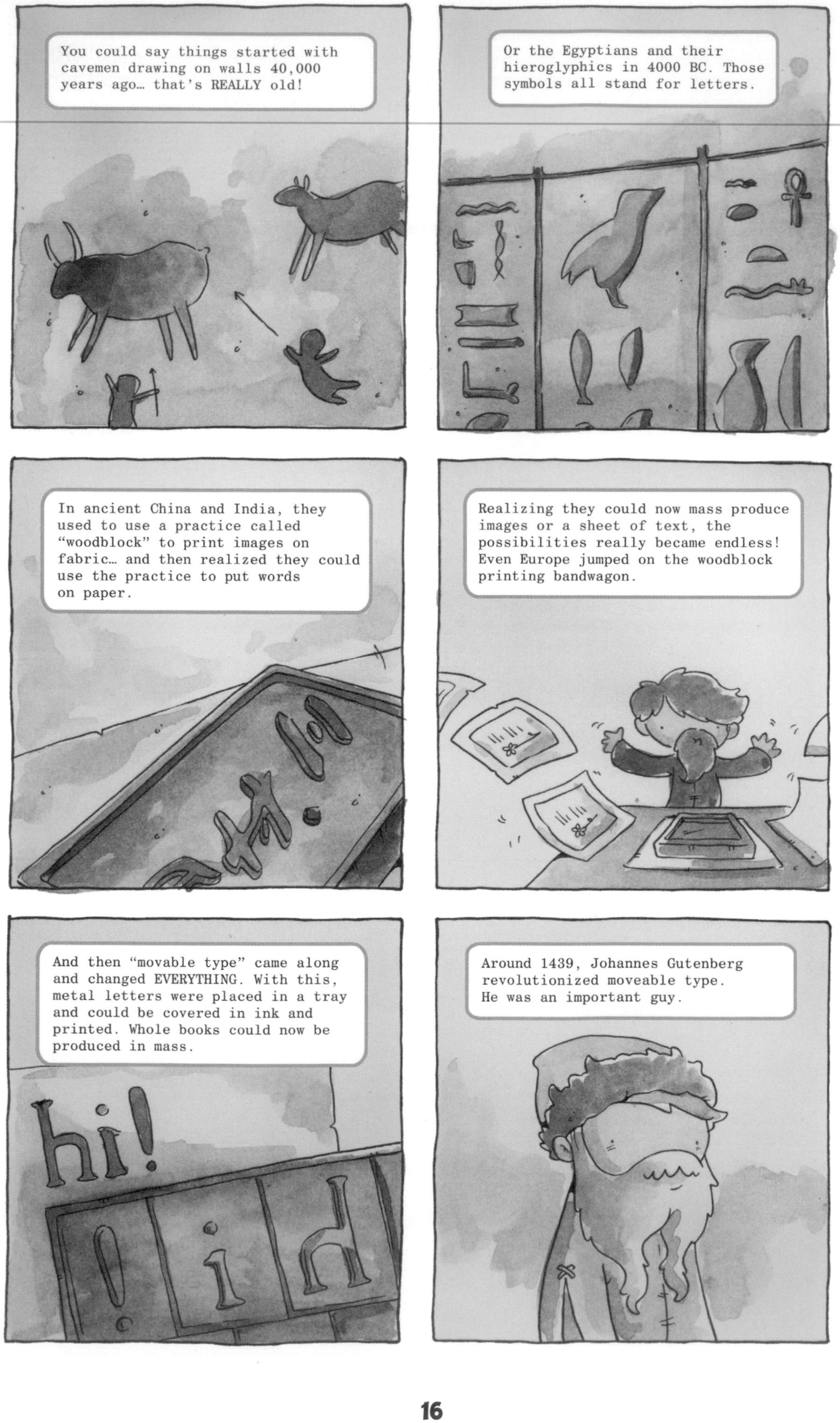
You could say things started with cavemen drawing on walls 40,000 years ago… that's REALLY old!
Or the Egyptians and their hieroglyphics in 4000 BC. Those symbols all stand for letters.
In ancient China and India, they used to use a practice called "woodblock" to print images on fabric… and then realized they could use the practice to put words on paper.
Realizing they could now mass produce images or a sheet of text, the possibilities really became endless! Even Europe jumped on the woodblock printing bandwagon.
And then "movable type" came along and changed EVERYTHING. With this, metal letters were placed in a tray and could be covered in ink and printed. Whole books could now be produced in mass.
hi!
Around 1439, Johannes Gutenberg revolutionized moveable type. He was an important guy.

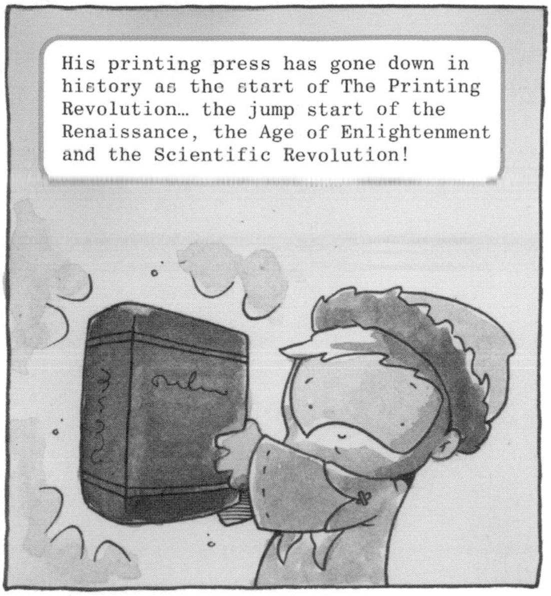
His printing press has gone down in history as the start of The Printing Revolution… the jump start of the Renaissance, the Age of Enlightenment and the Scientific Revolution!

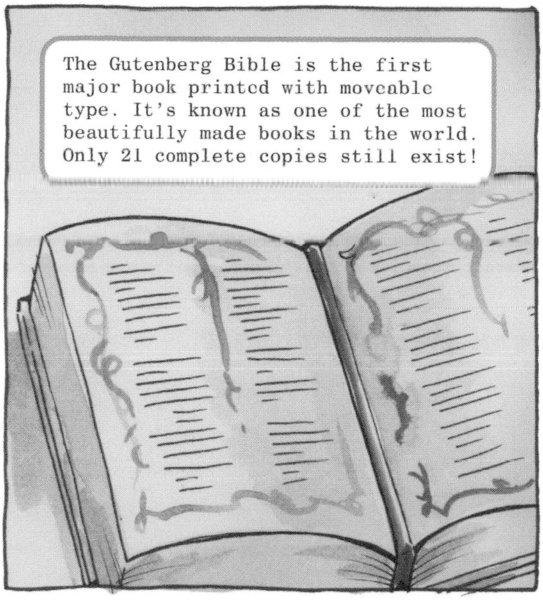
The Gutenberg Bible is the first major book printed with moveable type. It's known as one of the most beautifully made books in the world. Only 21 complete copies still exist!

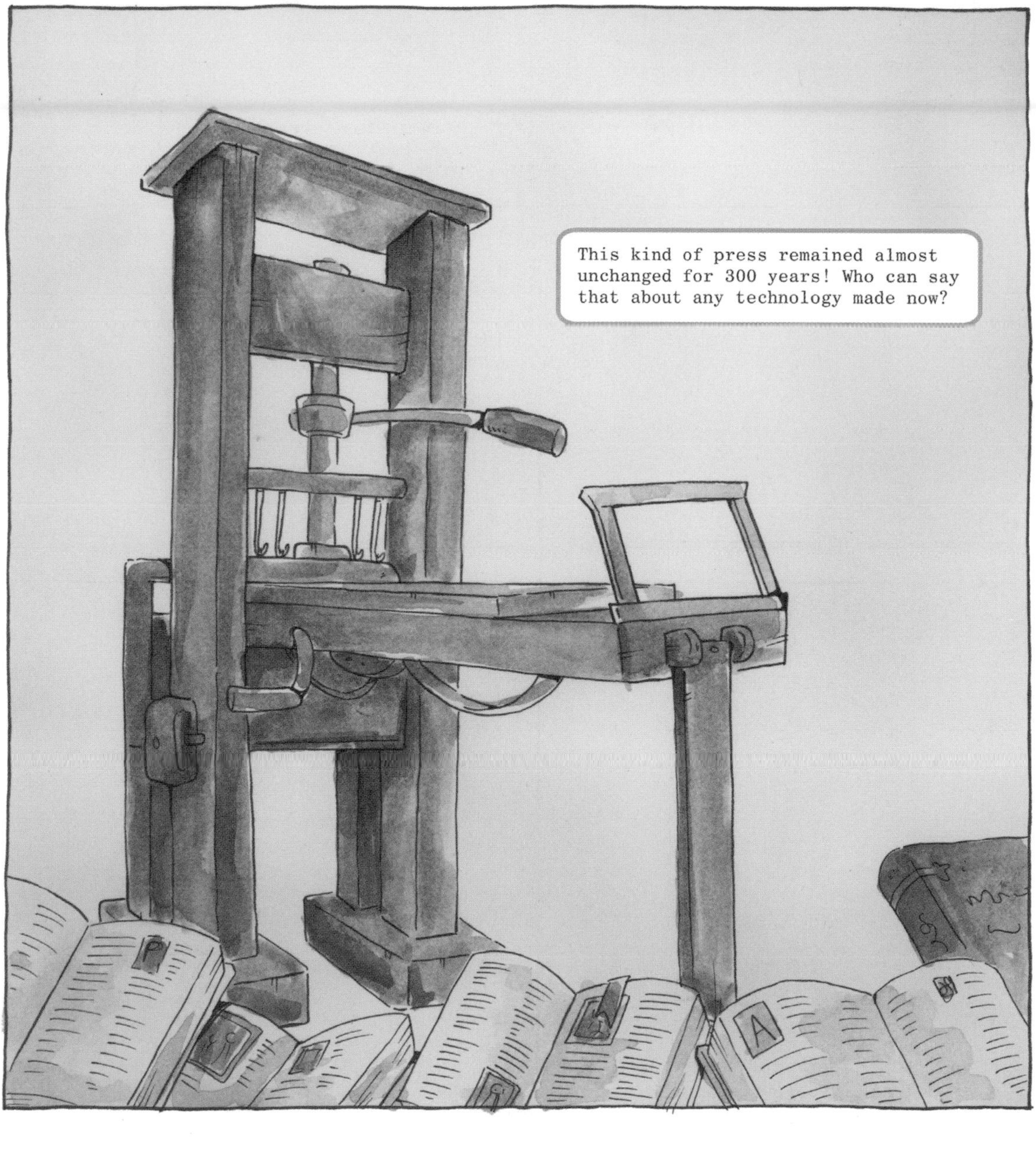
This kind of press remained almost unchanged for 300 years! Who can say that about any technology made now?

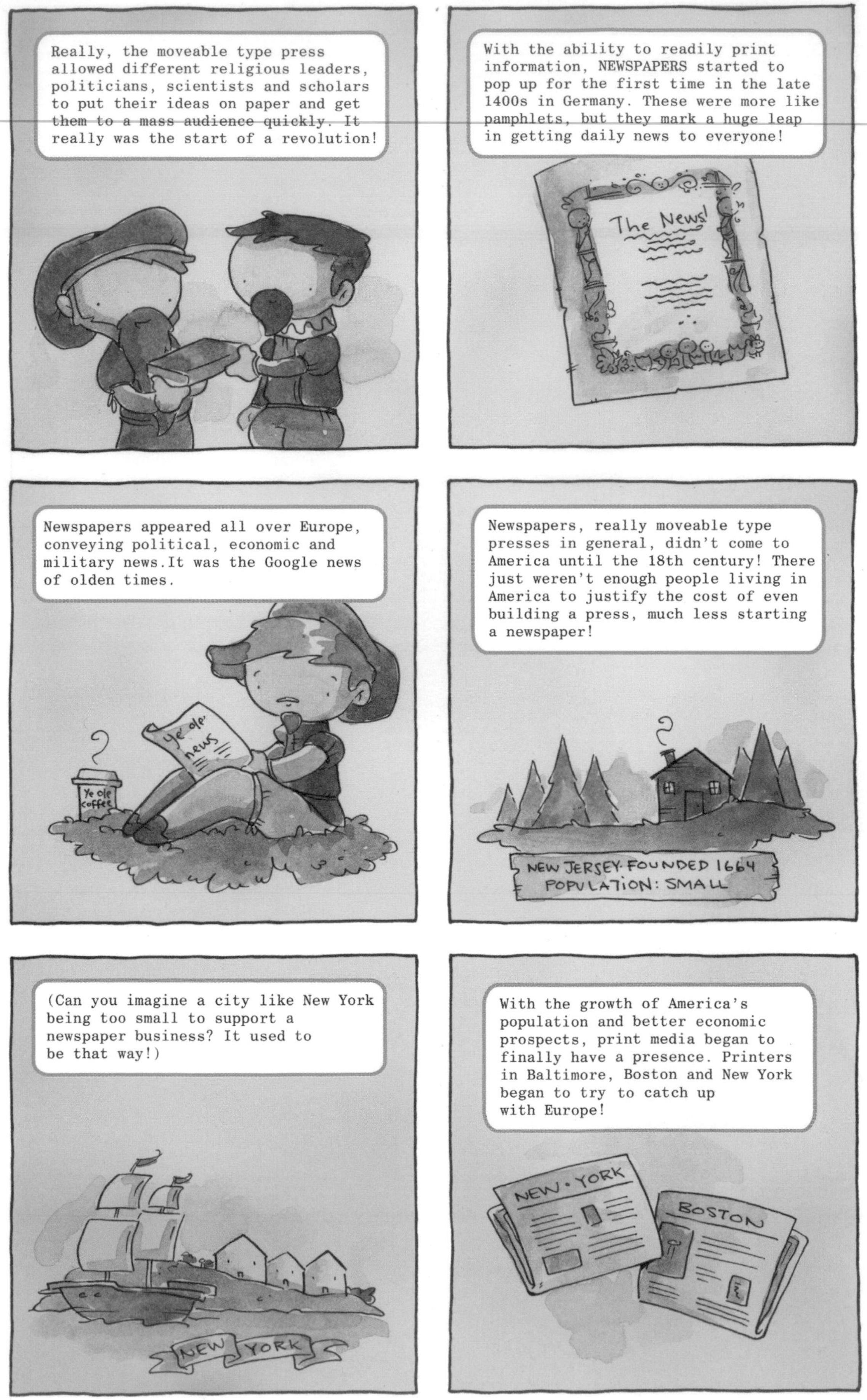
Really, the moveable type press allowed different religious leaders, politicians, scientists and scholars to put their ideas on paper and get them to a mass audience quickly. It really was the start of a revolution!
With the ability to readily print information, NEWSPAPERS started to pop up for the first time in the late 1400s in Germany. These were more like pamphlets, but they mark a huge leap in getting daily news to everyone!
The News!
Newspapers appeared all over Europe, conveying political, economic and military news.It was the Google news of olden times.
Ye ole news
Ye ole coffee
Newspapers, really moveable type presses in general, didn't come to America until the 18th century! There just weren't enough people living in America to justify the cost of even building a press, much less starting a newspaper!
NEW JERSEY· FOUNDED 1664
POPULATION: SMALL
(Can you imagine a city like New York being too small to support a newspaper business? It used to be that way!)
NEW YORK
With the growth of America's population and better economic prospects, print media began to finally have a presence. Printers in Baltimore, Boston and New York began to try to catch up with Europe!
NEW · YORK
BOSTON

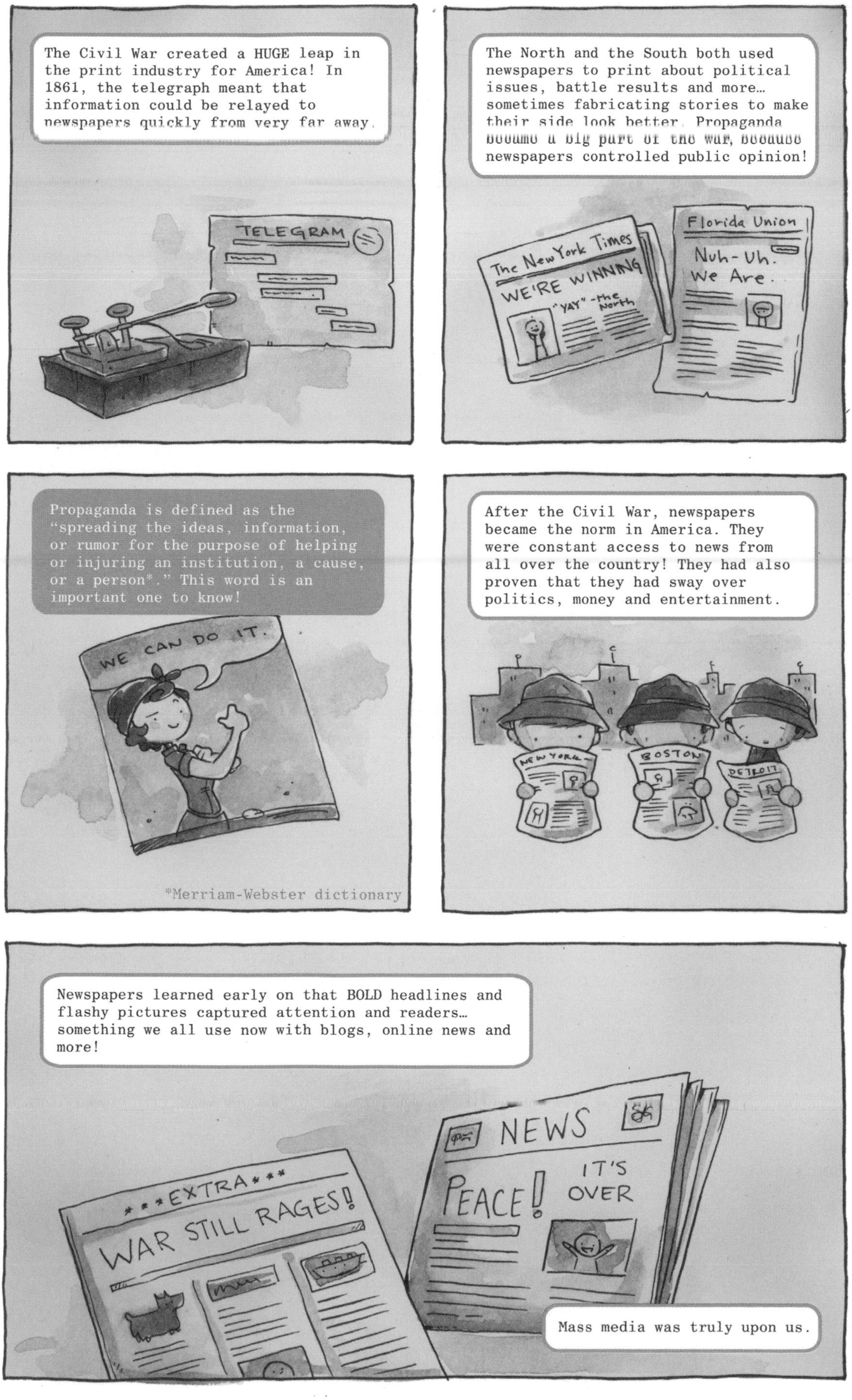
The Civil War created a HUGE leap in the print industry for America! In 1861, the telegraph meant that information could be relayed to newspapers quickly from very far away.
TELEGRAM
The North and the South both used newspapers to print about political issues, battle results and more… sometimes fabricating stories to make their side look better. Propaganda became a big part of the war, because newspapers controlled public opinion!
The New York Times
WE'RE WINNING
"YAY" -the North
Florida Union
Nuh-Uh. We Are.
Propaganda is defined as the "spreading the ideas, information, or rumor for the purpose of helping or injuring an institution, a cause, or a person*." This word is an important one to know!
WE CAN DO IT.
*Merriam-Webster dictionary
After the Civil War, newspapers became the norm in America. They were constant access to news from all over the country! They had also proven that they had sway over politics, money and entertainment.
NEW YORK
BOSTON
DETROIT
Newspapers learned early on that BOLD headlines and flashy pictures captured attention and readers… something we all use now with blogs, online news and more!
EXTRA
WAR STILL RAGES!
NEWS
PEACE!
IT'S OVER
Mass media was truly upon us.

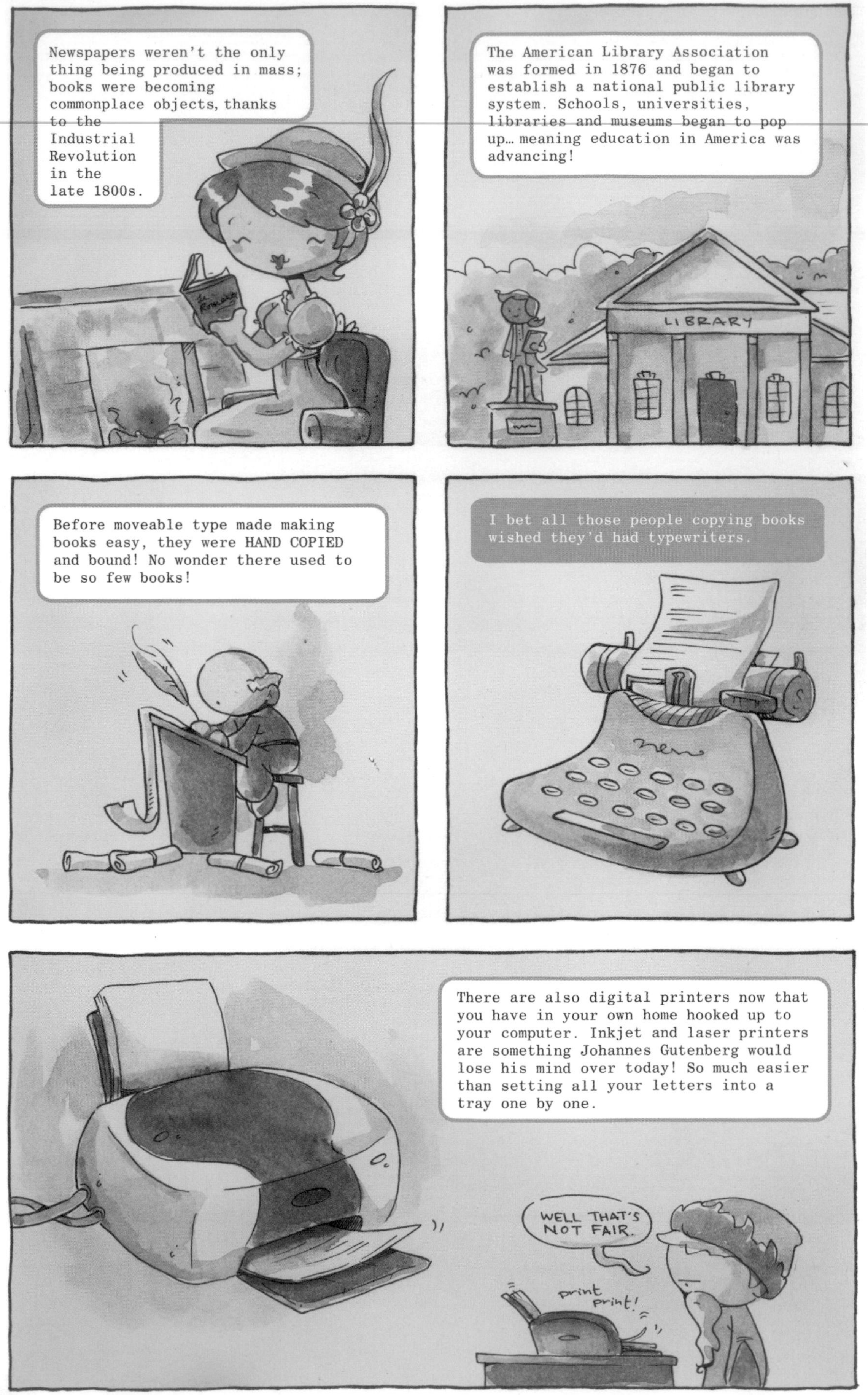
Newspapers weren't the only thing being produced in mass; books were becoming commonplace objects, thanks to the Industrial Revolution in the late 1800s.
The American Library Association was formed in 1876 and began to establish a national public library system. Schools, universities, libraries and museums began to pop up… meaning education in America was advancing!
LIBRARY
Before moveable type made making books easy, they were HAND COPIED and bound! No wonder there used to be so few books!
I bet all those people copying books wished they'd had typewriters.
There are also digital printers now that you have in your own home hooked up to your computer. Inkjet and laser printers are something Johannes Gutenberg would lose his mind over today! So much easier than setting all your letters into a tray one by one.
WELL THAT'S NOT FAIR.
print print!

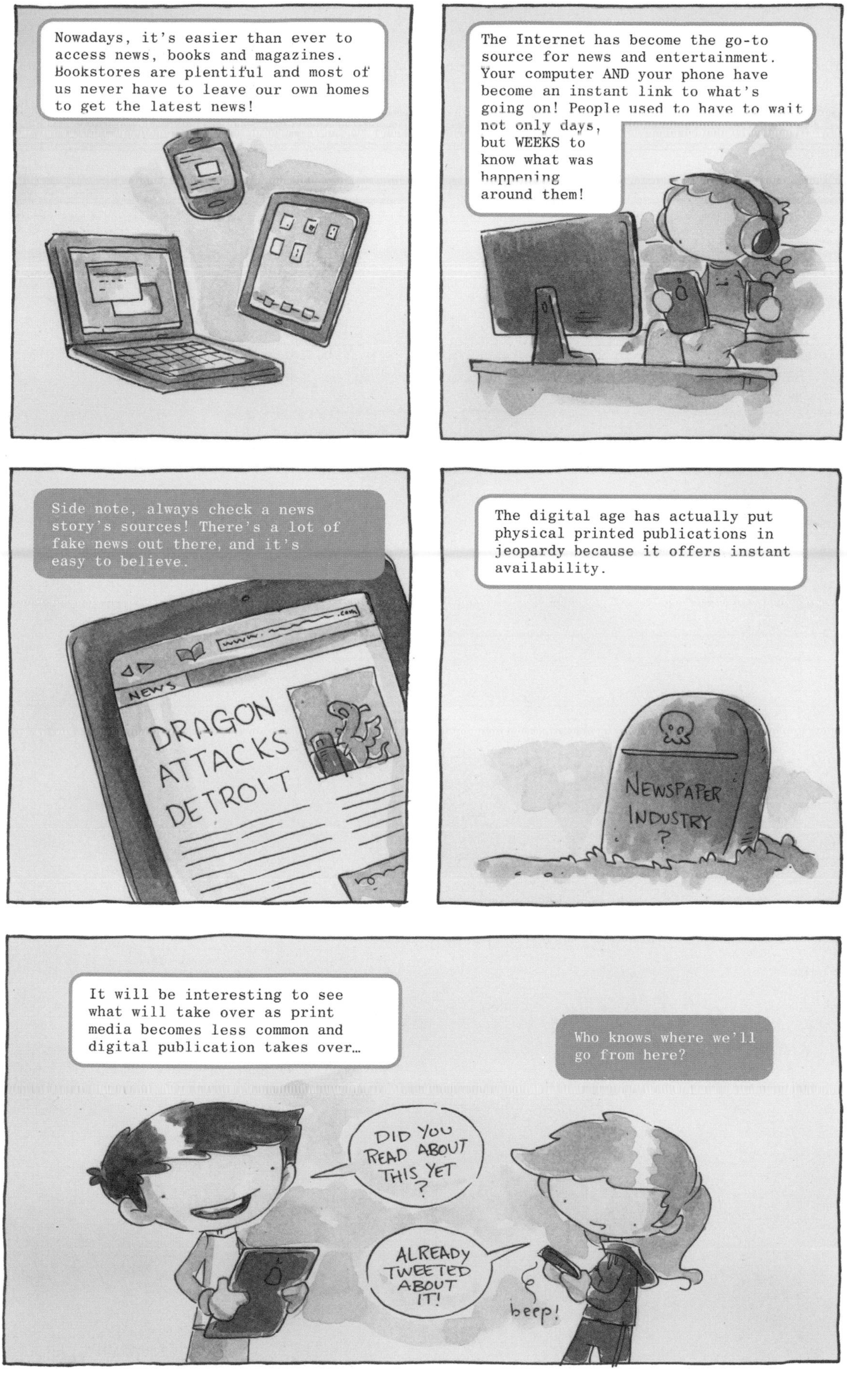
Nowadays, it's easier than ever to access news, books and magazines. Bookstores are plentiful and most of us never have to leave our own homes to get the latest news!
The Internet has become the go-to source for news and entertainment. Your computer AND your phone have become an instant link to what's going on! People used to have to wait not only days, but WEEKS to know what was happening around them!
Side note, always check a news story's sources! There's a lot of fake news out there, and it's easy to believe.
NEWS
DRAGON ATTACKS DETROIT
The digital age has actually put physical printed publications in jeopardy because it offers instant availability.
NEWSPAPER INDUSTRY ?
It will be interesting to see what will take over as print media becomes less common and digital publication takes over…
Who knows where we'll go from here?
DID YOU READ ABOUT THIS YET?
ALREADY TWEETED ABOUT IT!
beep!

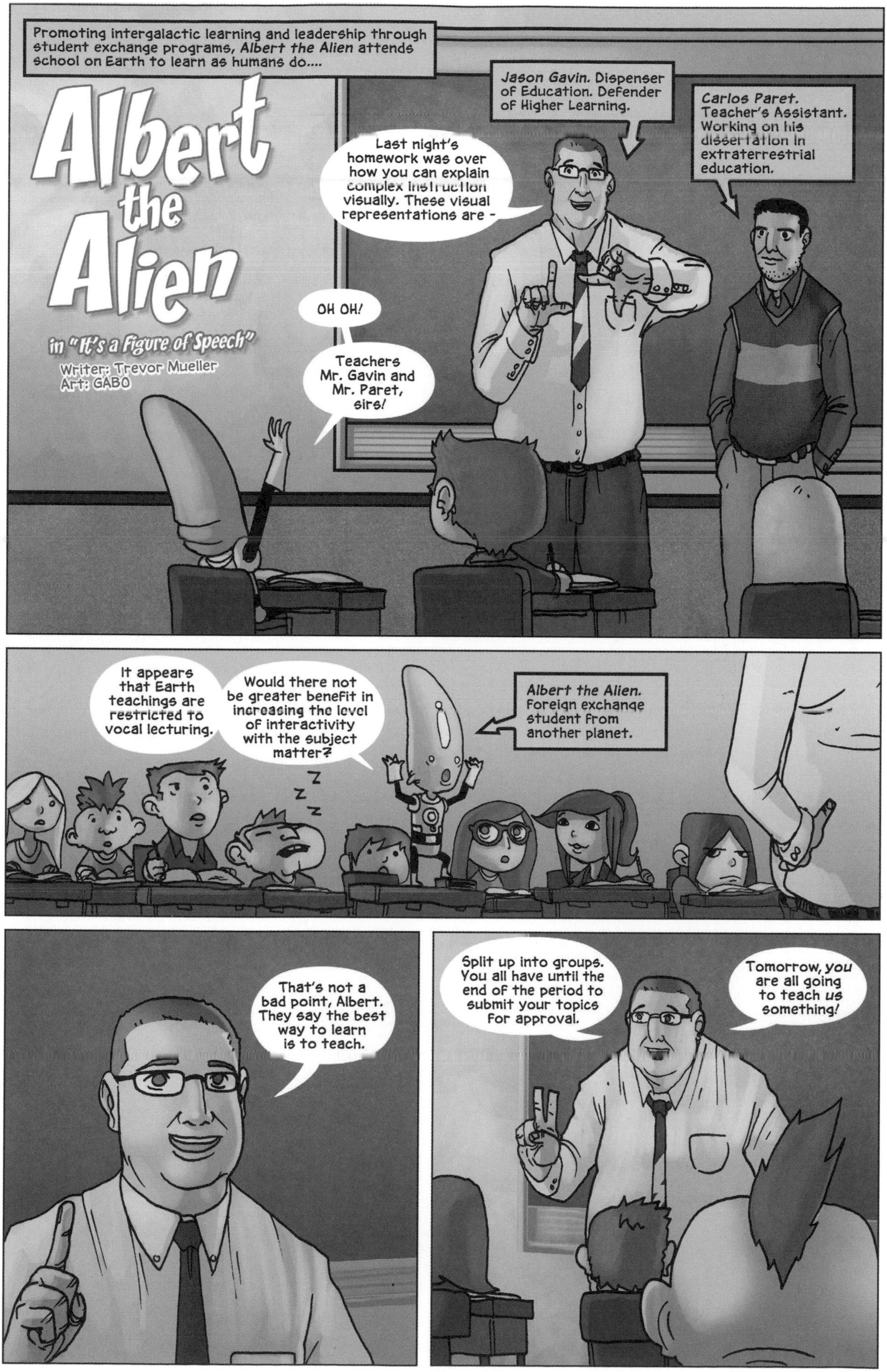
Promoting intergalactic learning and leadership through student exchange programs, Albert the Alien attends school on Earth to learn as humans do....
Albert the Alien
in "It's a Figure of Speech"
Writer: Trevor Mueller
Art: GABO
Jason Gavin. Dispenser of Education. Defender of Higher Learning.
Carlos Paret. Teacher's Assistant. Working on his dissertation in extraterrestrial education.
Last night's homework was over how you can explain complex instruction visually. These visual representations are -
OH OH!
Teachers Mr. Gavin and Mr. Paret, sirs!
It appears that Earth teachings are restricted to vocal lecturing.
Would there not be greater benefit in increasing the level of interactivity with the subject matter?
Albert the Alien. Foreign exchange student from another planet.
Z Z Z
That's not a bad point, Albert. They say the best way to learn is to teach.
Split up into groups. You all have until the end of the period to submit your topics for approval.
Tomorrow, you are all going to teach us something!

Nice idea, Jenny.

Oh, I'm looking forward to learning about that, Marcques.

Hmm, that might be too complex for the class, Veronica.

Wally, school bully. Not very good at school stuff.

Wally, I don't think that lesson is appropriate.

how 2 beet up kids 4 LUNCH MUNNY

Albert, I don't think the school will let you teach us how to implode a quantum singularity again. Not after last time.

$$S = \frac{\pi A K e^3}{2 \overline{W} G}$$

I'm seeing some really great ideas here. Keep racking your brains!

Racking... your... brain?

Why would anyone want to do that to their brain, friend Gerty?

Gerty Greyson, Albert's homestay sister and human friend.

24

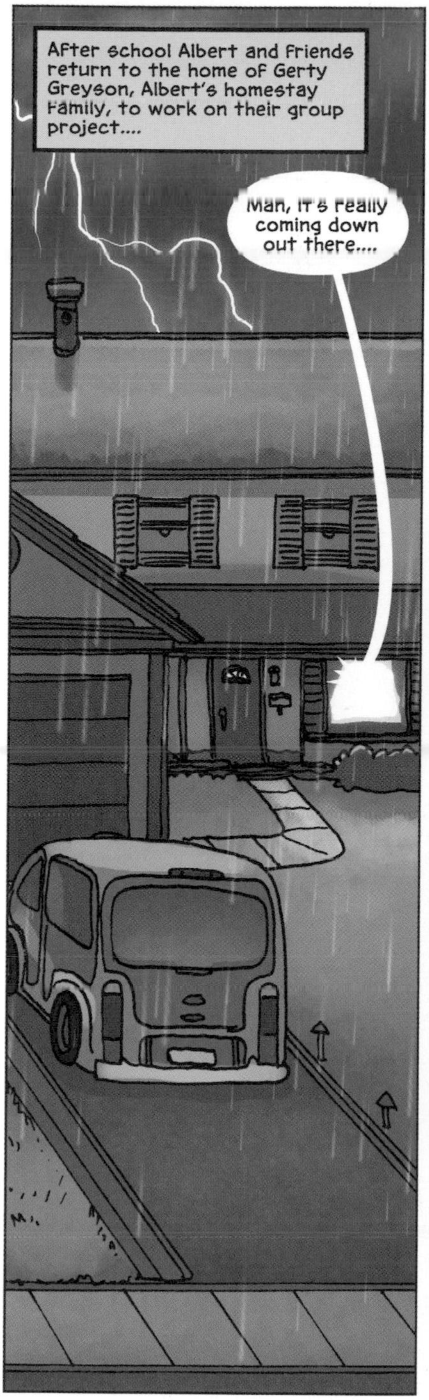
After school Albert and friends return to the home of Gerty Greyson, Albert's homestay family, to work on their group project....
Man, it's really coming down out there....

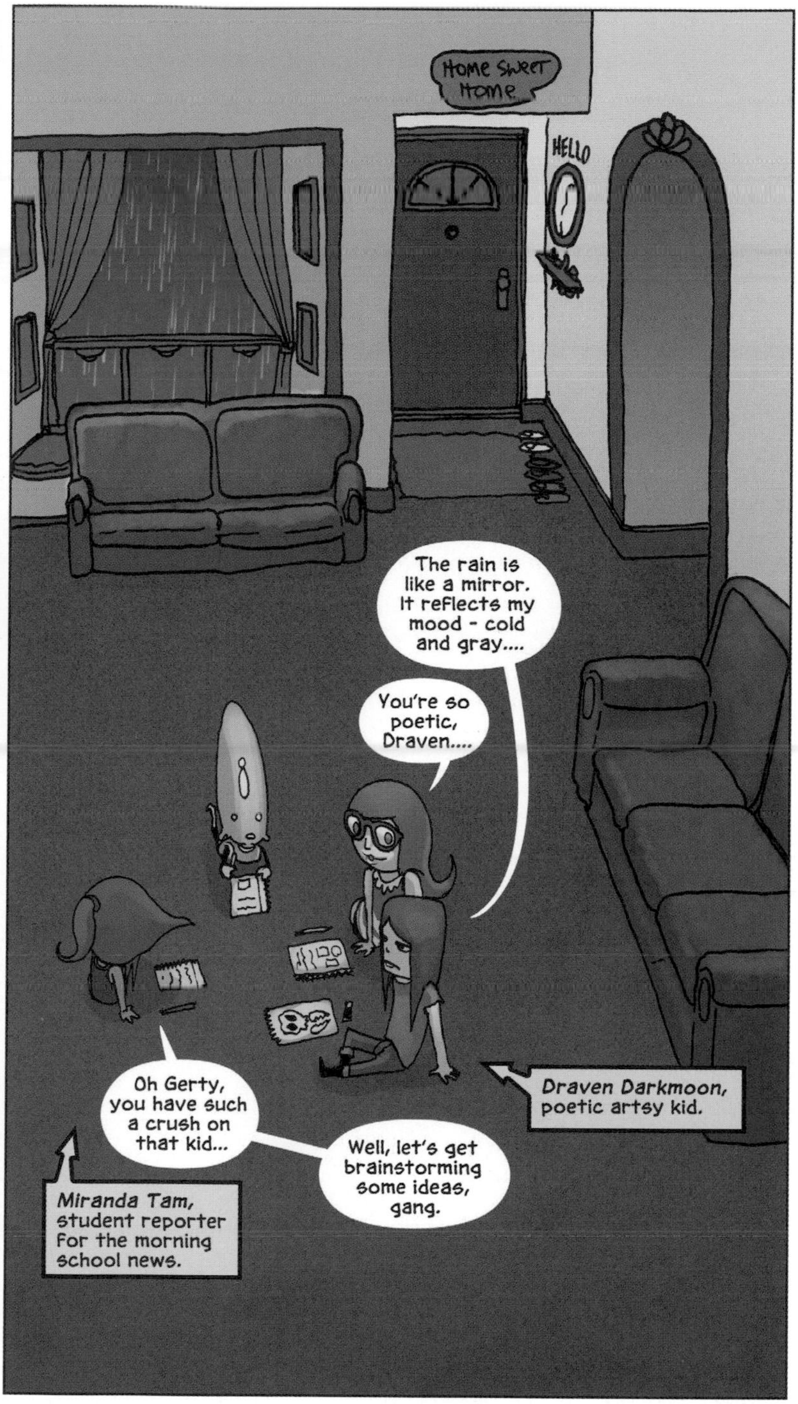
Home Sweet Home
HELLO
The rain is like a mirror. It reflects my mood - cold and gray....
You're so poetic, Draven....
Oh Gerty, you have such a crush on that kid...
Well, let's get brainstorming some ideas, gang.
Draven Darkmoon, poetic artsy kid.
Miranda Tam, student reporter for the morning school news.

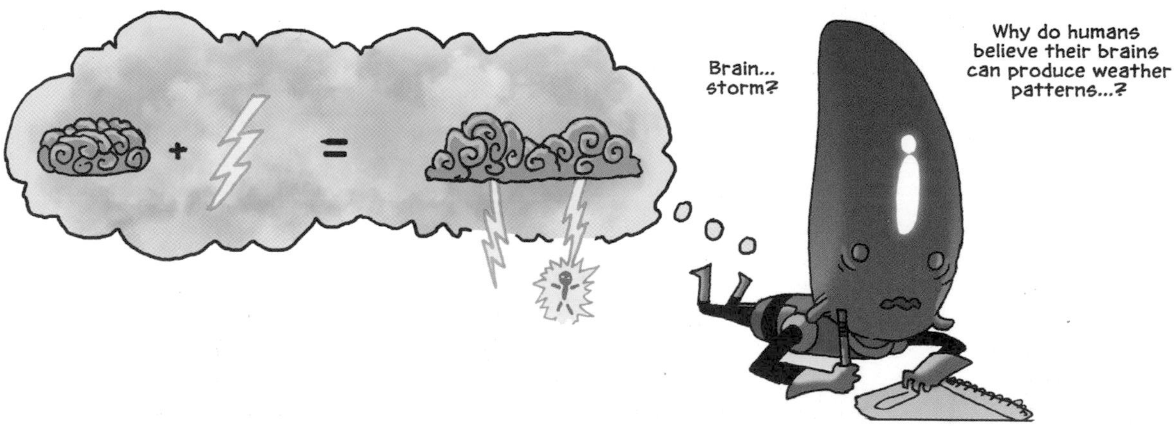
+
=
Brain... storm?
Why do humans believe their brains can produce weather patterns...?

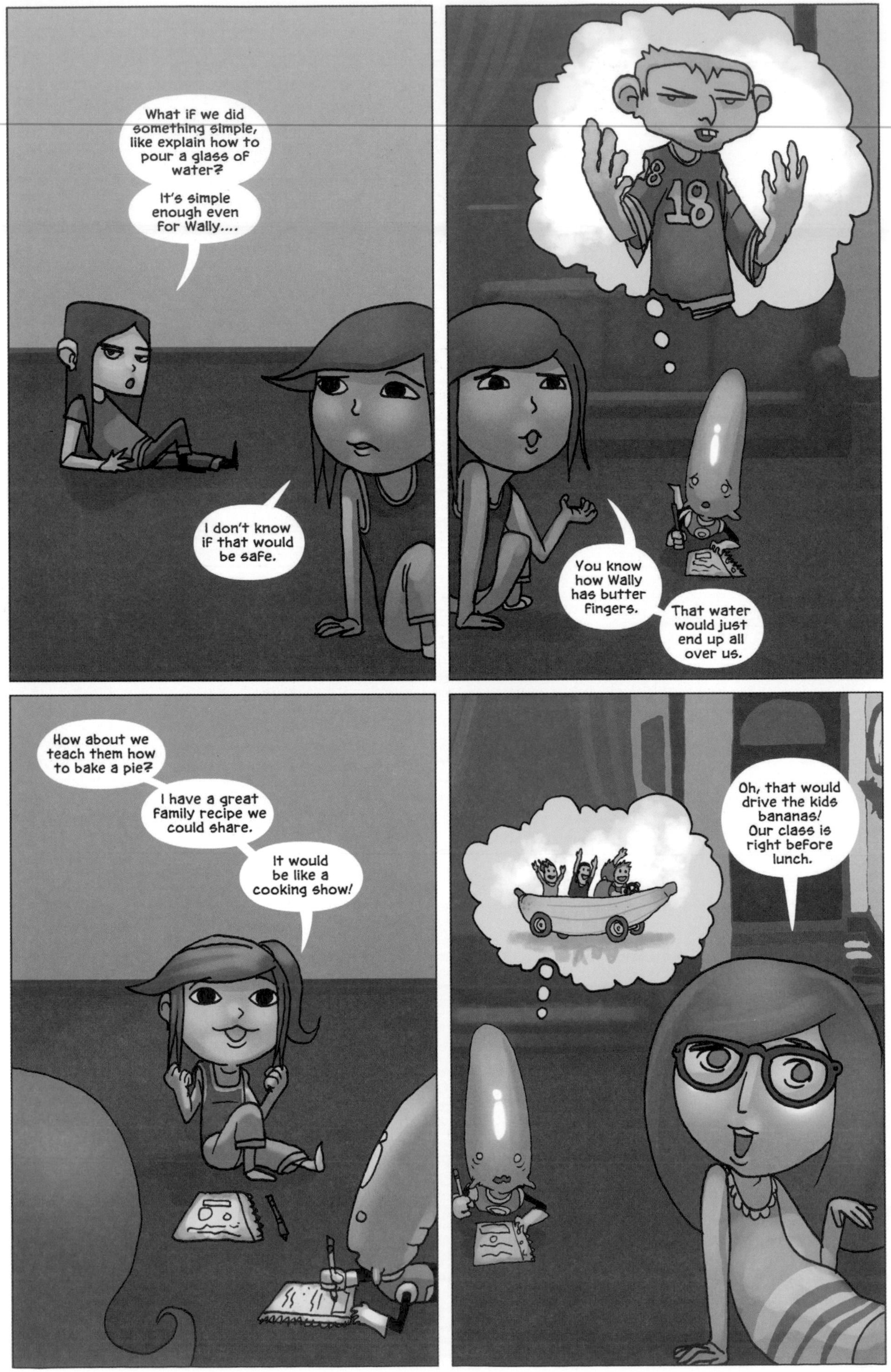
What if we did something simple, like explain how to pour a glass of water?
It's simple enough even for Wally....
I don't know if that would be safe.
You know how Wally has butter fingers.
That water would just end up all over us.
How about we teach them how to bake a pie?
I have a great family recipe we could share.
It would be like a cooking show!
Oh, that would drive the kids bananas! Our class is right before lunch.

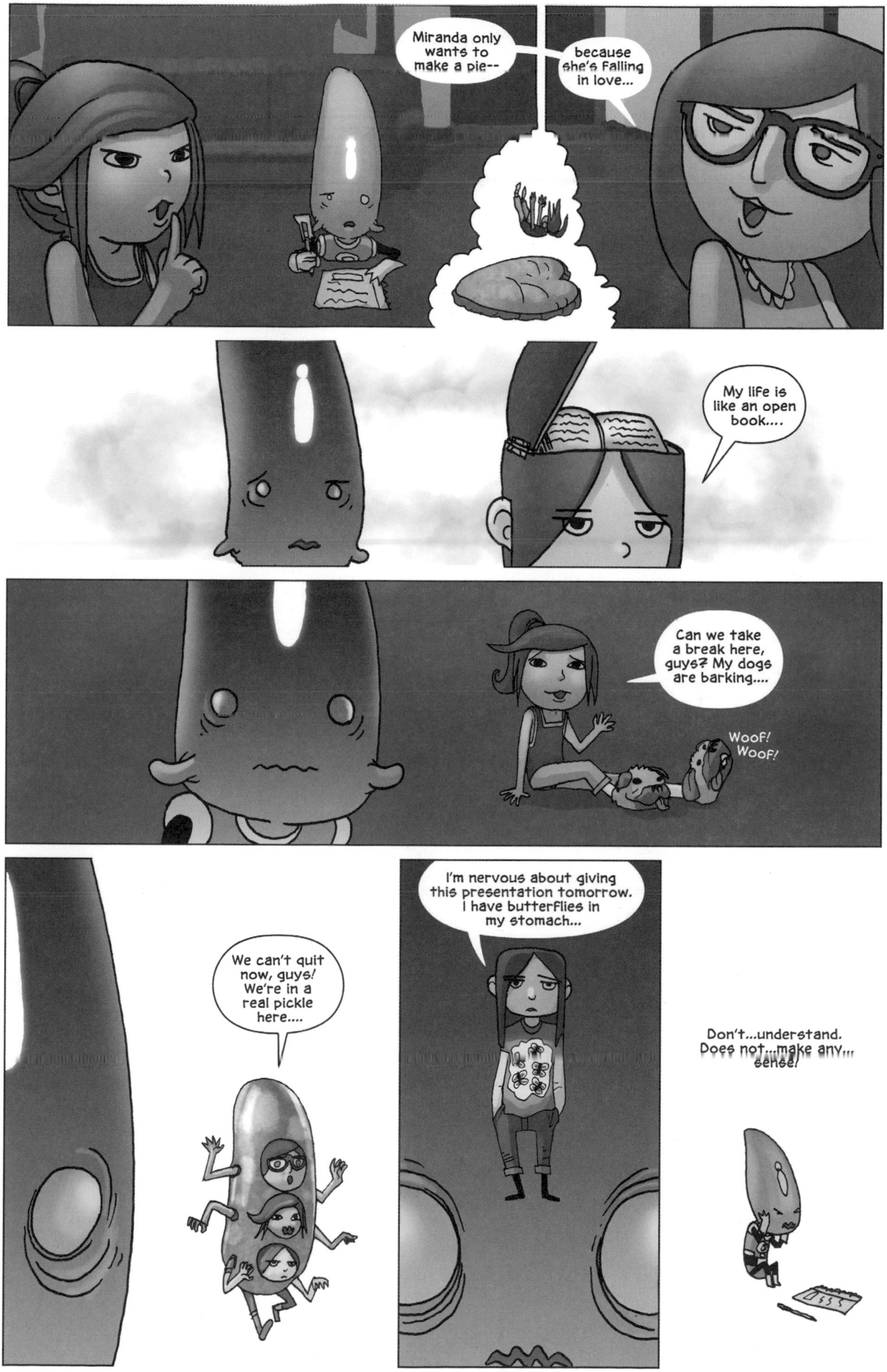
Miranda only wants to make a pie--
because she's falling in love...
My life is like an open book....
Can we take a break here, guys? My dogs are barking....
Woof! Woof!
We can't quit now, guys! We're in a real pickle here....
I'm nervous about giving this presentation tomorrow. I have butterflies in my stomach...
Don't...understand. Does not...make any... sense!

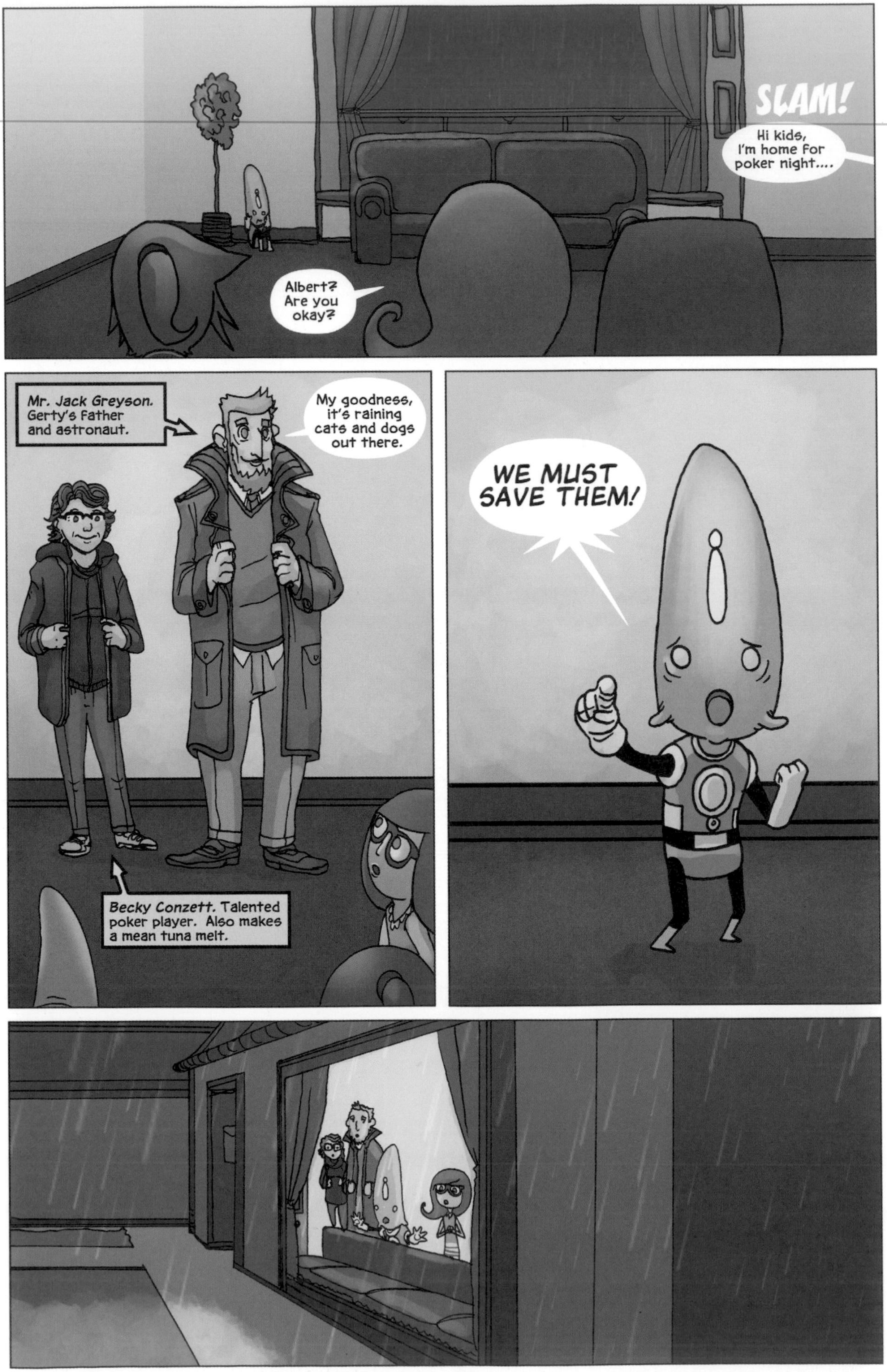
SLAM!
Hi kids, I'm home for poker night....
Albert? Are you okay?
Mr. Jack Greyson. Gerty's Father and astronaut.
My goodness, it's raining cats and dogs out there.
Becky Conzett. Talented poker player. Also makes a mean tuna melt.
WE MUST SAVE THEM!

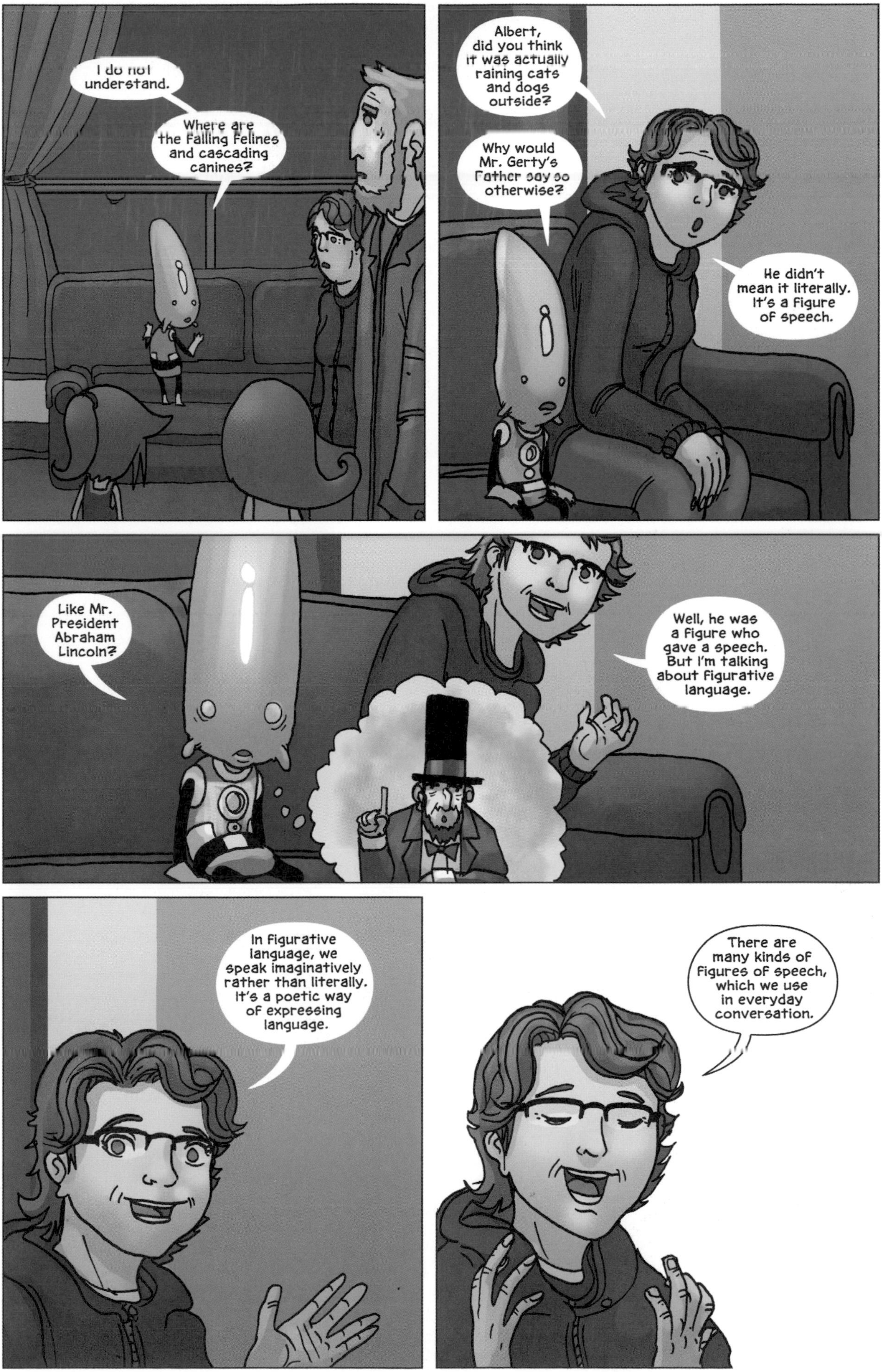

I do not understand.
Where are the Falling Felines and cascading canines?
Albert, did you think it was actually raining cats and dogs outside?
Why would Mr. Gerty's Father say so otherwise?
He didn't mean it literally. It's a figure of speech.
Like Mr. President Abraham Lincoln?
Well, he was a figure who gave a speech. But I'm talking about figurative language.
In figurative language, we speak imaginatively rather than literally. It's a poetic way of expressing language.
There are many kinds of figures of speech, which we use in everyday conversation.

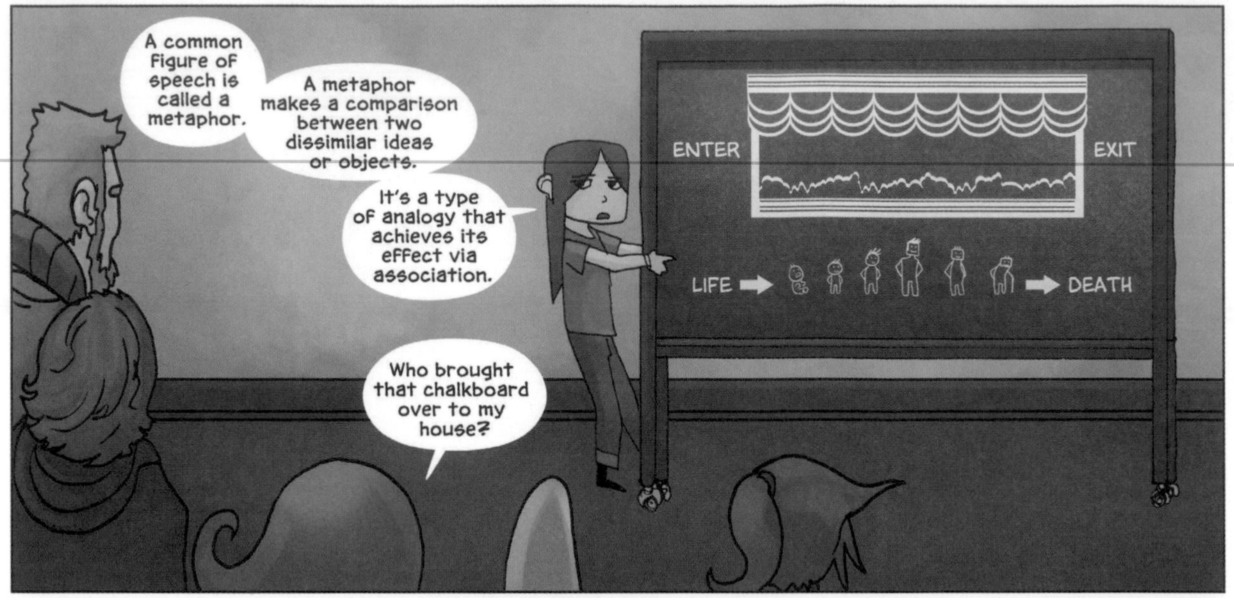
A common figure of speech is called a metaphor.
A metaphor makes a comparison between two dissimilar ideas or objects.
It's a type of analogy that achieves its effect via association.
ENTER
EXIT
LIFE
DEATH
Who brought that chalkboard over to my house?

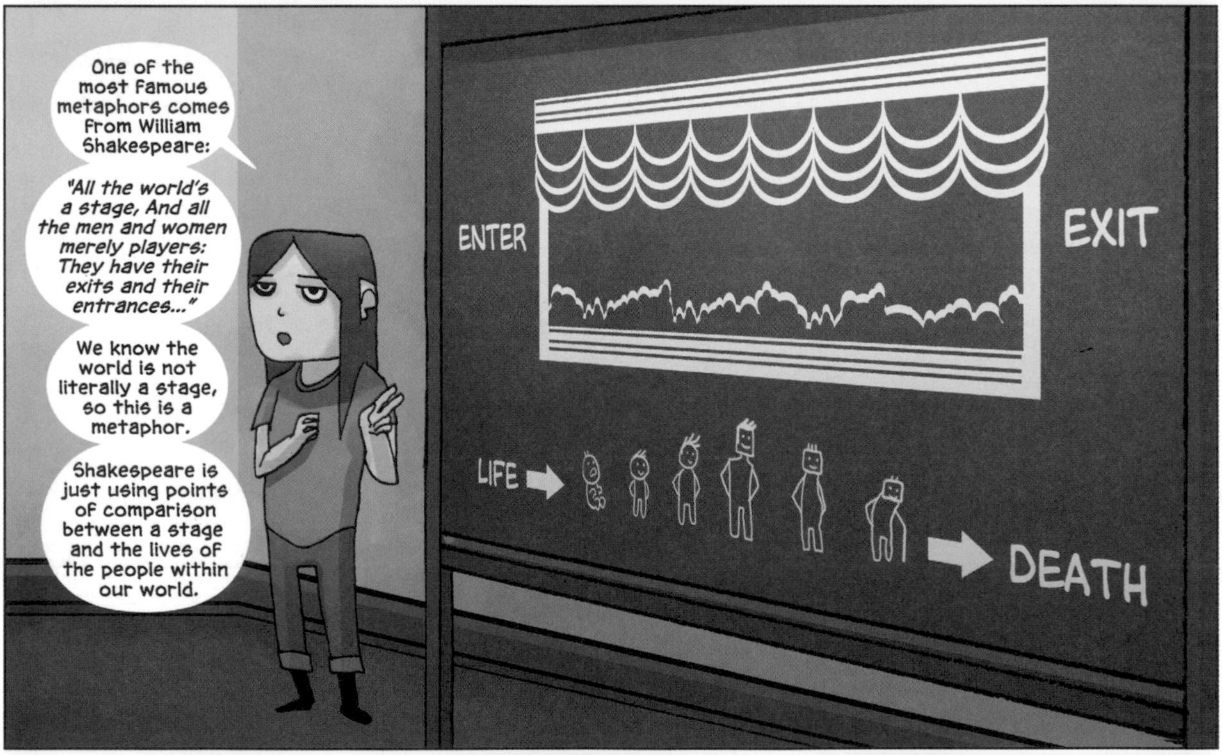
One of the most famous metaphors comes from William Shakespeare:
"All the world's a stage, And all the men and women merely players: They have their exits and their entrances..."
We know the world is not literally a stage, so this is a metaphor.
Shakespeare is just using points of comparison between a stage and the lives of the people within our world.
ENTER
EXIT
LIFE
DEATH

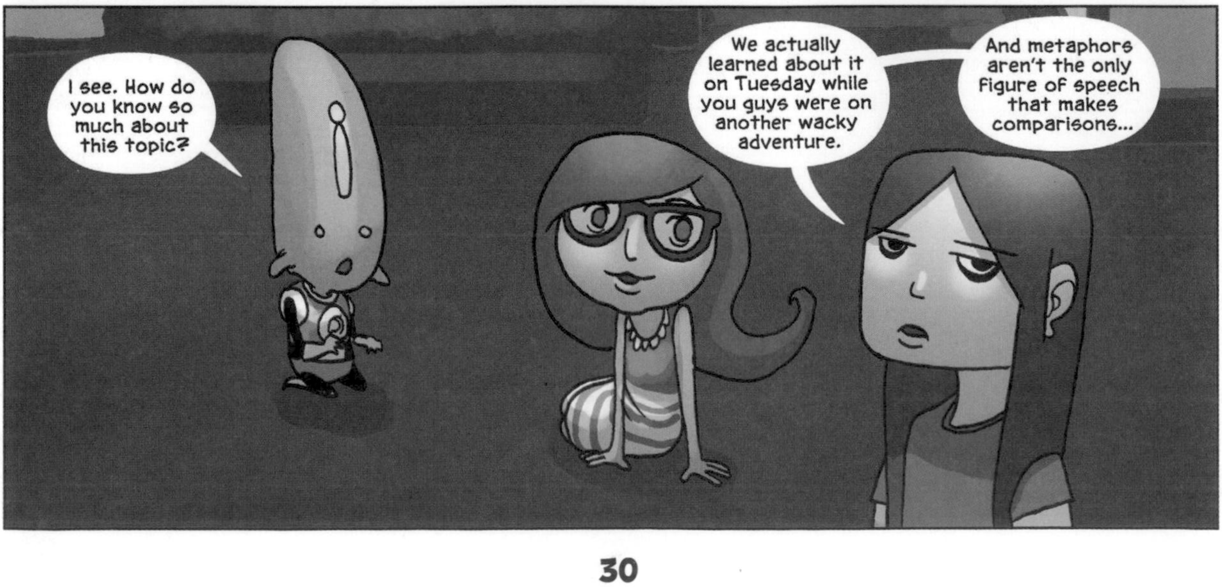
I see. How do you know so much about this topic?
We actually learned about it on Tuesday while you guys were on another wacky adventure.
And metaphors aren't the only figure of speech that makes comparisons...

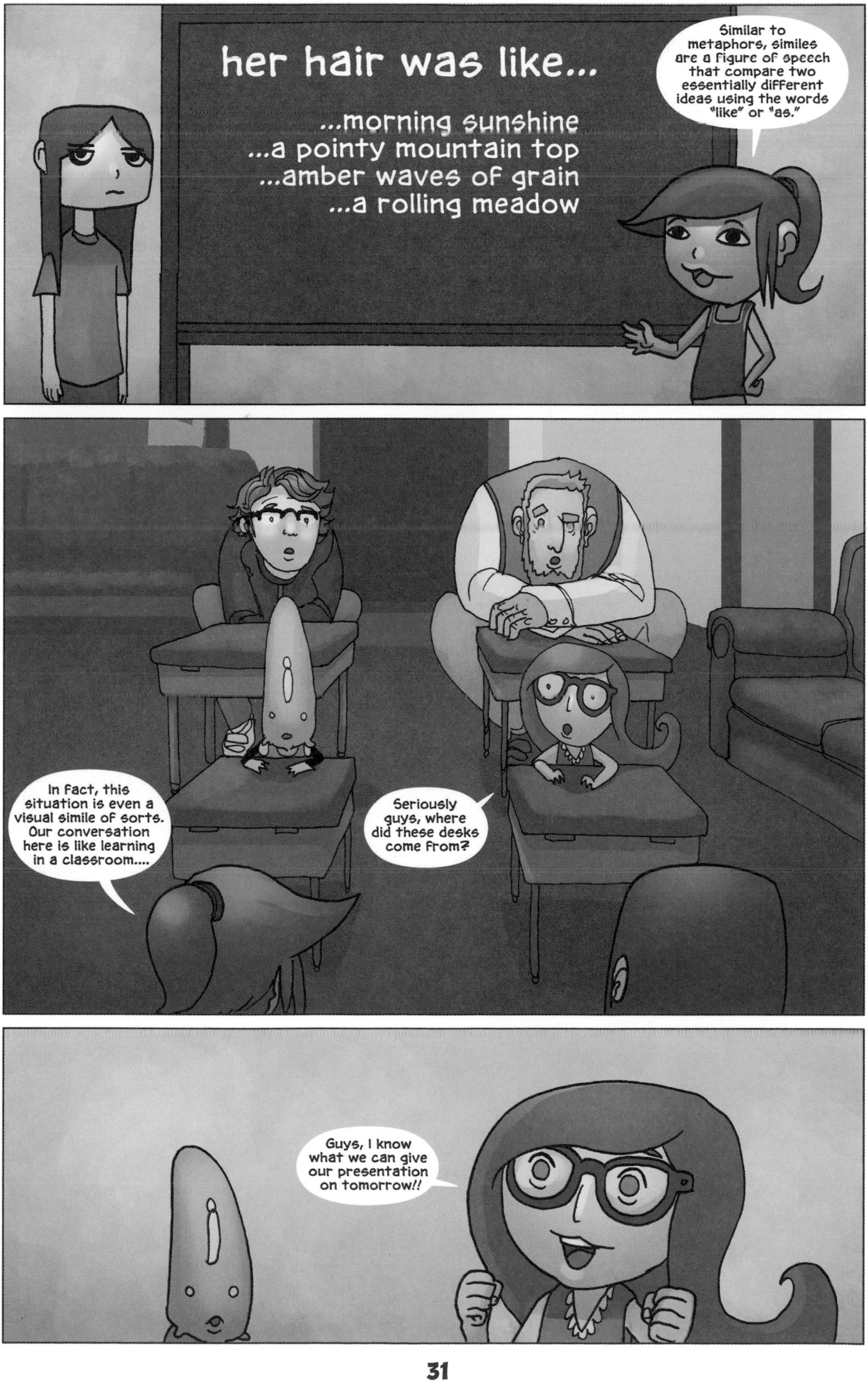
her hair was like...
...morning sunshine
...a pointy mountain top
...amber waves of grain
...a rolling meadow
Similar to metaphors, similes are a figure of speech that compare two essentially different ideas using the words "like" or "as."
In fact, this situation is even a visual simile of sorts. Our conversation here is like learning in a classroom....
Seriously guys, where did these desks come from?
Guys, I know what we can give our presentation on tomorrow!!

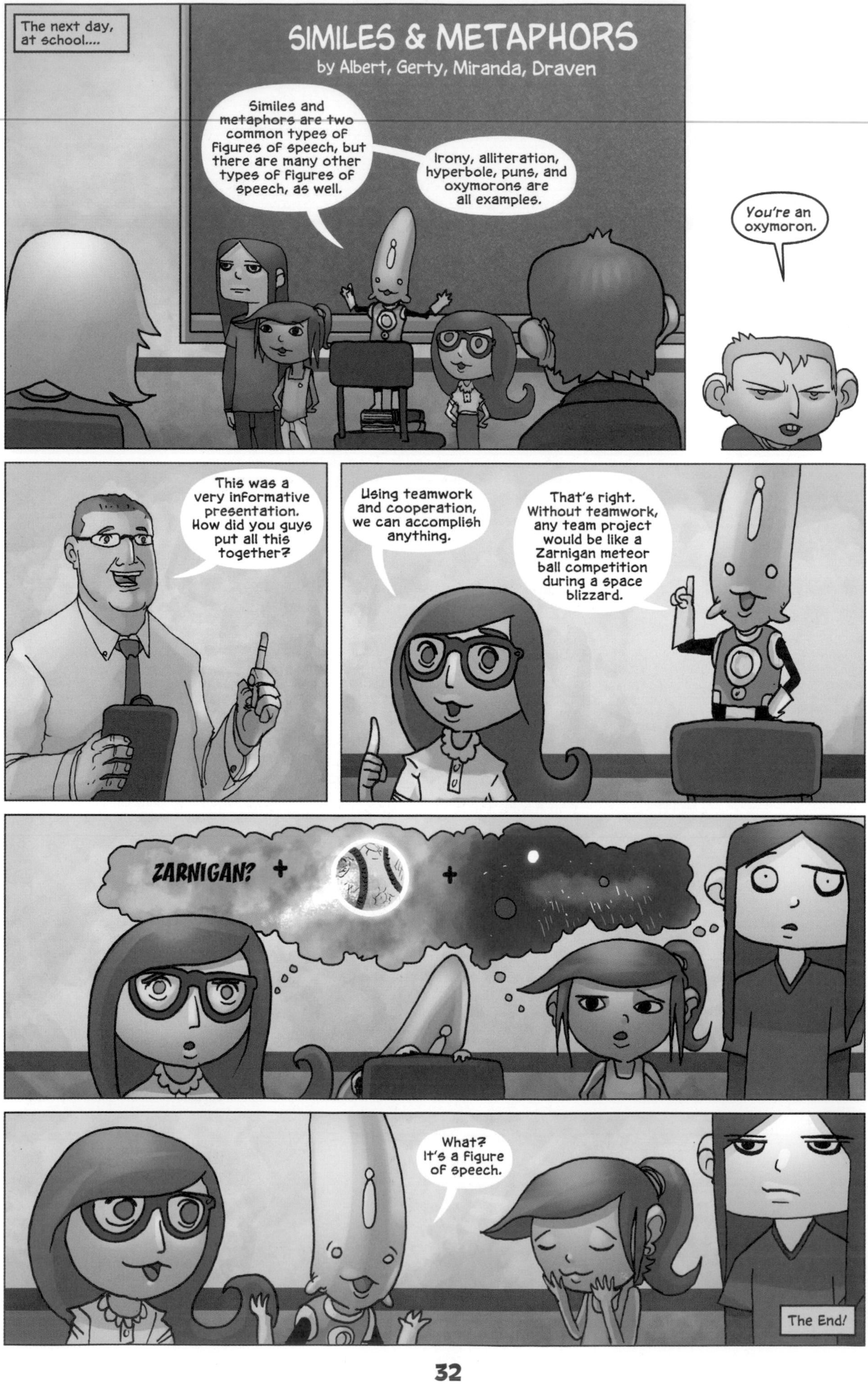
The next day, at school....
SIMILES & METAPHORS
by Albert, Gerty, Miranda, Draven
Similes and metaphors are two common types of figures of speech, but there are many other types of figures of speech, as well.
Irony, alliteration, hyperbole, puns, and oxymorons are all examples.
You're an oxymoron.
This was a very informative presentation. How did you guys put all this together?
Using teamwork and cooperation, we can accomplish anything.
That's right. Without teamwork, any team project would be like a Zarnigan meteor ball competition during a space blizzard.
ZARNIGAN? +
+
What? It's a figure of speech.
The End!

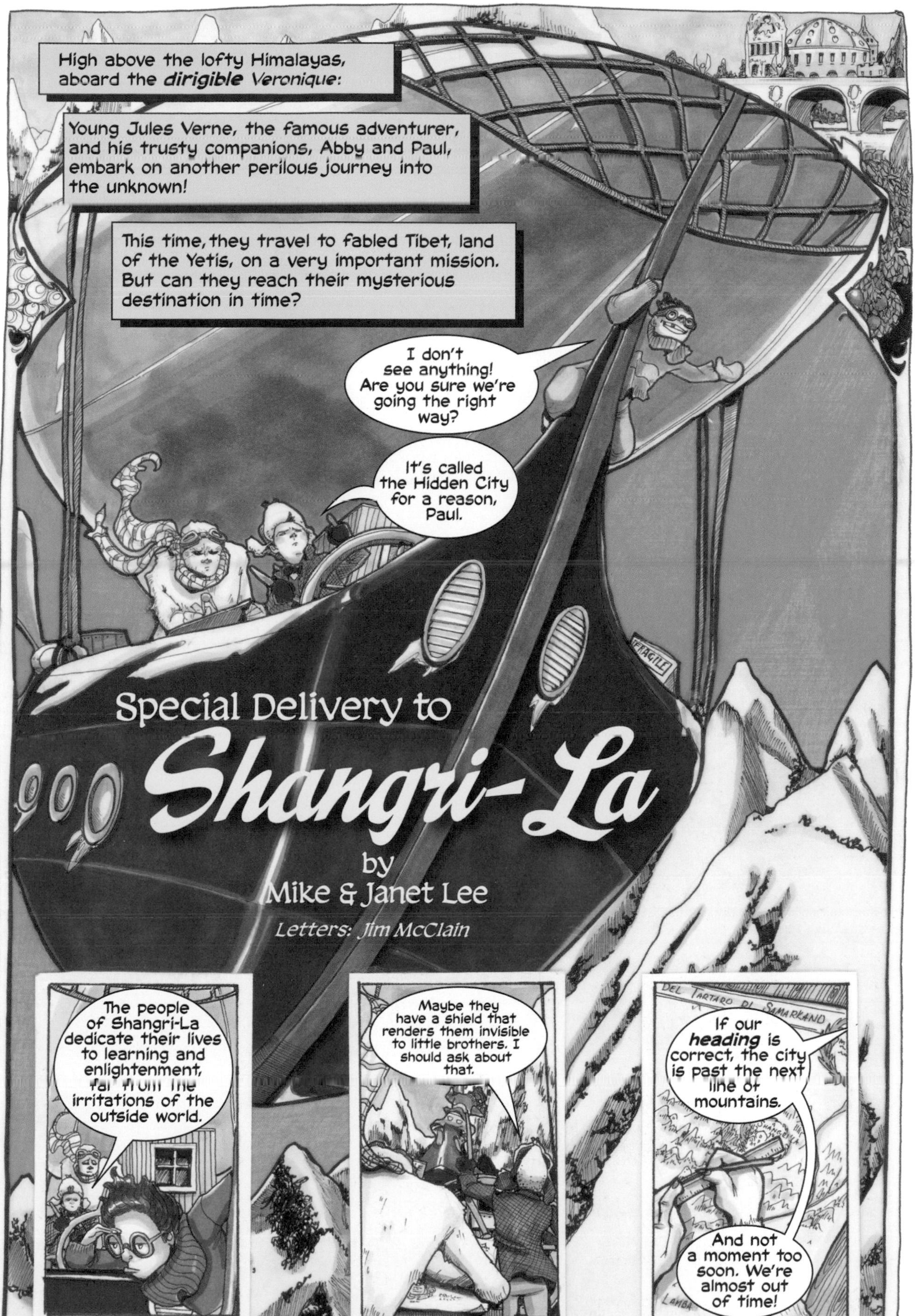

High above the lofty Himalayas, aboard the *dirigible* Veronique:
Young Jules Verne, the famous adventurer, and his trusty companions, Abby and Paul, embark on another perilous journey into the unknown!
This time, they travel to fabled Tibet, land of the Yetis, on a very important mission. But can they reach their mysterious destination in time?
I don't see anything! Are you sure we're going the right way?
It's called the Hidden City for a reason, Paul.
Special Delivery to
Shangri-La
by
Mike & Janet Lee
Letters: Jim McClain
The people of Shangri-La dedicate their lives to learning and enlightenment, far from the irritations of the outside world.
Maybe they have a shield that renders them invisible to little brothers. I should ask about that.
If our **heading** is correct, the city is past the next line of mountains.
And not a moment too soon. We're almost out of time!

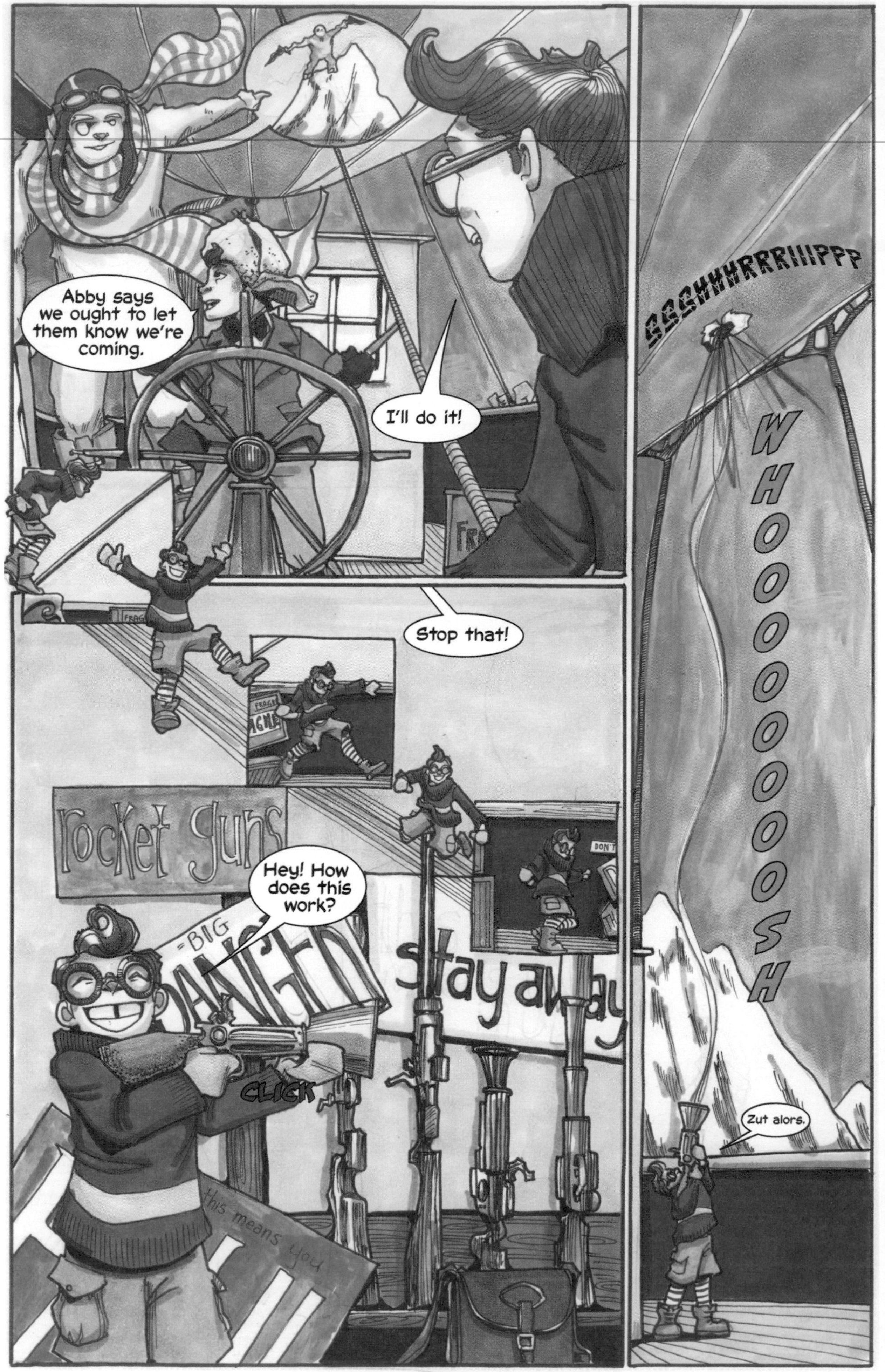
Abby says we ought to let them know we're coming.
I'll do it!
Stop that!
rocket guns
Hey! How does this work?
BIG DANGER
stay away
CLICK
this means you
SSSHHHRRRIIIPPP
WHOOOOOOOOOSH
Zut alors.

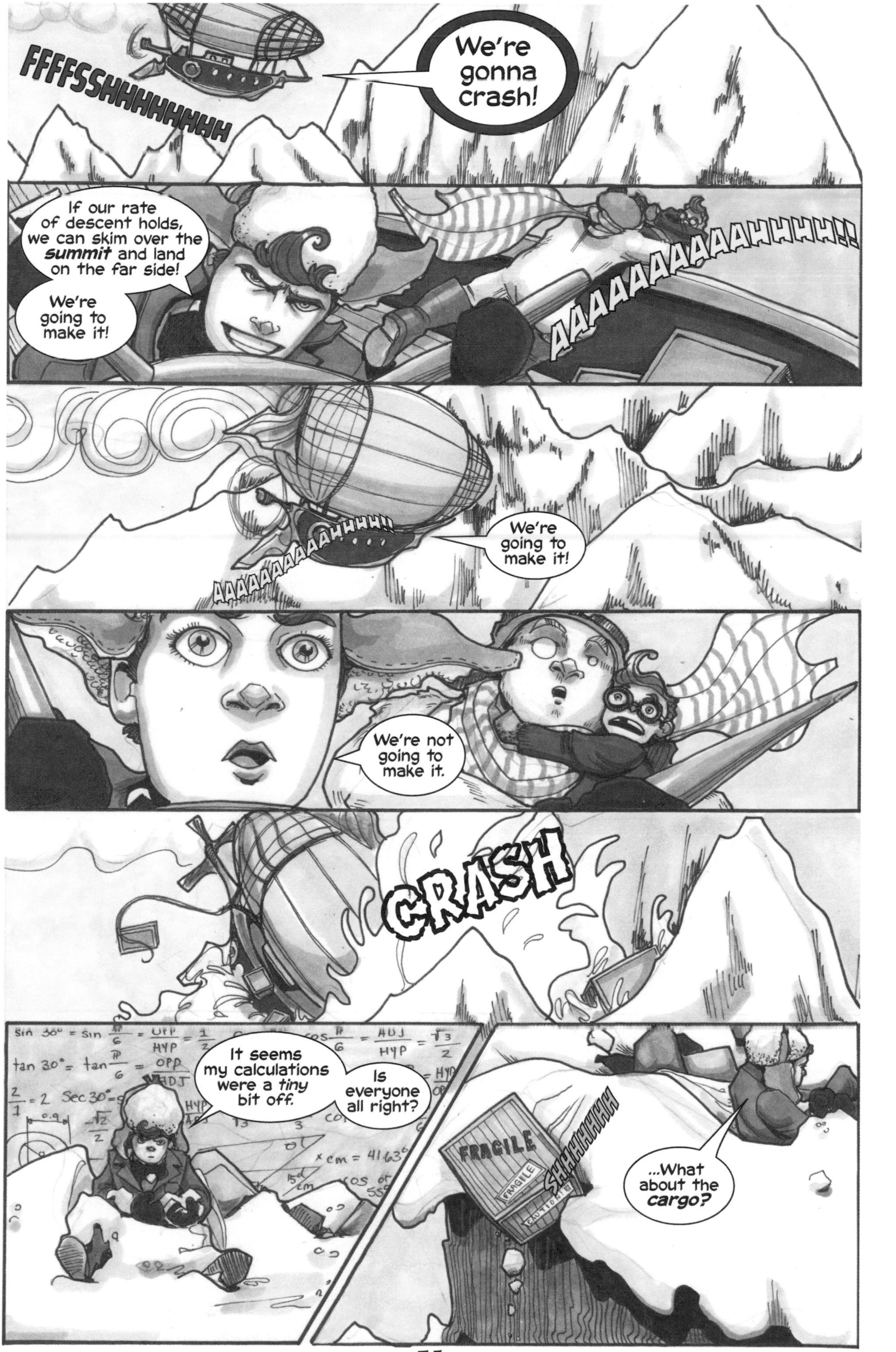
FFFFSSHHHHHHHHH
We're gonna crash!
If our rate of descent holds, we can skim over the *summit* and land on the far side!
We're going to make it!
AAAAAAAAAAAAHHHHH!!
AAAAAAAAAAAHHHH!!
We're going to make it!
We're not going to make it.
CRASH
It seems my calculations were a *tiny* bit off.
Is everyone all right?
FRAGILE
SHHHHHHH
...What about the *cargo?*

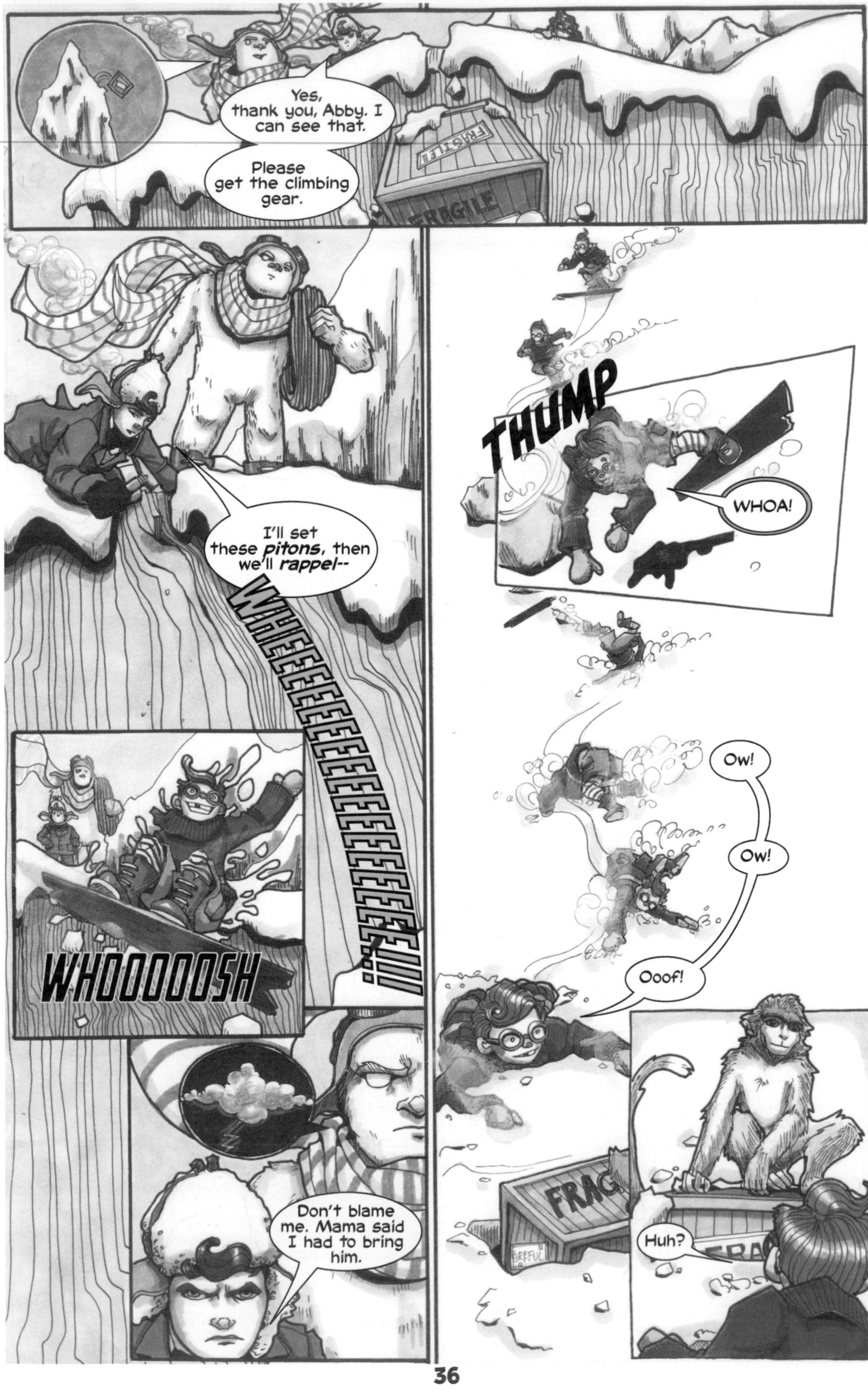

Yes, thank you, Abby. I can see that.
Please get the climbing gear.
FRAGILE
FRAGILE
I'll set these *pitons*, then we'll *rappel*--
WHEEEEEEEEEEEEEEEEE!!!!!
WHOOOOOOSH
THUMP
WHOA!
Ow!
Ow!
Ooof!
Don't blame me. Mama said I had to bring him.
FRAG
Huh?

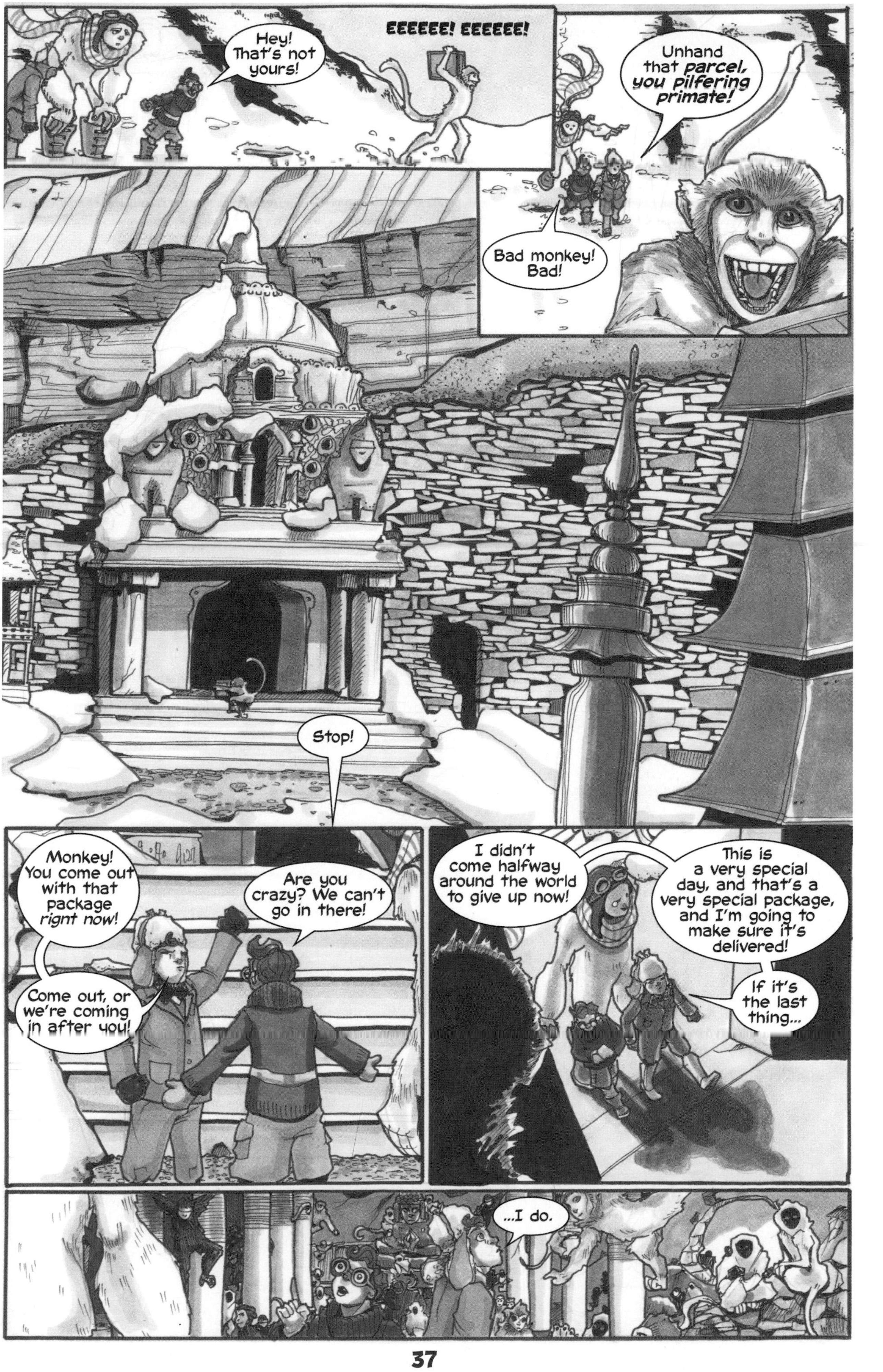
EEEEEE! EEEEEE!
Hey! That's not yours!
Unhand that parcel, you pilfering primate!
Bad monkey! Bad!
Stop!
Monkey! You come out with that package right now!
Come out, or we're coming in after you!
Are you crazy? We can't go in there!
I didn't come halfway around the world to give up now!
This is a very special day, and that's a very special package, and I'm going to make sure it's delivered!
If it's the last thing...
...I do.

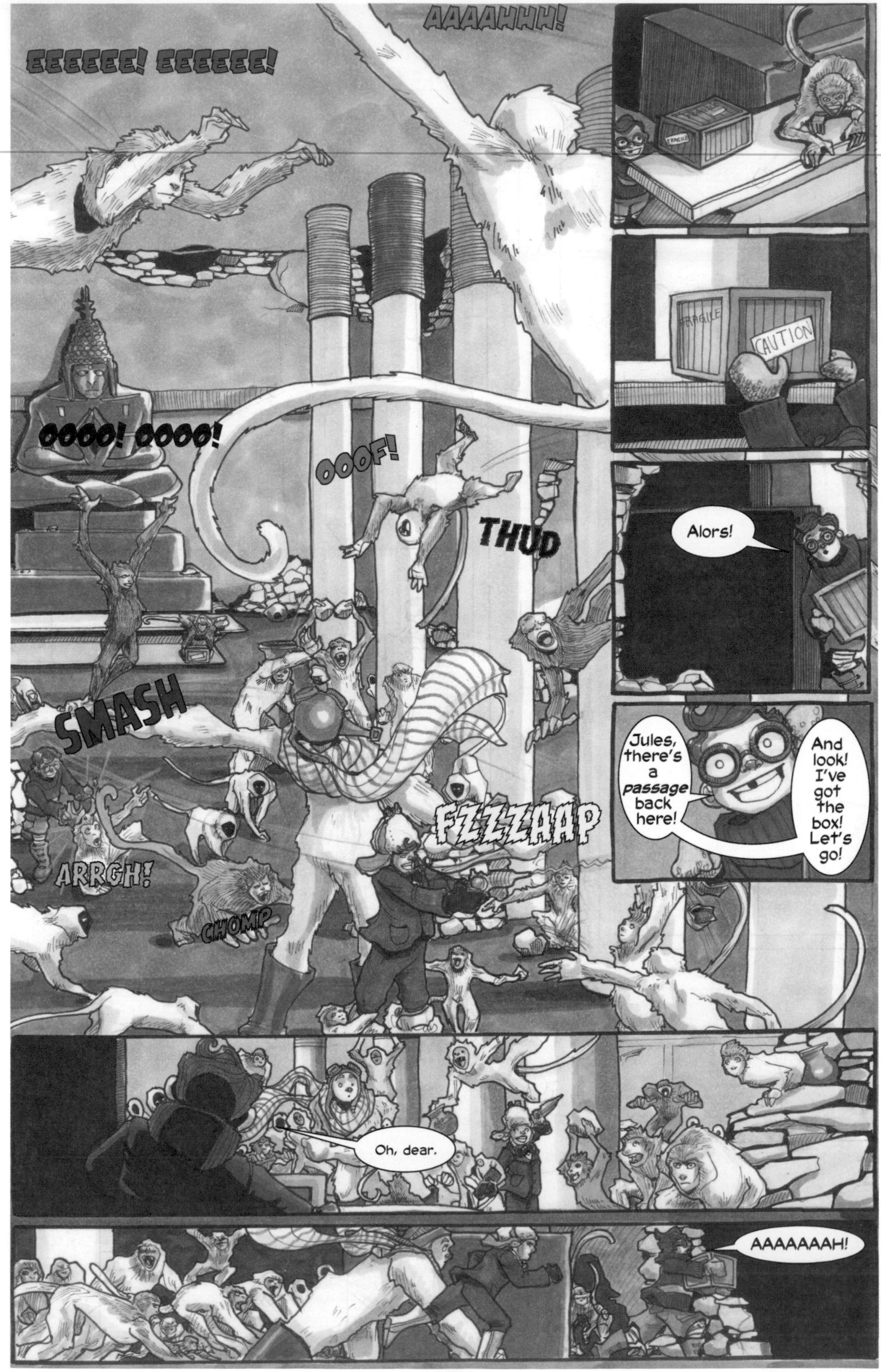
EEEEEE! EEEEEE!
AAAAHHH!
OOOO! OOOO!
OOOF!
THUD
SMASH
FZZZAAP
ARRGH!
CHOMP
FRAGILE
FRAGILE
CAUTION
Alors!
Jules, there's a *passage* back here!
And look! I've got the box! Let's go!
Oh, dear.
AAAAAAAH!

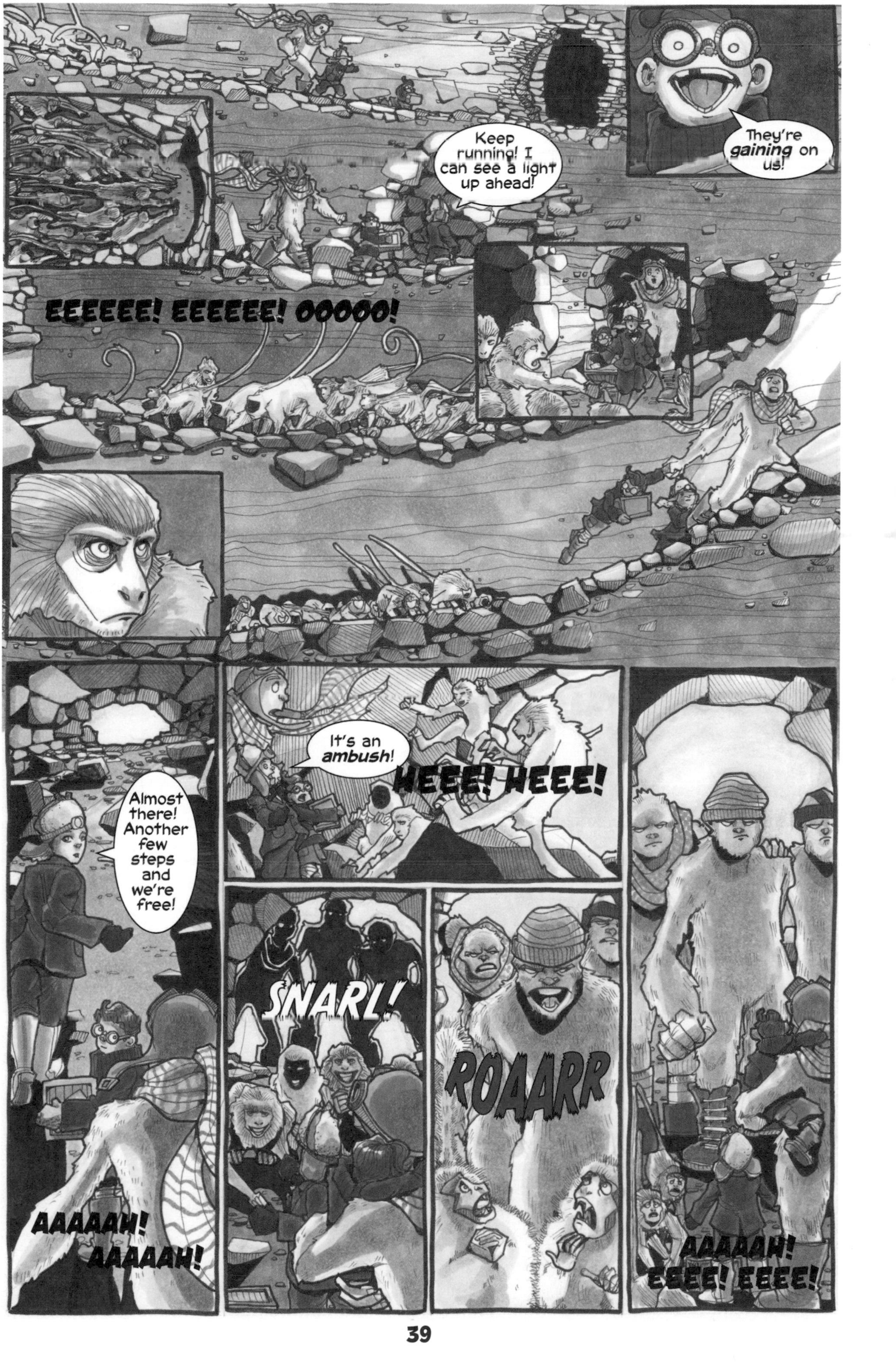

Keep running! I can see a light up ahead!
They're *gaining* on us!
EEEEEE! EEEEEE! OOOOO!
Almost there! Another few steps and we're free!
It's an *ambush*!
HEEE! HEEE!
SNARL!
ROAARR
AAAAAH! AAAAAH!
AAAAAH! EEEE! EEEE!

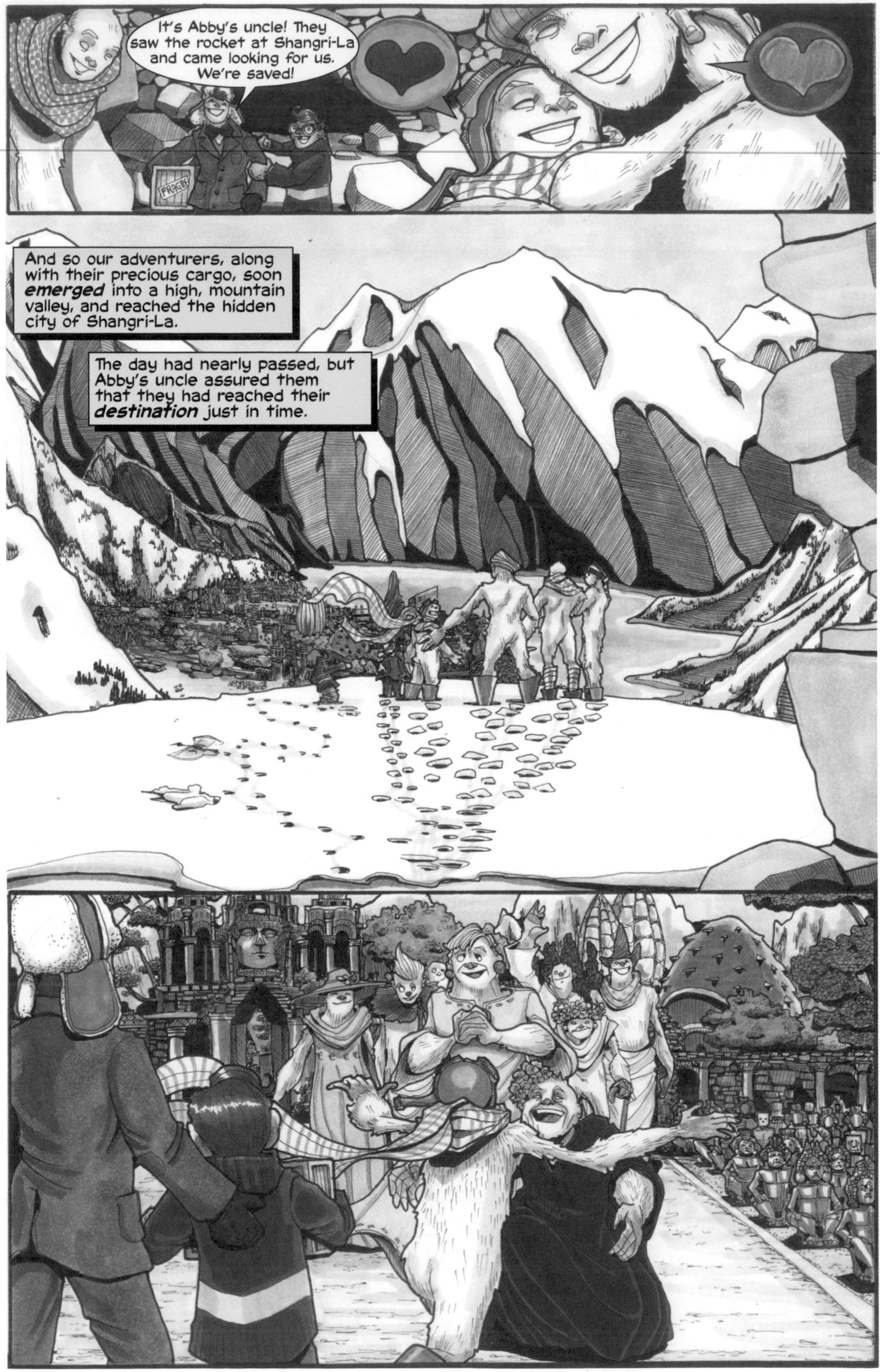
It's Abby's uncle! They saw the rocket at Shangri-La and came looking for us. We're saved!
And so our adventurers, along with their precious cargo, soon ***emerged*** into a high, mountain valley, and reached the hidden city of Shangri-La.
The day had nearly passed, but Abby's uncle assured them that they had reached their ***destination*** just in time.

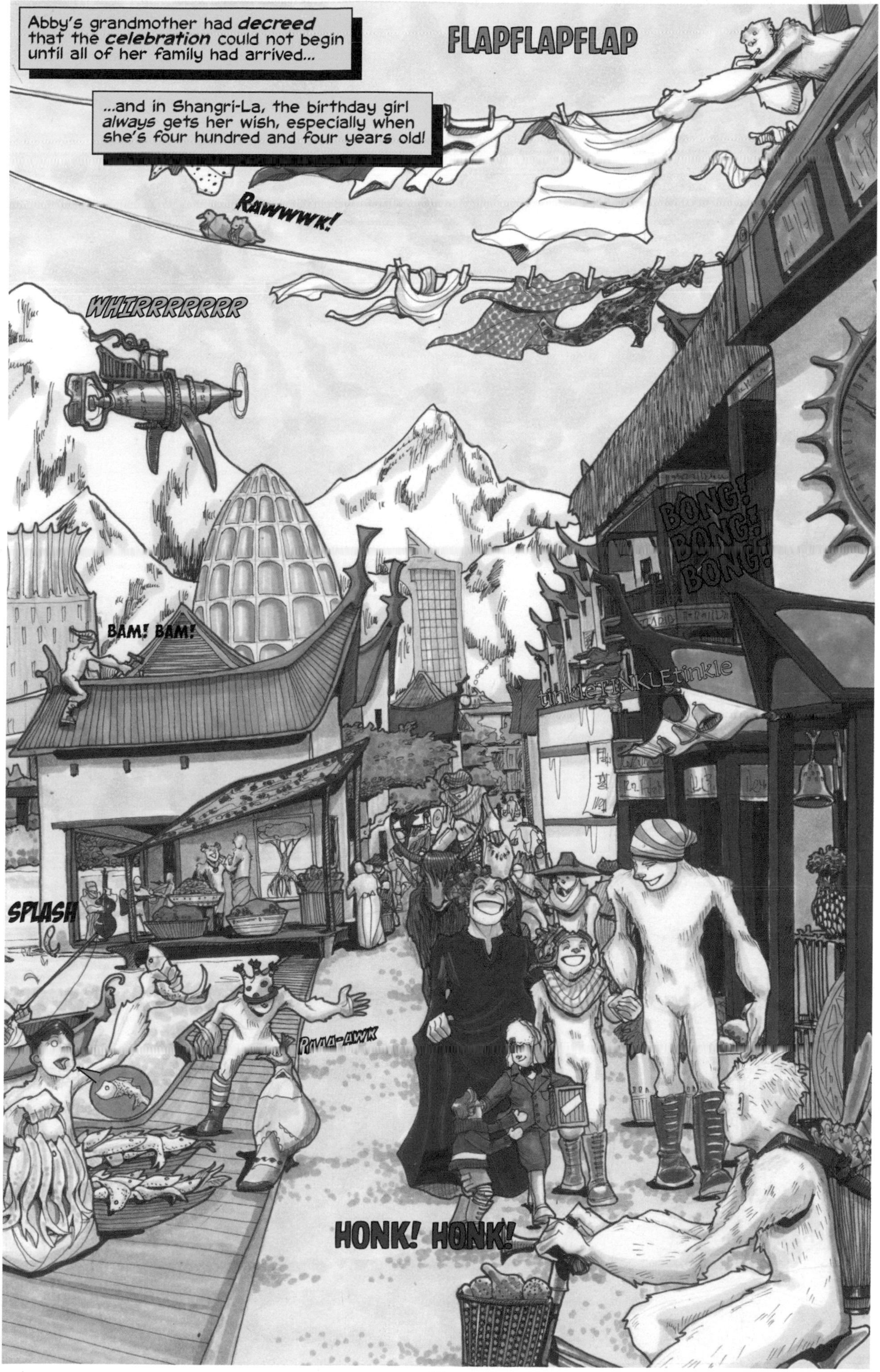
Abby's grandmother had *decreed* that the *celebration* could not begin until all of her family had arrived...
...and in Shangri-La, the birthday girl *always* gets her wish, especially when she's four hundred and four years old!
FLAPFLAPFLAP
RAWWWWK!
WHIRRRRRRRR
BONG! BONG! BONG!
BAM! BAM!
tinkleTINKLEtinkle
SPLASH
RWAA-AWK
HONK! HONK!

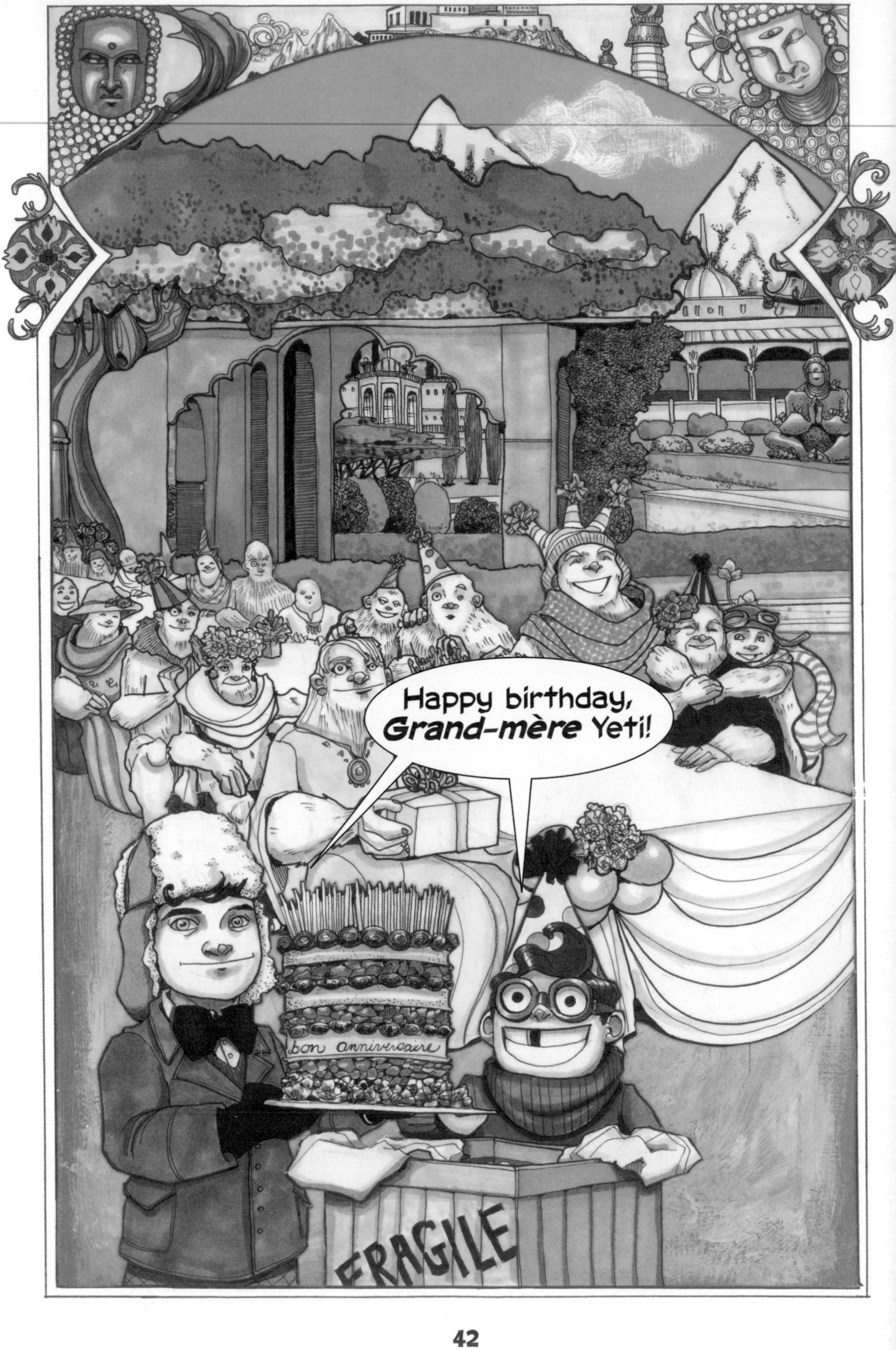
Happy birthday, Grand-mère Yeti!
bon anniversaire
FRAGILE

SCIENCE

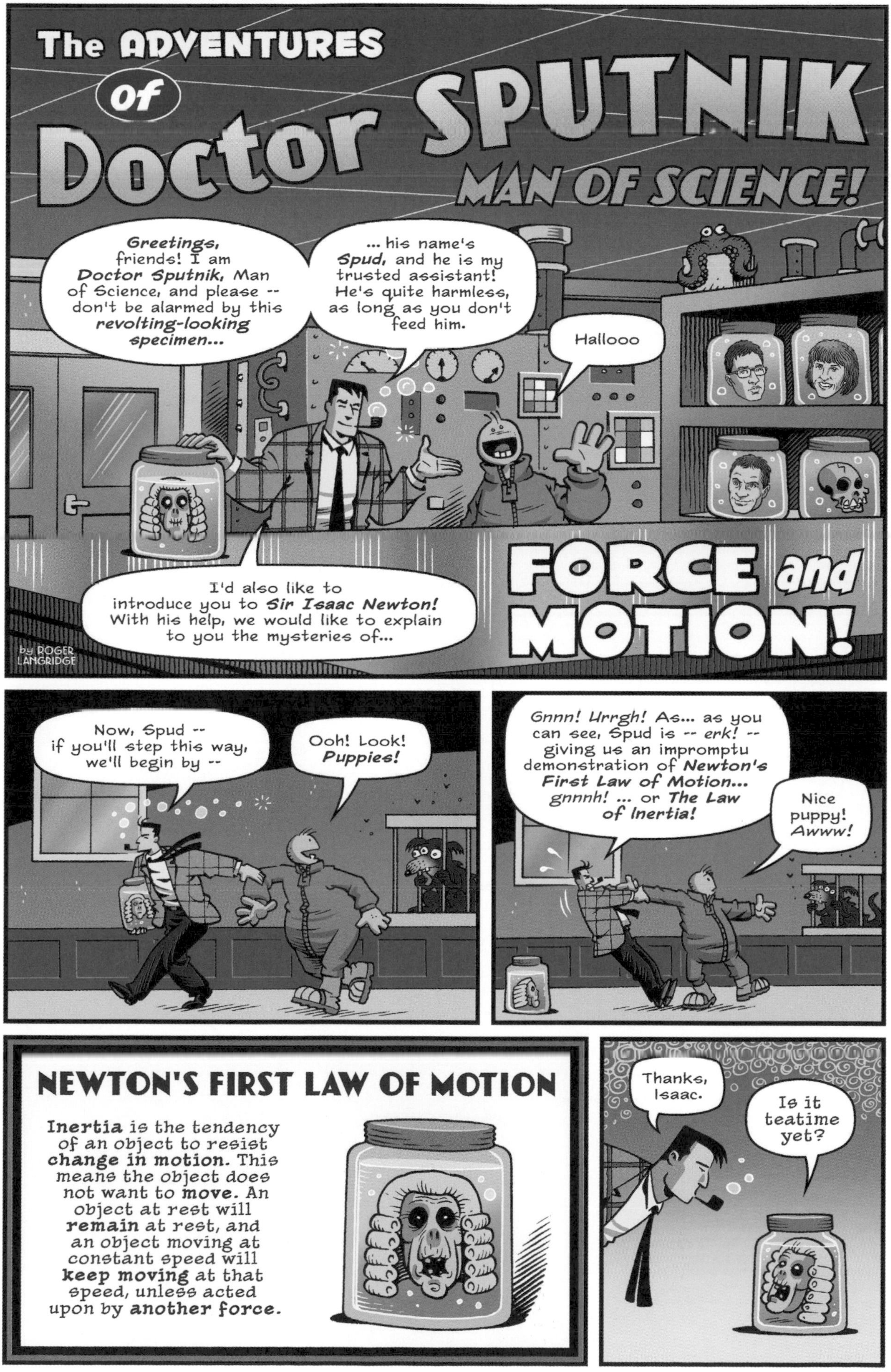

The ADVENTURES of Doctor SPUTNIK MAN OF SCIENCE!
Greetings, friends! I am Doctor Sputnik, Man of Science, and please -- don't be alarmed by this revolting-looking specimen...
... his name's Spud, and he is my trusted assistant! He's quite harmless, as long as you don't feed him.
Hallooo
I'd also like to introduce you to Sir Isaac Newton! With his help, we would like to explain to you the mysteries of...
FORCE and MOTION!
by ROGER LANGRIDGE
Now, Spud -- if you'll step this way, we'll begin by --
Ooh! Look! Puppies!
Gnnn! Urrgh! As... as you can see, Spud is -- erk! -- giving us an impromptu demonstration of Newton's First Law of Motion... gnnnh! ... or The Law of Inertia!
Nice puppy! Awww!
NEWTON'S FIRST LAW OF MOTION
Inertia is the tendency of an object to resist change in motion. This means the object does not want to move. An object at rest will remain at rest, and an object moving at constant speed will keep moving at that speed, unless acted upon by another force.
Thanks, Isaac.
Is it teatime yet?

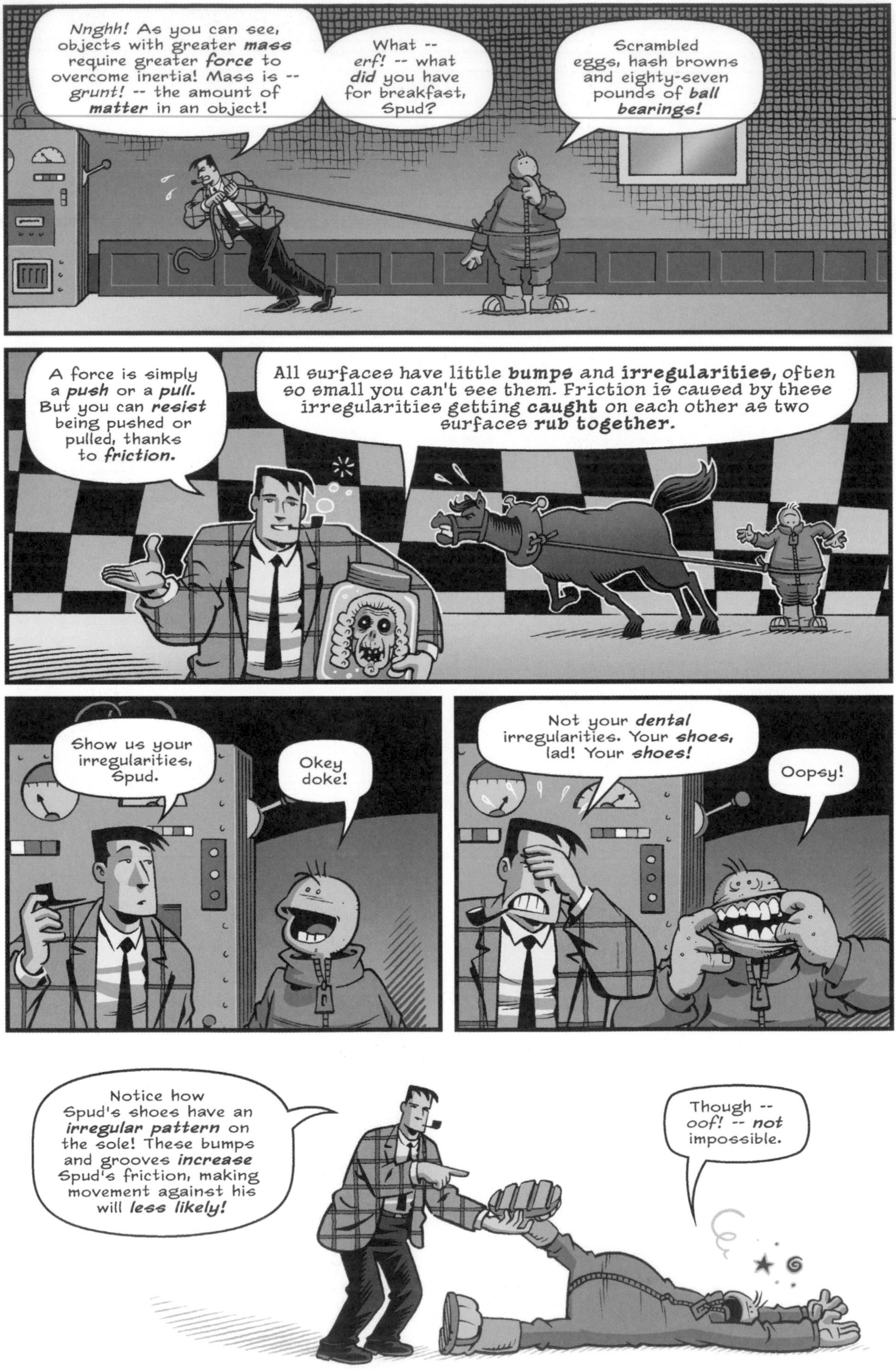

Nnghh! As you can see, objects with greater mass require greater force to overcome inertia! Mass is -- grunt! -- the amount of matter in an object!
What -- erf! -- what did you have for breakfast, Spud?
Scrambled eggs, hash browns and eighty-seven pounds of ball bearings!
A force is simply a push or a pull. But you can resist being pushed or pulled, thanks to friction.
All surfaces have little bumps and irregularities, often so small you can't see them. Friction is caused by these irregularities getting caught on each other as two surfaces rub together.
Show us your irregularities, Spud.
Okey doke!
Not your dental irregularities. Your shoes, lad! Your shoes!
Oopsy!
Notice how Spud's shoes have an irregular pattern on the sole! These bumps and grooves increase Spud's friction, making movement against his will less likely!
Though -- oof! -- not impossible.

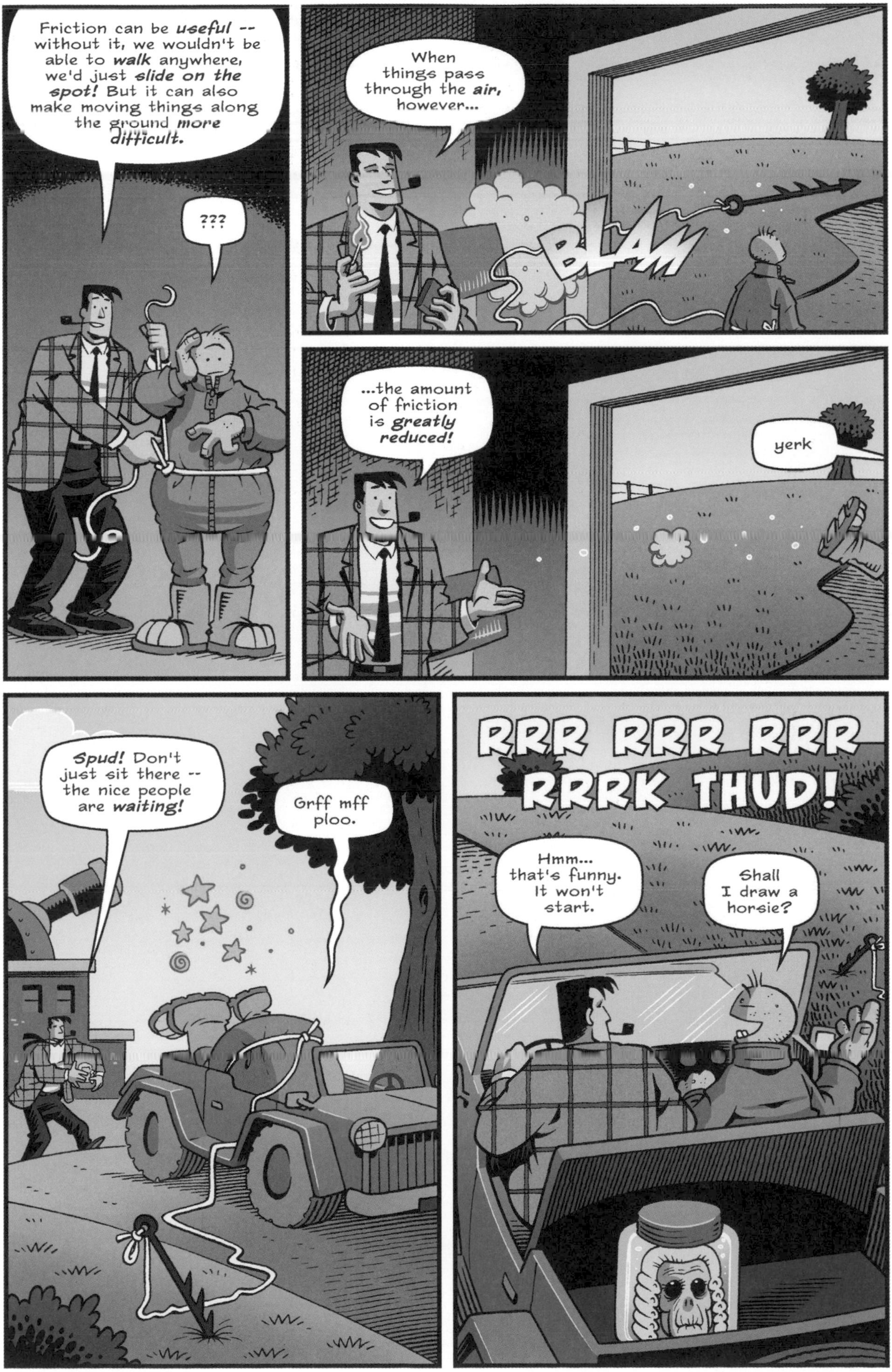
Friction can be useful -- without it, we wouldn't be able to walk anywhere, we'd just slide on the spot! But it can also make moving things along the ground more difficult.
???
When things pass through the air, however...
BLAM
...the amount of friction is greatly reduced!
yerk
Spud! Don't just sit there -- the nice people are waiting!
Grff mff ploo.
RRR RRR RRR RRRK THUD!
Hmm... that's funny. It won't start.
Shall I draw a horsie?

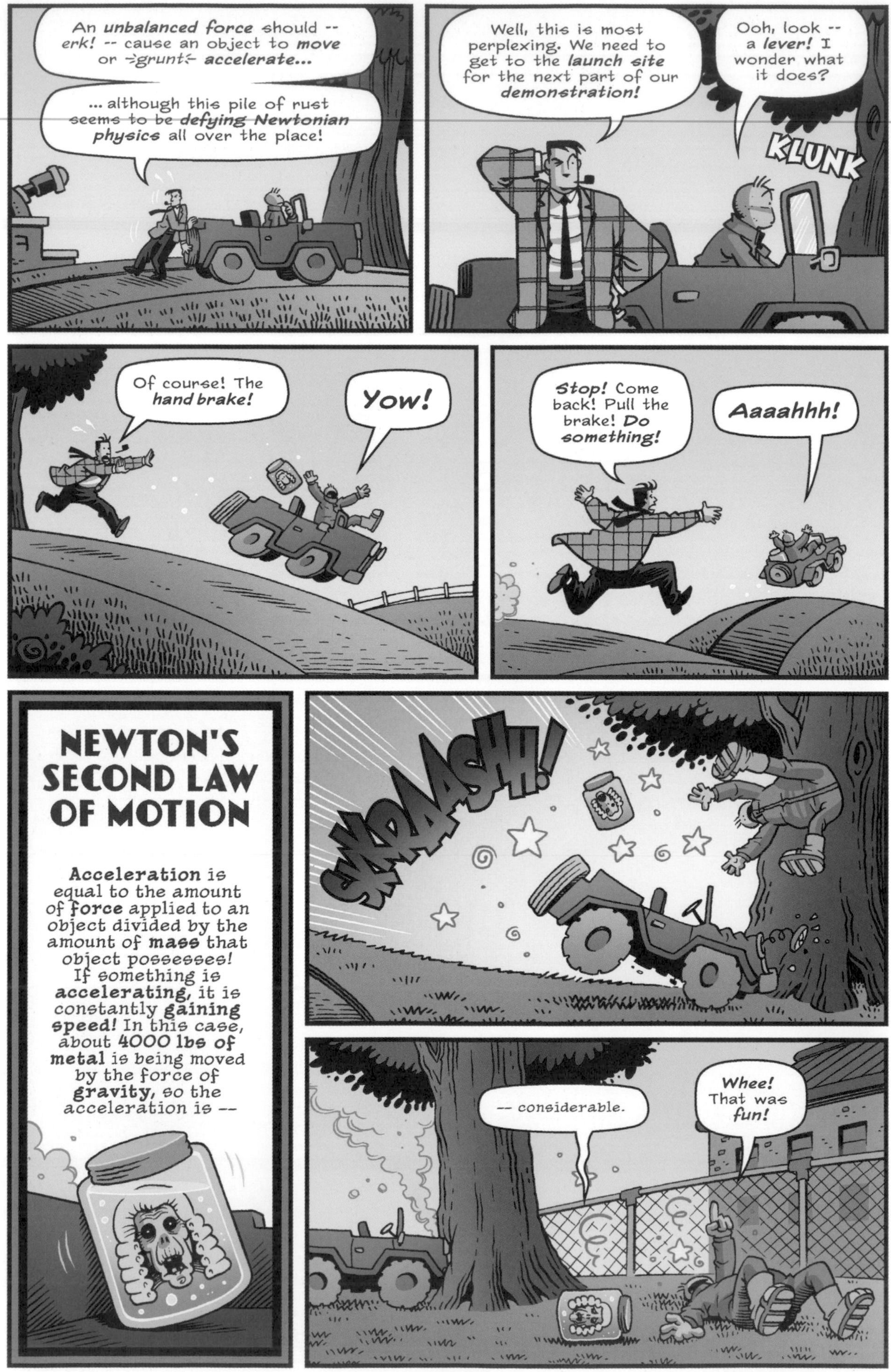
An unbalanced force should -- erk! -- cause an object to move or -grunt- accelerate...
... although this pile of rust seems to be defying Newtonian physics all over the place!
Well, this is most perplexing. We need to get to the launch site for the next part of our demonstration!
Ooh, look -- a lever! I wonder what it does?
KLUNK
Of course! The hand brake!
Yow!
Stop! Come back! Pull the brake! Do something!
Aaaahhh!
NEWTON'S SECOND LAW OF MOTION
Acceleration is equal to the amount of force applied to an object divided by the amount of mass that object possesses! If something is accelerating, it is constantly gaining speed! In this case, about 4000 lbs of metal is being moved by the force of gravity, so the acceleration is --
SKRAASHH!
-- considerable.
Whee! That was fun!

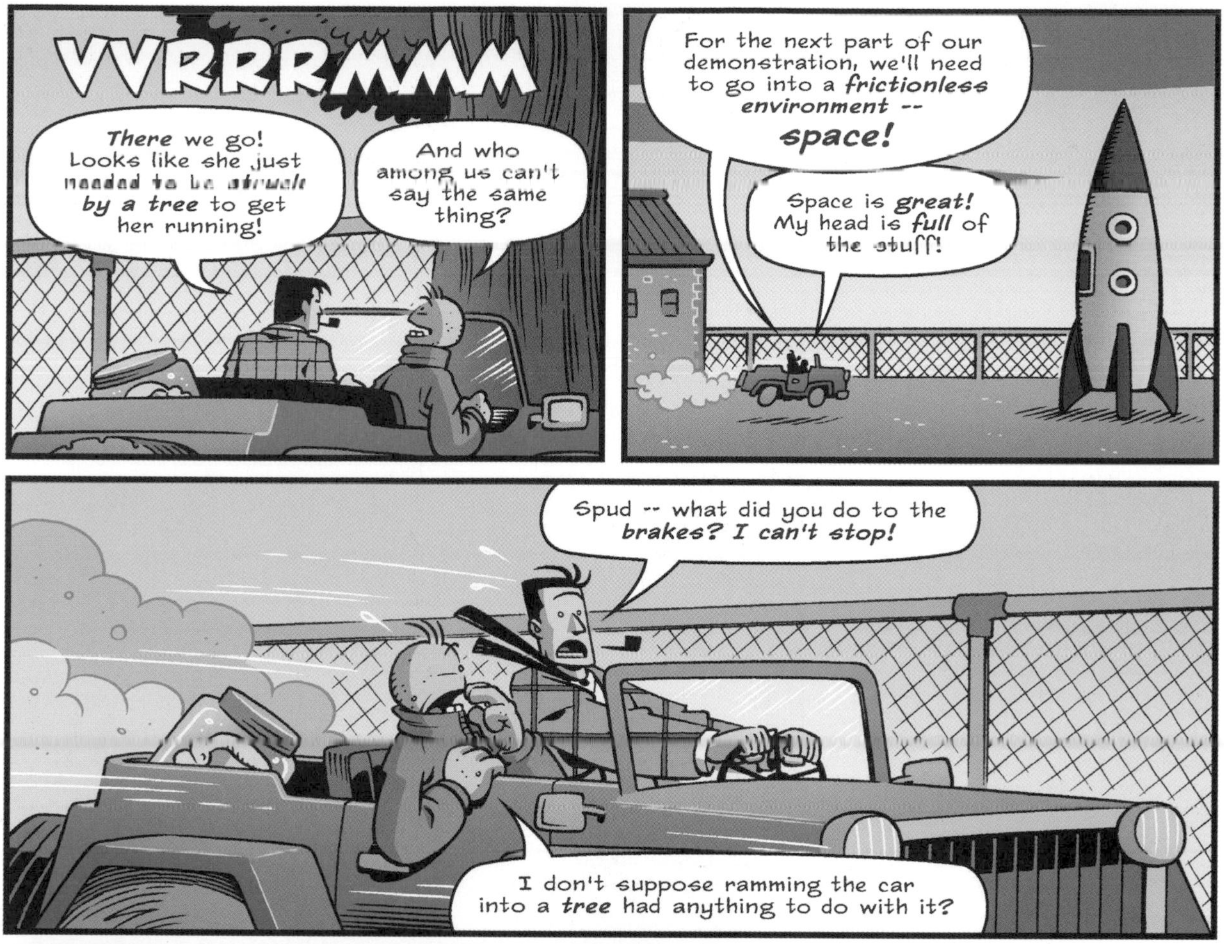
VVRRRMMM
There we go! Looks like she just needed to be struck by a tree to get her running!
And who among us can't say the same thing?
For the next part of our demonstration, we'll need to go into a frictionless environment -- space!
Space is great! My head is full of the stuff!
Spud -- what did you do to the brakes? I can't stop!
I don't suppose ramming the car into a tree had anything to do with it?

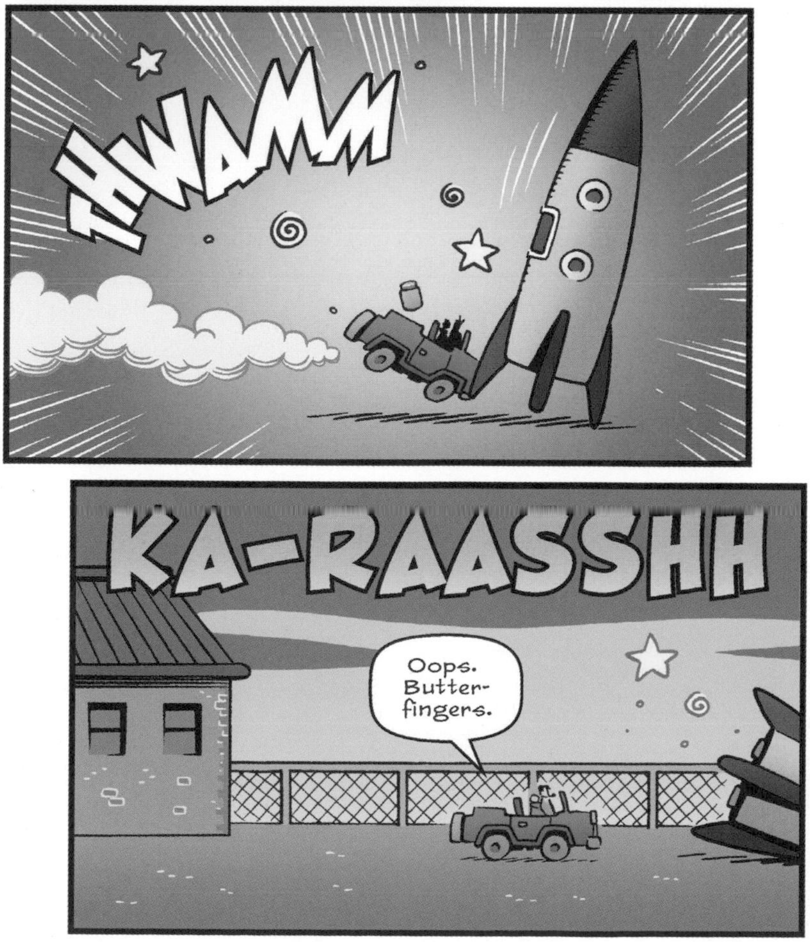
THWAMM
KA-RAASSHH
Oops. Butter-fingers.

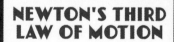

NEWTON'S THIRD LAW OF MOTION

For every **action**, there is an equal, but opposite, ***reaction!*** That is to say, if an object (say, a ***car***) should strike **another** object (say, a ***rocket***), the force of the moving car would exert itself on the stationary rocket and cause the rocket to **move!** In return, the rocket would exert equal, but opposite, stationary force upon the moving car, causing it to **stop!**

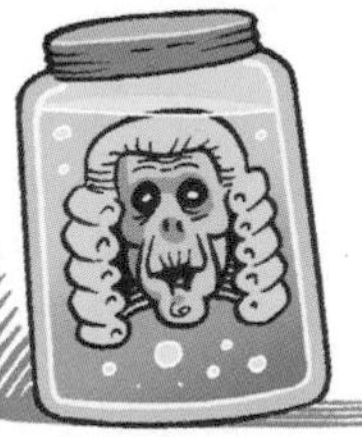

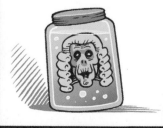

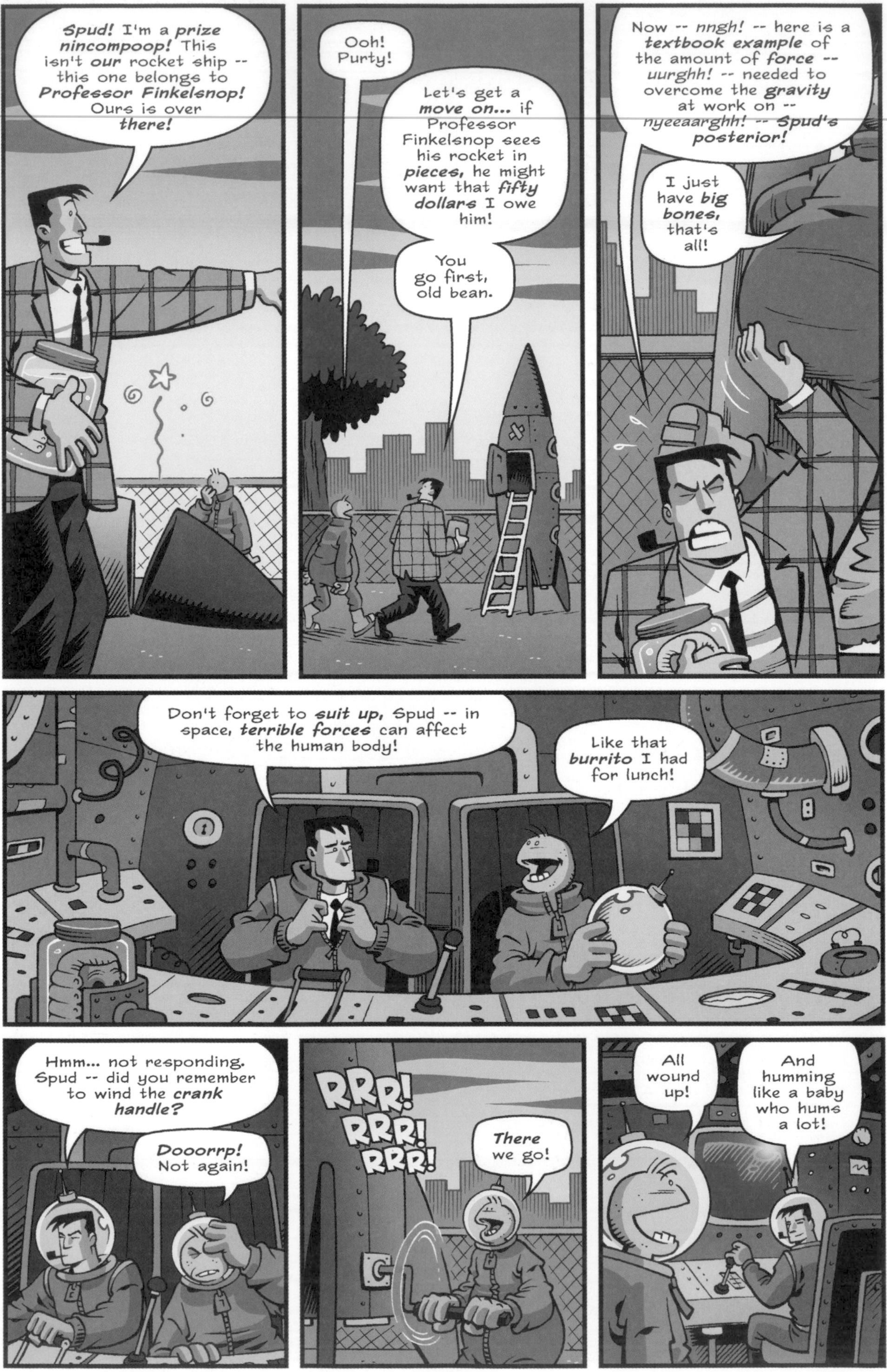
Spud! I'm a prize nincompoop! This isn't our rocket ship -- this one belongs to Professor Finkelsnop! Ours is over there!
Ooh! Purty!
Let's get a move on... if Professor Finkelsnop sees his rocket in pieces, he might want that fifty dollars I owe him!
You go first, old bean.
Now -- nngh! -- here is a textbook example of the amount of force -- uurghh! -- needed to overcome the gravity at work on -- nyeeaarghh! -- Spud's posterior!
I just have big bones, that's all!
Don't forget to suit up, Spud -- in space, terrible forces can affect the human body!
Like that burrito I had for lunch!
Hmm... not responding. Spud -- did you remember to wind the crank handle?
Dooorrp! Not again!
RRR! RRR! RRR!
There we go!
All wound up!
And humming like a baby who hums a lot!

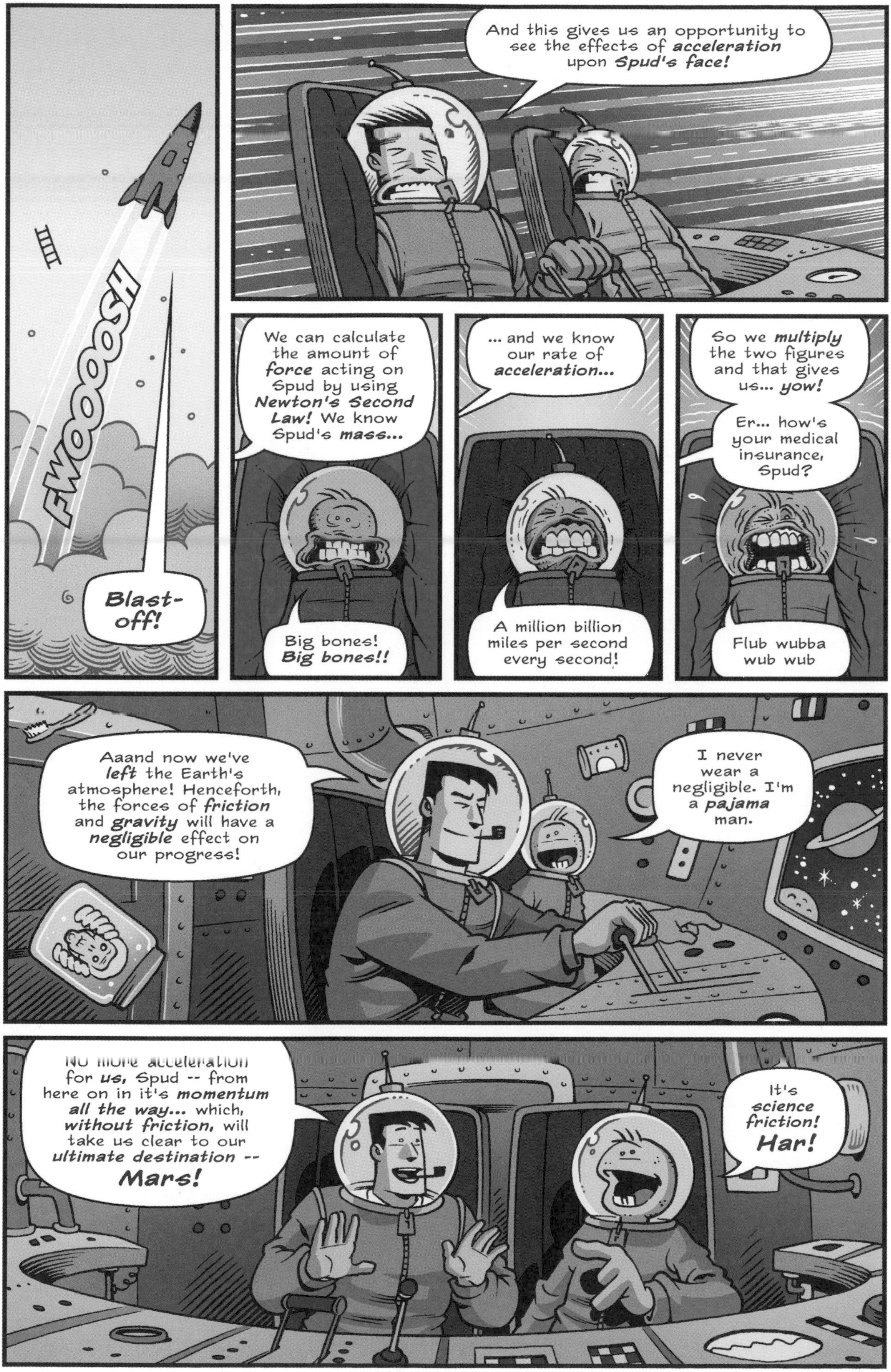
FWOOOOSH
Blast-off!
And this gives us an opportunity to see the effects of acceleration upon Spud's face!
We can calculate the amount of force acting on Spud by using Newton's Second Law! We know Spud's mass...
Big bones! Big bones!!
... and we know our rate of acceleration...
A million billion miles per second every second!
So we multiply the two figures and that gives us... yow!
Er... how's your medical insurance, Spud?
Flub wubba wub wub
Aaand now we've left the Earth's atmosphere! Henceforth, the forces of friction and gravity will have a negligible effect on our progress!
I never wear a negligible. I'm a pajama man.
No more acceleration for us, Spud -- from here on in it's momentum all the way... which, without friction, will take us clear to our ultimate destination -- Mars!
It's science friction! Har!

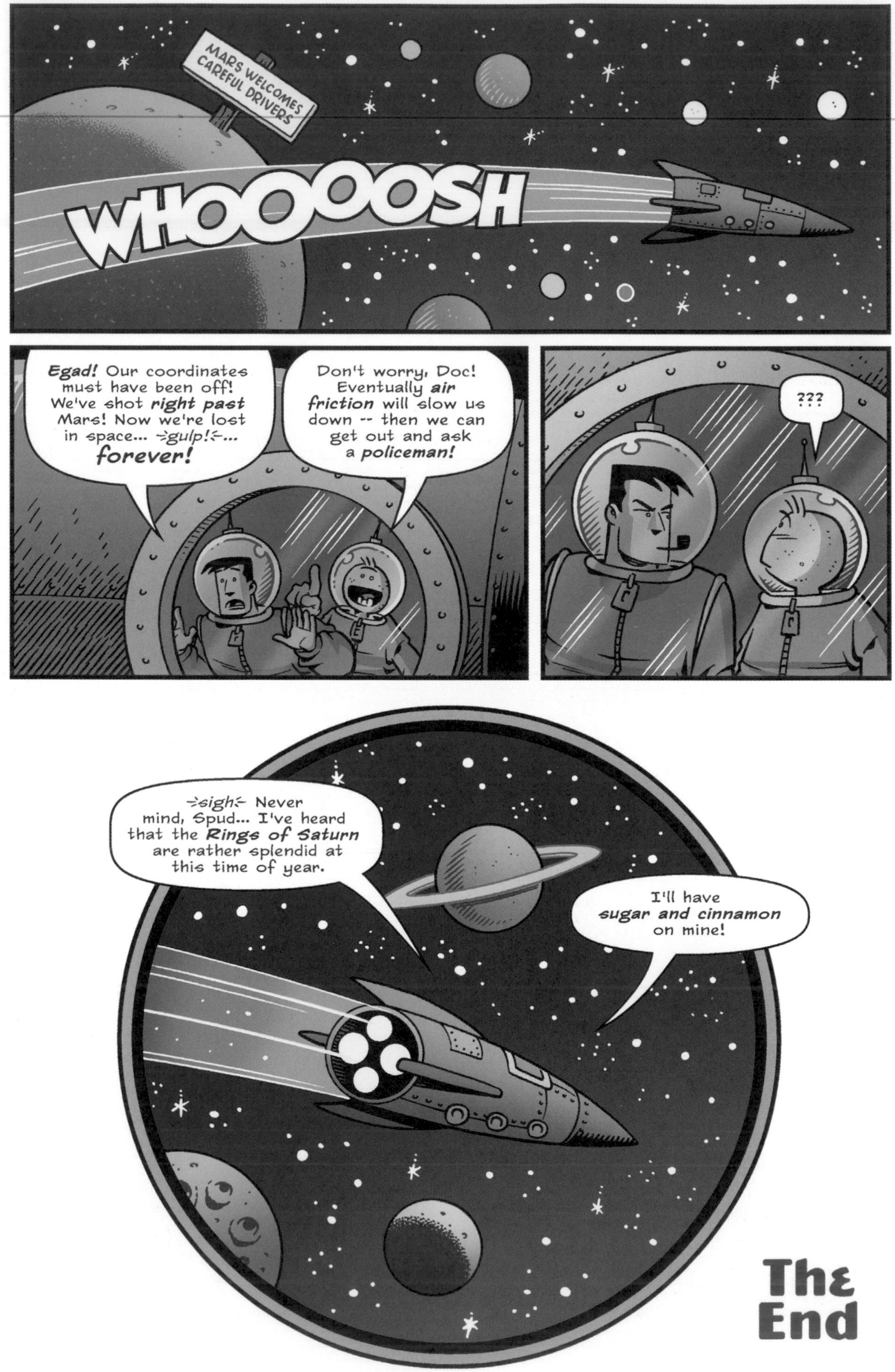
MARS WELCOMES CAREFUL DRIVERS
WHOOOOSH
Egad! Our coordinates must have been off! We've shot right past Mars! Now we're lost in space... gulp!... forever!
Don't worry, Doc! Eventually air friction will slow us down -- then we can get out and ask a policeman!
???
sigh Never mind, Spud... I've heard that the Rings of Saturn are rather splendid at this time of year.
I'll have sugar and cinnamon on mine!
The End

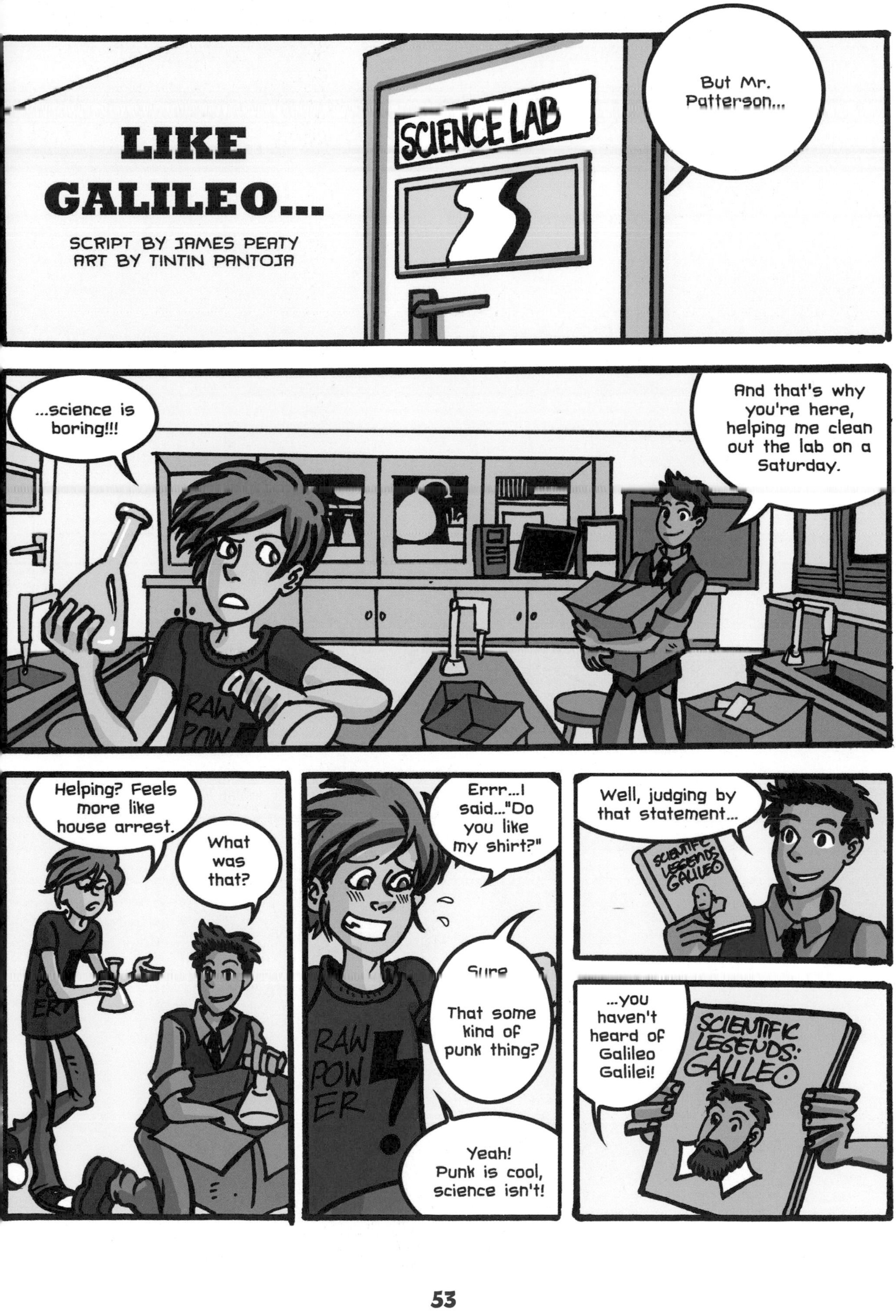
LIKE GALILEO...
SCRIPT BY JAMES PEATY
ART BY TINTIN PANTOJA
SCIENCE LAB
But Mr. Patterson...
...science is boring!!!
And that's why you're here, helping me clean out the lab on a Saturday.
RAW POW
Helping? Feels more like house arrest.
What was that?
Errr...I said..."Do you like my shirt?"
Sure
That some kind of punk thing?
RAW POW ER
Yeah! Punk is cool, science isn't!
Well, judging by that statement...
SCIENTIFIC LEGENDS GALILEO
...you haven't heard of Galileo Galilei!
SCIENTIFIC LEGENDS: GALILEO

Read panels from left to right across both pages.

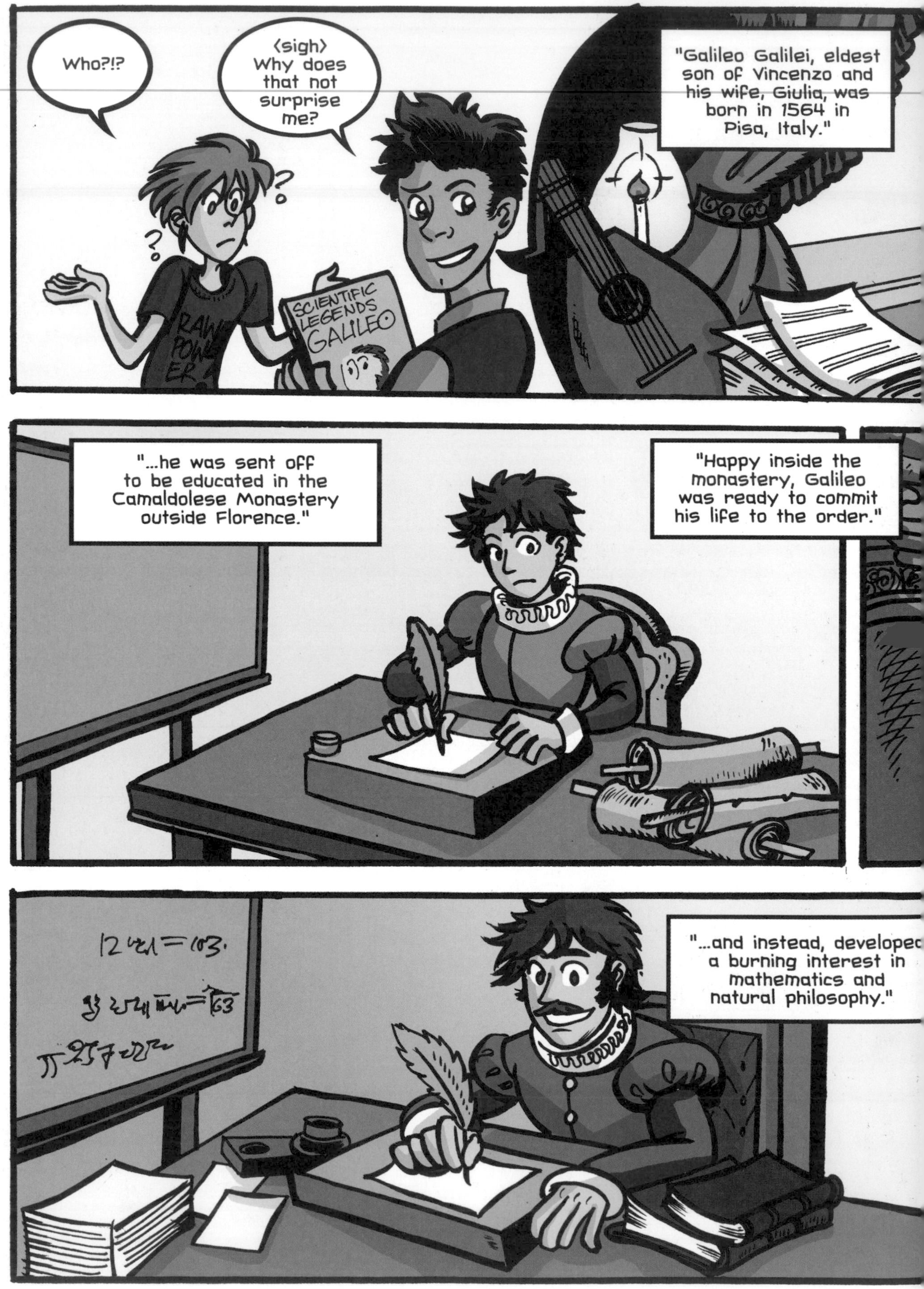

Who?!?
<sigh> Why does that not surprise me?
"Galileo Galilei, eldest son of Vincenzo and his wife, Giulia, was born in 1564 in Pisa, Italy."
SCIENTIFIC LEGENDS GALILEO
RAW POWER
"...he was sent off to be educated in the Camaldolese Monastery outside Florence."
"Happy inside the monastery, Galileo was ready to commit his life to the order."
"...and instead, developed a burning interest in mathematics and natural philosophy."

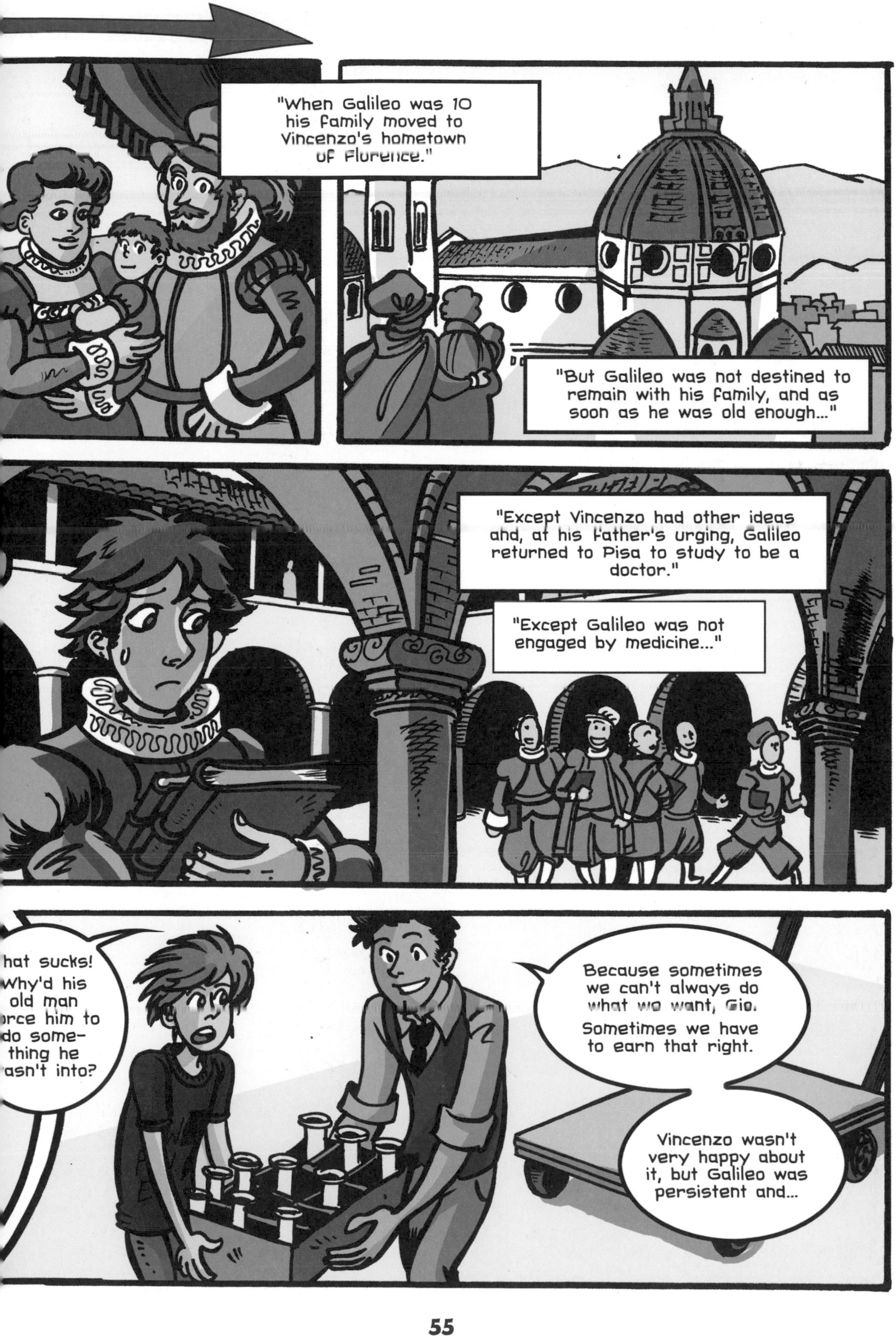
"When Galileo was 10 his family moved to Vincenzo's hometown of Florence."
"But Galileo was not destined to remain with his family, and as soon as he was old enough..."
"Except Vincenzo had other ideas and, at his father's urging, Galileo returned to Pisa to study to be a doctor."
"Except Galileo was not engaged by medicine..."
hat sucks! Why'd his old man orce him to do some-thing he asn't into?
Because sometimes we can't always do what we want, Gio.
Sometimes we have to earn that right.
Vincenzo wasn't very happy about it, but Galileo was persistent and...

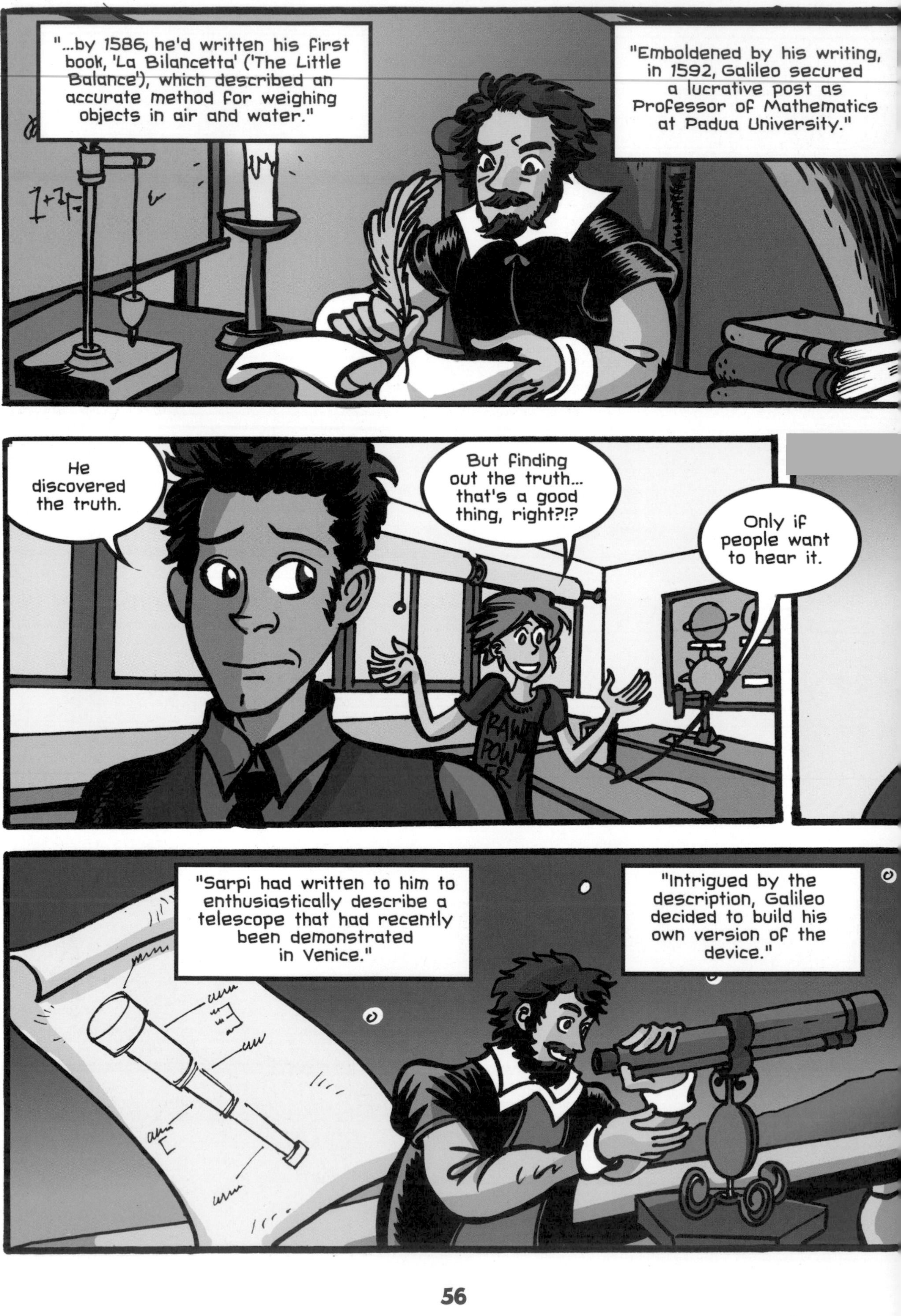
"...by 1586, he'd written his first book, 'La Bilancetta' ('The Little Balance'), which described an accurate method for weighing objects in air and water."
"Emboldened by his writing, in 1592, Galileo secured a lucrative post as Professor of Mathematics at Padua University."
He discovered the truth.
But finding out the truth... that's a good thing, right?!?
Only if people want to hear it.
RAW POWER
"Sarpi had written to him to enthusiastically describe a telescope that had recently been demonstrated in Venice."
"Intrigued by the description, Galileo decided to build his own version of the device."

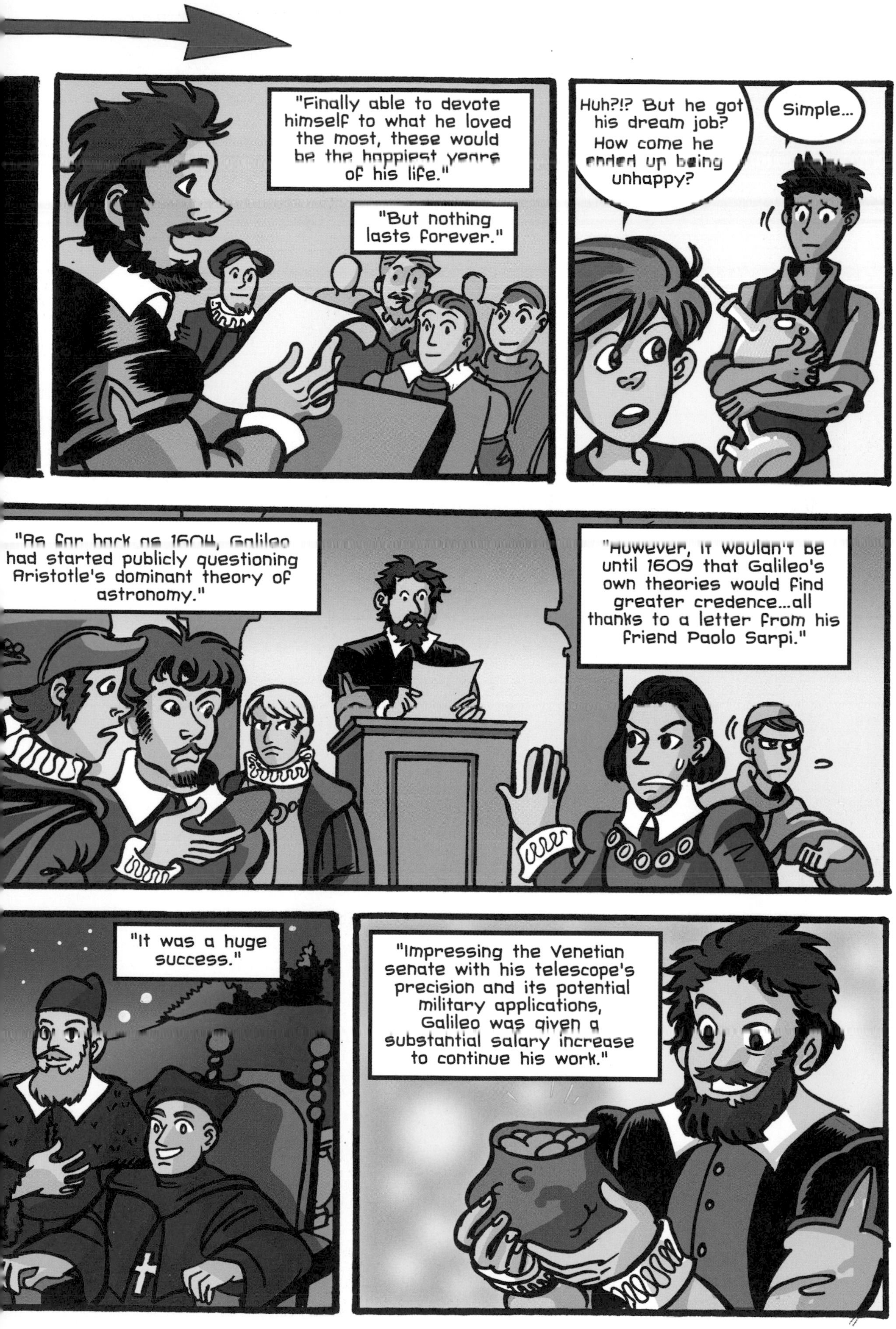
"Finally able to devote himself to what he loved the most, these would be the happiest years of his life."
"But nothing lasts forever."
Huh?!? But he got his dream job? How come he ended up being unhappy?
Simple...
"As far back as 1604, Galileo had started publicly questioning Aristotle's dominant theory of astronomy."
"However, it wouldn't be until 1609 that Galileo's own theories would find greater credence...all thanks to a letter from his friend Paolo Sarpi."
"It was a huge success."
"Impressing the Venetian senate with his telescope's precision and its potential military applications, Galileo was given a substantial salary increase to continue his work."

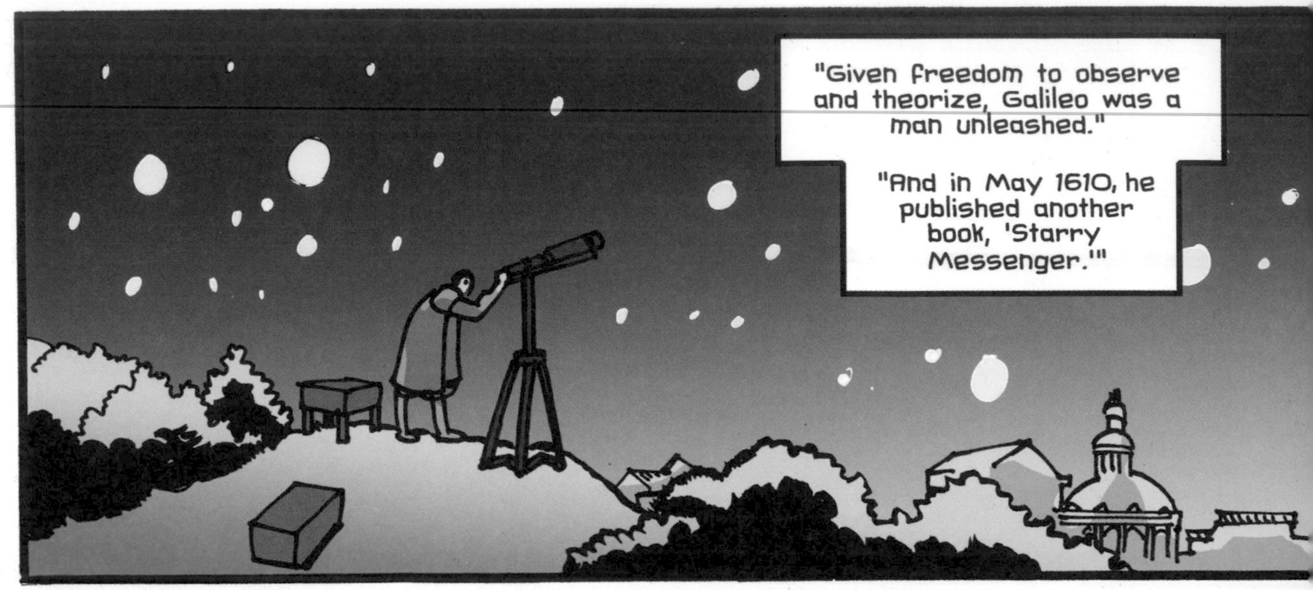
"Given freedom to observe and theorize, Galileo was a man unleashed."
"And in May 1610, he published another book, 'Starry Messenger.'"

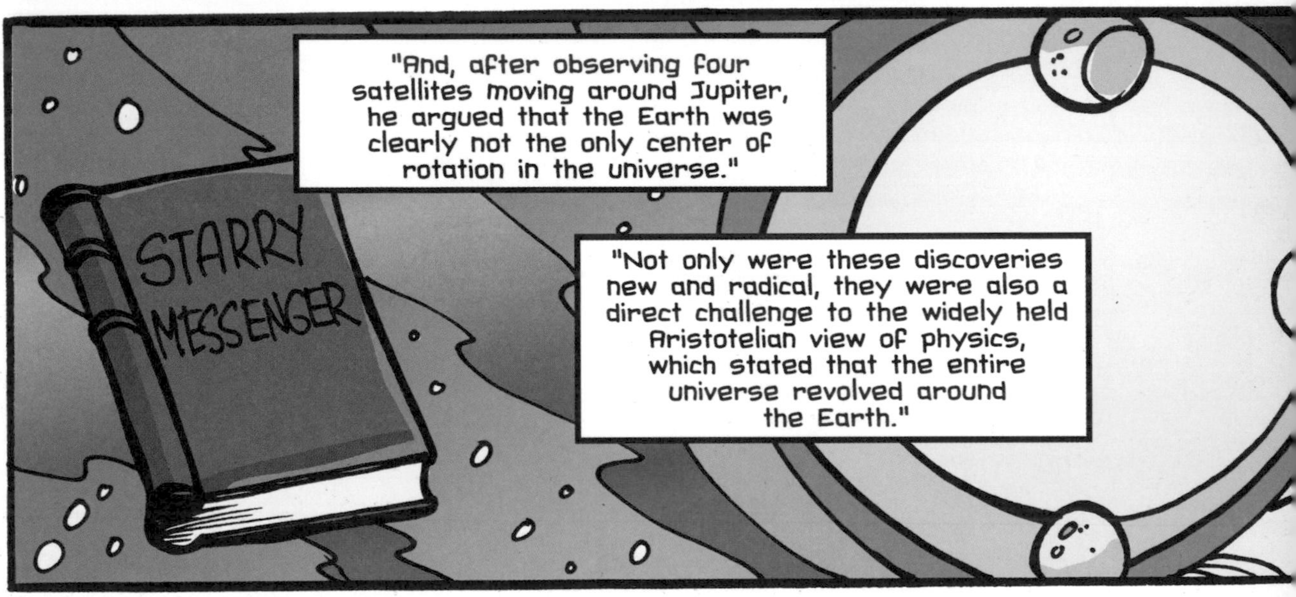
"And, after observing four satellites moving around Jupiter, he argued that the Earth was clearly not the only center of rotation in the universe."
STARRY MESSENGER
"Not only were these discoveries new and radical, they were also a direct challenge to the widely held Aristotelian view of physics, which stated that the entire universe revolved around the Earth."

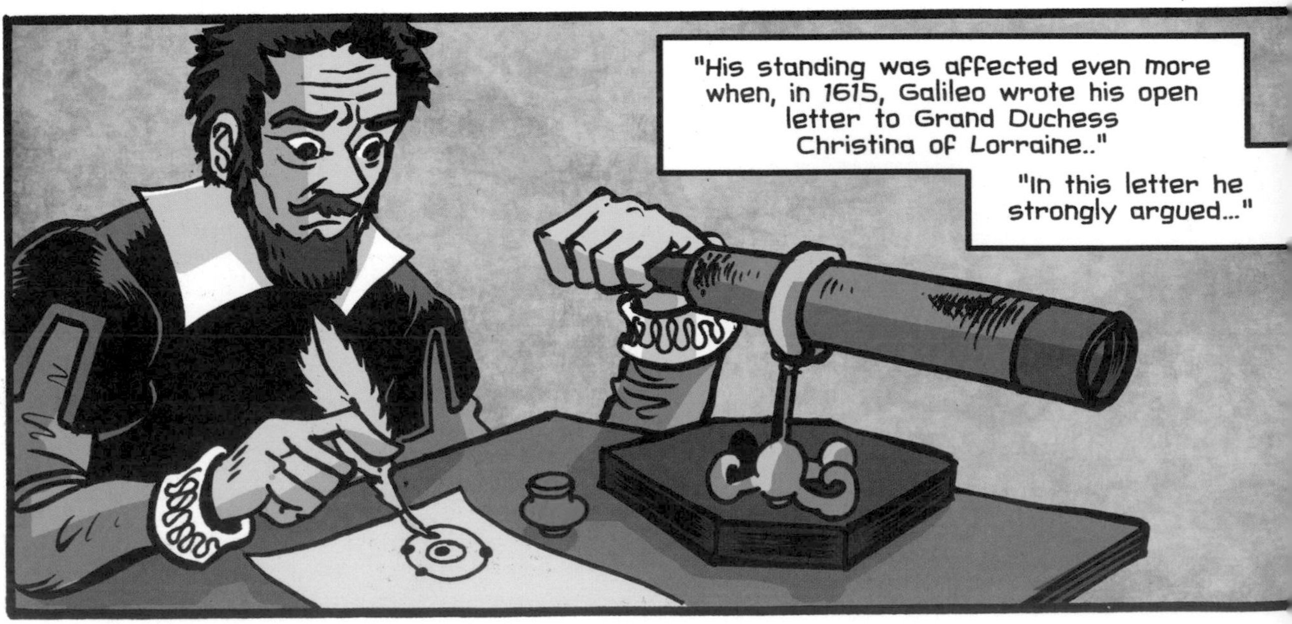
"His standing was affected even more when, in 1615, Galileo wrote his open letter to Grand Duchess Christina of Lorraine.."
"In this letter he strongly argued..."

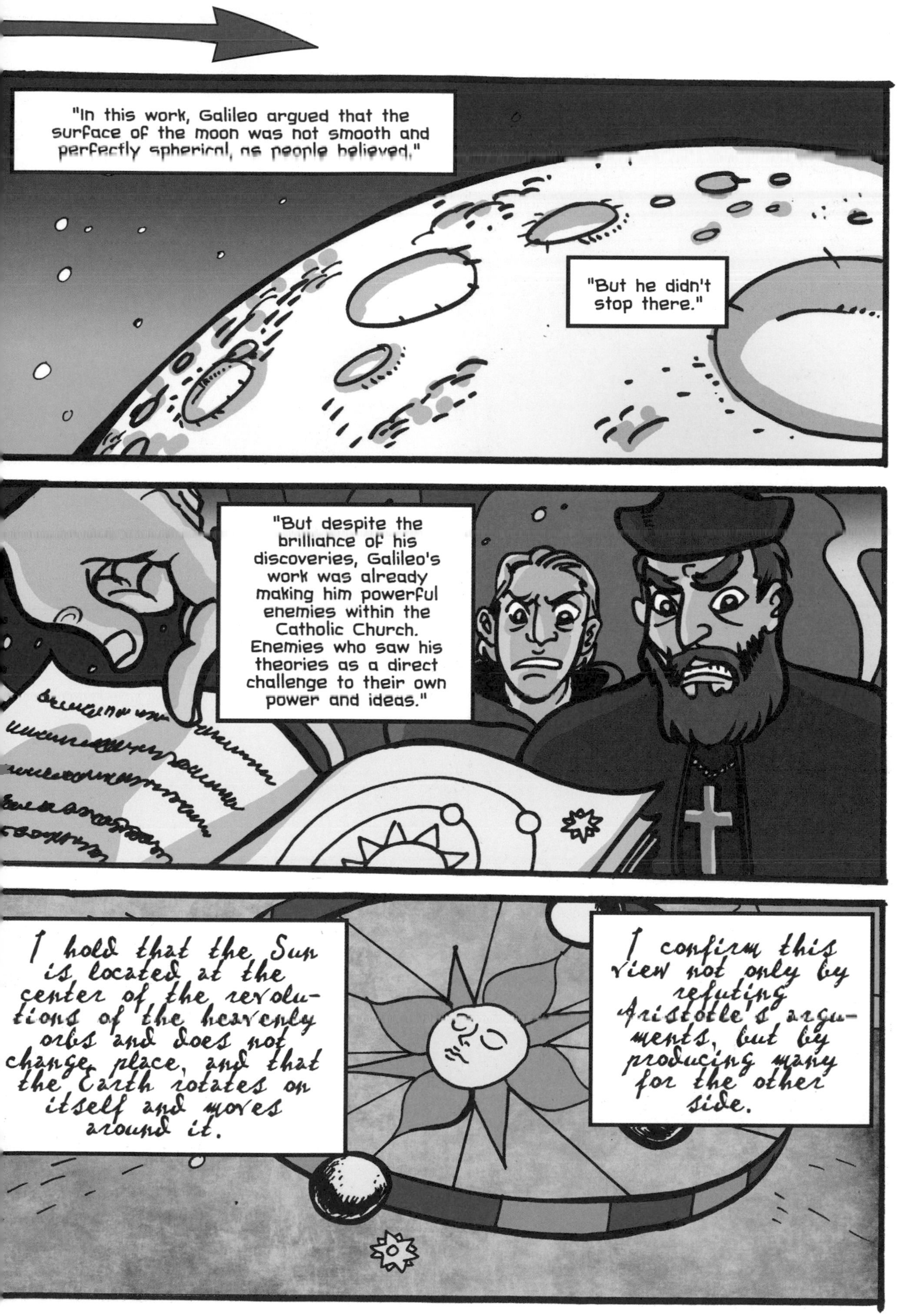
"In this work, Galileo argued that the surface of the moon was not smooth and perfectly spherical, as people believed."
"But he didn't stop there."
"But despite the brilliance of his discoveries, Galileo's work was already making him powerful enemies within the Catholic Church. Enemies who saw his theories as a direct challenge to their own power and ideas."
I hold that the Sun is located at the center of the revolutions of the heavenly orbs and does not change place, and that the Earth rotates on itself and moves around it.
I confirm this view not only by refuting Aristotle's arguments, but by producing many for the other side.

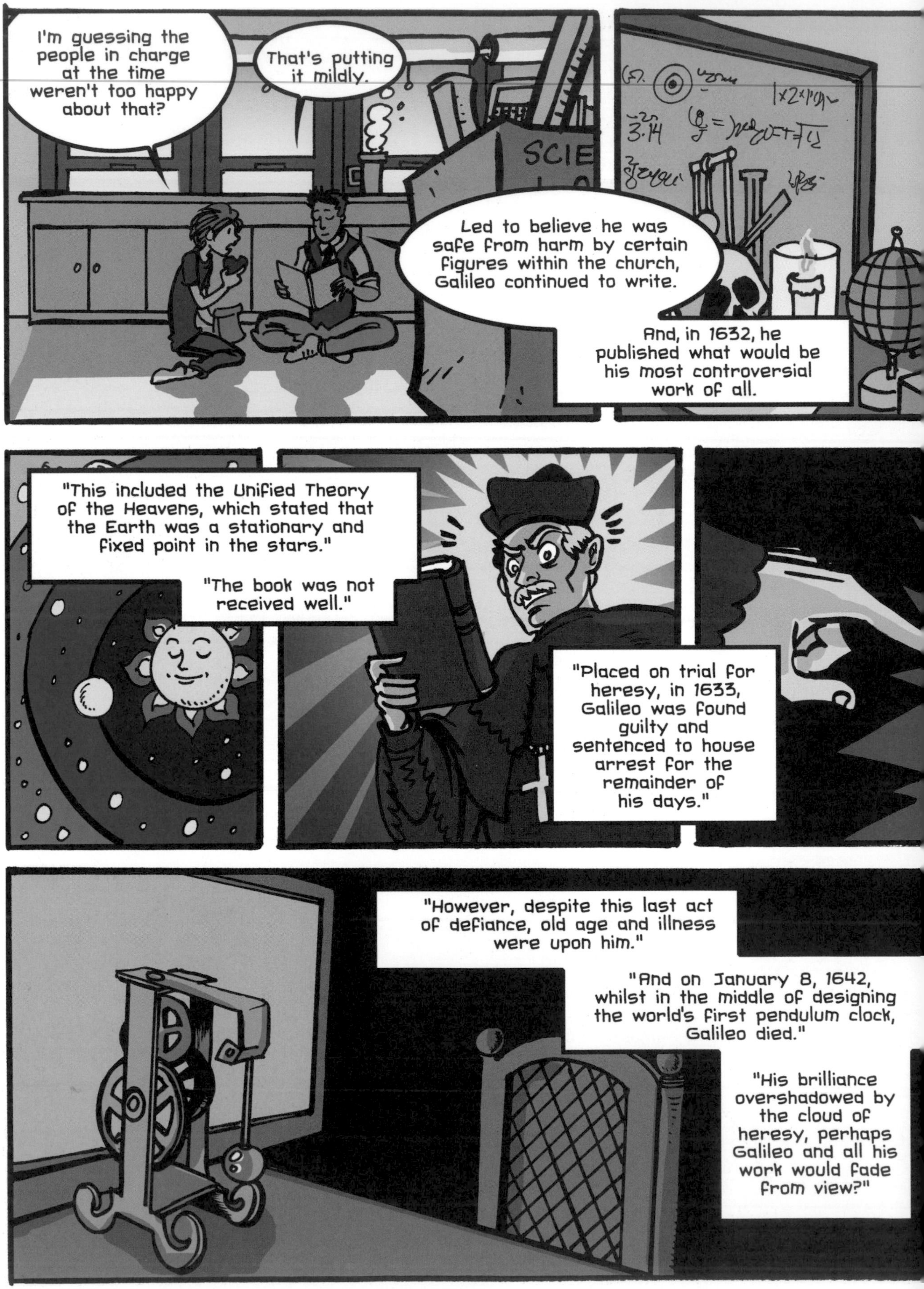
I'm guessing the people in charge at the time weren't too happy about that?
That's putting it mildly.
SCIE
Led to believe he was safe from harm by certain figures within the church, Galileo continued to write.
And, in 1632, he published what would be his most controversial work of all.
"This included the Unified Theory of the Heavens, which stated that the Earth was a stationary and fixed point in the stars."
"The book was not received well."
"Placed on trial for heresy, in 1633, Galileo was found guilty and sentenced to house arrest for the remainder of his days."
"However, despite this last act of defiance, old age and illness were upon him."
"And on January 8, 1642, whilst in the middle of designing the world's first pendulum clock, Galileo died."
"His brilliance overshadowed by the cloud of heresy, perhaps Galileo and all his work would fade from view?"

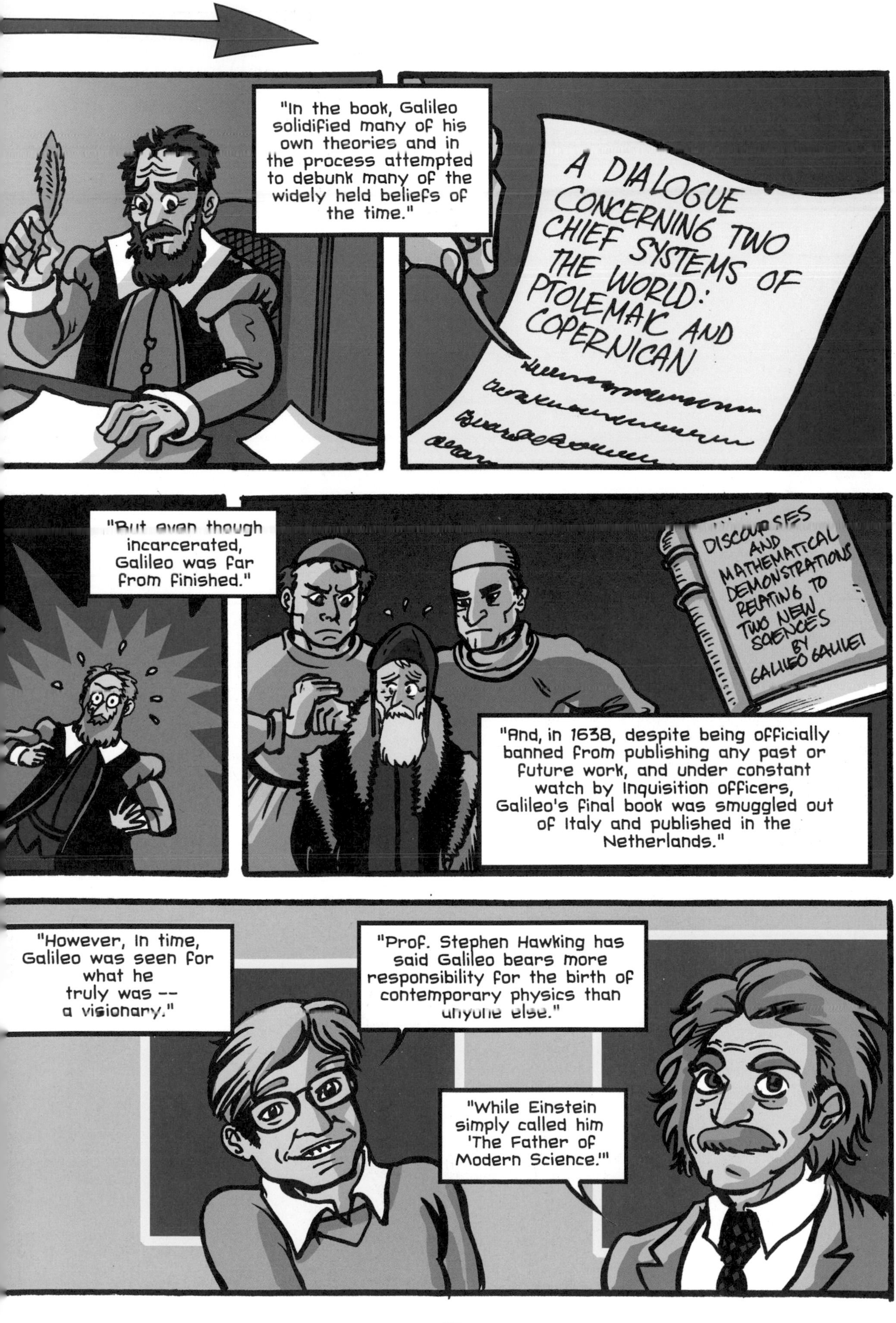

"In the book, Galileo solidified many of his own theories and in the process attempted to debunk many of the widely held beliefs of the time."
A DIALOGUE CONCERNING TWO CHIEF SYSTEMS OF THE WORLD: PTOLEMAIC AND COPERNICAN
"But even though incarcerated, Galileo was far from finished."
DISCOURSES AND MATHEMATICAL DEMONSTRATIONS RELATING TO TWO NEW SCIENCES BY GALILEO GALILEI
"And, in 1638, despite being officially banned from publishing any past or future work, and under constant watch by Inquisition officers, Galileo's final book was smuggled out of Italy and published in the Netherlands."
"However, in time, Galileo was seen for what he truly was -- a visionary."
"Prof. Stephen Hawking has said Galileo bears more responsibility for the birth of contemporary physics than anyone else."
"While Einstein simply called him 'The Father of Modern Science.'"

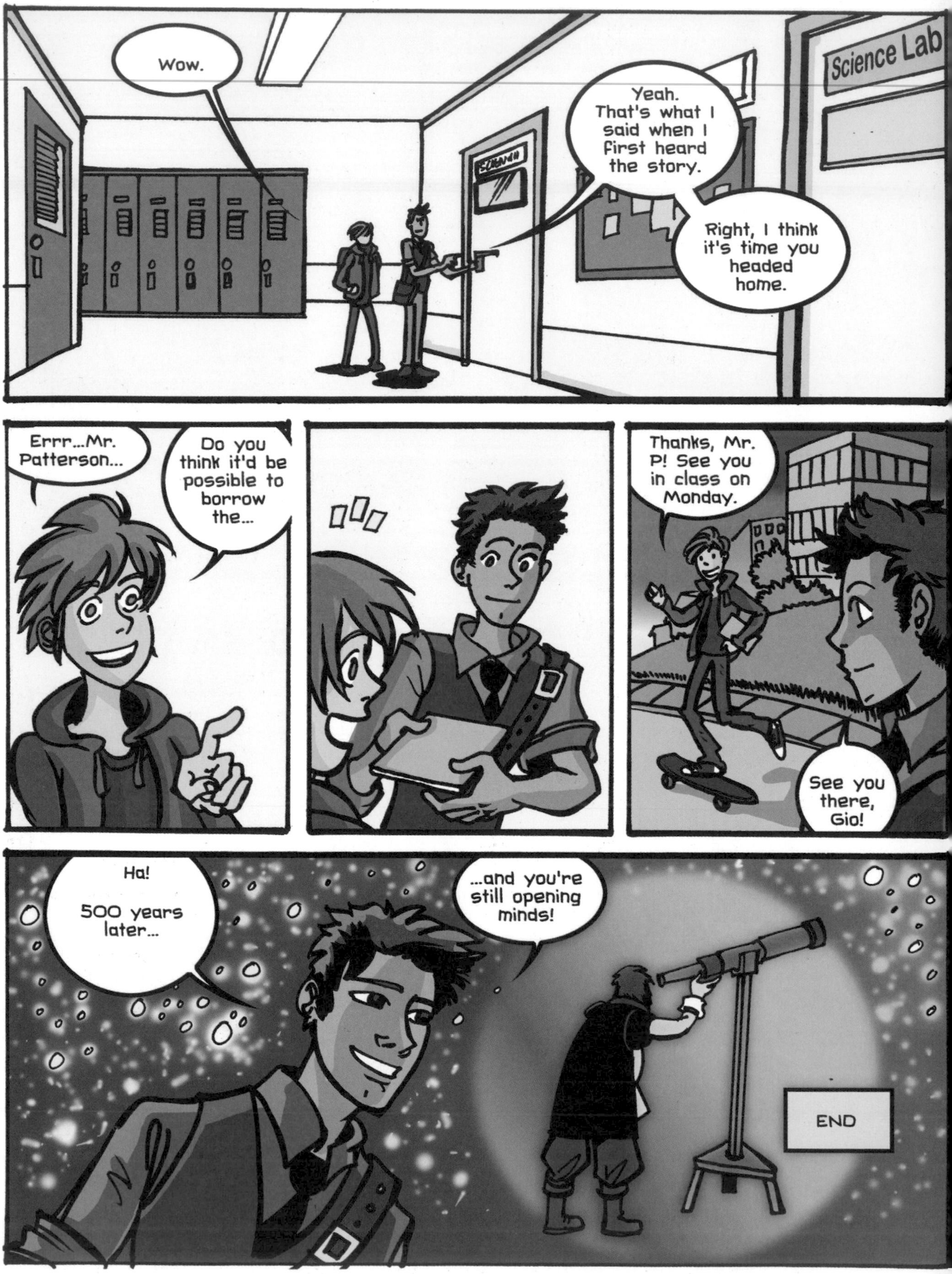
Science Lab
Wow.
Yeah. That's what I said when I first heard the story.
Right, I think it's time you headed home.
Errr...Mr. Patterson...
Do you think it'd be possible to borrow the...
Thanks, Mr. P! See you in class on Monday.
See you there, Gio!
Ha!
500 years later...
...and you're still opening minds!
END

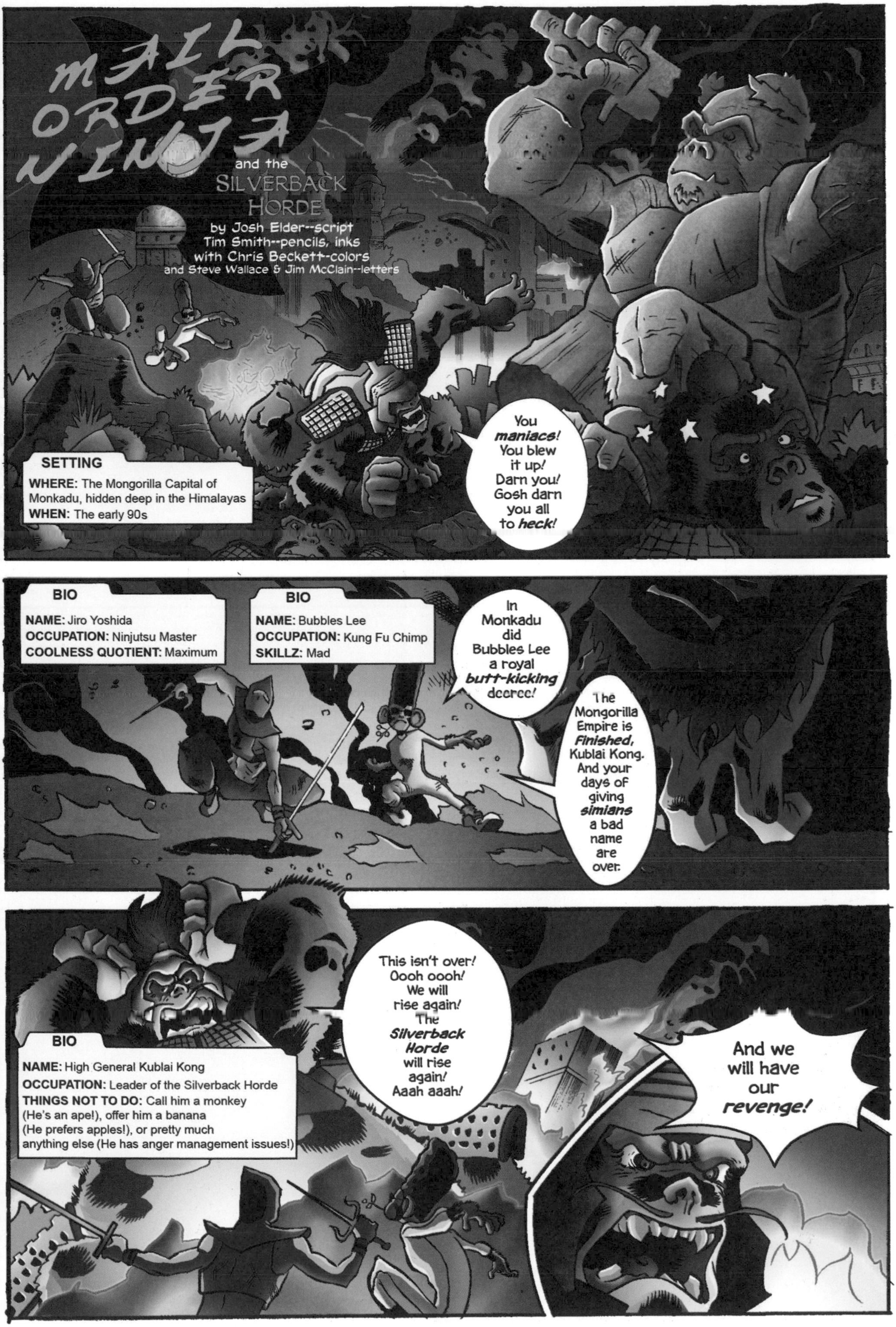

MAIL ORDER NINJA
and the SILVERBACK HORDE
by Josh Elder--script
Tim Smith--pencils, inks
with Chris Beckett--colors
and Steve Wallace & Jim McClain--letters
SETTING
WHERE: The Mongorilla Capital of Monkadu, hidden deep in the Himalayas
WHEN: The early 90s
You *maniacs!* You blew it up! Darn you! Gosh darn you all to *heck!*
BIO
NAME: Jiro Yoshida
OCCUPATION: Ninjutsu Master
COOLNESS QUOTIENT: Maximum
BIO
NAME: Bubbles Lee
OCCUPATION: Kung Fu Chimp
SKILLZ: Mad
In Monkadu did Bubbles Lee a royal *butt-kicking* decree!
The Mongorilla Empire is *Finished,* Kublai Kong. And your days of giving *simians* a bad name are over.
BIO
NAME: High General Kublai Kong
OCCUPATION: Leader of the Silverback Horde
THINGS NOT TO DO: Call him a monkey (He's an ape!), offer him a banana (He prefers apples!), or pretty much anything else (He has anger management issues!)
This isn't over! Oooh oooh! We will rise again! The *Silverback Horde* will rise again! Aaah aaah!
And we will have our *revenge!*

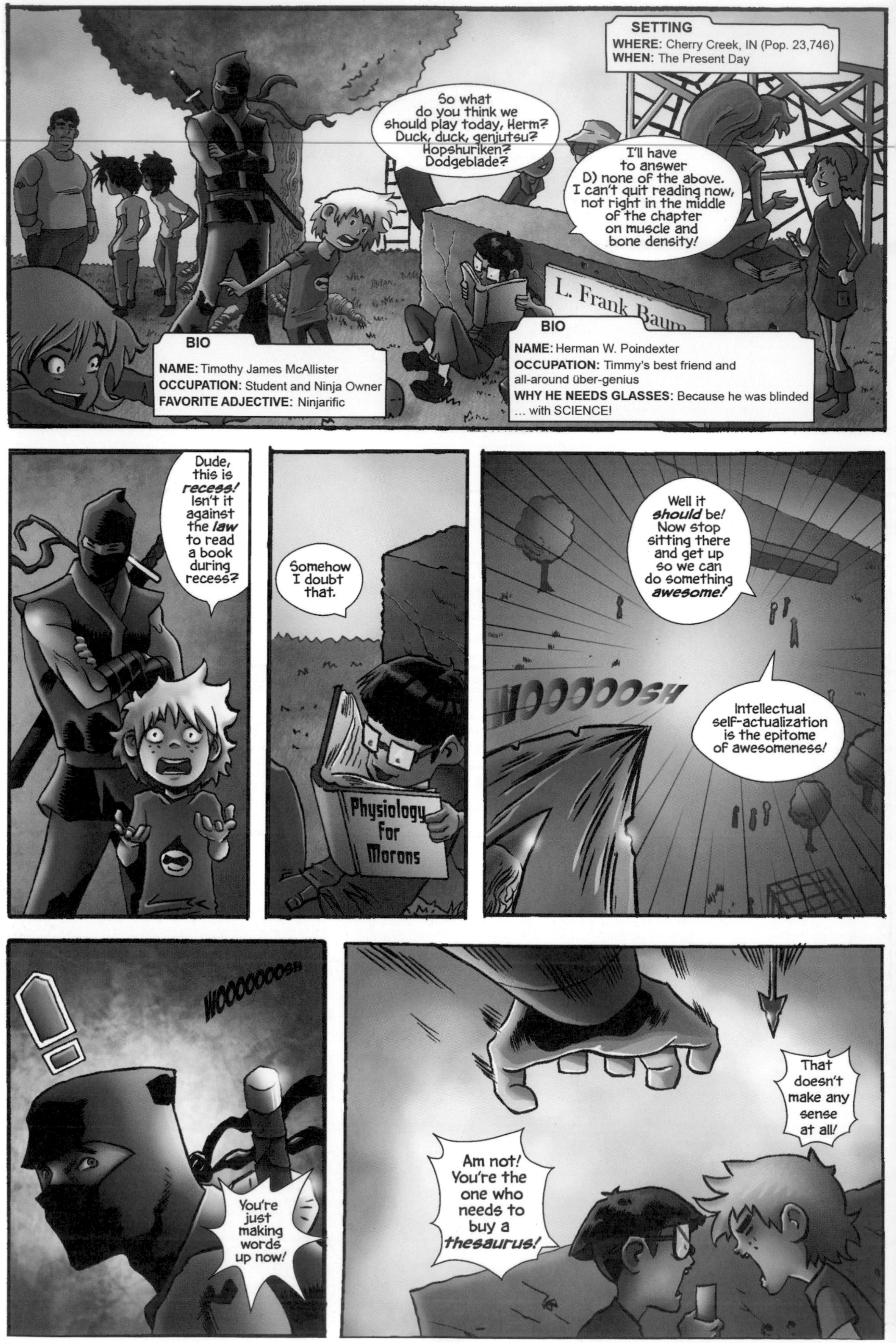
SETTING
WHERE: Cherry Creek, IN (Pop. 23,746)
WHEN: The Present Day
So what do you think we should play today, Herm? Duck, duck, genjutsu? Hopshuriken? Dodgeblade?
I'll have to answer D) none of the above. I can't quit reading now, not right in the middle of the chapter on muscle and bone density!
L. Frank Baum
BIO
NAME: Timothy James McAllister
OCCUPATION: Student and Ninja Owner
FAVORITE ADJECTIVE: Ninjarific
BIO
NAME: Herman W. Poindexter
OCCUPATION: Timmy's best friend and all-around über-genius
WHY HE NEEDS GLASSES: Because he was blinded … with SCIENCE!
Dude, this is recess! Isn't it against the law to read a book during recess?
Somehow I doubt that.
Physiology For Morons
Well it should be! Now stop sitting there and get up so we can do something awesome!
WOOOOOSH
Intellectual self-actualization is the epitome of awesomeness!
WOOOOOOOSH
You're just making words up now!
Am not! You're the one who needs to buy a thesaurus!
That doesn't make any sense at all!

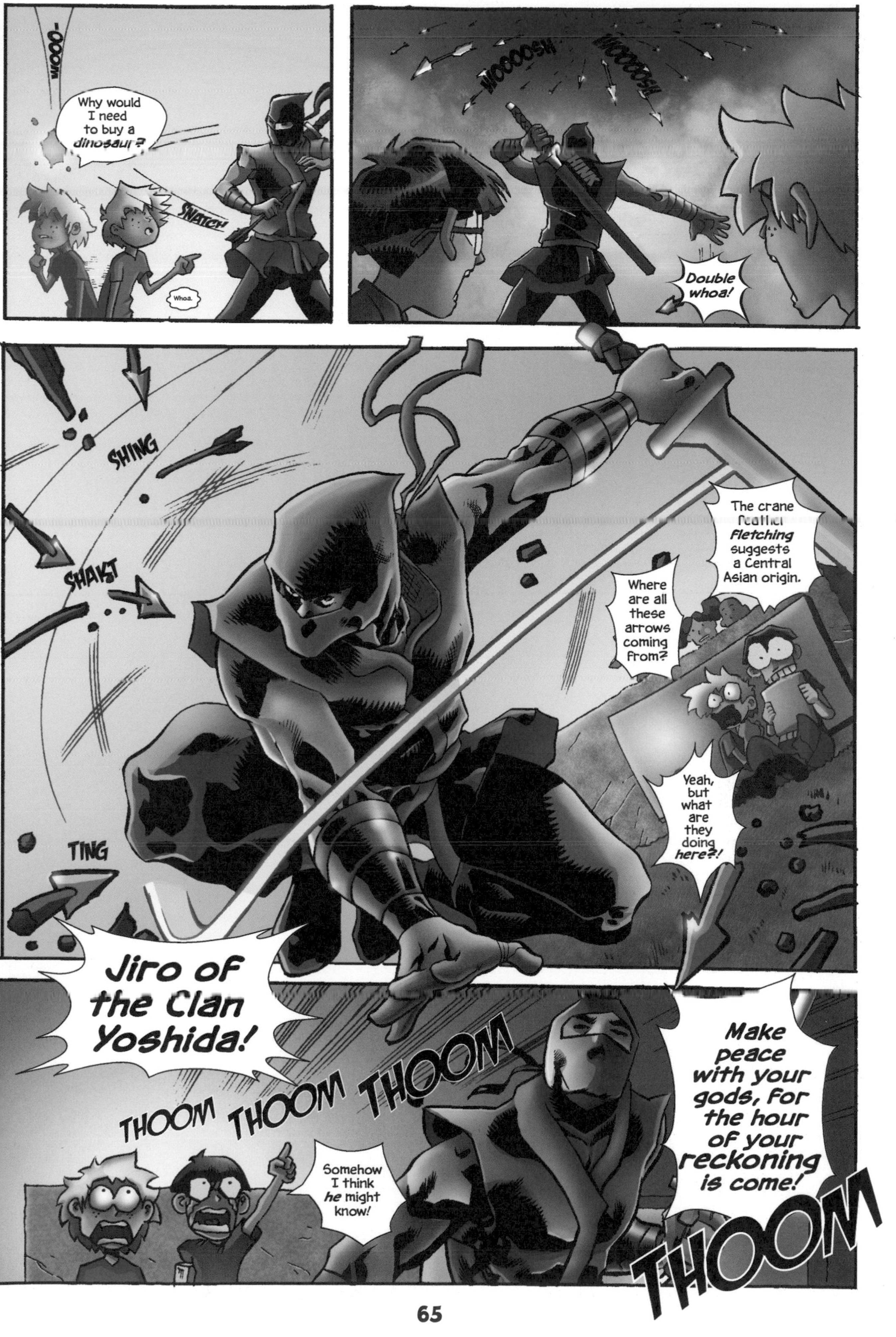
WOOO-
Why would I need to buy a dinosaur?
SNATCH
Whoa.
WOOOOSH
WOOOOSH
WOOOOSH
Double whoa!
SHING
SHAKT
TING
The crane feather *fletching* suggests a Central Asian origin.
Where are all these arrows coming from?
Yeah, but what are they doing *here?!*
Jiro of the Clan Yoshida!
THOOM THOOM THOOM
Somehow I think *he* might know!
Make peace with your gods, for the hour of your reckoning is come!
THOOM

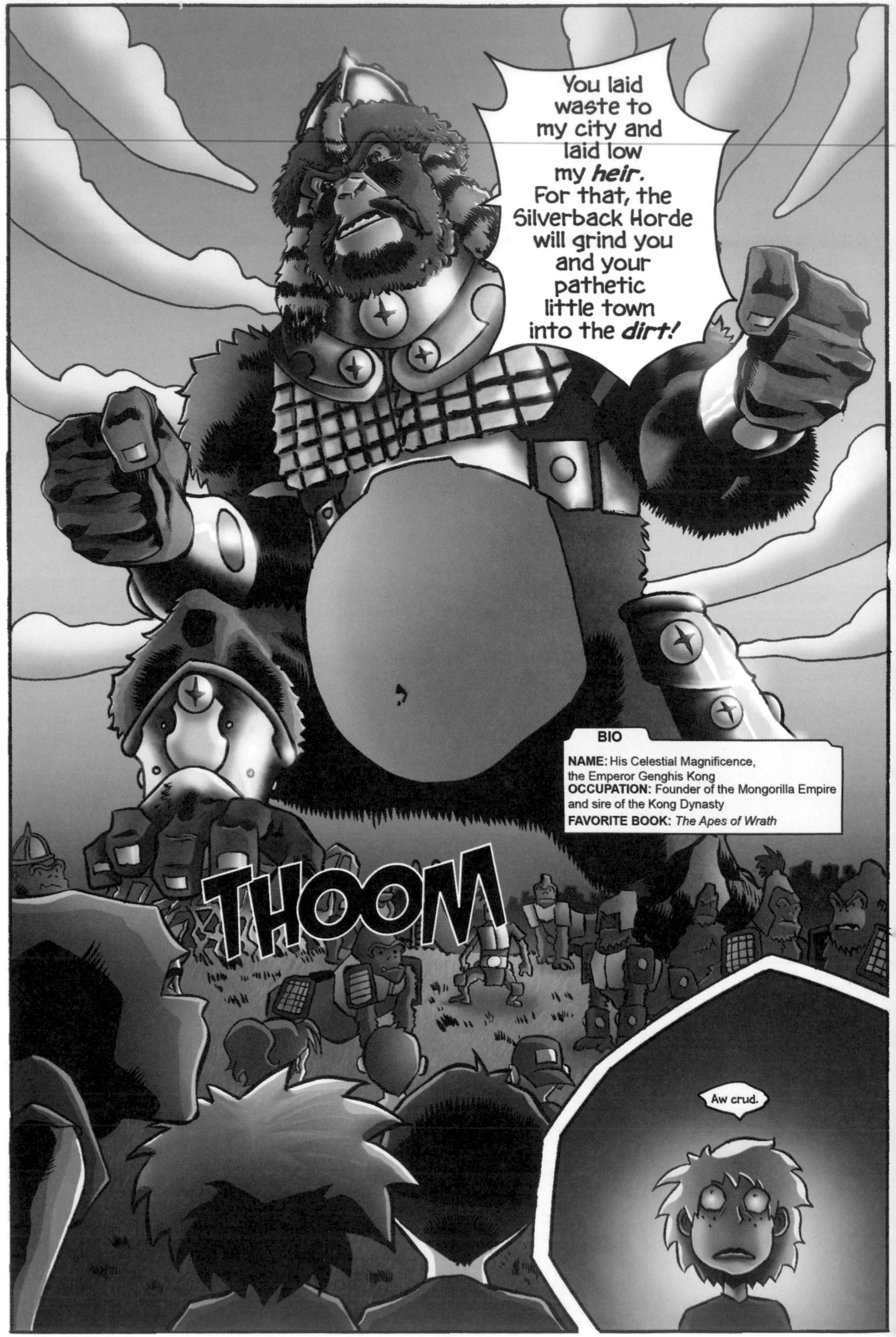
You laid waste to my city and laid low my *heir*. For that, the Silverback Horde will grind you and your pathetic little town into the *dirt!*
BIO
NAME: His Celestial Magnificence, the Emperor Genghis Kong
OCCUPATION: Founder of the Mongorilla Empire and sire of the Kong Dynasty
FAVORITE BOOK: *The Apes of Wrath*
THOOM
Aw crud.

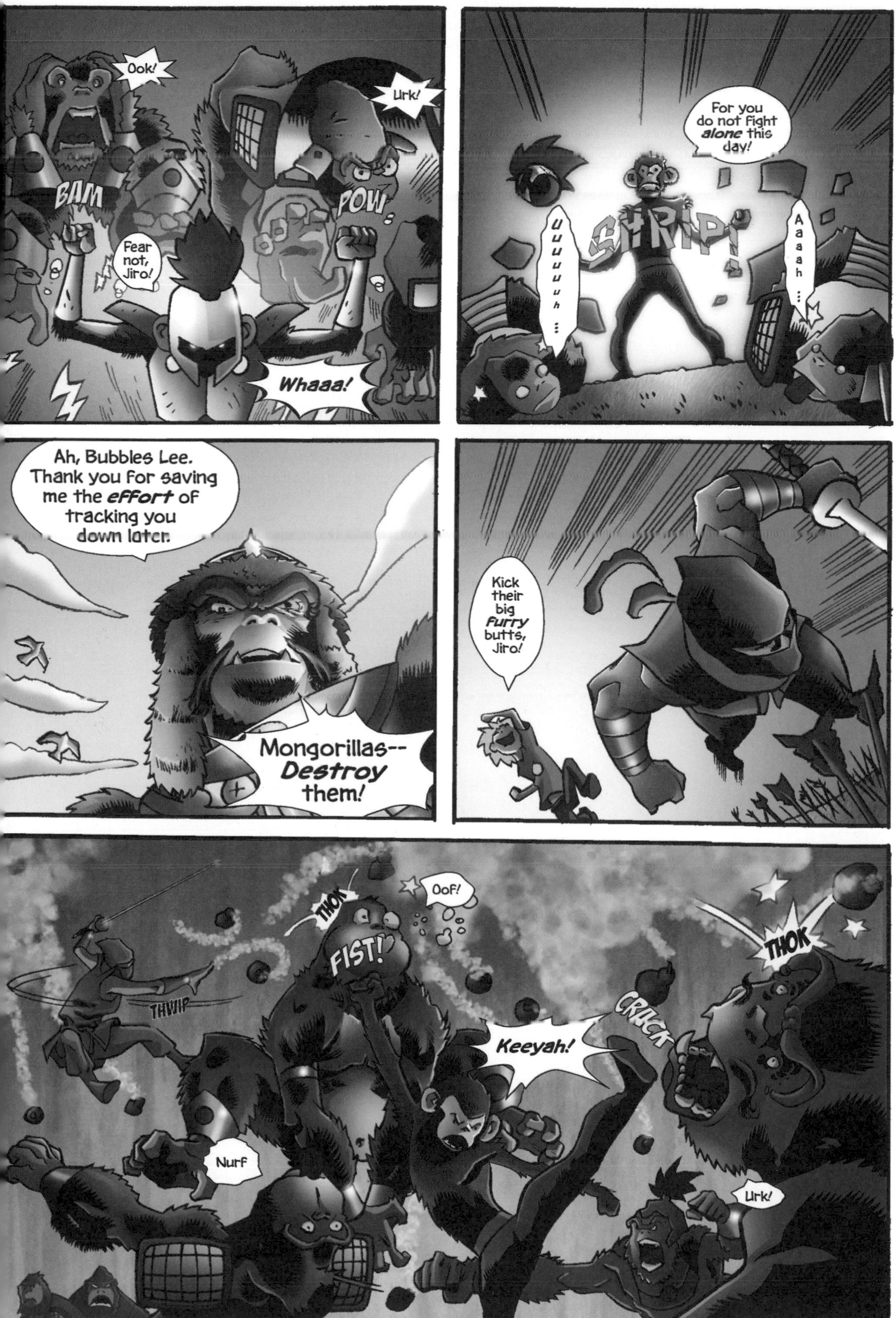
Ook!
Urk!
BAM
POW
Fear not, Jiro!
Whaaa!
For you do not fight *alone* this day!
SHRIP!
Uuuuuuh...
Aaaah...
Ah, Bubbles Lee. Thank you for saving me the *effort* of tracking you down later.
Mongorillas-- *Destroy* them!
Kick their big *furry* butts, Jiro!
THOK
Oof!
FIST!
THOK
THWIP
CRACK
Keeyah!
Nurf
Urk!

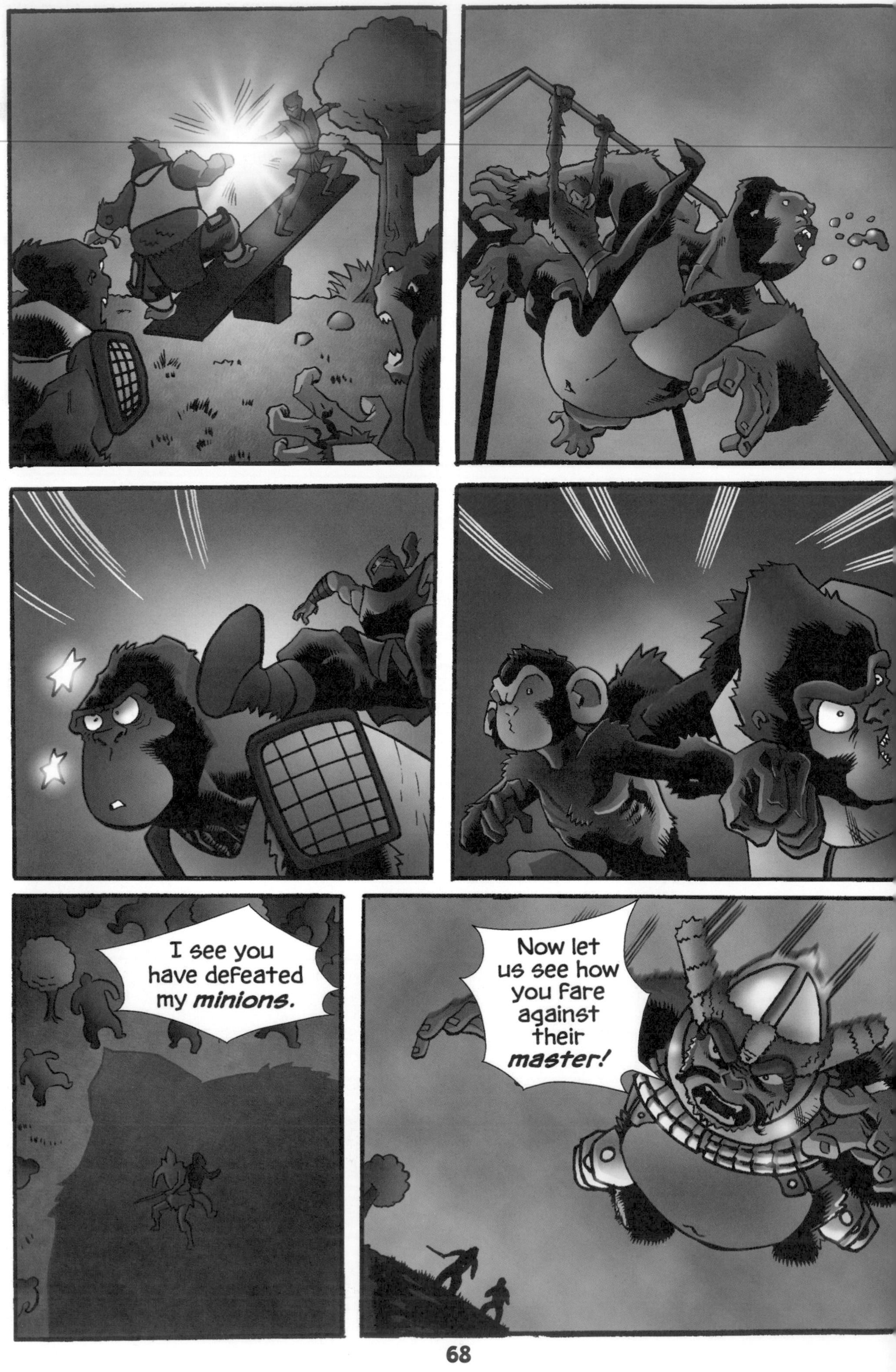

I see you have defeated my *minions.*
Now let us see how you fare against their *master!*

Ooh... *That's* gonna leave a mark.

Indubitably.

FWACK!

SNAP

FOOT TO FACE

KRUNCH

TWHAP!

VICTORY!

THUMP! THUMP! THUMP!

No way! Jiro can't get *punked* by some overgrown monkey!

First, gorillas aren't monkeys. They're apes. Second, the *square-cube law* proves that it's impossible for any monkey or ape to ever get *that* overgrown.

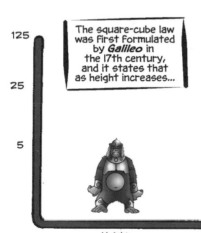

125
25
5

Height
Strength
Weight

The square-cube law was first formulated by *Galileo* in the 17th century, and it states that as height increases...

...surface area-- which determines *strength*-- increases by a squared factor, while volume-- which determines *weight*-- increases by a cubed factor.

So Genghis Kong is 30 feet tall, five times taller than an ordinary gorilla.

What... *sorcery*... is...this?

Which means his strength is 5^2 or 25 times greater that that of an ordinary gorilla, but his weight is 5^3 or 125 times greater than that of an ordinary gorilla.

Feel... so... *heavy*...

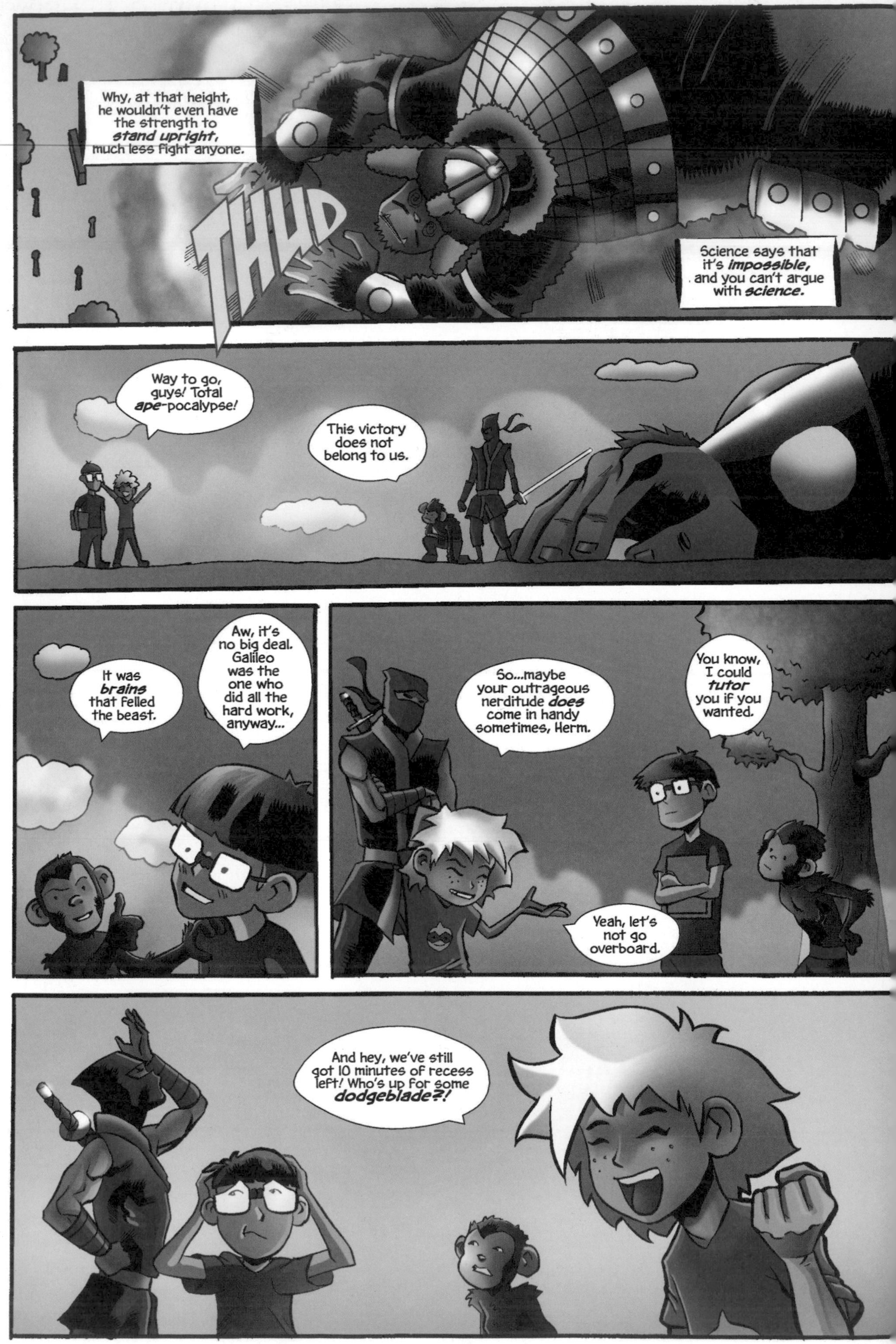
Why, at that height, he wouldn't even have the strength to *stand upright,* much less fight anyone.
THUD
Science says that it's *impossible,* and you can't argue with *science.*
Way to go, guys! Total *ape*-pocalypse!
This victory does not belong to us.
It was *brains* that felled the beast.
Aw, it's no big deal. Galileo was the one who did all the hard work, anyway...
So...maybe your outrageous nerditude *does* come in handy sometimes, Herm.
You know, I could *tutor* you if you wanted.
Yeah, let's not go overboard.
And hey, we've still got 10 minutes of recess left! Who's up for some *dodgeblade?!*

MATHEMATICS

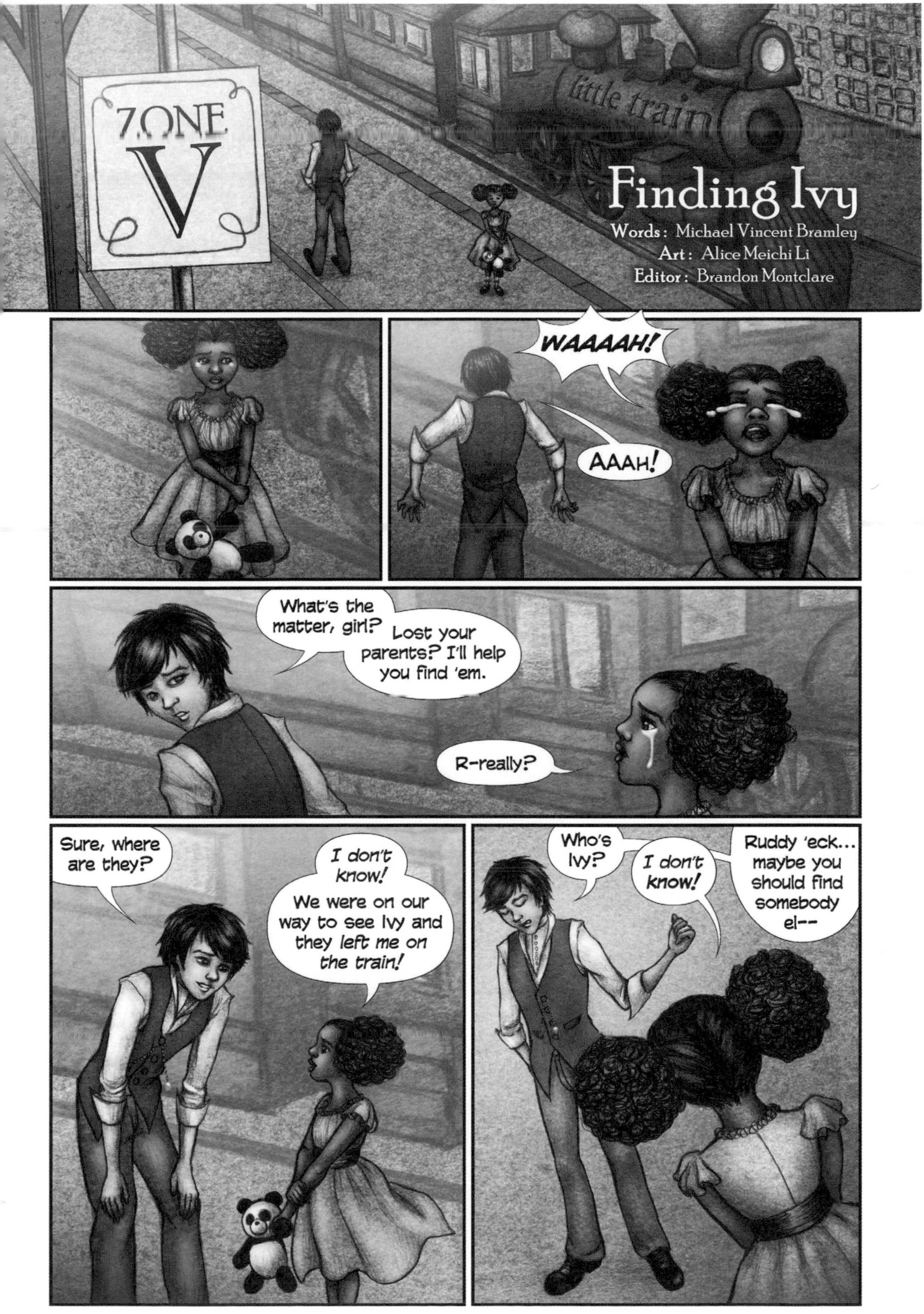

ZONE V
little train
Finding Ivy
Words: Michael Vincent Bramley
Art: Alice Meichi Li
Editor: Brandon Montclare
WAAAAH!
AAAH!
What's the matter, girl?
Lost your parents? I'll help you find 'em.
R-really?
Sure, where are they?
I don't know!
We were on our way to see Ivy and they *left me on the train!*
Who's Ivy?
I don't know!
Ruddy 'eck... maybe you should find somebody el--

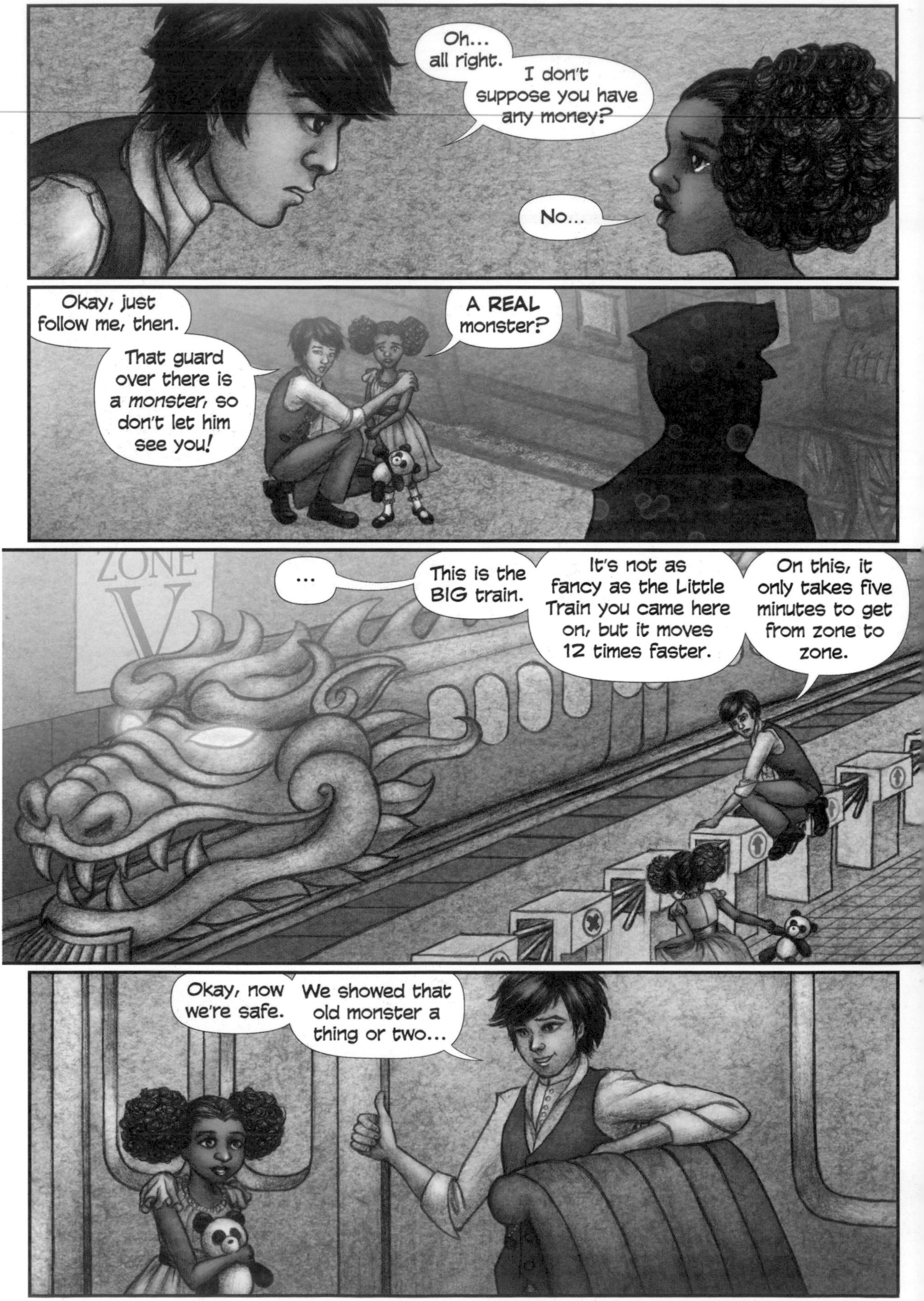
Oh... all right.
I don't suppose you have any money?
No...
Okay, just follow me, then.
That guard over there is a *monster*, so don't let him see you!
A **REAL** monster?
ZONE V
...
This is the BIG train.
It's not as fancy as the Little Train you came here on, but it moves 12 times faster.
On this, it only takes five minutes to get from zone to zone.
Okay, now we're safe.
We showed that old monster a thing or two...

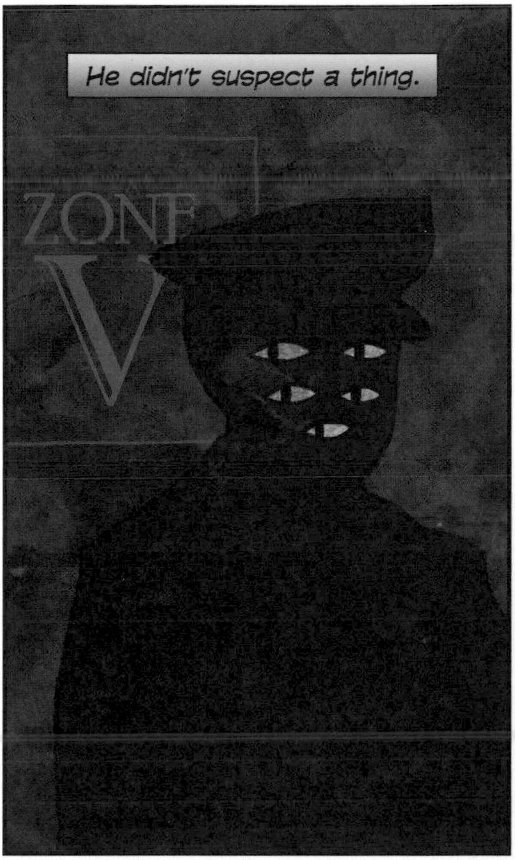
He didn't suspect a thing.
ZONE V

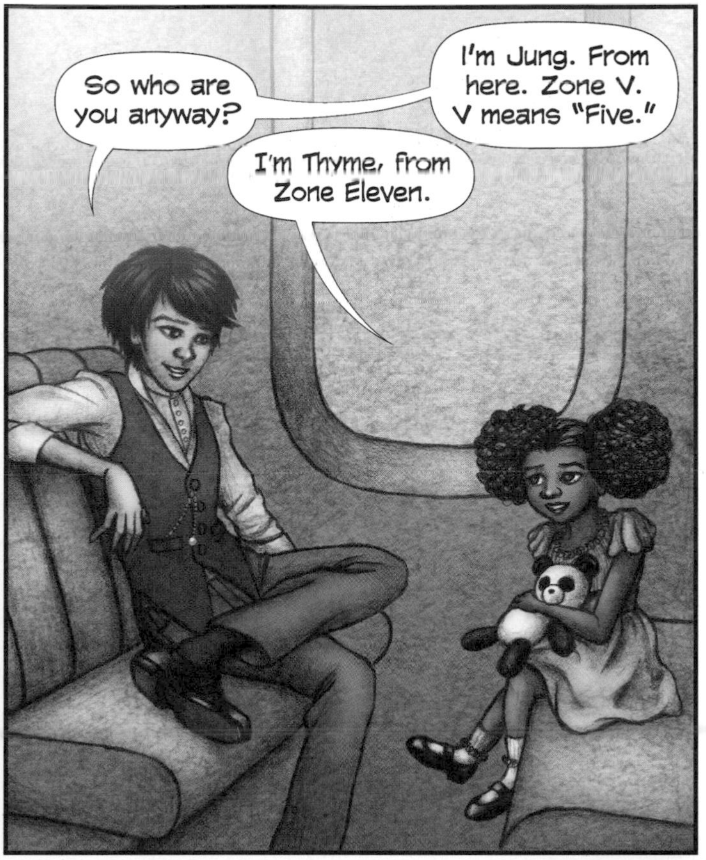
So who are you anyway?
I'm Jung. From here. Zone V. V means "Five."
I'm Thyme, from Zone Eleven.

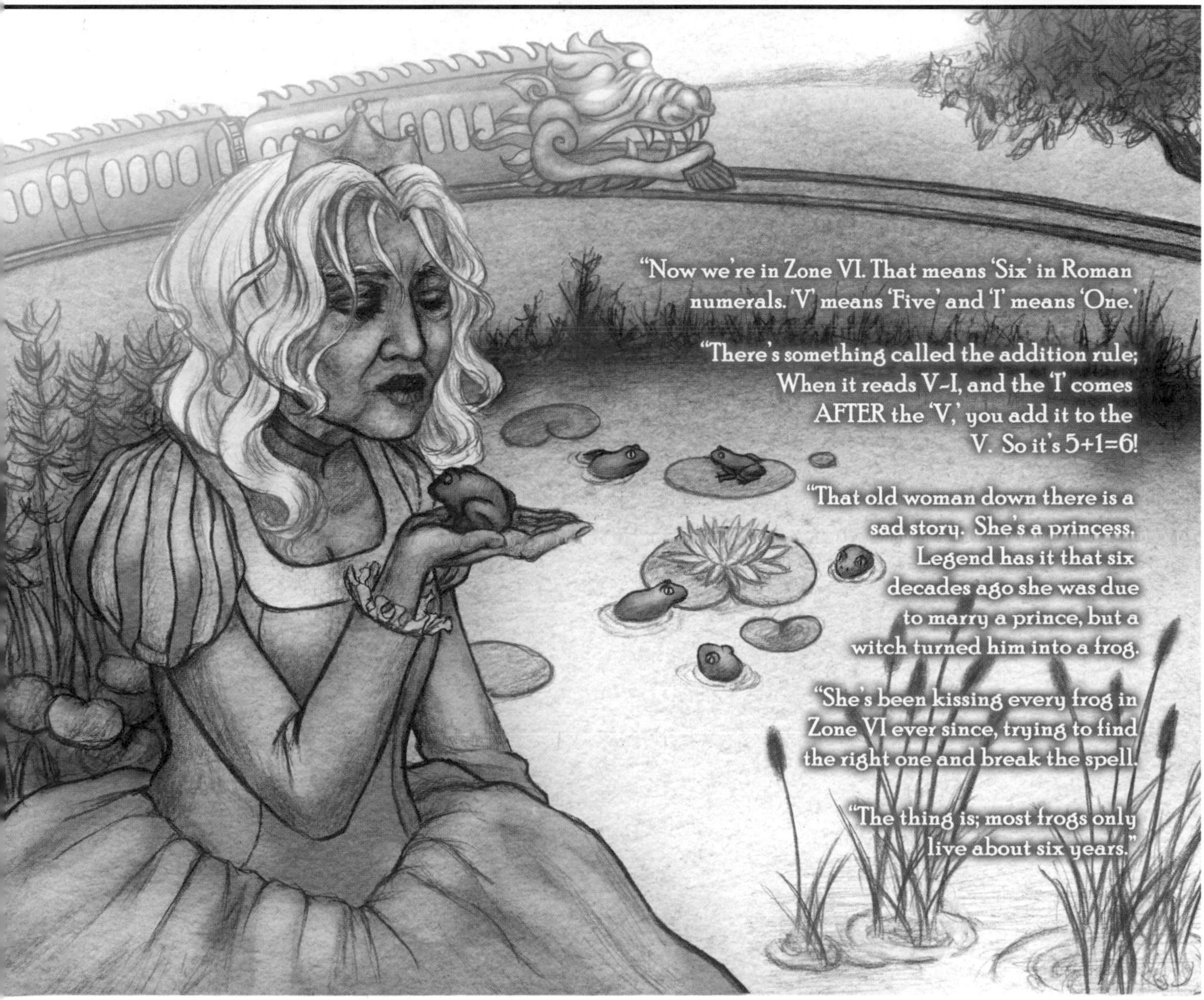
"Now we're in Zone VI. That means 'Six' in Roman numerals. 'V' means 'Five' and 'I' means 'One.'
"There's something called the addition rule; When it reads V-I, and the 'I' comes AFTER the 'V,' you add it to the V. So it's 5+1=6!
"That old woman down there is a sad story. She's a princess. Legend has it that six decades ago she was due to marry a prince, but a witch turned him into a frog.
"She's been kissing every frog in Zone VI ever since, trying to find the right one and break the spell.
"The thing is; most frogs only live about six years."

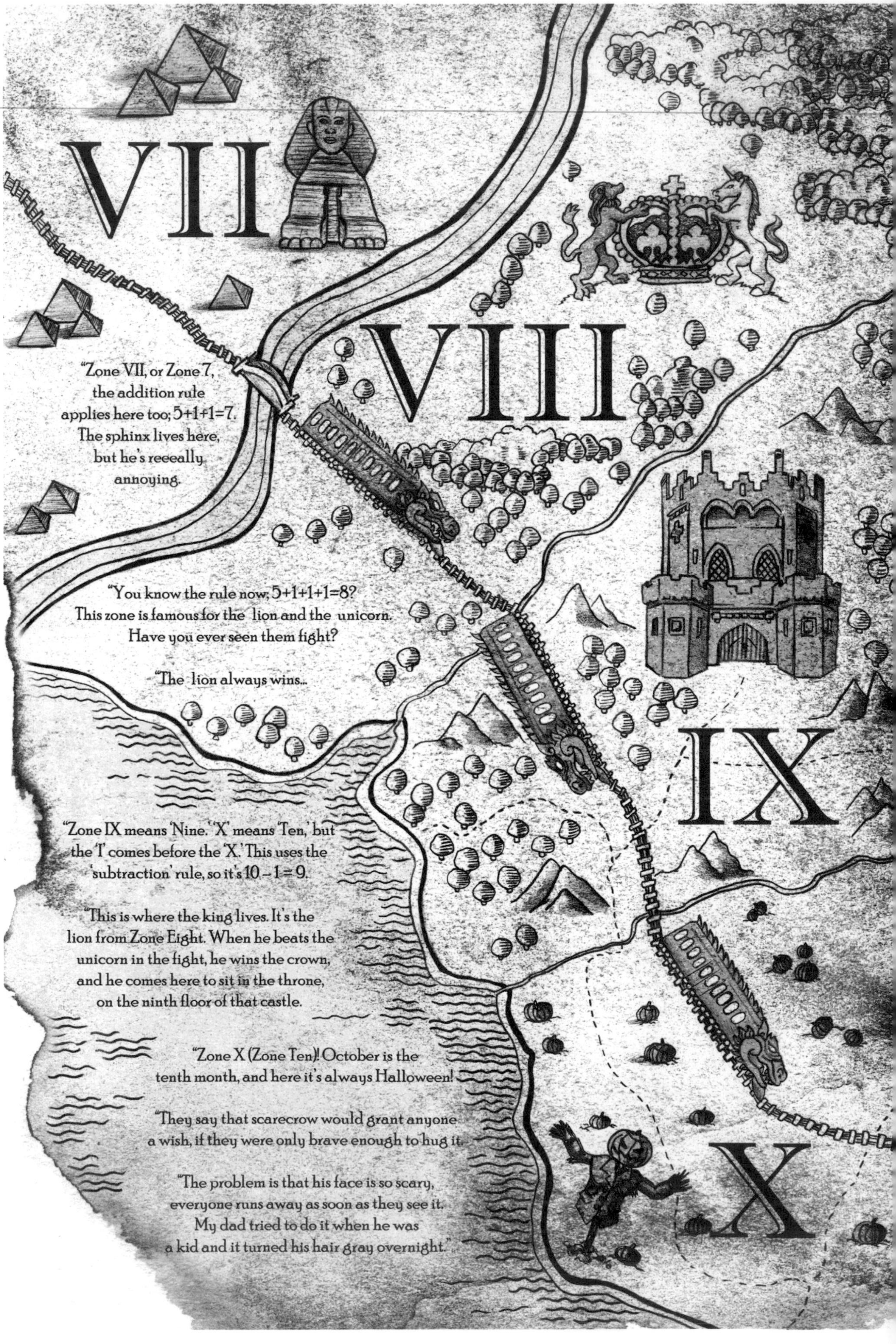

VII
VIII
IX
X

"Zone VII, or Zone 7,
the addition rule
applies here too; 5+1+1=7.
The sphinx lives here,
but he's reeeally
annoying.

"You know the rule now, 5+1+1+1=8?
This zone is famous for the lion and the unicorn.
Have you ever seen them fight?

"The lion always wins...

"Zone IX means 'Nine.' 'X' means 'Ten,' but
the 'I' comes before the 'X.' This uses the
'subtraction' rule, so it's 10 – 1 = 9.

"This is where the king lives. It's the
lion from Zone Eight. When he beats the
unicorn in the fight, he wins the crown,
and he comes here to sit in the throne,
on the ninth floor of that castle.

"Zone X (Zone Ten)! October is the
tenth month, and here it's always Halloween!

"They say that scarecrow would grant anyone
a wish, if they were only brave enough to hug it.

"The problem is that his face is so scary,
everyone runs away as soon as they see it.
My dad tried to do it when he was
a kid and it turned his hair gray overnight."

Zone XI. Eleven. Back to the addition rule! 10+1=11! Hey, this cold place is your zone, right?

Can I just drop you off with someone here?

You don't have a rich aunt or grandmother or something?

No, we only moved here a few weeks ago. My family are all out at Ivy's place...

Ah shoot. Just a thought.

Well we must be catching up with them, if they didn't get as far as my zone...

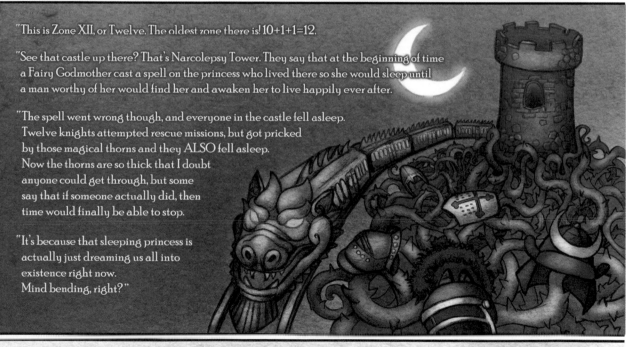

"This is Zone XII, or Twelve. The oldest zone there is! 10+1+1=12.

"See that castle up there? That's Narcolepsy Tower. They say that at the beginning of time a Fairy Godmother cast a spell on the princess who lived there so she would sleep until a man worthy of her would find her and awaken her to live happily ever after.

"The spell went wrong though, and everyone in the castle fell asleep. Twelve knights attempted rescue missions, but got pricked by those magical thorns and they ALSO fell asleep. Now the thorns are so thick that I doubt anyone could get through, but some say that if someone actually did, then time would finally be able to stop.

"It's because that sleeping princess is actually just dreaming us all into existence right now. Mind bending, right?"

"Zone I, or One. Here there is only one person with one problem. He sits up on that one wall and tries to figure it all out."

To scramble, or not to scramble...

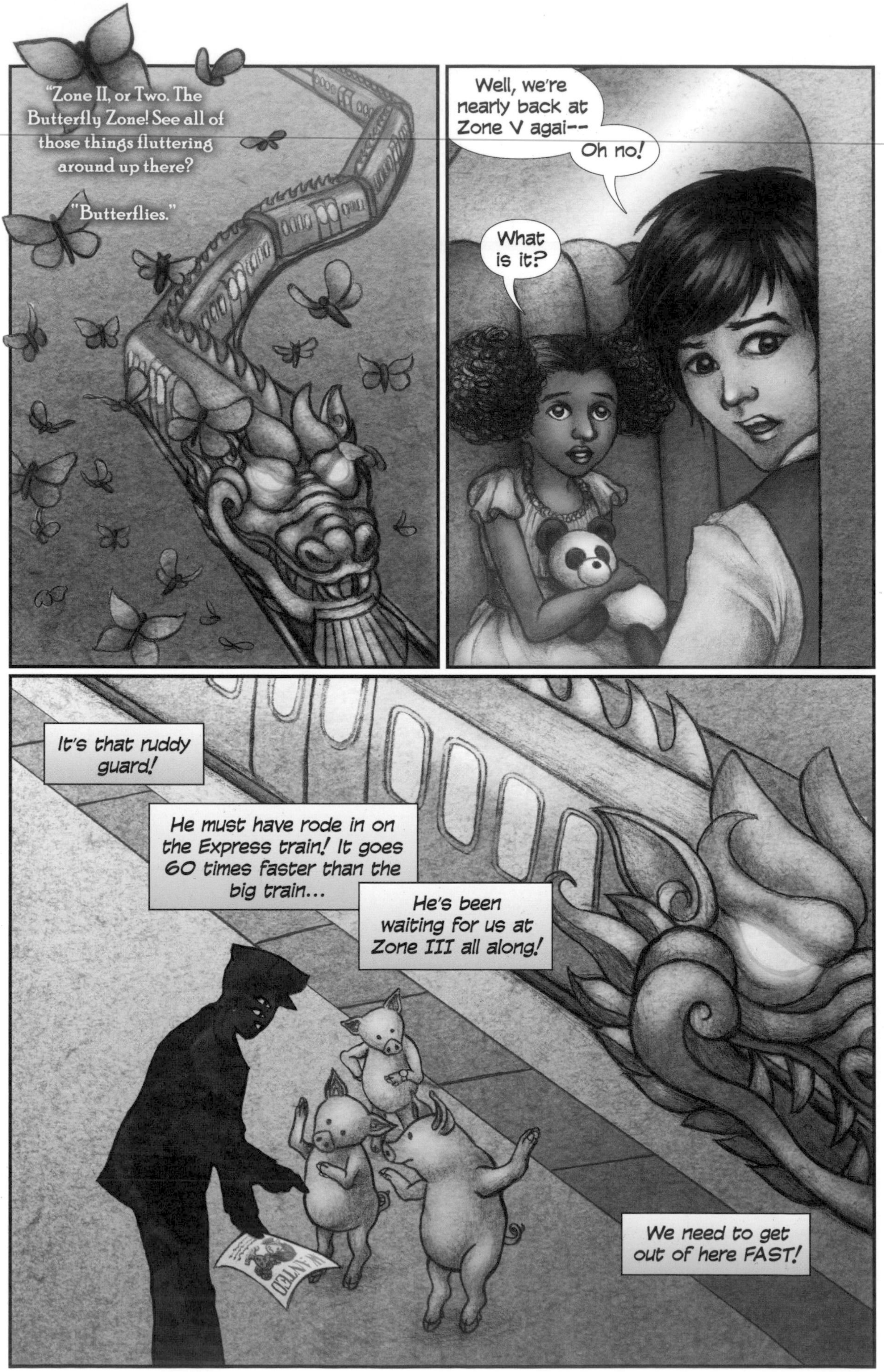
"Zone II, or Two. The Butterfly Zone! See all of those things fluttering around up there?
"Butterflies."
Well, we're nearly back at Zone V agai--
Oh no!
What is it?
It's that ruddy guard!
He must have rode in on the Express train! It goes 60 times faster than the big train...
He's been waiting for us at Zone III all along!
We need to get out of here FAST!

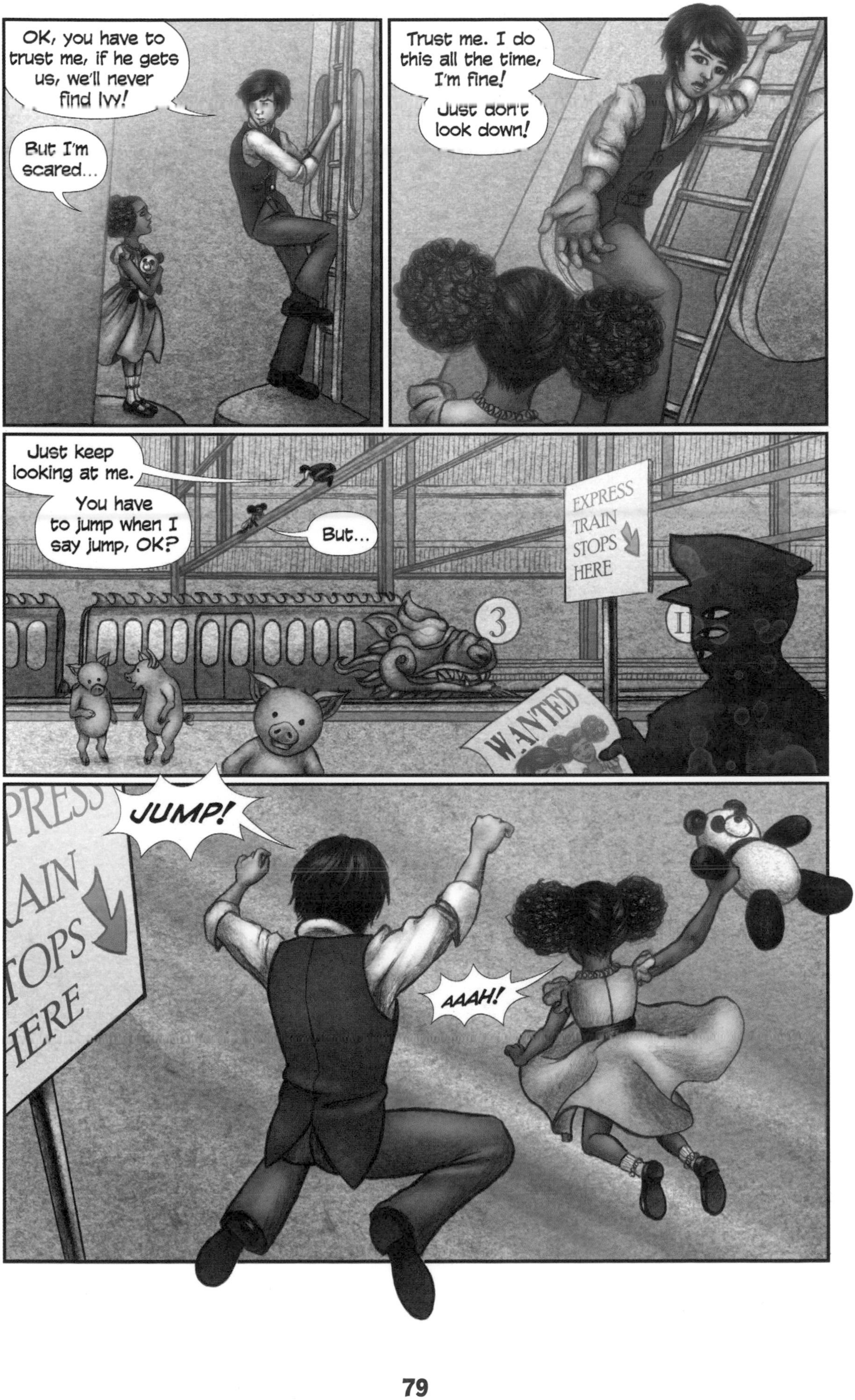
OK, you have to trust me, if he gets us, we'll never find Ivy!
But I'm scared...
Trust me. I do this all the time, I'm fine!
Just don't look down!
Just keep looking at me.
You have to jump when I say jump, OK?
But...
EXPRESS TRAIN STOPS HERE
3
WANTED
JUMP!
AAAH!

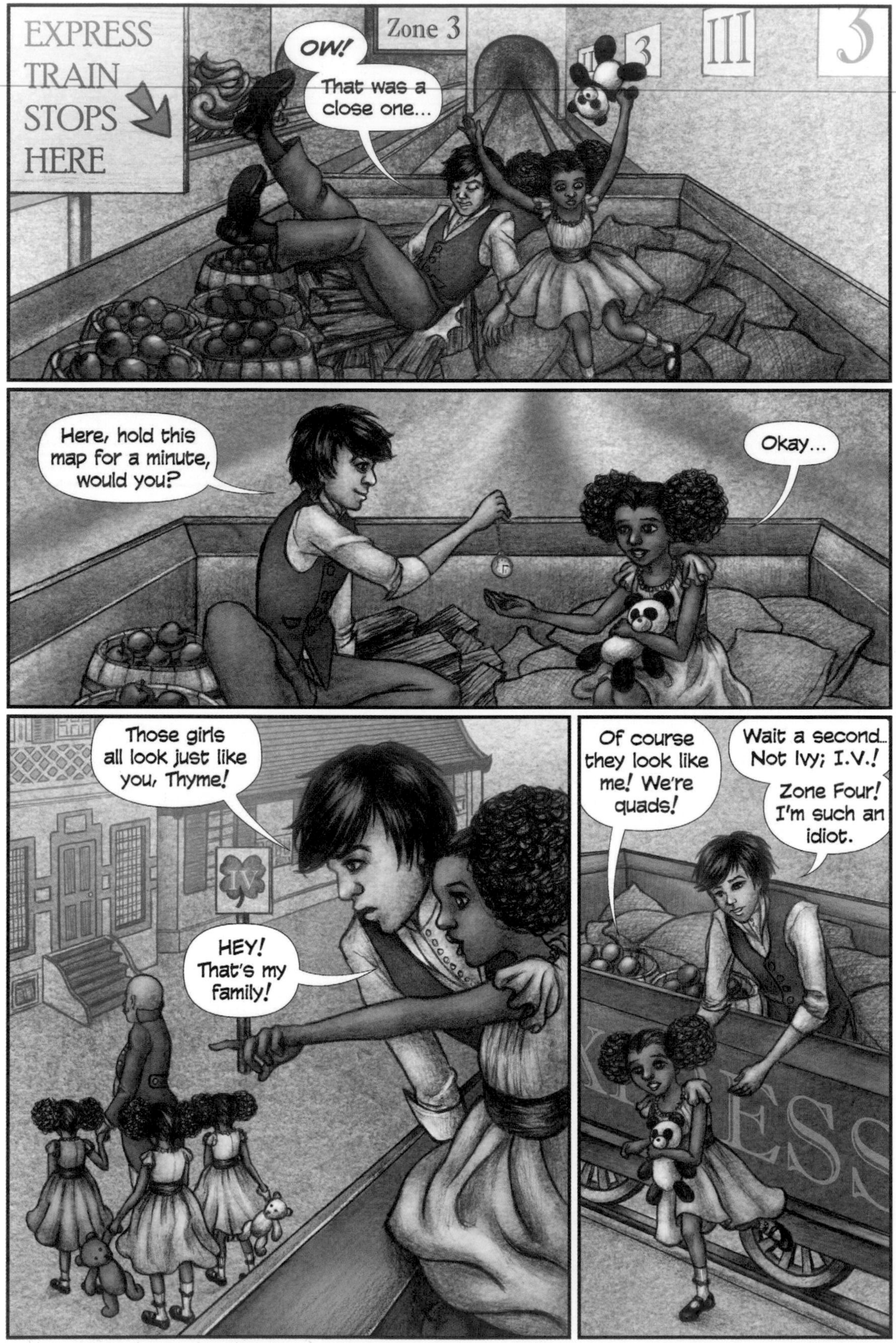
EXPRESS TRAIN STOPS HERE
Zone 3
III
OW!
That was a close one...
Here, hold this map for a minute, would you?
Okay...
Those girls all look just like you, Thyme!
HEY! That's my family!
Of course they look like me! We're quads!
Wait a second... Not Ivy; I.V.!
Zone Four! I'm such an idiot.
EXPRESS

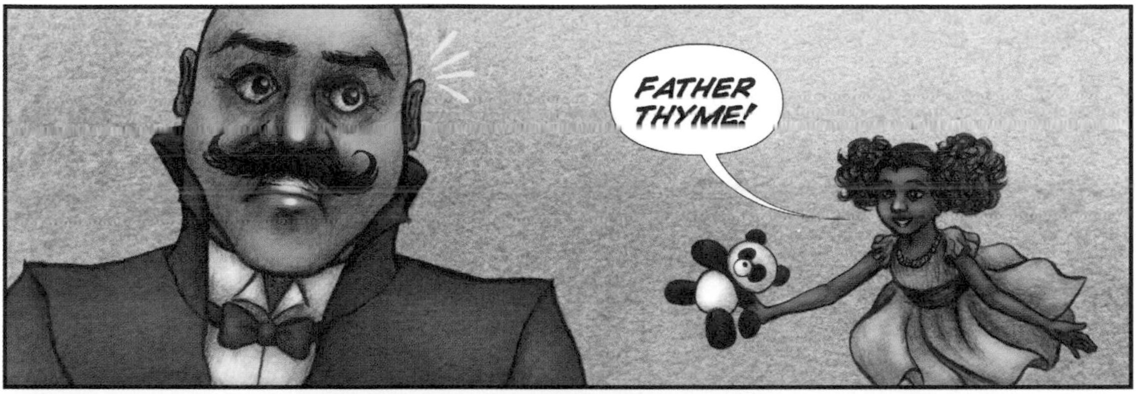
FATHER THYME!

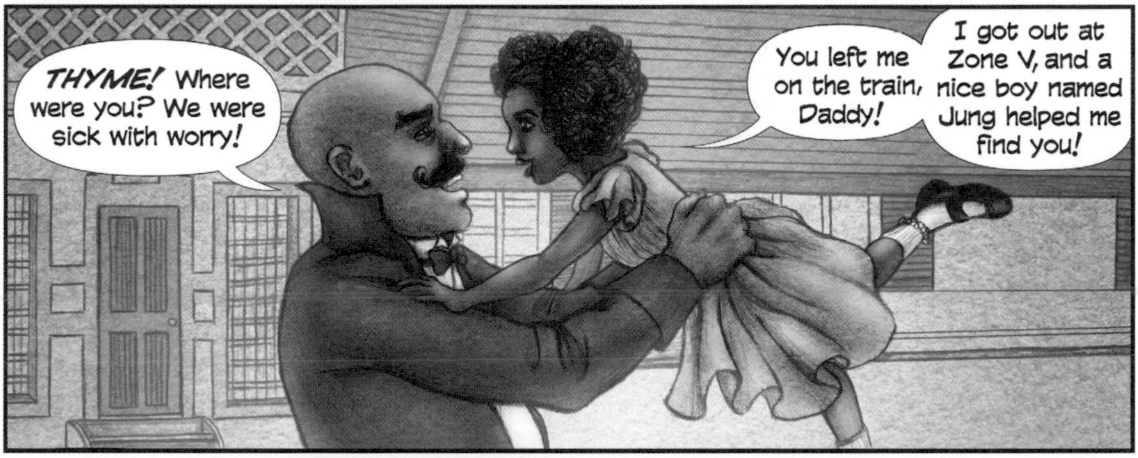
THYME! Where were you? We were sick with worry!
You left me on the train, Daddy!
I got out at Zone V, and a nice boy named Jung helped me find you!

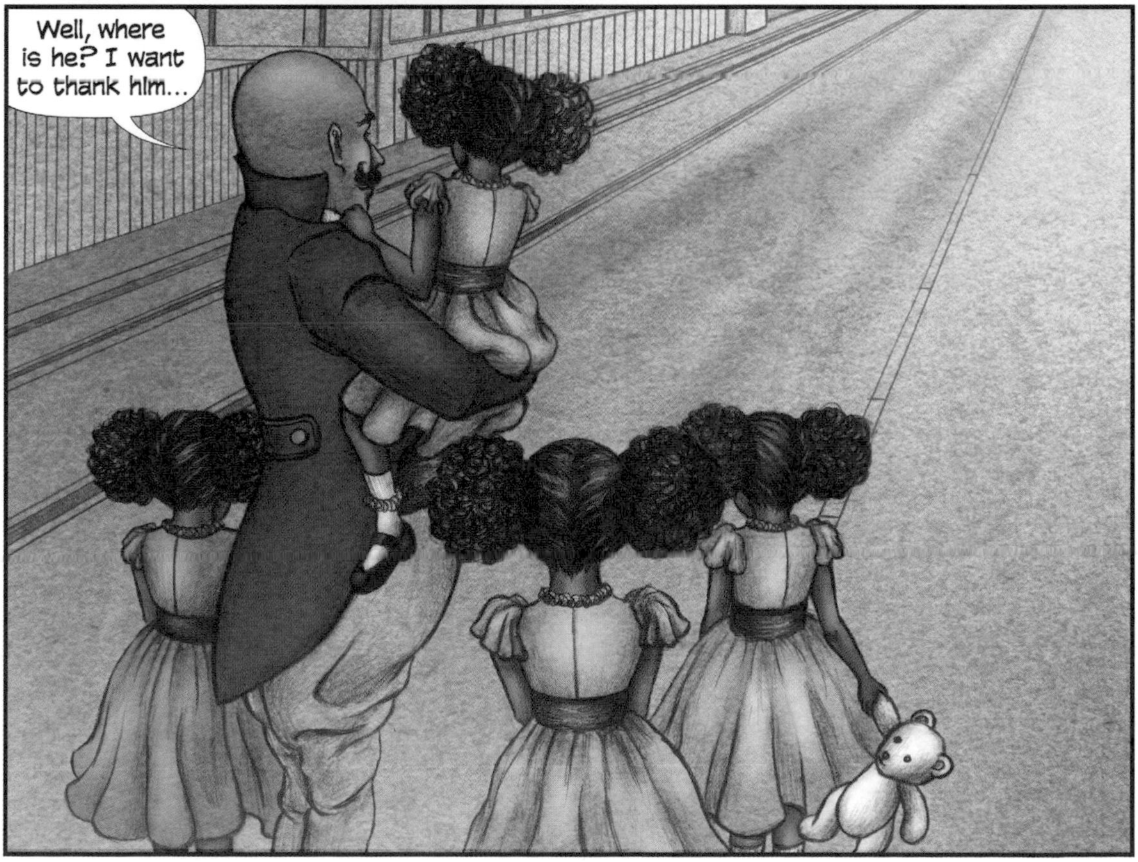
Well, where is he? I want to thank him...

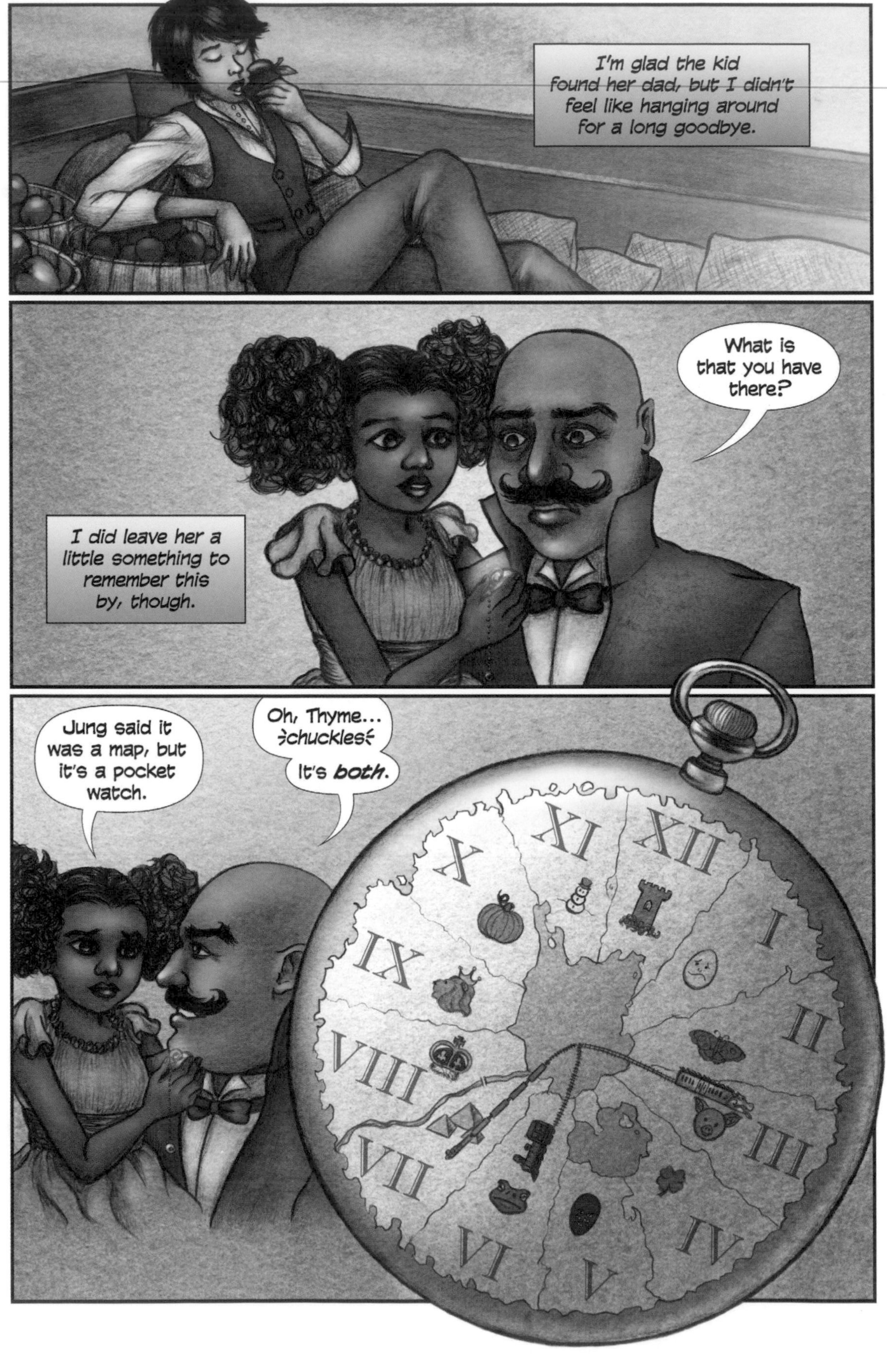
I'm glad the kid found her dad, but I didn't feel like hanging around for a long goodbye.
What is that you have there?
I did leave her a little something to remember this by, though.
Jung said it was a map, but it's a pocket watch.
Oh, Thyme... ⊰chuckles⊱ It's **both**.

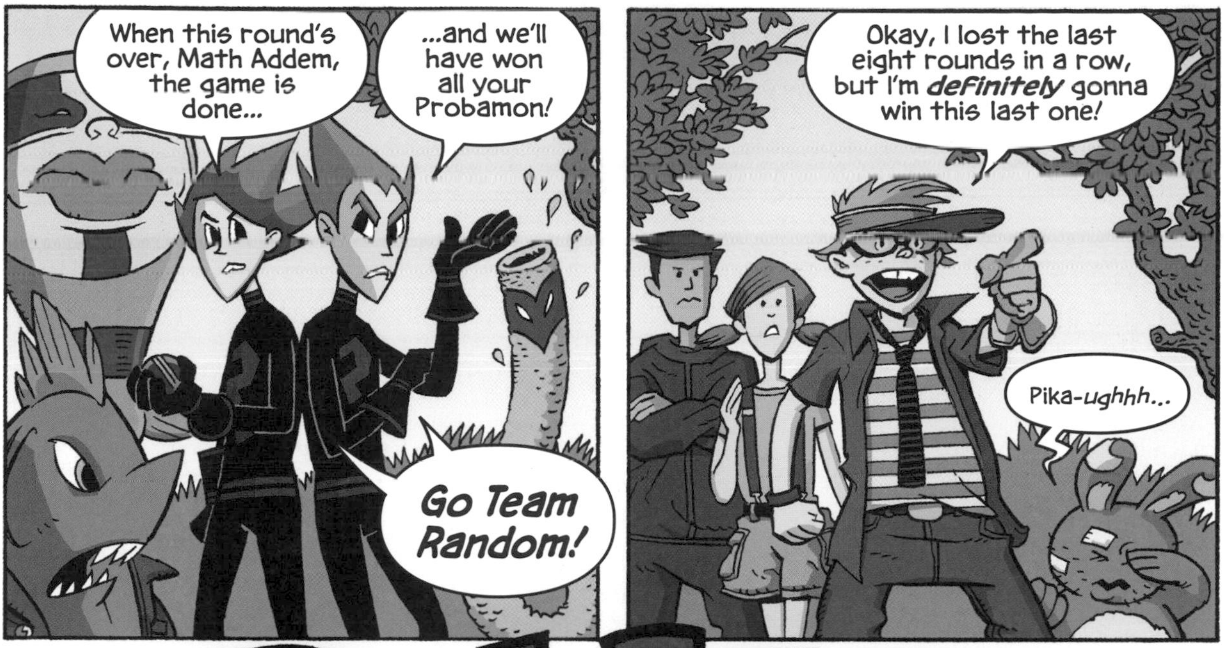
When this round's over, Math Addem, the game is done...
...and we'll have won all your Probamon!
Go Team Random!
Okay, I lost the last eight rounds in a row, but I'm *definitely* gonna win this last one!
Pika-*ughhh*...

Probamon!
"Gotta Chance 'em All!"

Writer
Geoffrey Golden

Artist
Nate Pride

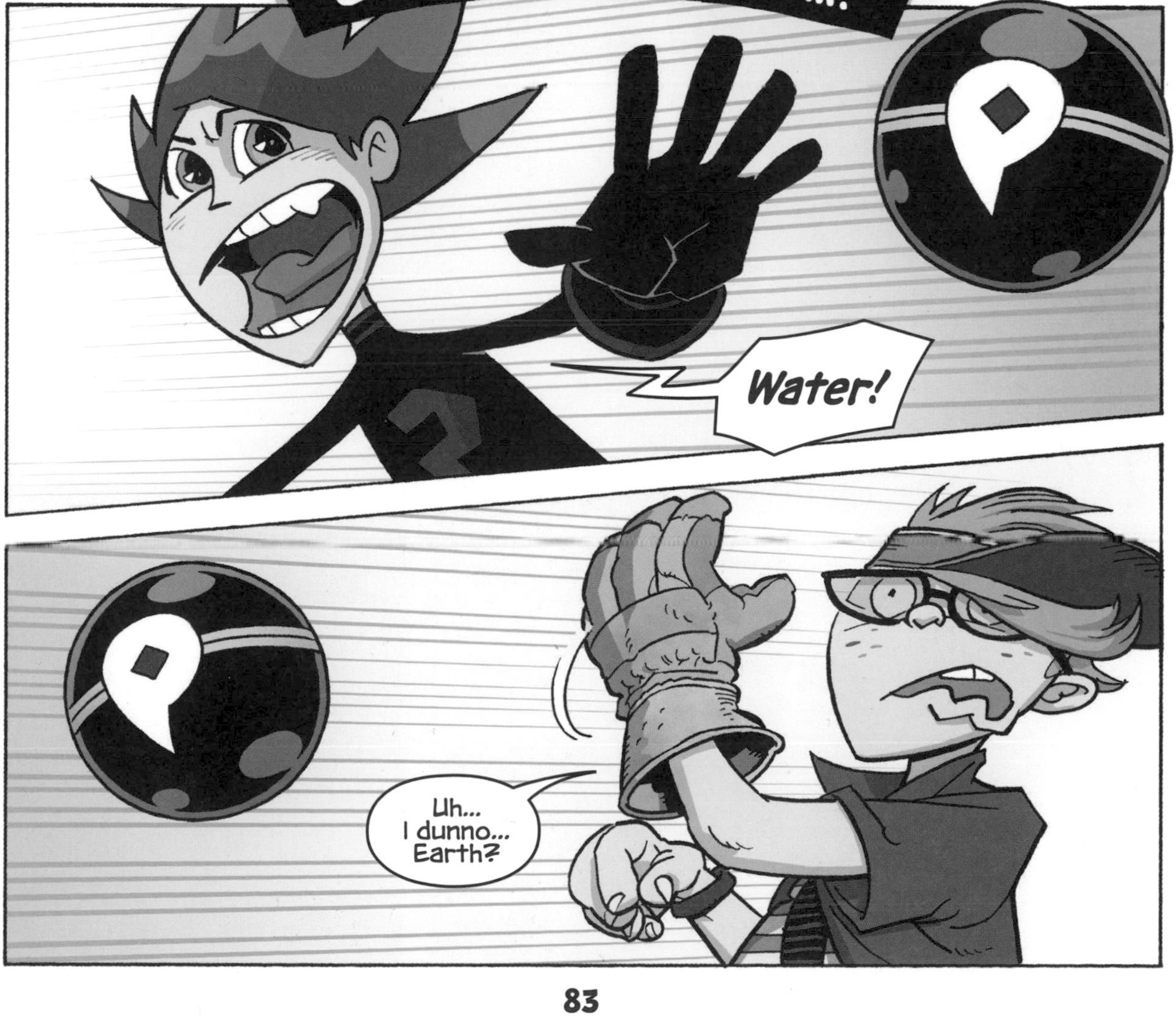
Water!
Uh... I dunno... Earth?

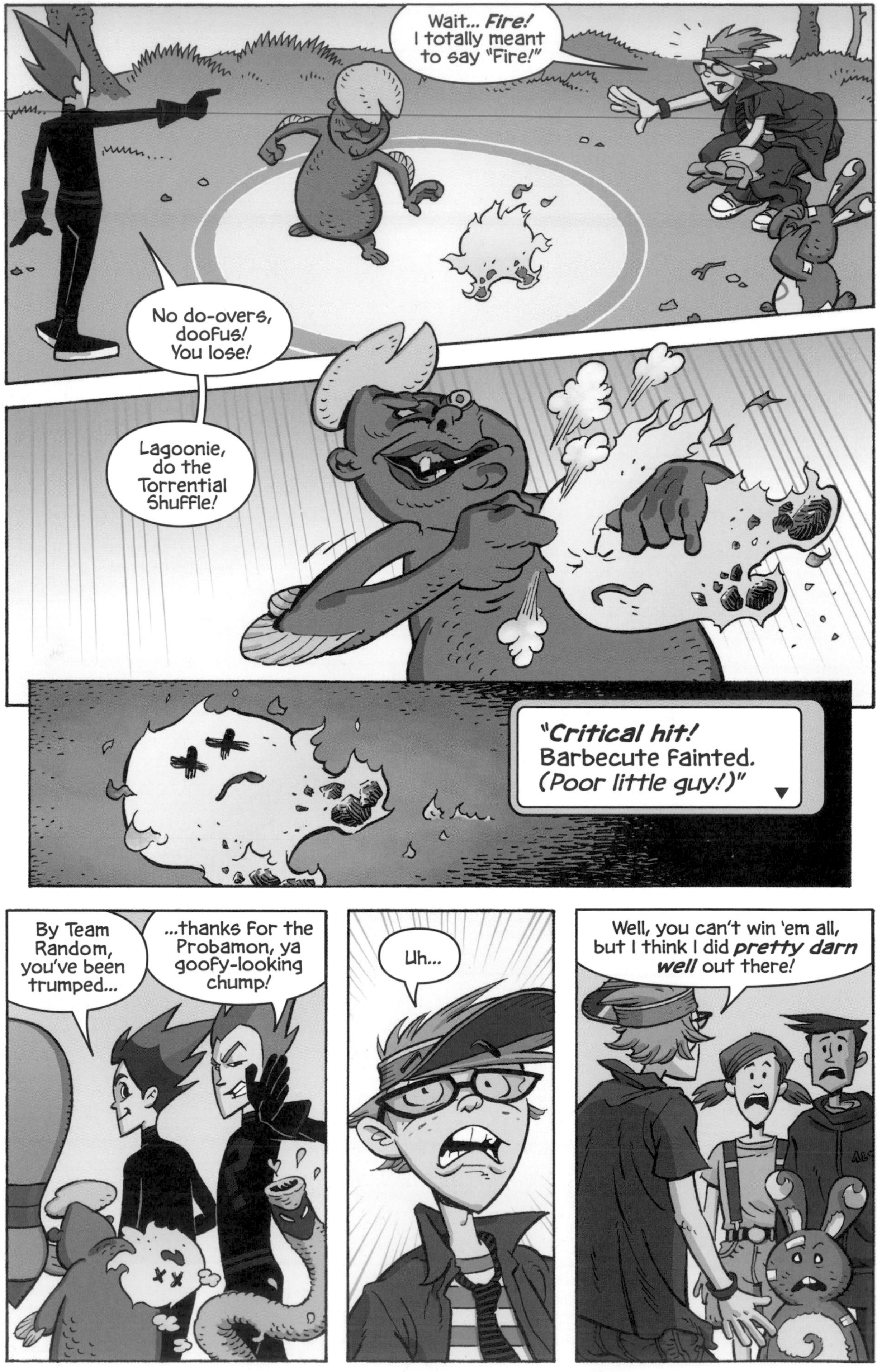
Wait... Fire!
I totally meant to say "Fire!"
No do-overs, doofus! You lose!
Lagoonie, do the Torrential Shuffle!
"Critical hit!
Barbecute fainted.
(Poor little guy!)"
By Team Random, you've been trumped...
...thanks for the Probamon, ya goofy-looking chump!
Uh...
Well, you can't win 'em all, but I think I did pretty darn well out there!

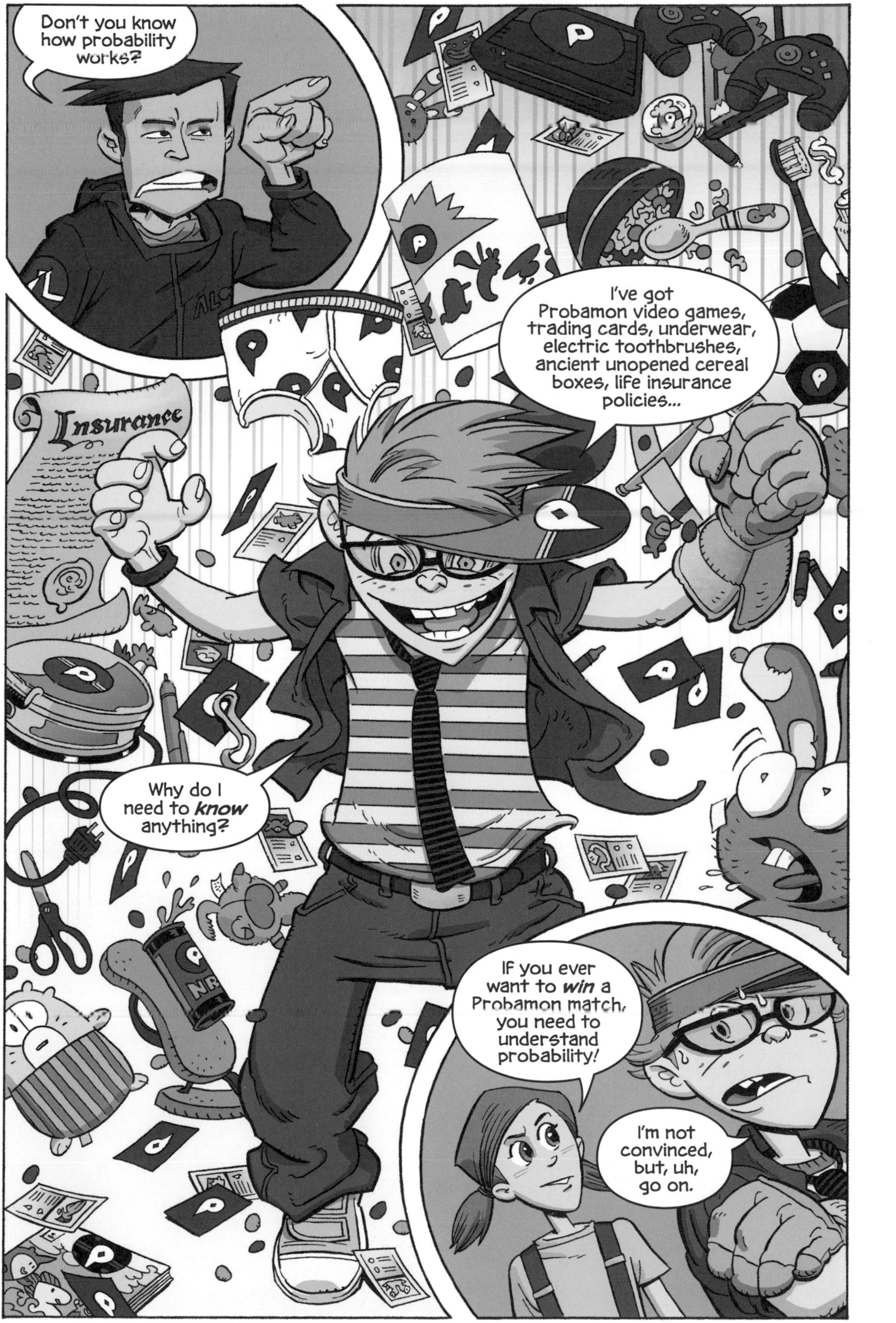

Don't you know how probability works?
I've got Probamon video games, trading cards, underwear, electric toothbrushes, ancient unopened cereal boxes, life insurance policies...
Insurance
Why do I need to *know* anything?
If you ever want to *win* a Probamon match, you need to understand probability!
I'm not convinced, but, uh, go on.

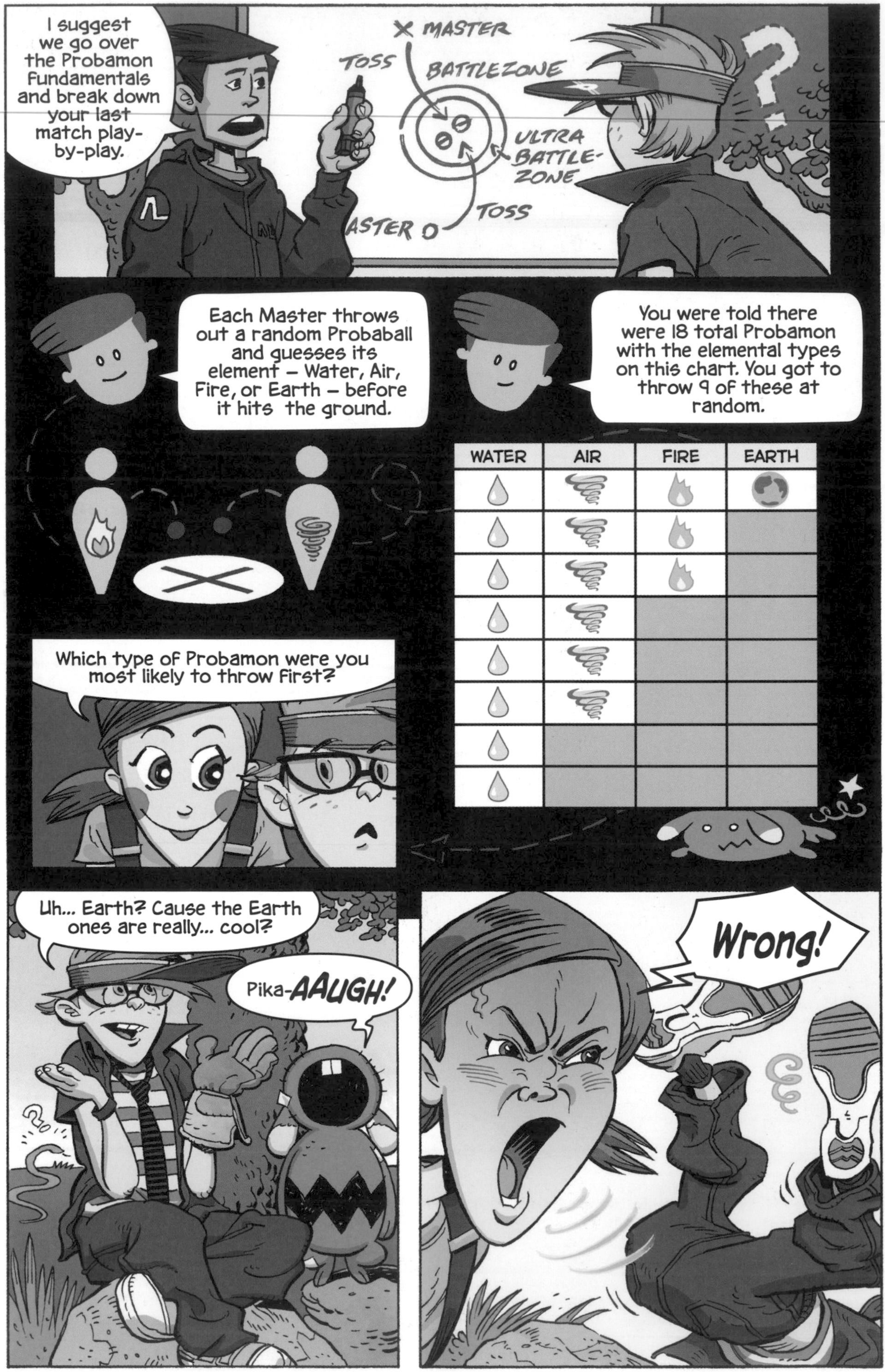
I suggest we go over the Probamon Fundamentals and break down your last match play-by-play.
MASTER
TOSS
BATTLEZONE
ULTRA BATTLE-ZONE
TOSS
ASTER
Each Master throws out a random Probaball and guesses its element – Water, Air, Fire, or Earth – before it hits the ground.
You were told there were 18 total Probamon with the elemental types on this chart. You got to throw 9 of these at random.
WATER
AIR
FIRE
EARTH
Which type of Probamon were you most likely to throw first?
Uh... Earth? Cause the Earth ones are really... cool?
Pika-AAUGH!
Wrong!

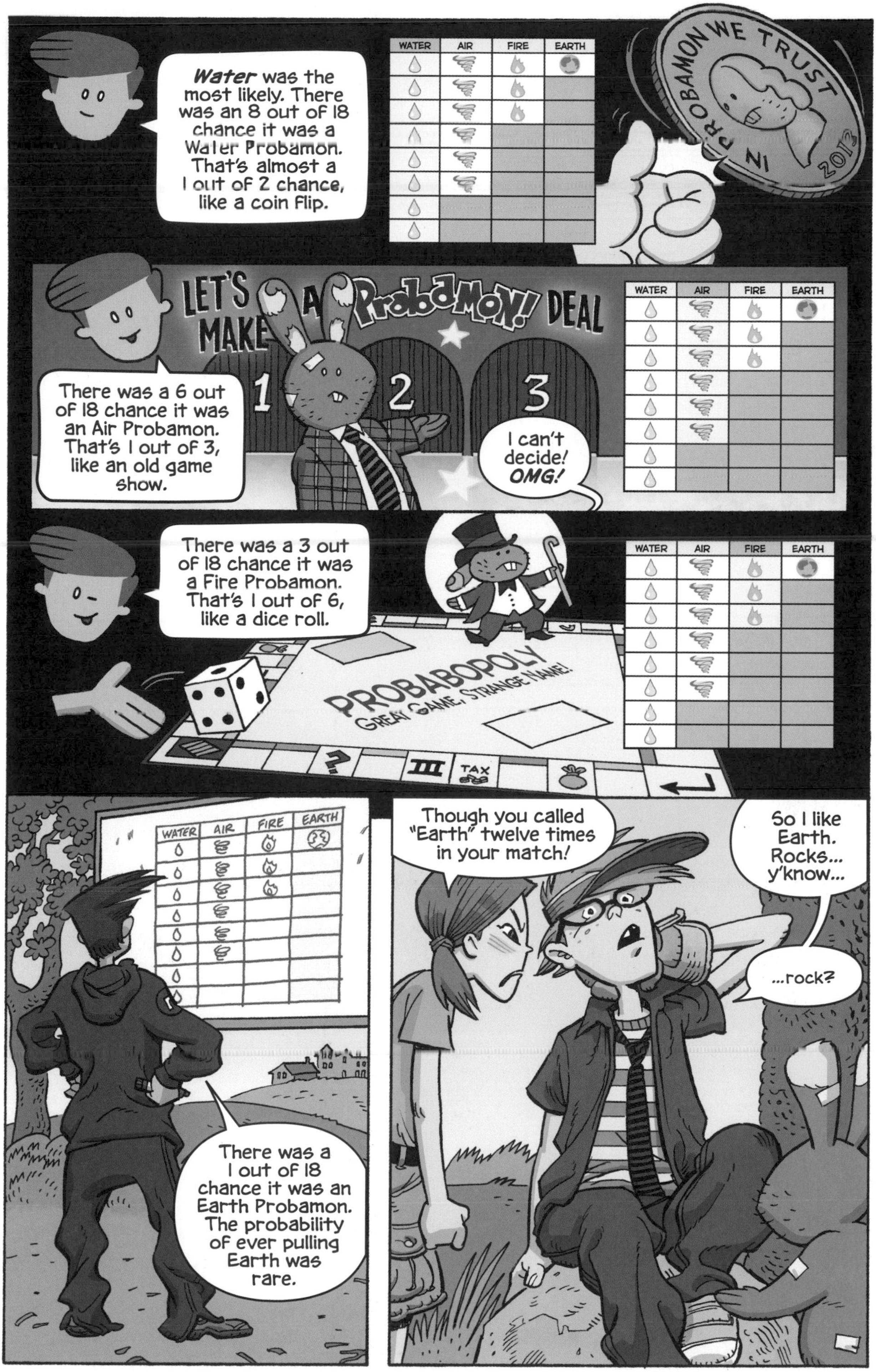
WATER AIR FIRE EARTH
IN PROBAMON WE TRUST 2013
Water was the most likely. There was an 8 out of 18 chance it was a Water Probamon. That's almost a 1 out of 2 chance, like a coin flip.
LET'S MAKE A PROBAMON! DEAL
1 2 3
There was a 6 out of 18 chance it was an Air Probamon. That's 1 out of 3, like an old game show.
I can't decide! ***OMG!***
There was a 3 out of 18 chance it was a Fire Probamon. That's 1 out of 6, like a dice roll.
PROBABOPOLY
GREAT GAME, STRANGE NAME!
TAX
There was a 1 out of 18 chance it was an Earth Probamon. The probability of ever pulling Earth was rare.
Though you called "Earth" twelve times in your match!
So I like Earth. Rocks... y'know...
...rock?

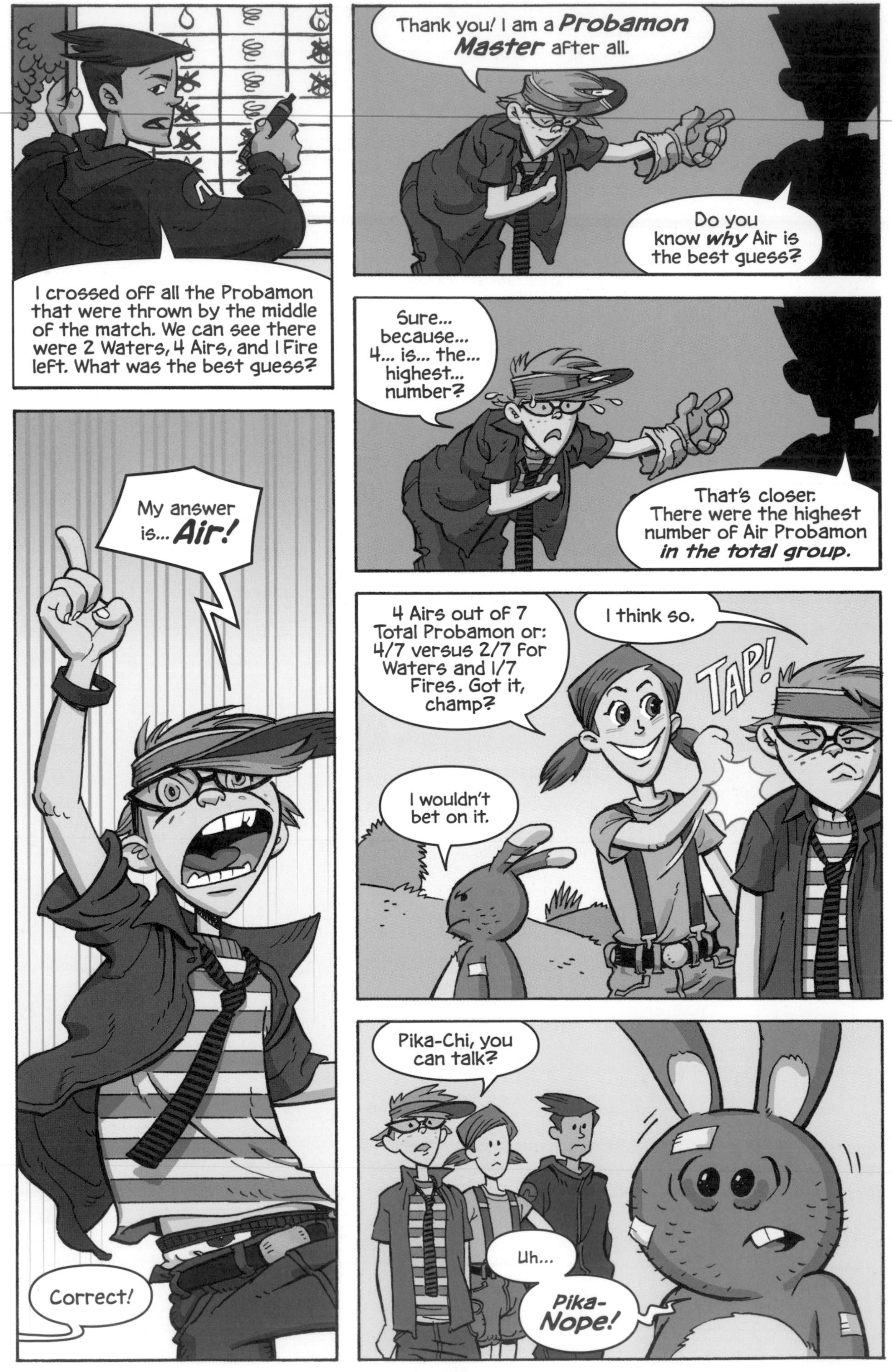
I crossed off all the Probamon that were thrown by the middle of the match. We can see there were 2 Waters, 4 Airs, and 1 Fire left. What was the best guess?
My answer is... Air!
Correct!
Thank you! I am a Probamon Master after all.
Do you know why Air is the best guess?
Sure... because... 4... is... the... highest... number?
That's closer. There were the highest number of Air Probamon in the total group.
4 Airs out of 7 Total Probamon or: 4/7 versus 2/7 for Waters and 1/7 Fires. Got it, champ?
I think so.
TAP!
I wouldn't bet on it.
Pika-Chi, you can talk?
Uh...
Pika-Nope!

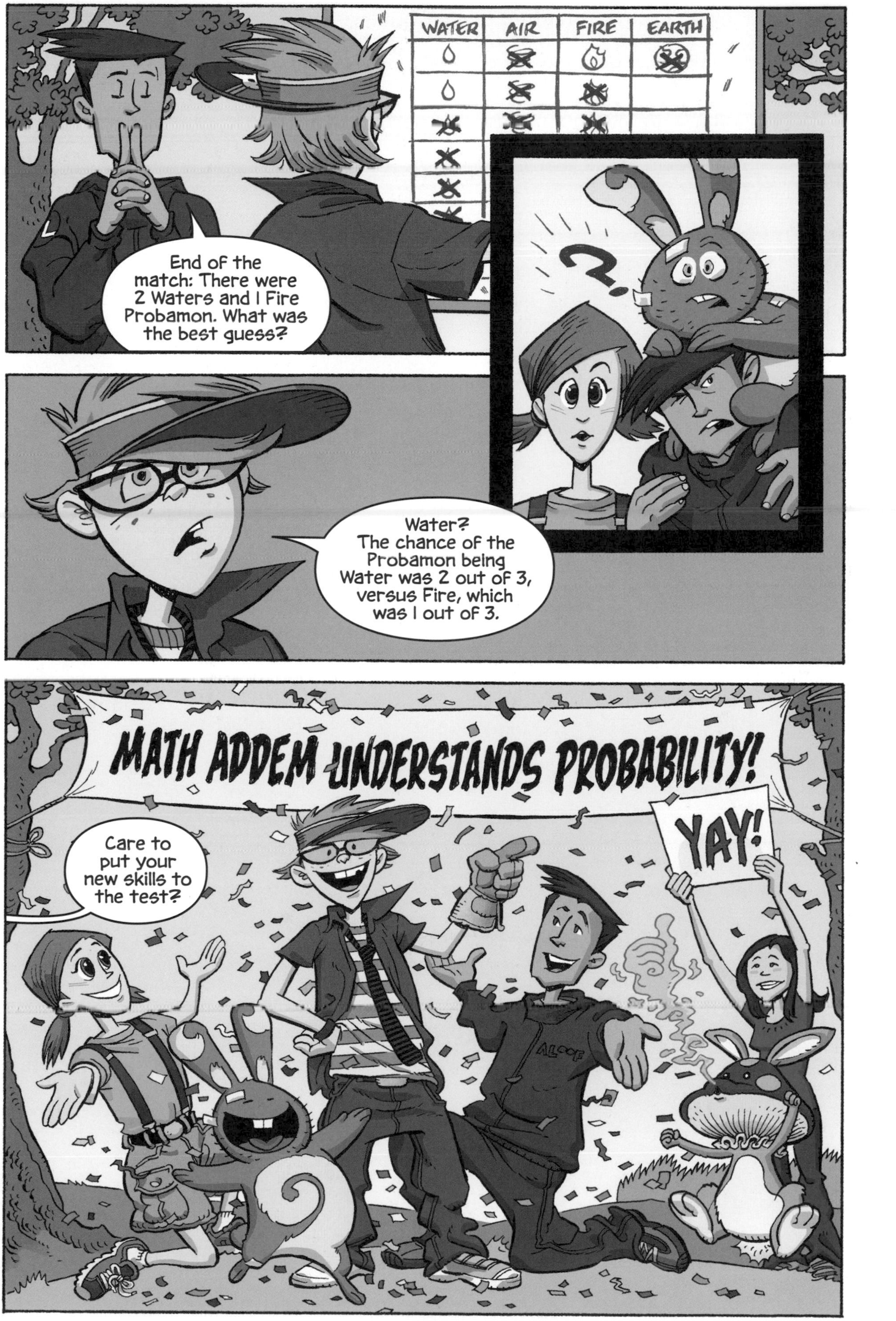
WATER
AIR
FIRE
EARTH
End of the match: There were 2 Waters and 1 Fire Probamon. What was the best guess?
Water? The chance of the Probamon being Water was 2 out of 3, versus Fire, which was 1 out of 3.
MATH ADDEM UNDERSTANDS PROBABILITY!
YAY!
Care to put your new skills to the test?

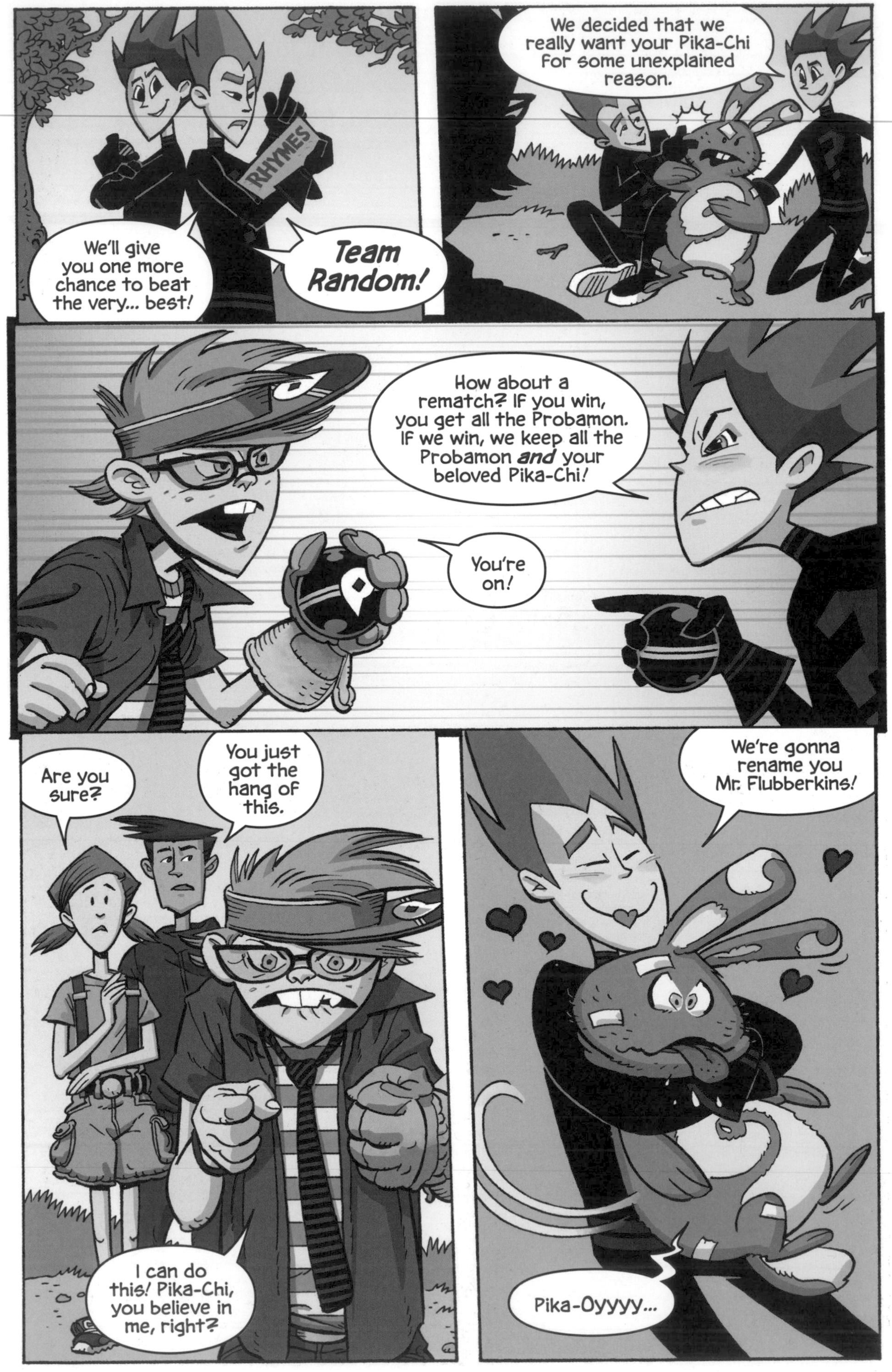

We'll give you one more chance to beat the very... best!
Team Random!
We decided that we really want your Pika-Chi for some unexplained reason.
RHYMES
How about a rematch? If you win, you get all the Probamon. If we win, we keep all the Probamon *and* your beloved Pika-Chi!
You're on!
Are you sure?
You just got the hang of this.
I can do this! Pika-Chi, you believe in me, right?
We're gonna rename you Mr. Flubberkins!
Pika-Oyyyy...

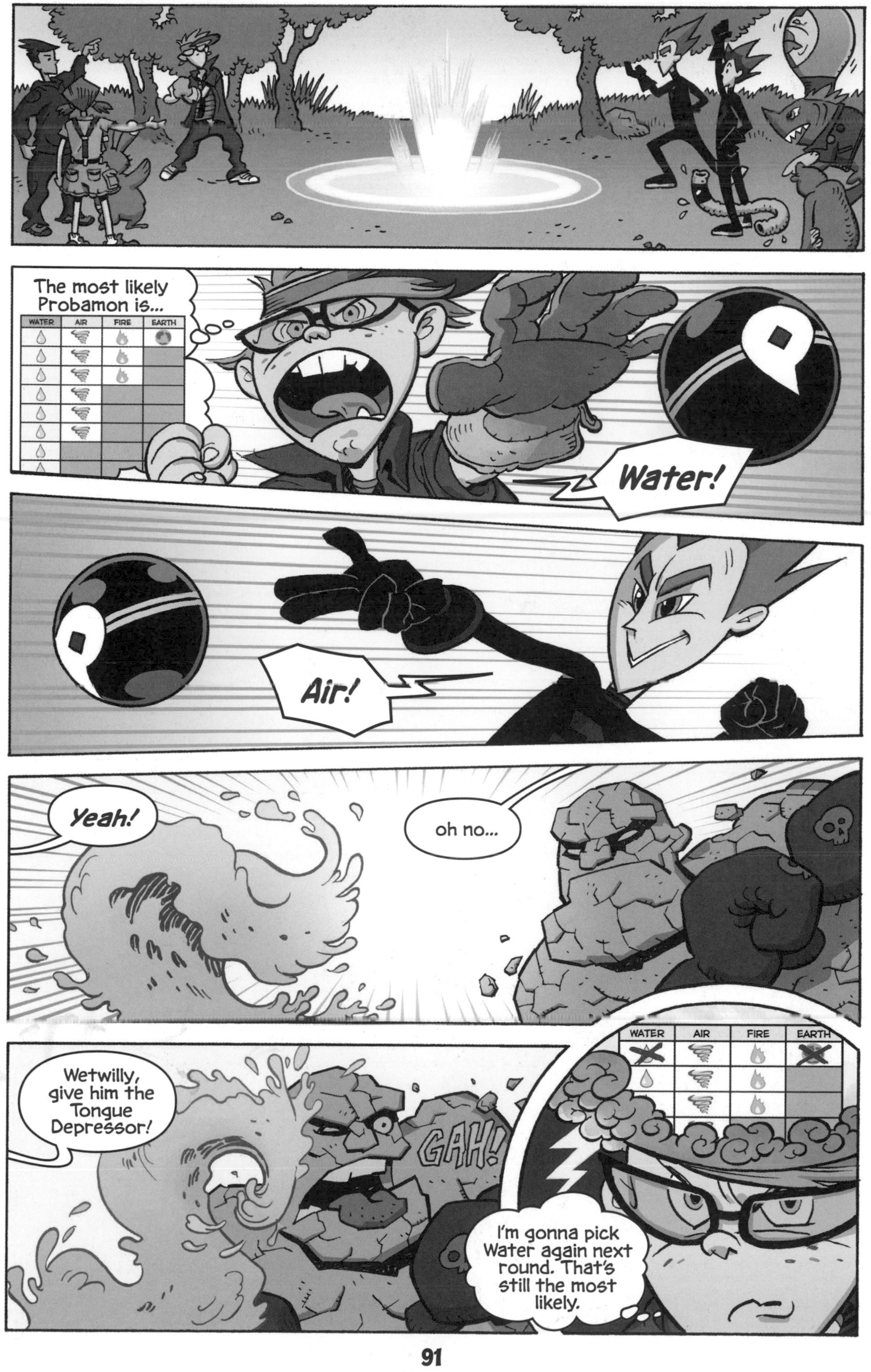

The most likely Probamon is...
WATER AIR FIRE EARTH
Water!
Air!
Yeah!
oh no...
Wetwilly, give him the Tongue Depressor!
GAH!
WATER AIR FIRE EARTH
I'm gonna pick Water again next round. That's still the most likely.

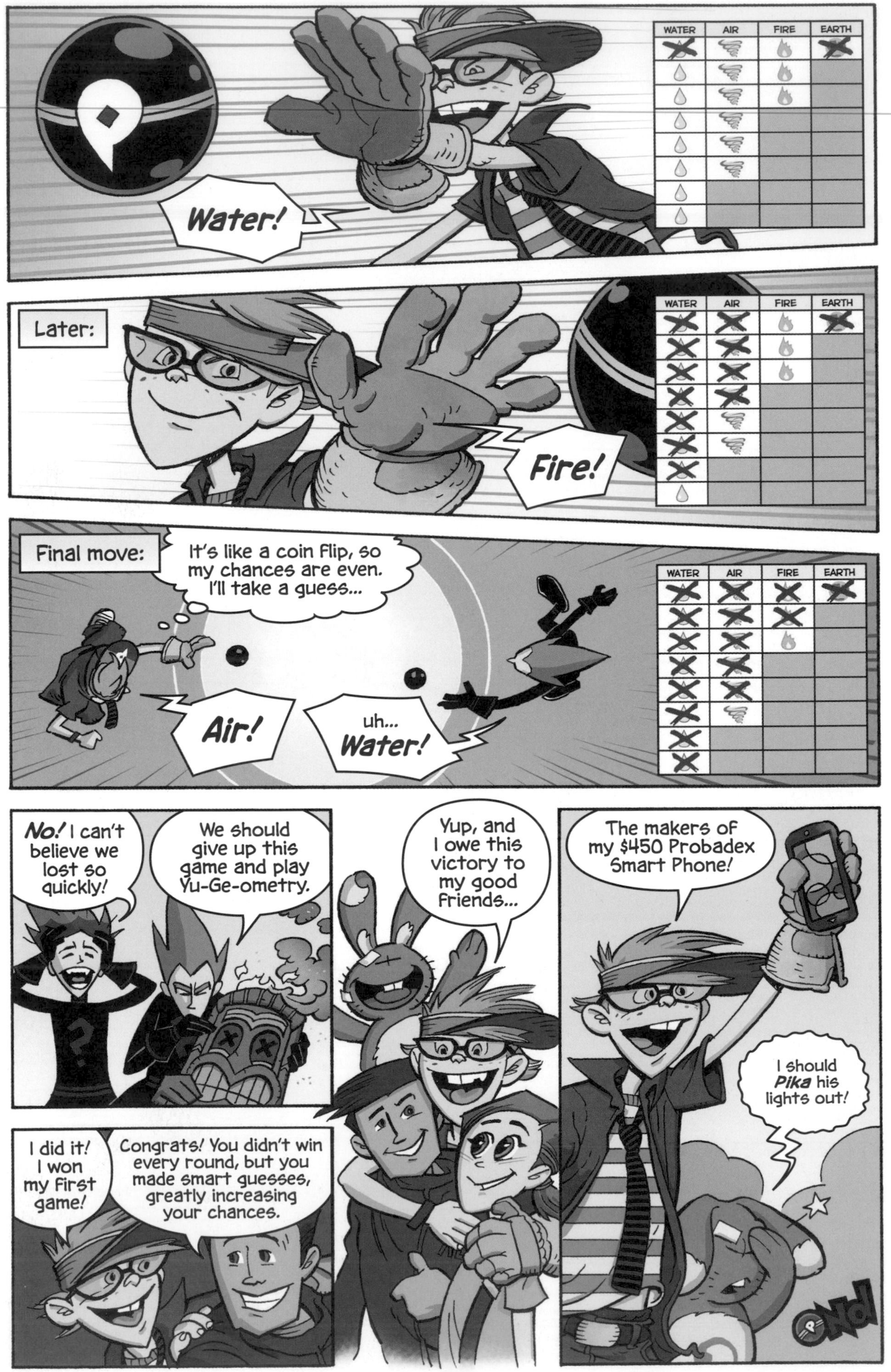

WATER AIR FIRE EARTH
Water!
Later:
WATER AIR FIRE EARTH
Fire!
Final move:
It's like a coin flip, so my chances are even. I'll take a guess...
WATER AIR FIRE EARTH
Air!
uh... Water!
No! I can't believe we lost so quickly!
We should give up this game and play Yu-Ge-ometry.
Yup, and I owe this victory to my good friends...
The makers of my $450 Probadex Smart Phone!
I should Pika his lights out!
I did it! I won my first game!
Congrats! You didn't win every round, but you made smart guesses, greatly increasing your chances.

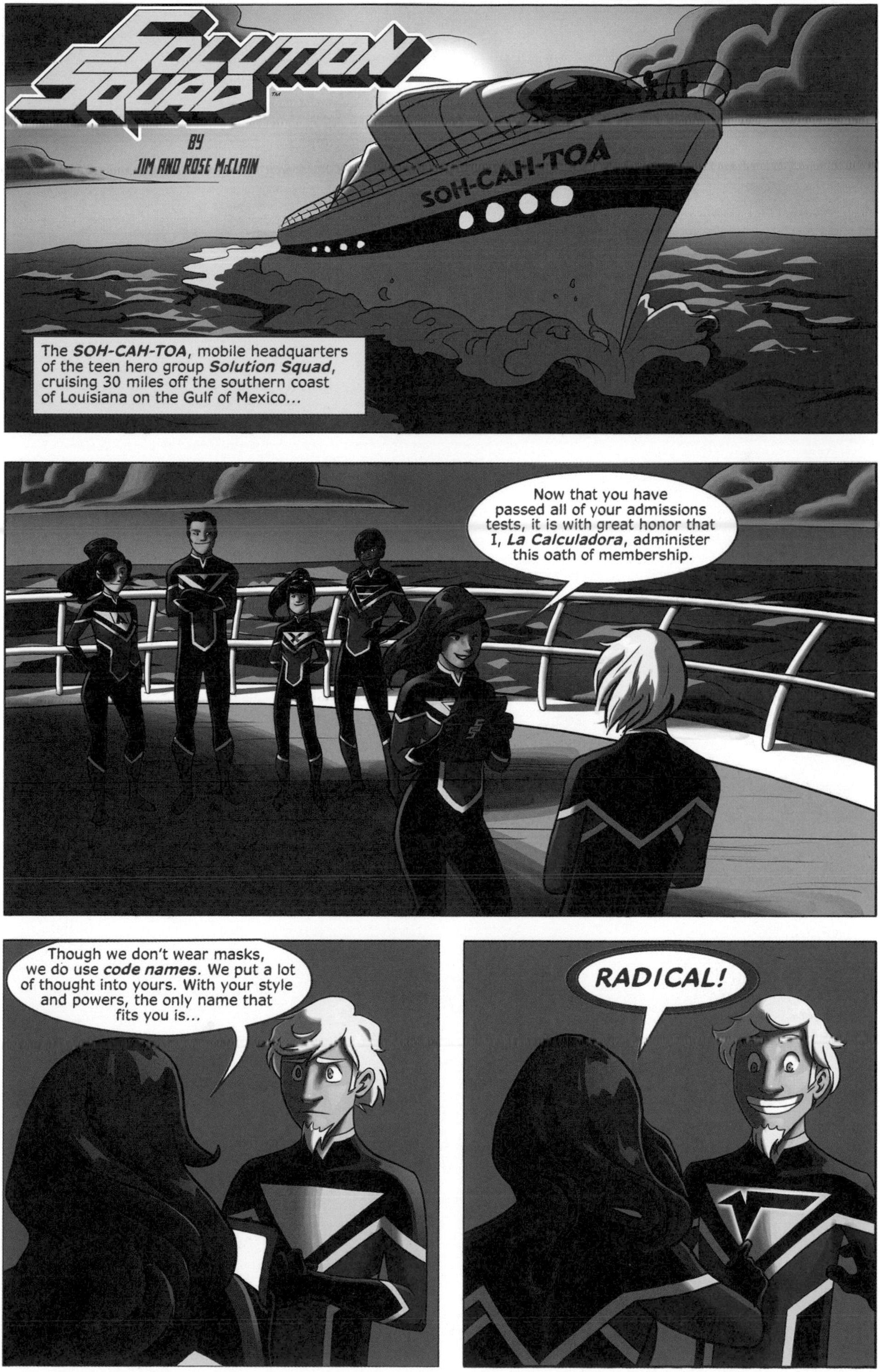
SOLUTION SQUAD™
BY
JIM AND ROSE McCLAIN
SOH-CAH-TOA
The SOH-CAH-TOA, mobile headquarters of the teen hero group Solution Squad, cruising 30 miles off the southern coast of Louisiana on the Gulf of Mexico...
Now that you have passed all of your admissions tests, it is with great honor that I, La Calculadora, administer this oath of membership.
Though we don't wear masks, we do use code names. We put a lot of thought into yours. With your style and powers, the only name that fits you is...
RADICAL!

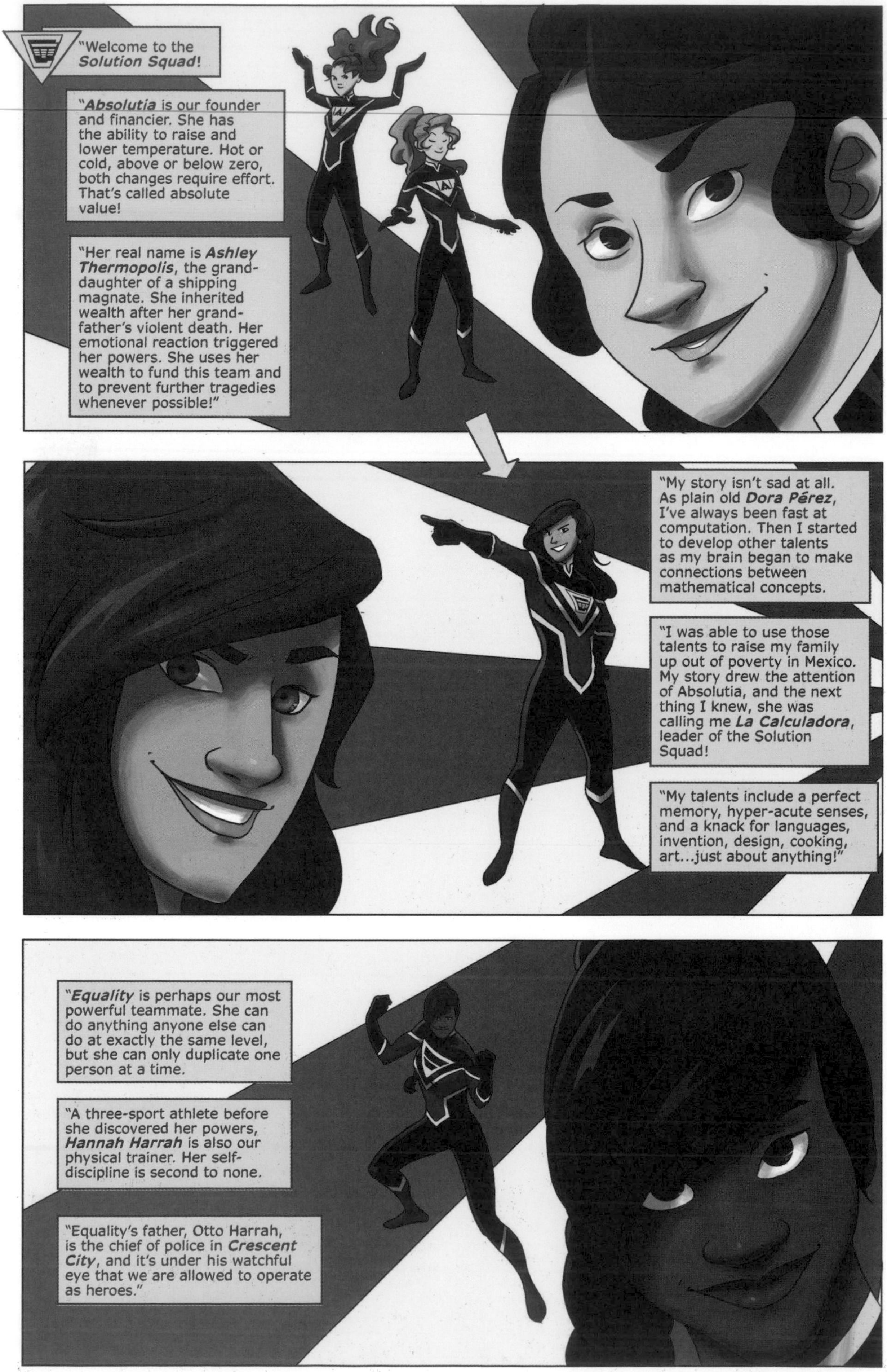
"Welcome to the Solution Squad!
"Absolutia is our founder and financier. She has the ability to raise and lower temperature. Hot or cold, above or below zero, both changes require effort. That's called absolute value!
"Her real name is Ashley Thermopolis, the granddaughter of a shipping magnate. She inherited wealth after her grandfather's violent death. Her emotional reaction triggered her powers. She uses her wealth to fund this team and to prevent further tragedies whenever possible!"
"My story isn't sad at all. As plain old Dora Pérez, I've always been fast at computation. Then I started to develop other talents as my brain began to make connections between mathematical concepts.
"I was able to use those talents to raise my family up out of poverty in Mexico. My story drew the attention of Absolutia, and the next thing I knew, she was calling me La Calculadora, leader of the Solution Squad!
"My talents include a perfect memory, hyper-acute senses, and a knack for languages, invention, design, cooking, art...just about anything!"
"Equality is perhaps our most powerful teammate. She can do anything anyone else can do at exactly the same level, but she can only duplicate one person at a time.
"A three-sport athlete before she discovered her powers, Hannah Harrah is also our physical trainer. Her self-discipline is second to none.
"Equality's father, Otto Harrah, is the chief of police in Crescent City, and it's under his watchful eye that we are allowed to operate as heroes."

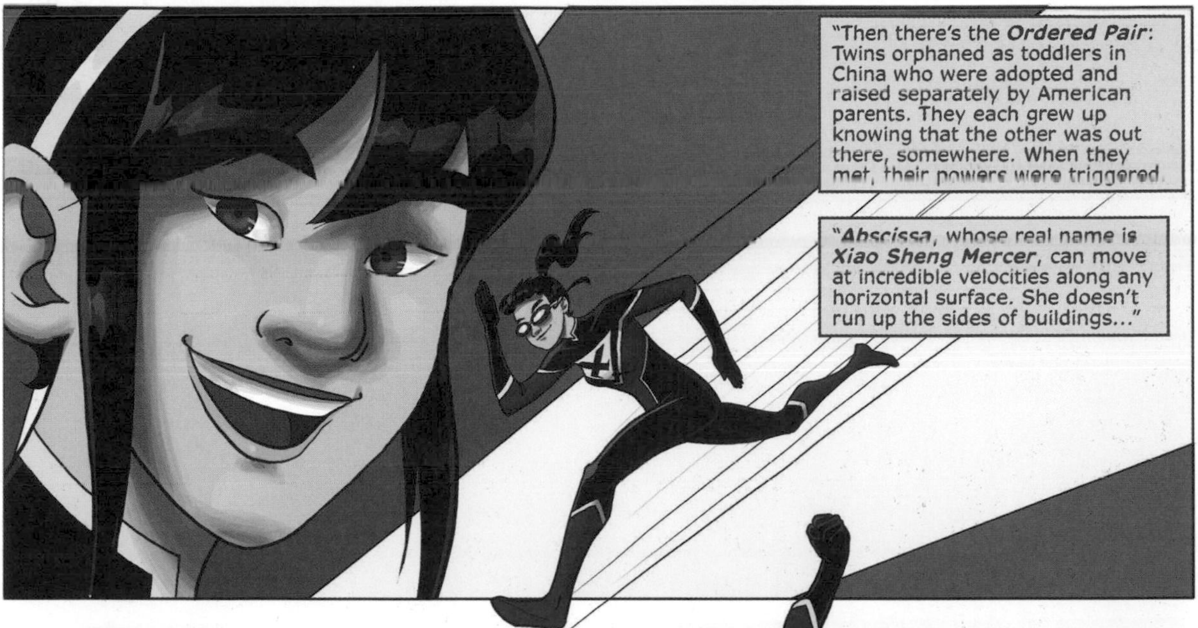
"Then there's the ***Ordered Pair***: Twins orphaned as toddlers in China who were adopted and raised separately by American parents. They each grew up knowing that the other was out there, somewhere. When they met, their powers were triggered.
"***Abscissa***, whose real name is ***Xiao Sheng Mercer***, can move at incredible velocities along any horizontal surface. She doesn't run up the sides of buildings..."

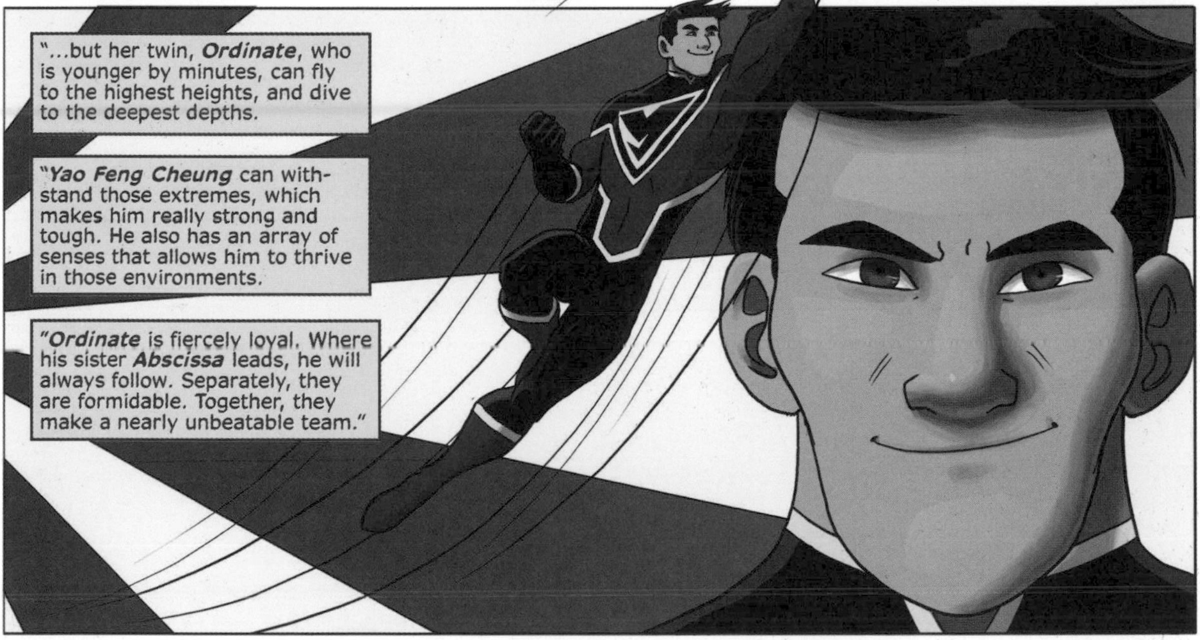
"...but her twin, ***Ordinate***, who is younger by minutes, can fly to the highest heights, and dive to the deepest depths.
"***Yao Feng Cheung*** can with-stand those extremes, which makes him really strong and tough. He also has an array of senses that allows him to thrive in those environments.
"***Ordinate*** is fiercely loyal. Where his sister ***Abscissa*** leads, he will always follow. Separately, they are formidable. Together, they make a nearly unbeatable team."

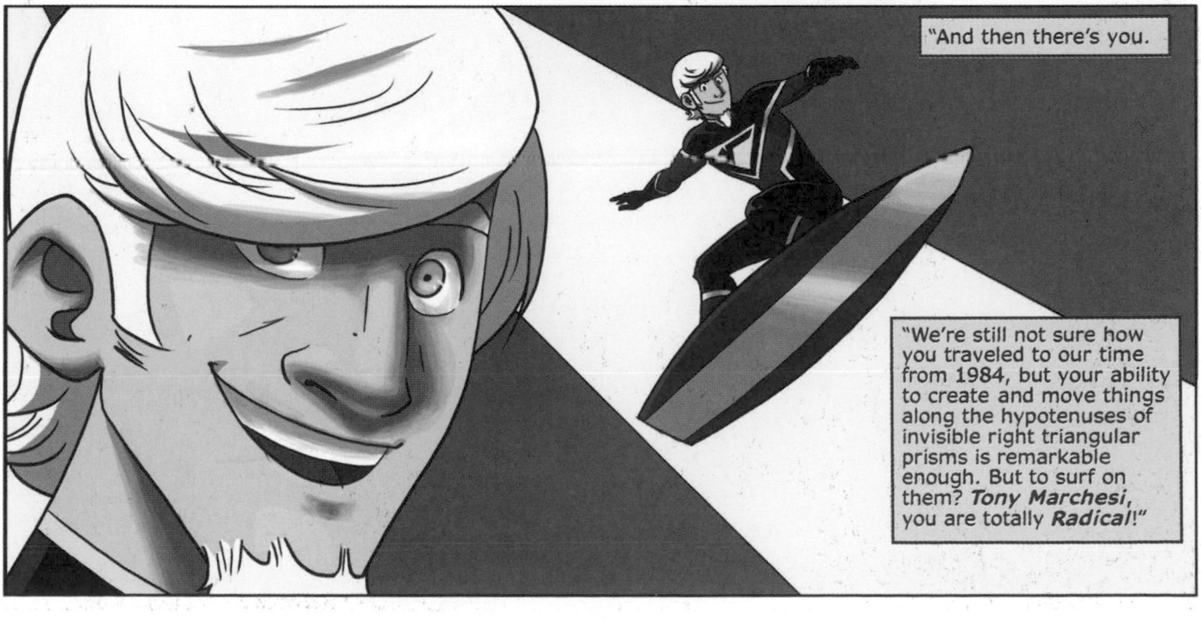
"And then there's you.
"We're still not sure how you traveled to our time from 1984, but your ability to create and move things along the hypotenuses of invisible right triangular prisms is remarkable enough. But to surf on them? ***Tony Marchesi***, you are totally ***Radical***!"

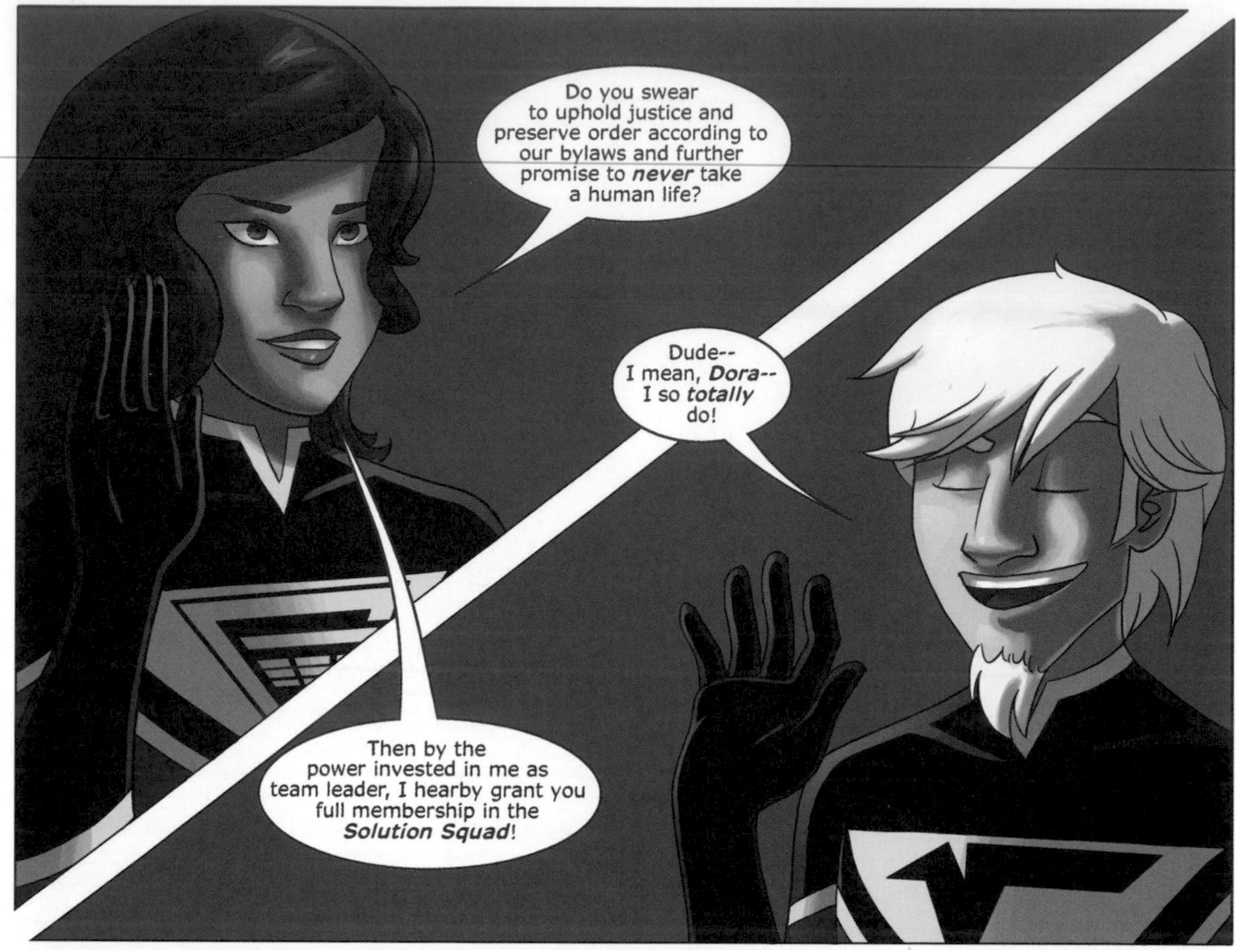
Do you swear to uphold justice and preserve order according to our bylaws and further promise to *never* take a human life?
Dude-- I mean, *Dora*-- I so *totally* do!
Then by the power invested in me as team leader, I hearby grant you full membership in the *Solution Squad*!

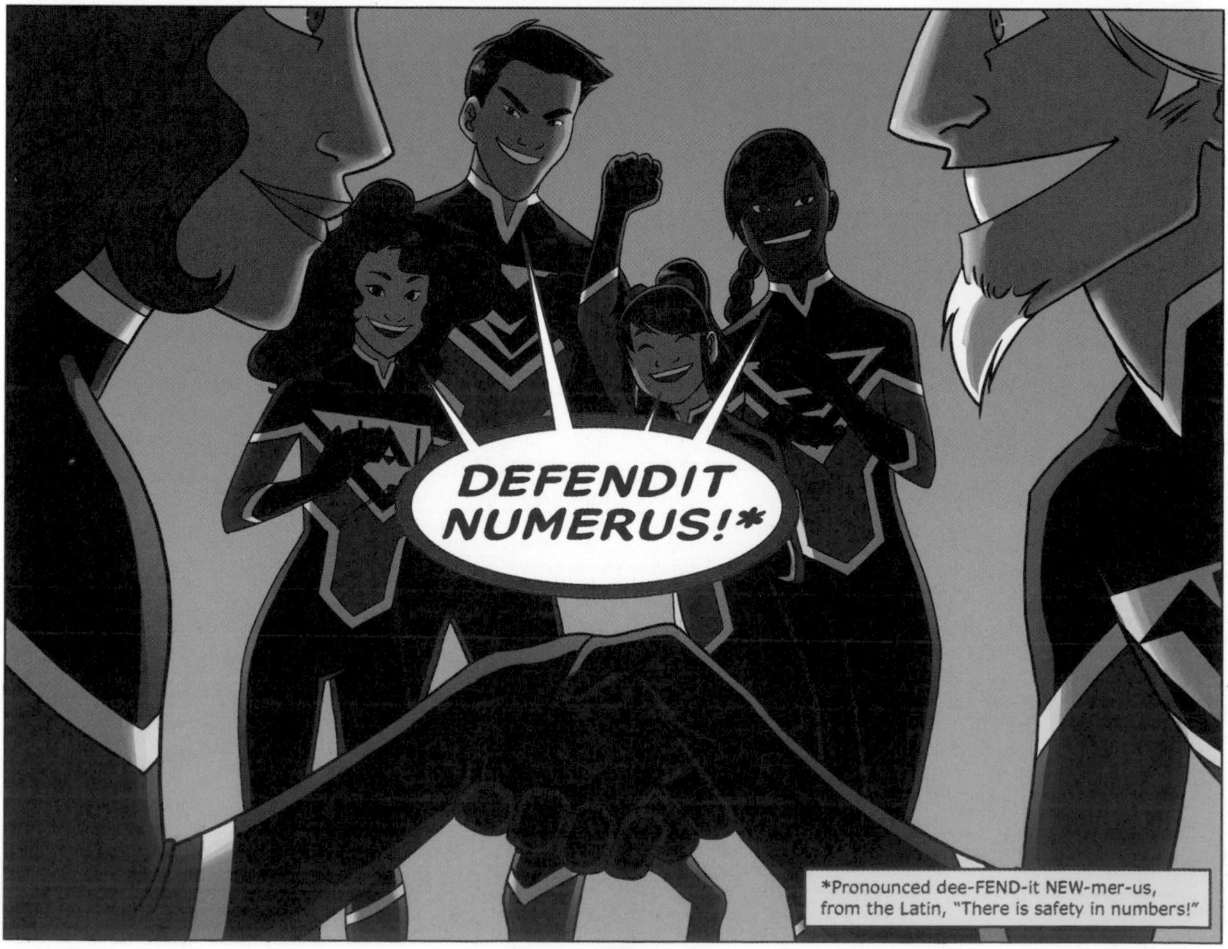
DEFENDIT NUMERUS!*
*Pronounced dee-FEND-it NEW-mer-us, from the Latin, "There is safety in numbers!"

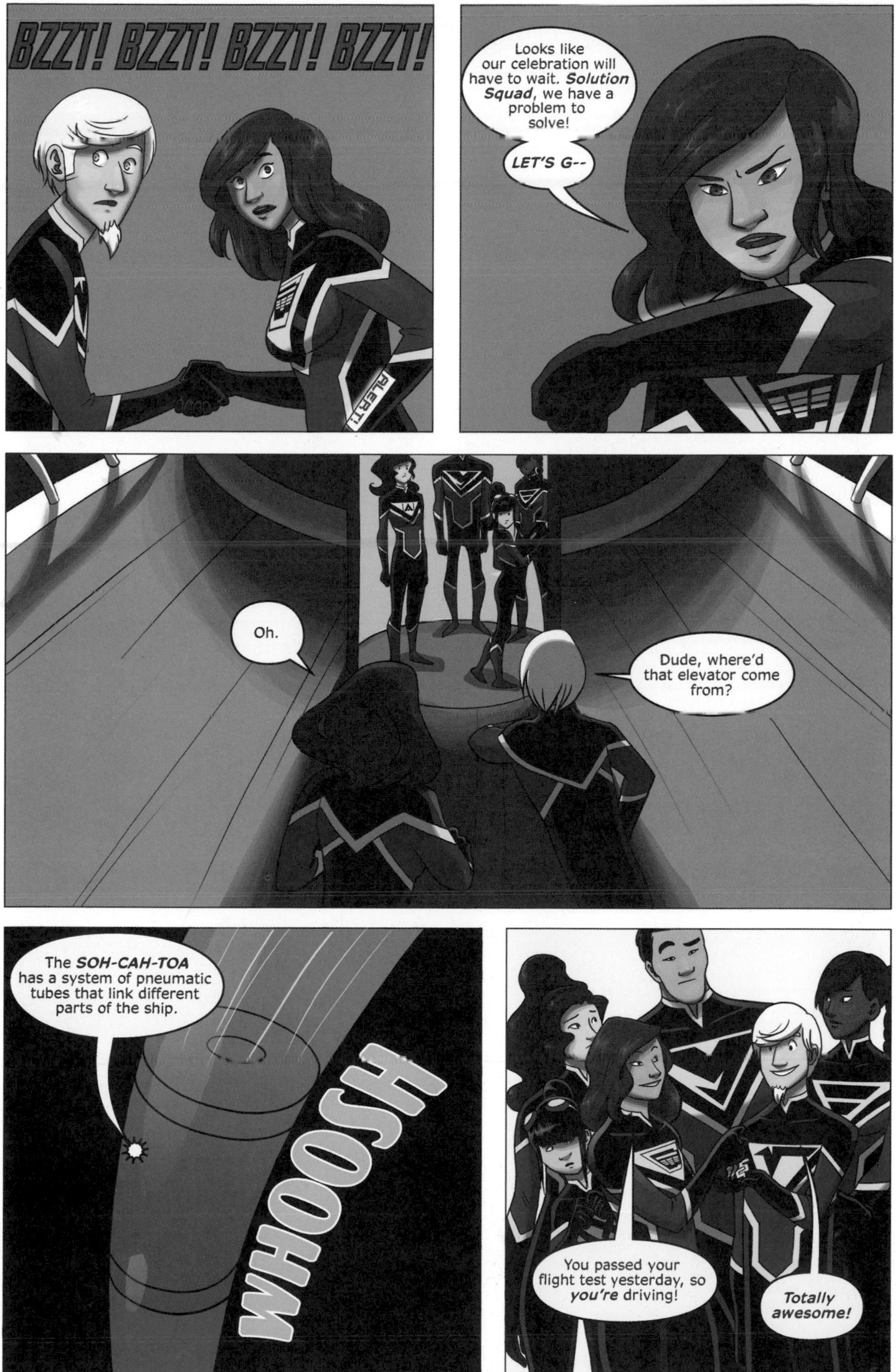
BZZT! BZZT! BZZT! BZZT!
ALERT!
Looks like our celebration will have to wait. *Solution Squad*, we have a problem to solve!
LET'S G--
Oh.
Dude, where'd that elevator come from?
The *SOH-CAH-TOA* has a system of pneumatic tubes that link different parts of the ship.
WHOOSH
You passed your flight test yesterday, so *you're* driving!
Totally awesome!

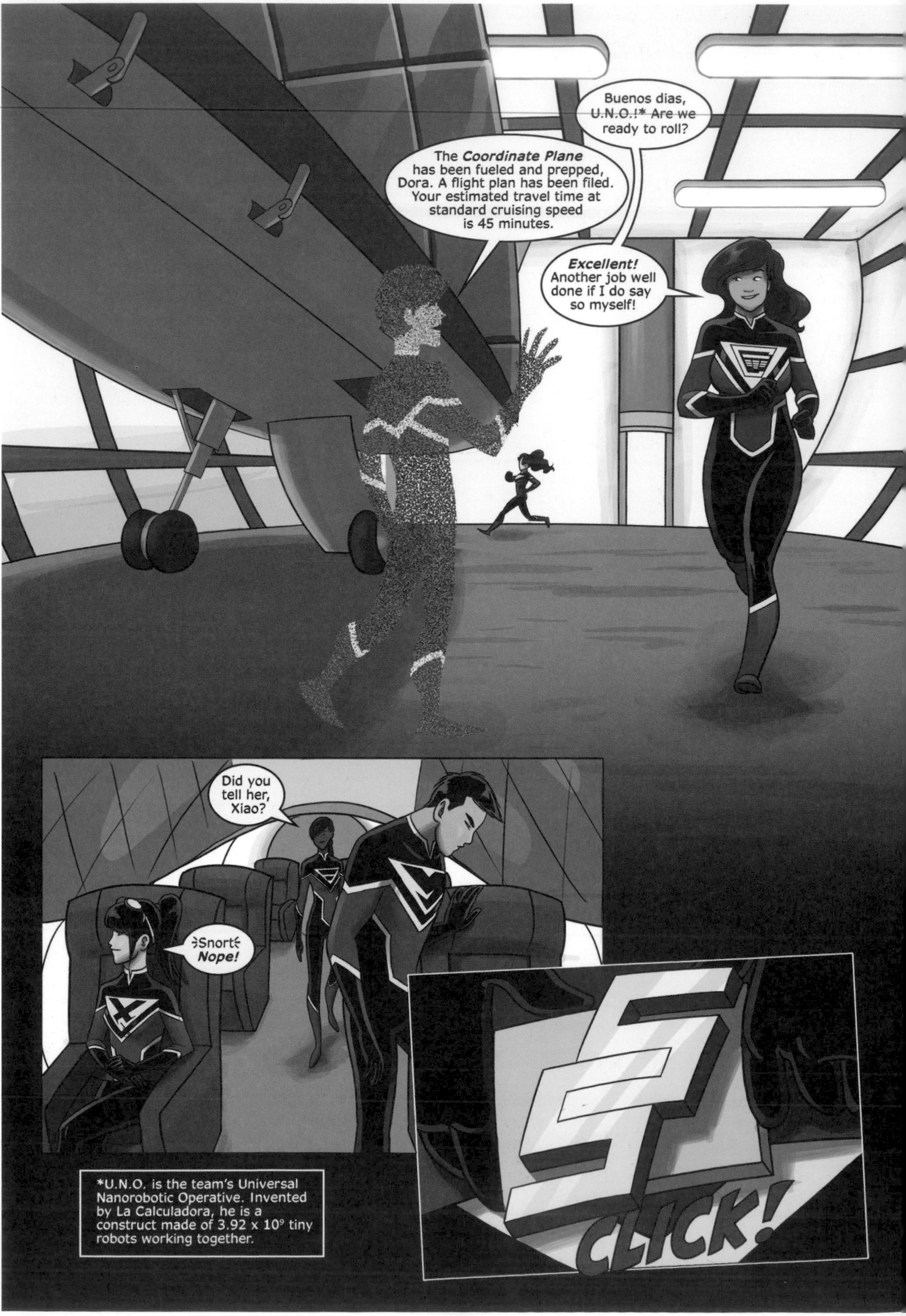

Buenos dias, U.N.O.!* Are we ready to roll?
The *Coordinate Plane* has been fueled and prepped, Dora. A flight plan has been filed. Your estimated travel time at standard cruising speed is 45 minutes.
Excellent! Another job well done if I do say so myself!
Did you tell her, Xiao?
⁑Snort⁑ *Nope!*
CLICK!

*U.N.O. is the team's Universal Nanorobotic Operative. Invented by La Calculadora, he is a construct made of 3.92×10^9 tiny robots working together.

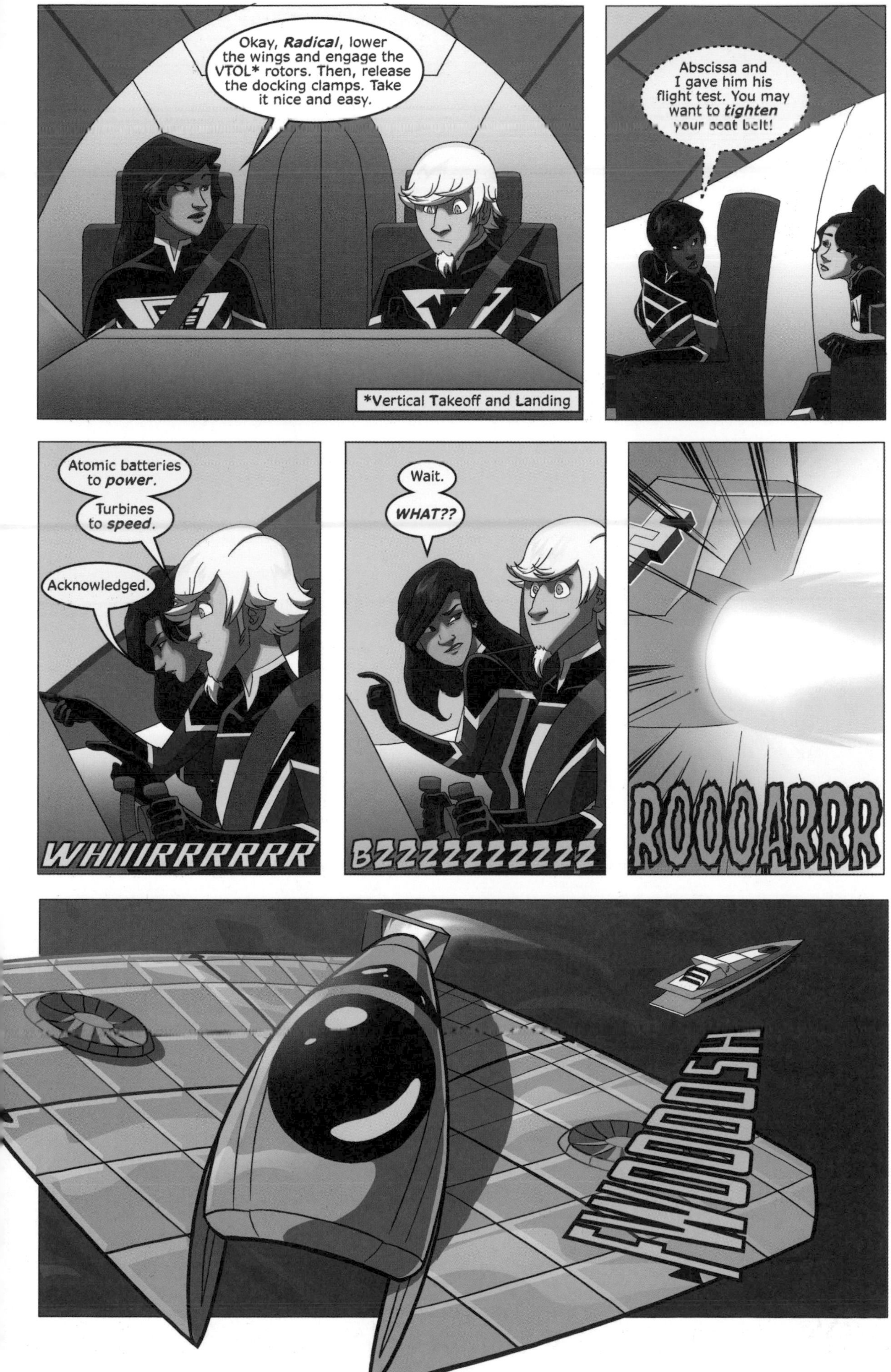
Okay, *Radical*, lower the wings and engage the VTOL* rotors. Then, release the docking clamps. Take it nice and easy.
*Vertical Takeoff and Landing
Abscissa and I gave him his flight test. You may want to *tighten* your seat belt!
Atomic batteries to *power*.
Turbines to *speed*.
Acknowledged.
WHIIIRRRRRR
Wait.
WHAT??
BZZZZZZZZZZ
ROOOARRR
WHOOOOSH

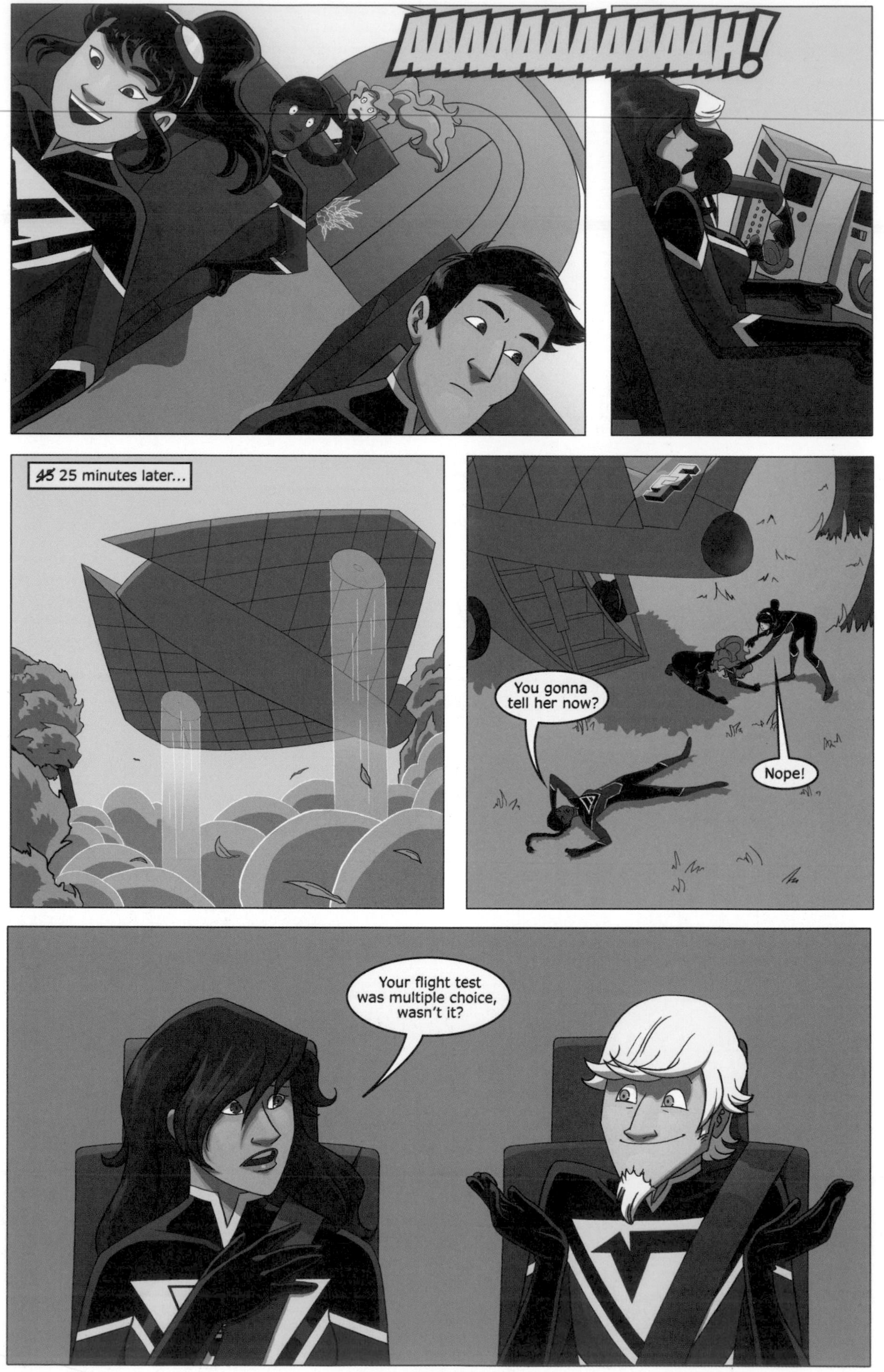
AAAAAAAAAAAH!
~~45~~ 25 minutes later...
You gonna tell her now?
Nope!
Your flight test was multiple choice, wasn't it?

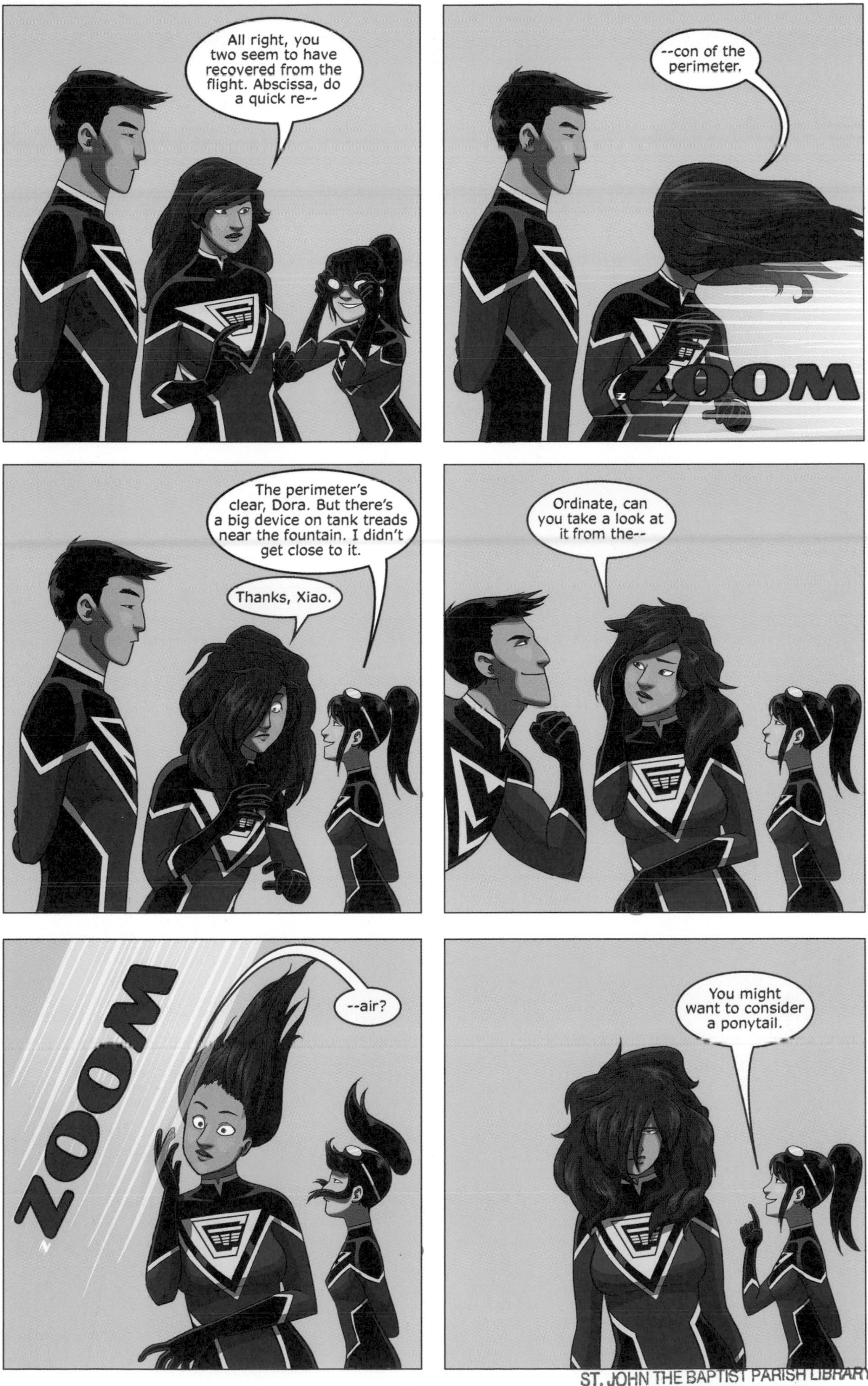
All right, you two seem to have recovered from the flight. Abscissa, do a quick re--
--con of the perimeter.
ZOOM
The perimeter's clear, Dora. But there's a big device on tank treads near the fountain. I didn't get close to it.
Thanks, Xiao.
Ordinate, can you take a look at it from the--
ZOOM
--air?
You might want to consider a ponytail.

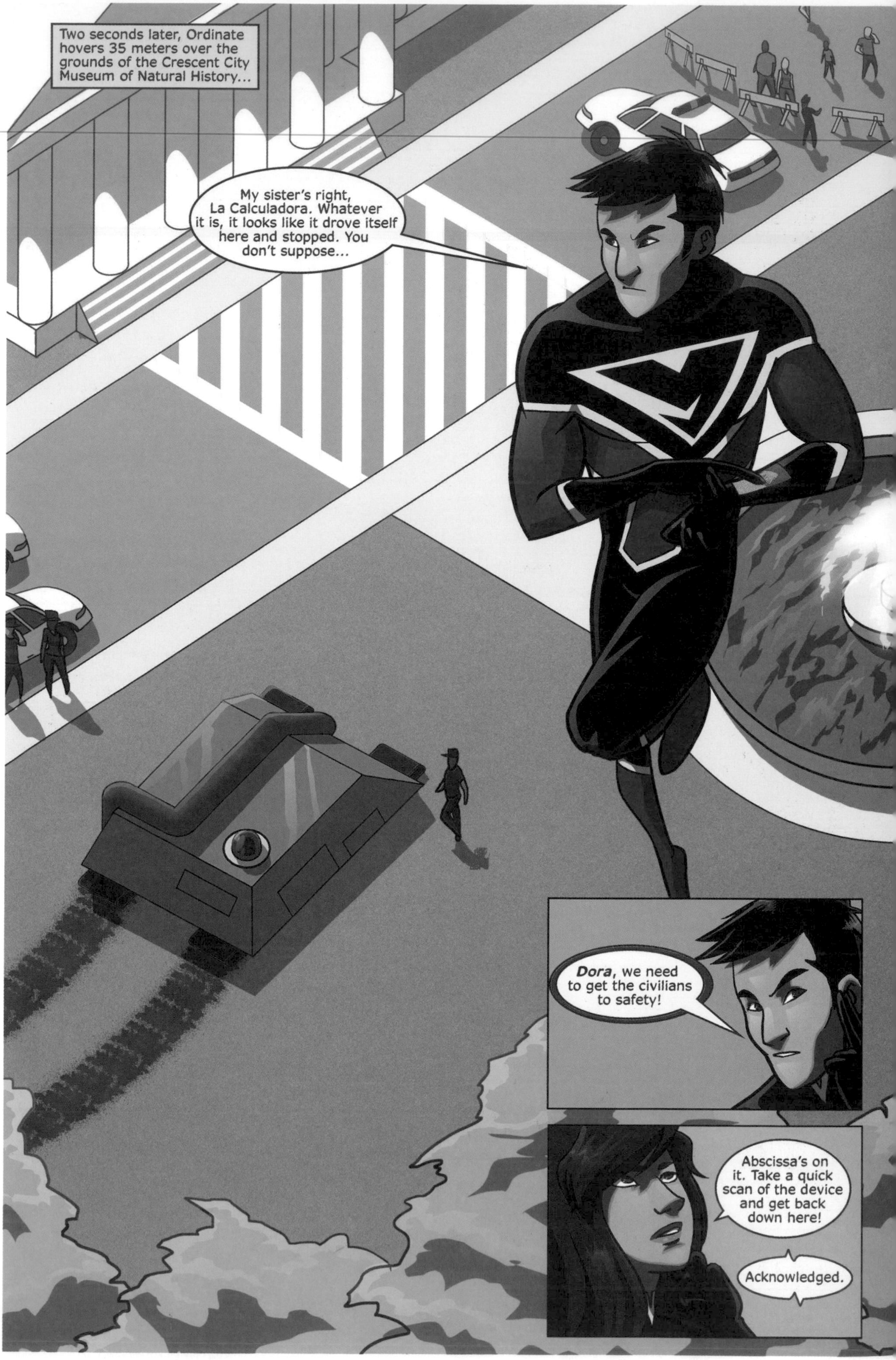
Two seconds later, Ordinate hovers 35 meters over the grounds of the Crescent City Museum of Natural History...
My sister's right, La Calculadora. Whatever it is, it looks like it drove itself here and stopped. You don't suppose...
Dora, we need to get the civilians to safety!
Abscissa's on it. Take a quick scan of the device and get back down here!
Acknowledged.

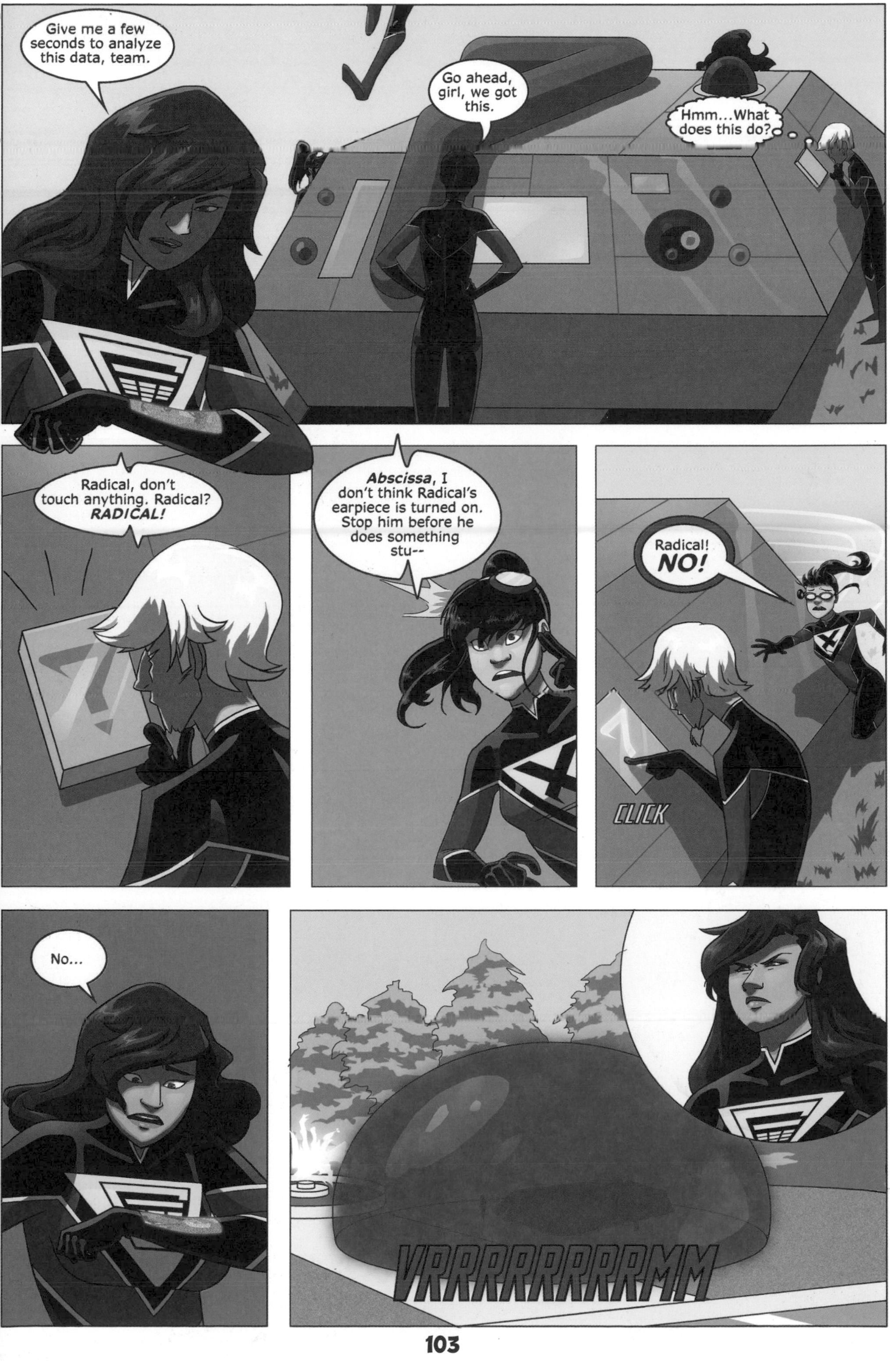
Give me a few seconds to analyze this data, team.
Go ahead, girl, we got this.
Hmm...What does this do?
Radical, don't touch anything. Radical? ***RADICAL!***
Abscissa, I don't think Radical's earpiece is turned on. Stop him before he does something stu--
Radical! ***NO!***
CLICK
No...
VRRRRRRRRRMM

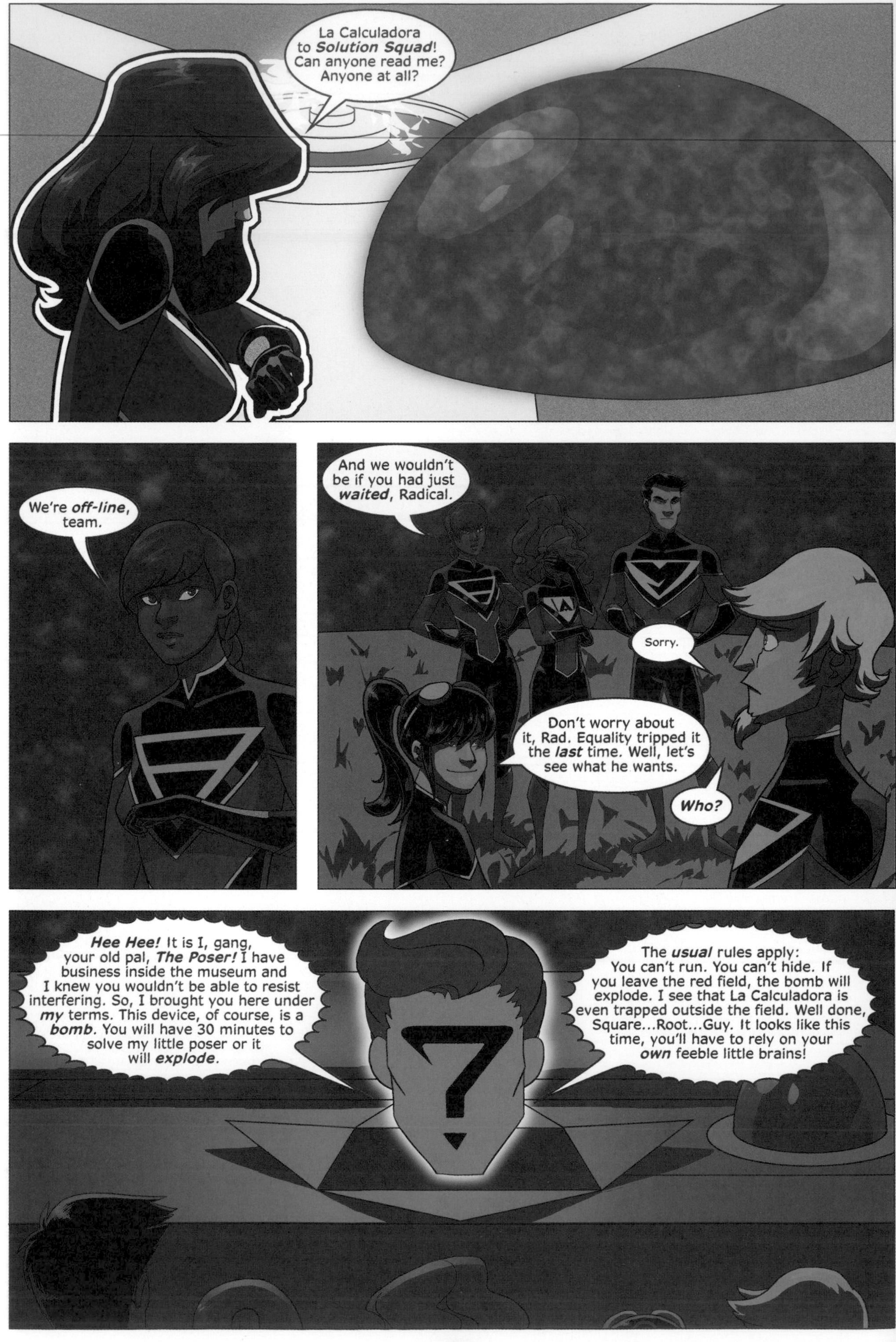
La Calculadora to Solution Squad! Can anyone read me? Anyone at all?
We're off-line, team.
And we wouldn't be if you had just waited, Radical.
Sorry.
Don't worry about it, Rad. Equality tripped it the last time. Well, let's see what he wants.
Who?
Hee Hee! It is I, gang, your old pal, The Poser! I have business inside the museum and I knew you wouldn't be able to resist interfering. So, I brought you here under my terms. This device, of course, is a bomb. You will have 30 minutes to solve my little poser or it will explode.
The usual rules apply: You can't run. You can't hide. If you leave the red field, the bomb will explode. I see that La Calculadora is even trapped outside the field. Well done, Square...Root...Guy. It looks like this time, you'll have to rely on your own feeble little brains!

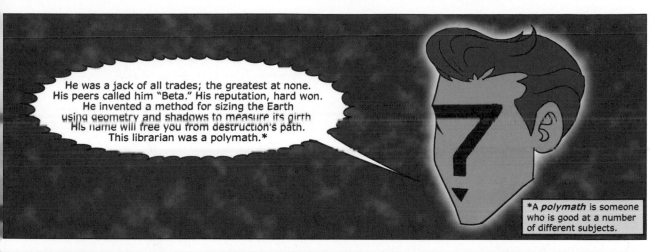

He was a jack of all trades; the greatest at none.
His peers called him "Beta." His reputation, hard won.
He invented a method for sizing the Earth
using geometry and shadows to measure its girth.
His name will free you from destruction's path.
This librarian was a polymath.*

*A *polymath* is someone who is good at a number of different subjects.

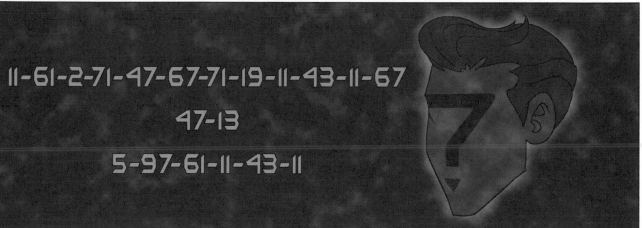

11-61-2-71-47-67-71-19-11-43-11-67

47-13

5-97-61-11-43-11

What's that?

Looks like a code.

They're *prime numbers*-- whole numbers greater than one that can only be divided by one and themselves.

A math puzzle? I guess it's a good thing the Linguistic Six didn't show up.

What do we do? I left my spare prime number list in my other uniform.

If La Calculadora were here, she'd just rattle them off. But since she's not...

We'll make a prime number sieve!

Yes! If each number stands for a letter, we can decode the message!

A prime number s--what now?

105

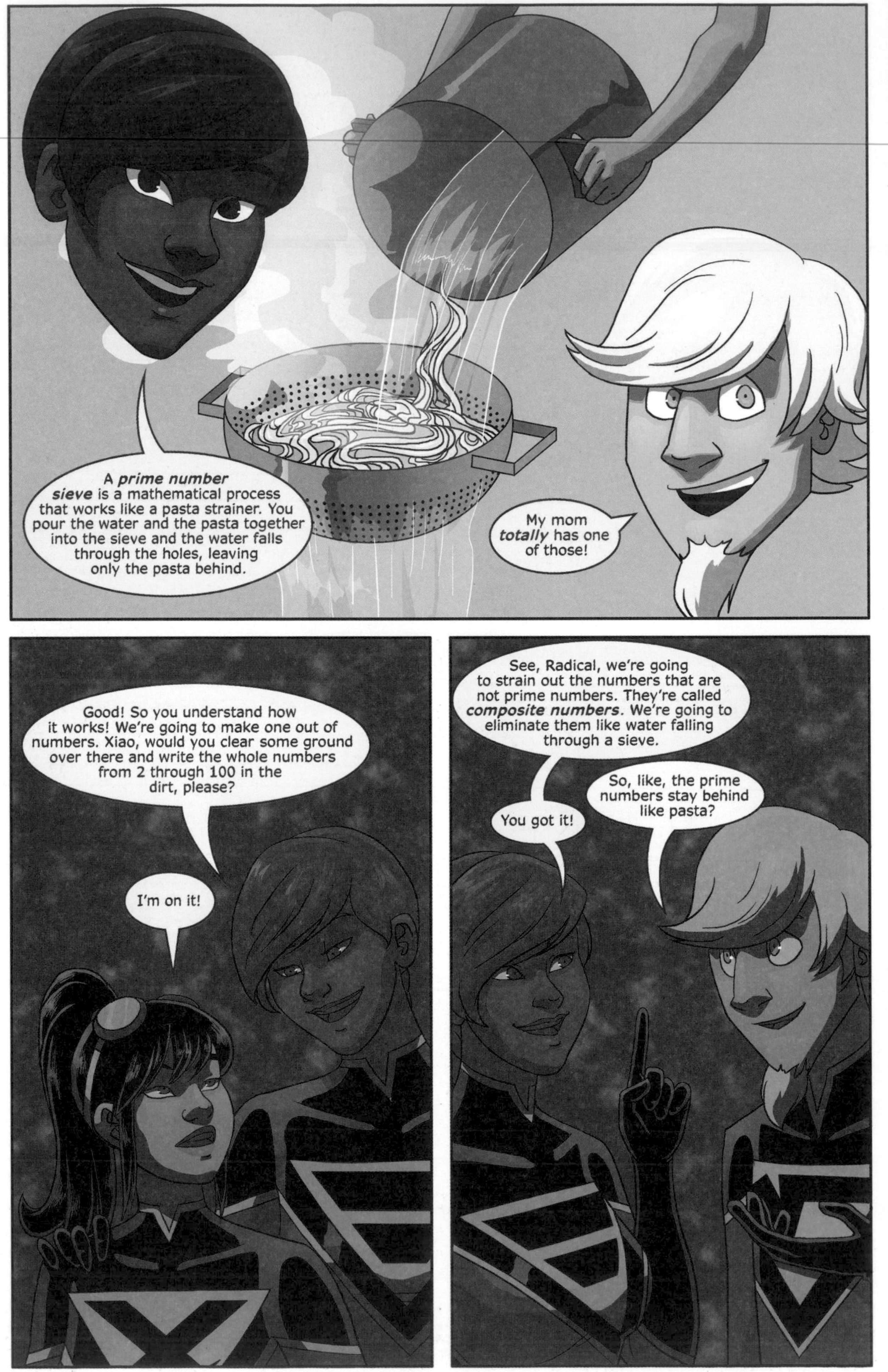
A *prime number sieve* is a mathematical process that works like a pasta strainer. You pour the water and the pasta together into the sieve and the water falls through the holes, leaving only the pasta behind.
My mom *totally* has one of those!
Good! So you understand how it works! We're going to make one out of numbers. Xiao, would you clear some ground over there and write the whole numbers from 2 through 100 in the dirt, please?
I'm on it!
See, Radical, we're going to strain out the numbers that are not prime numbers. They're called *composite numbers*. We're going to eliminate them like water falling through a sieve.
So, like, the prime numbers stay behind like pasta?
You got it!

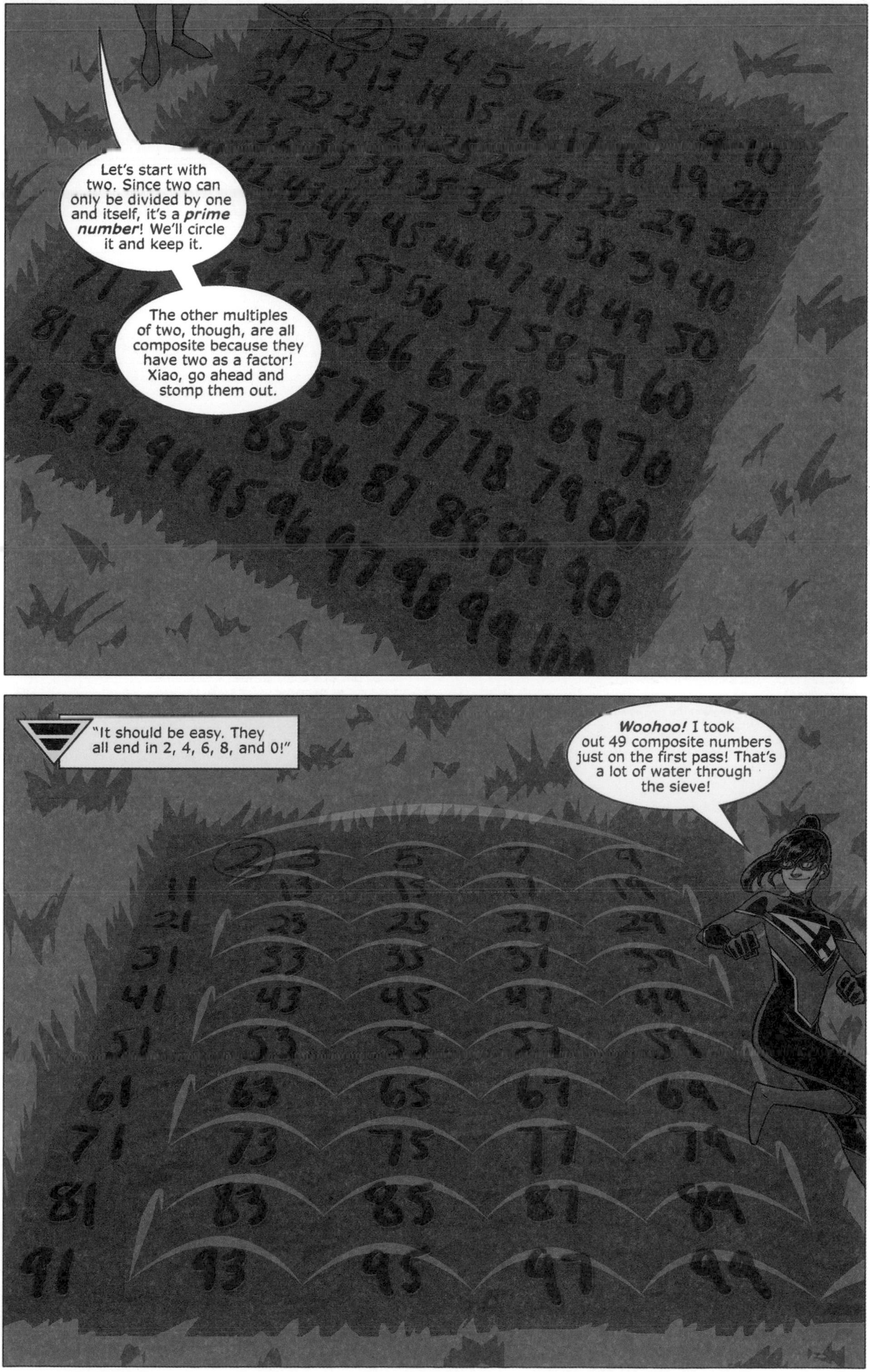
Let's start with two. Since two can only be divided by one and itself, it's a ***prime number***! We'll circle it and keep it.
The other multiples of two, though, are all composite because they have two as a factor! Xiao, go ahead and stomp them out.
"It should be easy. They all end in 2, 4, 6, 8, and 0!"
Woohoo! I took out 49 composite numbers just on the first pass! That's a lot of water through the sieve!

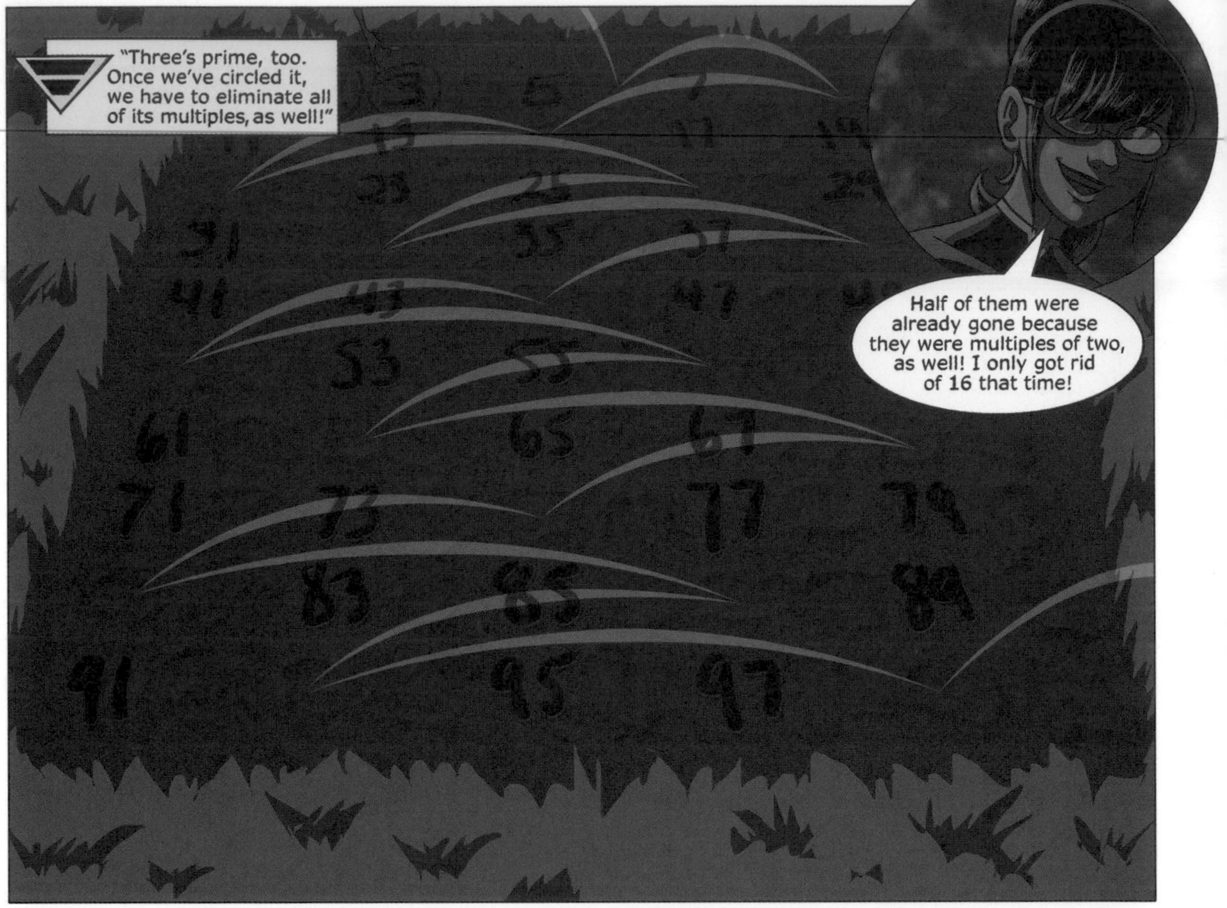
"Three's prime, too. Once we've circled it, we have to eliminate all of its multiples, as well!"
Half of them were already gone because they were multiples of two, as well! I only got rid of 16 that time!

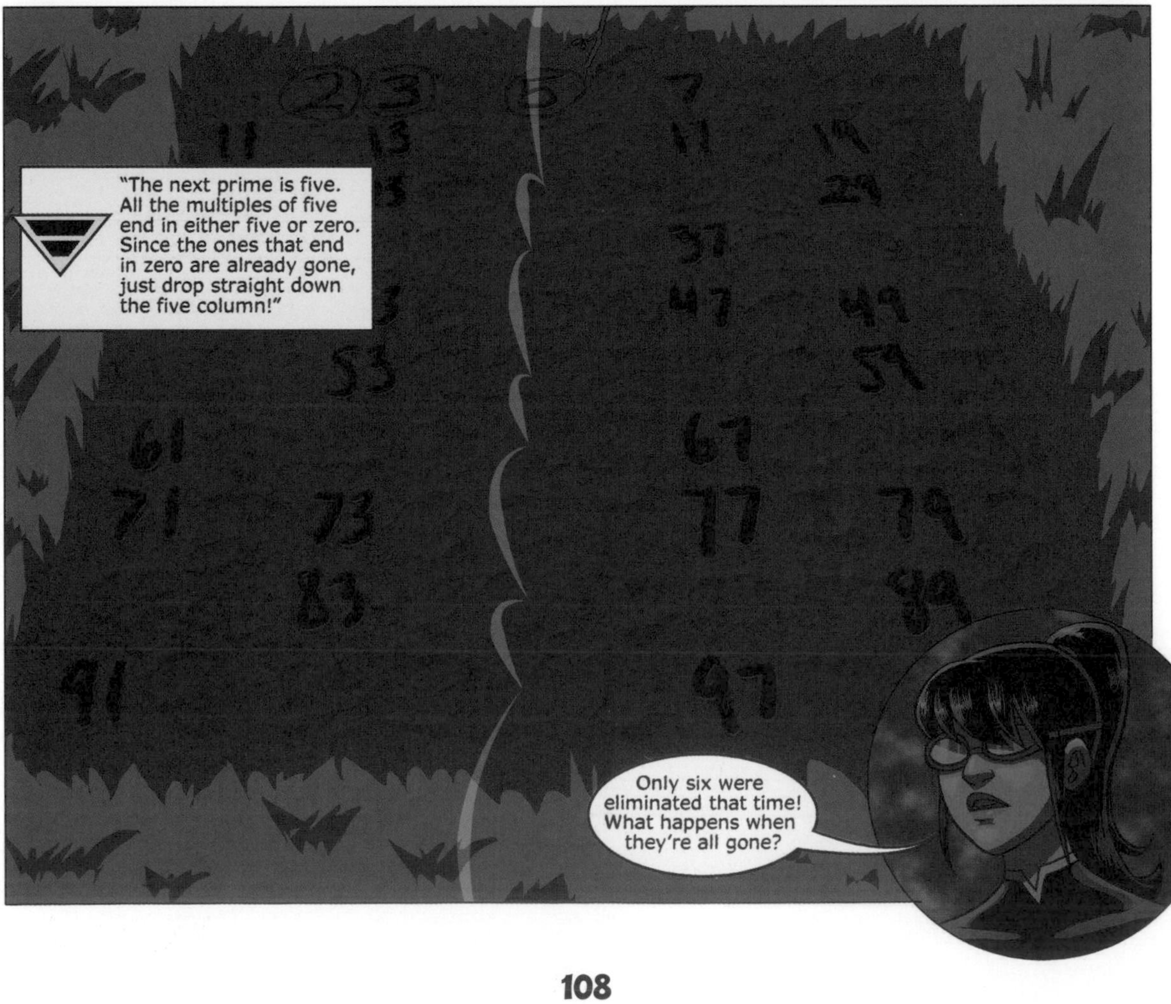
"The next prime is five. All the multiples of five end in either five or zero. Since the ones that end in zero are already gone, just drop straight down the five column!"
Only six were eliminated that time! What happens when they're all gone?

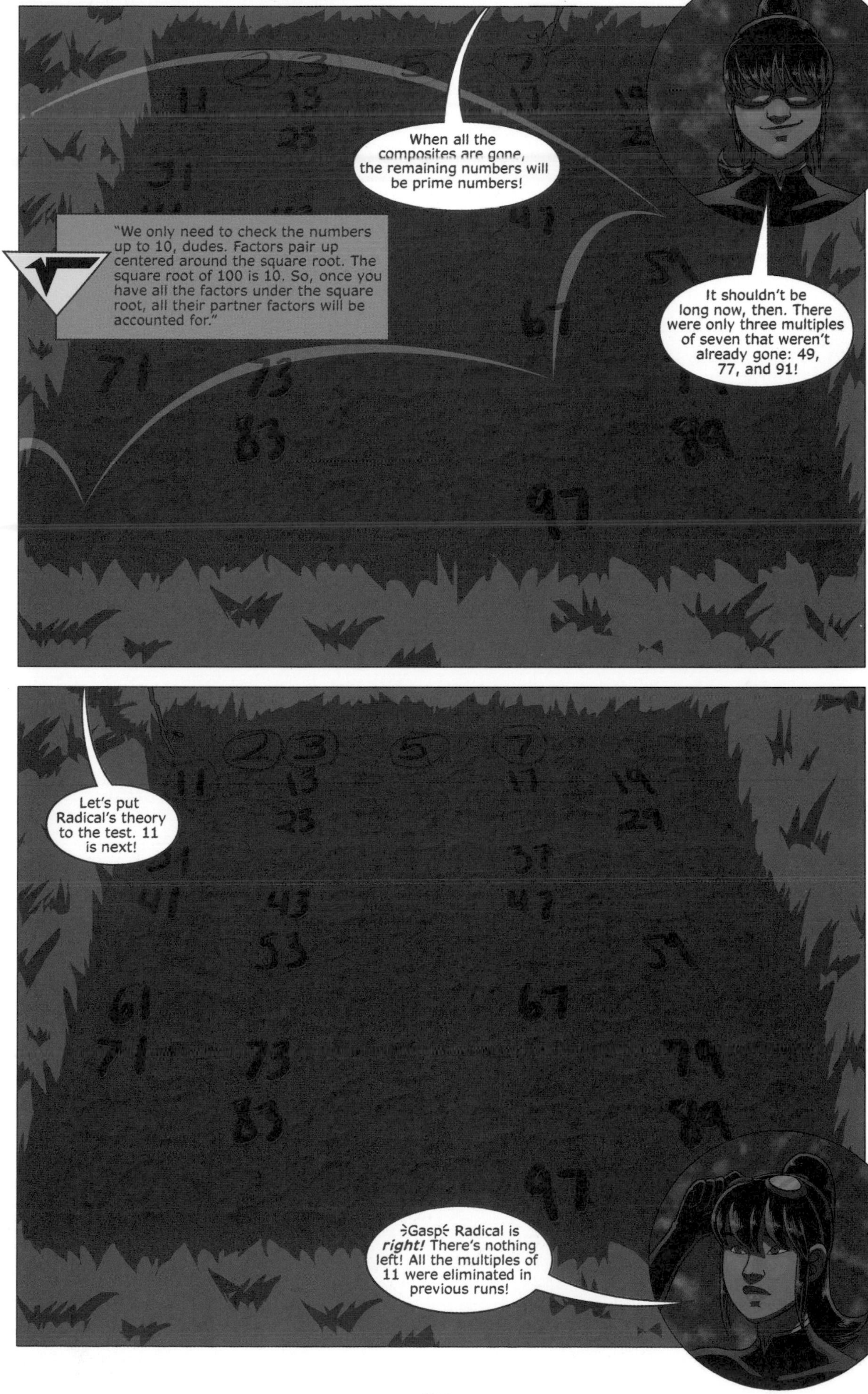
When all the composites are gone, the remaining numbers will be prime numbers!
It shouldn't be long now, then. There were only three multiples of seven that weren't already gone: 49, 77, and 91!
"We only need to check the numbers up to 10, dudes. Factors pair up centered around the square root. The square root of 100 is 10. So, once you have all the factors under the square root, all their partner factors will be accounted for."
Let's put Radical's theory to the test. 11 is next!
Gasp Radical is *right!* There's nothing left! All the multiples of 11 were eliminated in previous runs!

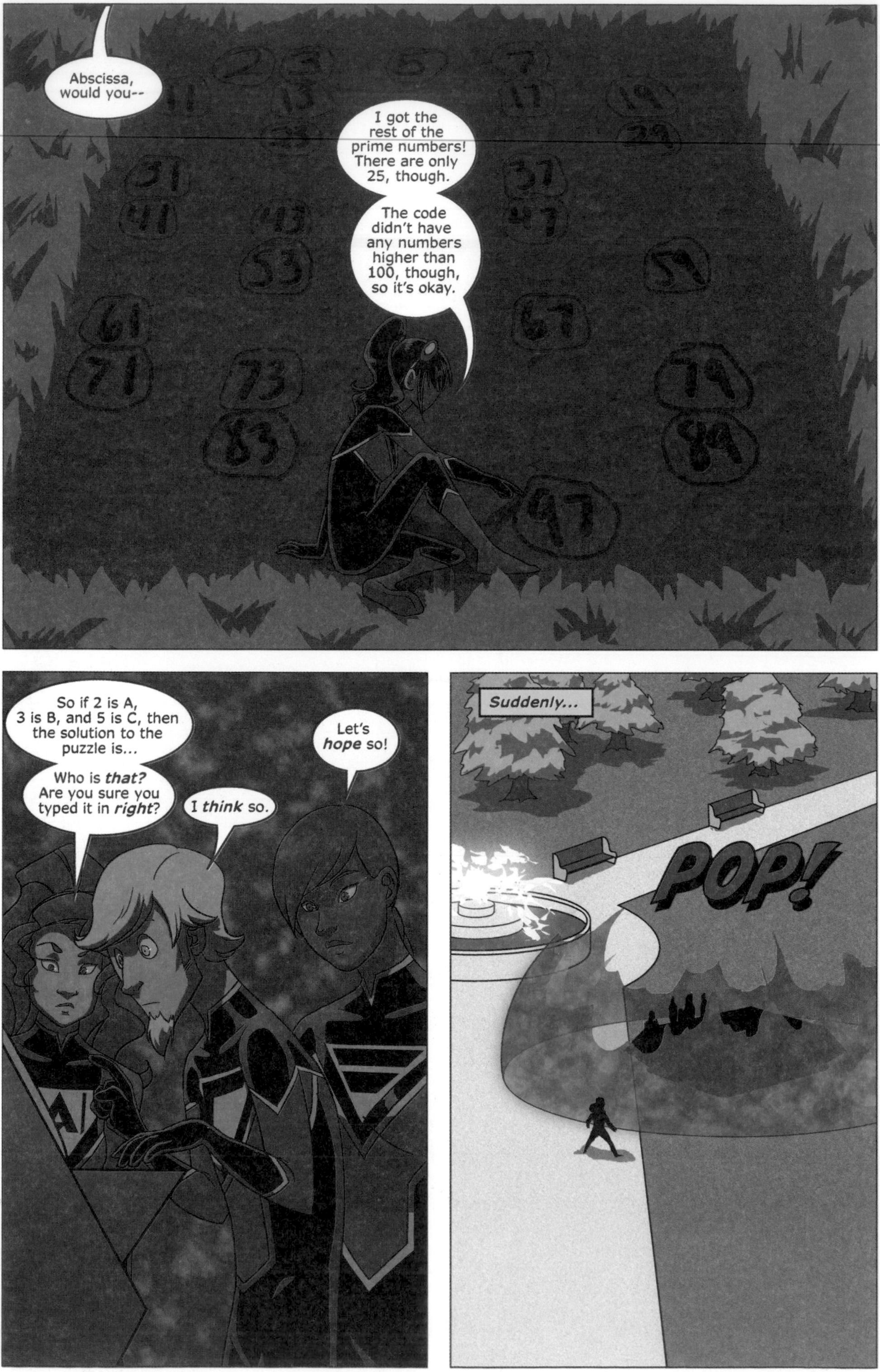

Abscissa, would you--
I got the rest of the prime numbers! There are only 25, though.
The code didn't have any numbers higher than 100, though, so it's okay.
So if 2 is A, 3 is B, and 5 is C, then the solution to the puzzle is...
Who is *that?* Are you sure you typed it in *right*?
I *think* so.
Let's *hope* so!
Suddenly...
POP!

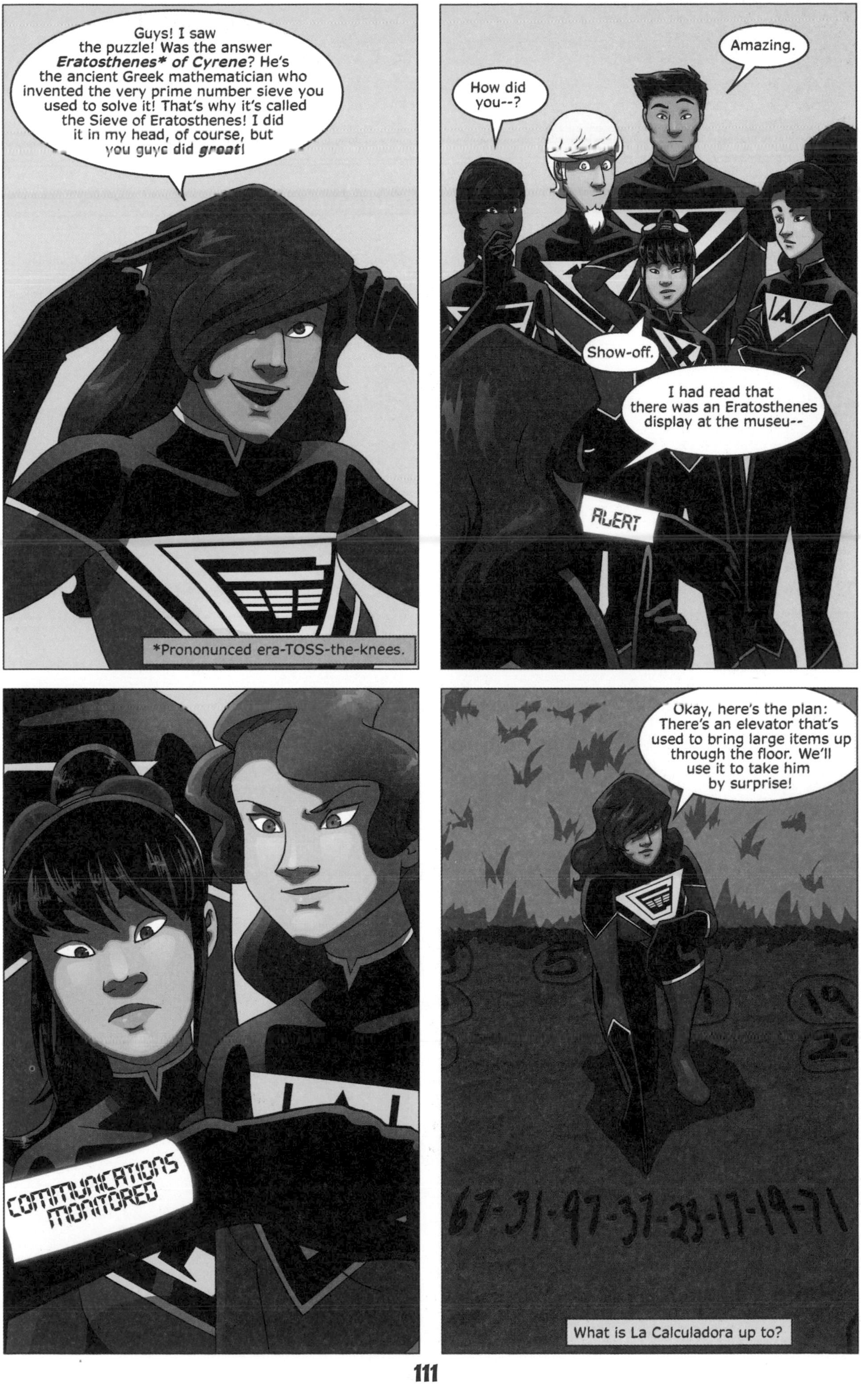
Guys! I saw the puzzle! Was the answer ***Eratosthenes* of Cyrene***? He's the ancient Greek mathematician who invented the very prime number sieve you used to solve it! That's why it's called the Sieve of Eratosthenes! I did it in my head, of course, but you guys did ***great***!
*Prononunced era-TOSS-the-knees.
How did you--?
Amazing.
Show-off.
I had read that there was an Eratosthenes display at the museu--
ALERT
COMMUNICATIONS MONITORED
Okay, here's the plan: There's an elevator that's used to bring large items up through the floor. We'll use it to take him by surprise!
67-31-97-37-23-17-19-71
What is La Calculadora up to?

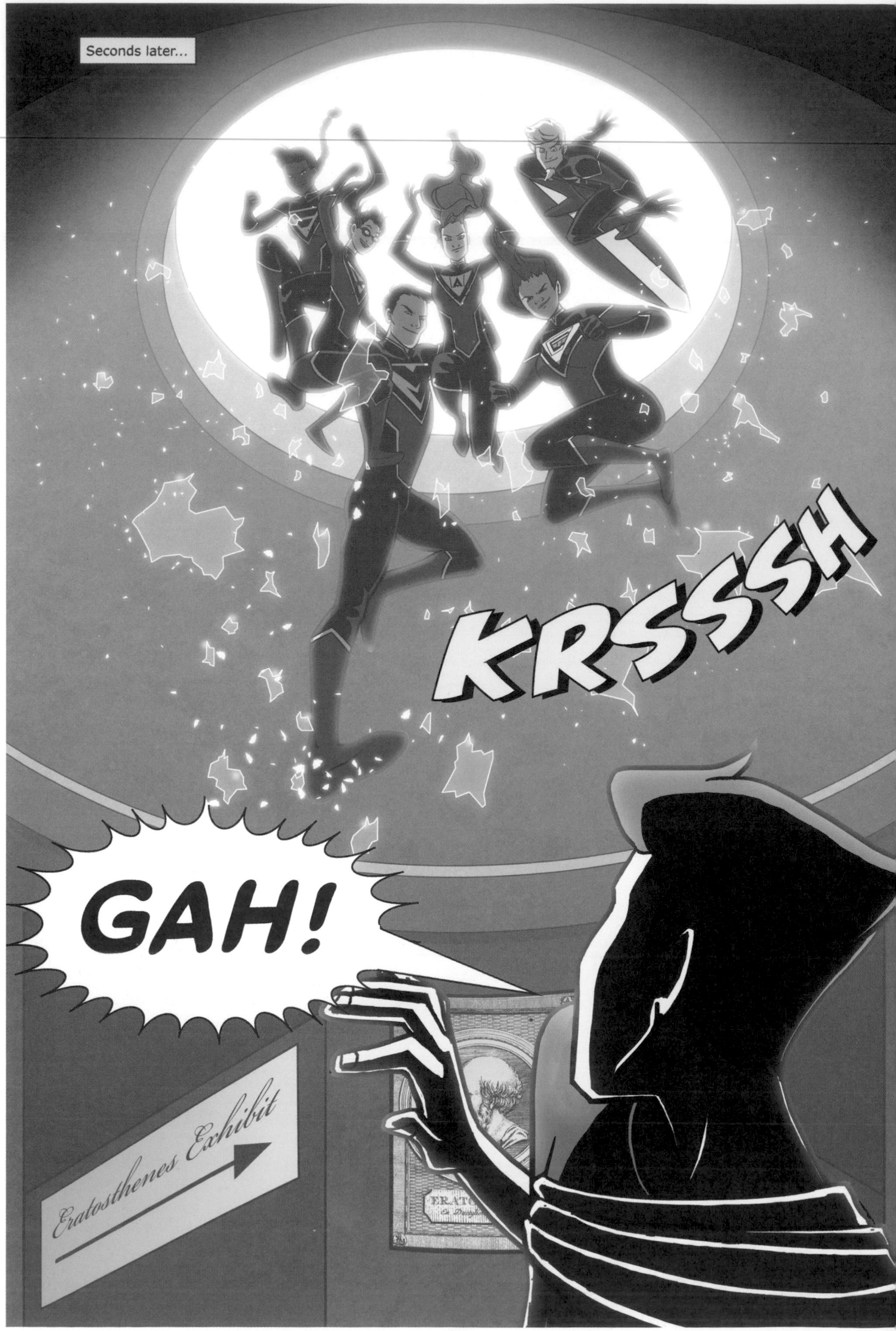
Seconds later...
KRSSSSH
GAH!
Eratosthenes Exhibit

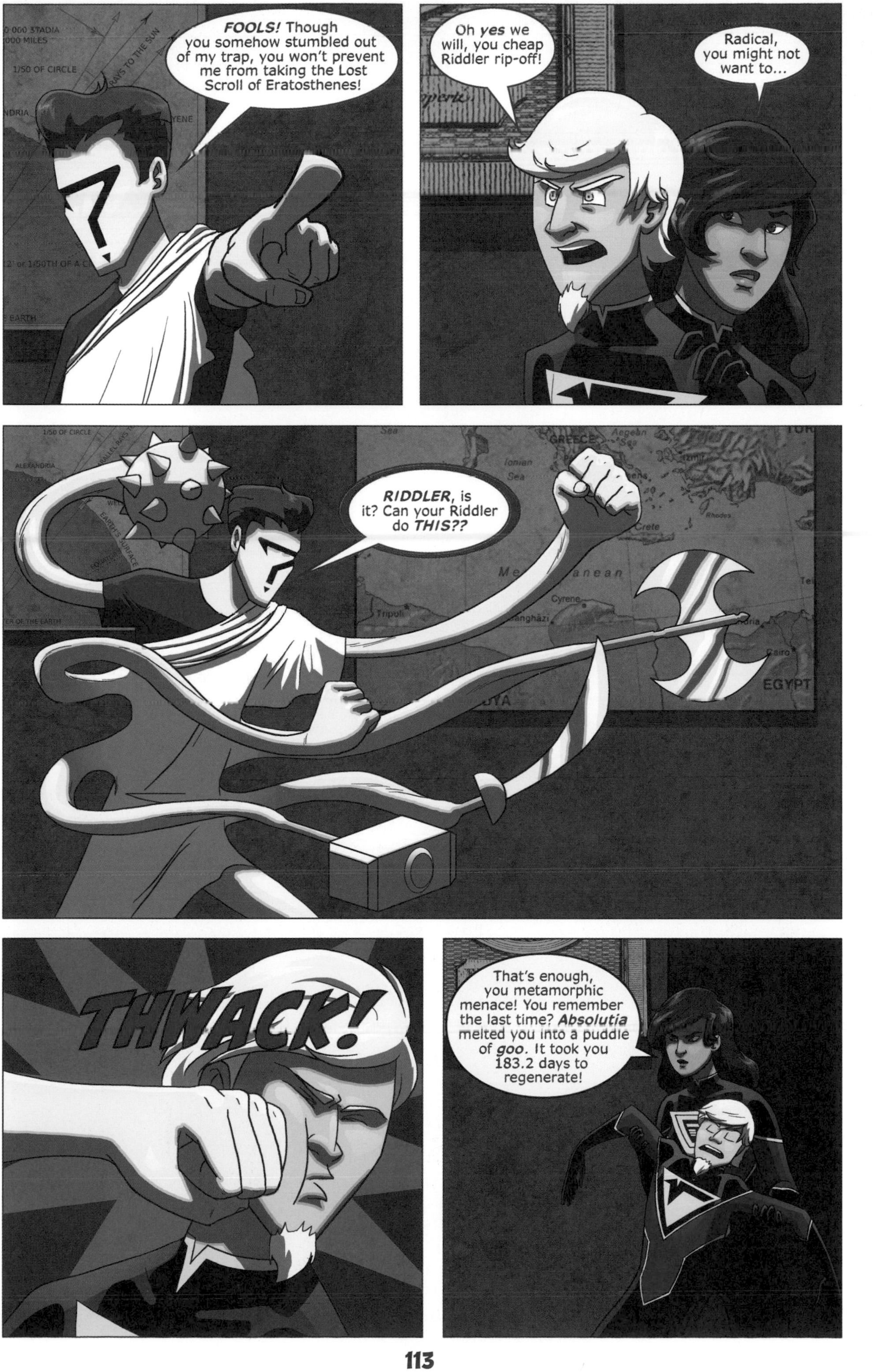
FOOLS! Though you somehow stumbled out of my trap, you won't prevent me from taking the Lost Scroll of Eratosthenes!
Oh yes we will, you cheap Riddler rip-off!
Radical, you might not want to...
RIDDLER, is it? Can your Riddler do THIS??
THWACK!
That's enough, you metamorphic menace! You remember the last time? Absolutia melted you into a puddle of goo. It took you 183.2 days to regenerate!

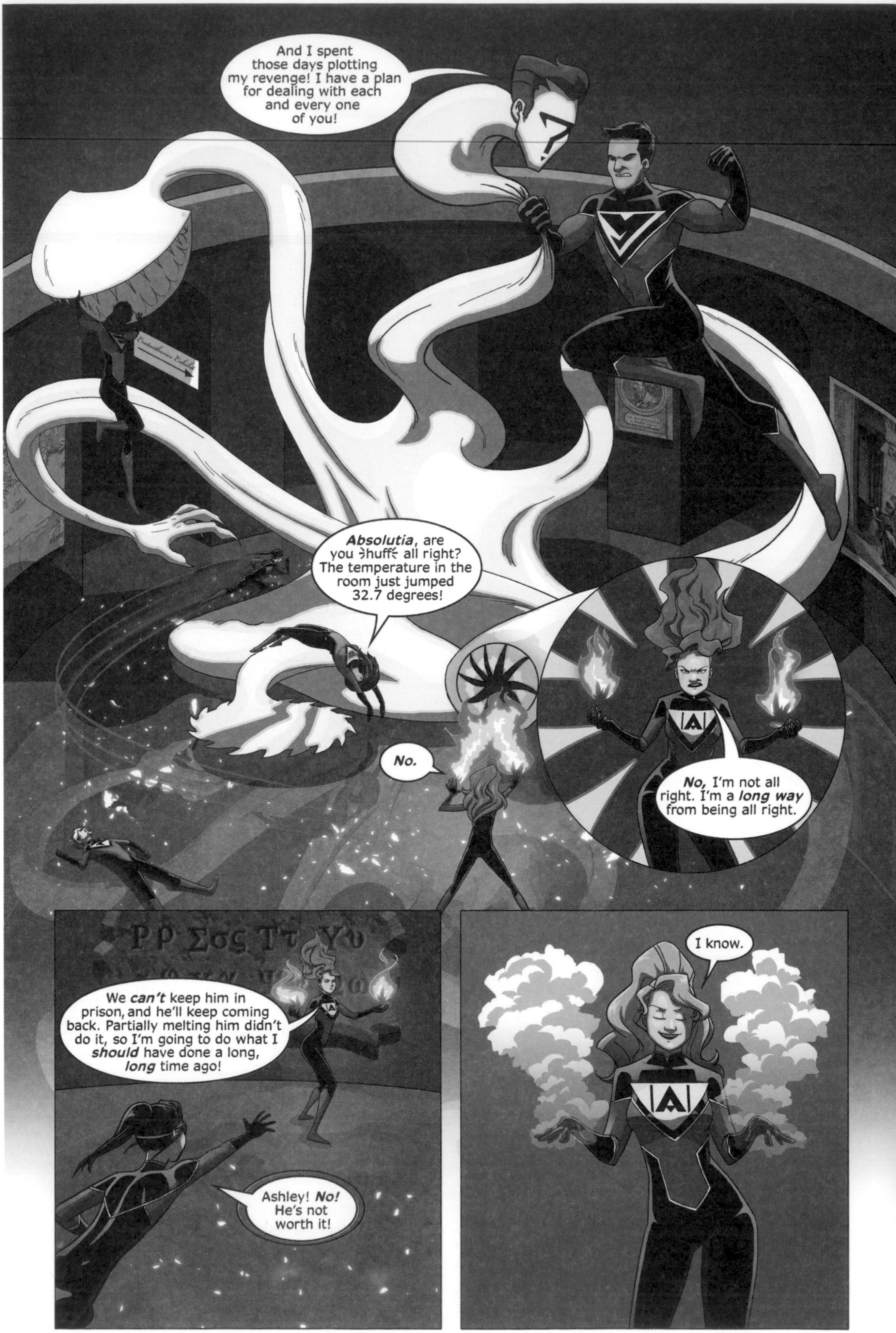
And I spent those days plotting my revenge! I have a plan for dealing with each and every one of you!
Absolutia, are you huff all right? The temperature in the room just jumped 32.7 degrees!
No.
No, I'm not all right. I'm a long way from being all right.
Ρρ Σσς Ττ Υυ
We can't keep him in prison, and he'll keep coming back. Partially melting him didn't do it, so I'm going to do what I should have done a long, long time ago!
Ashley! No! He's not worth it!
I know.

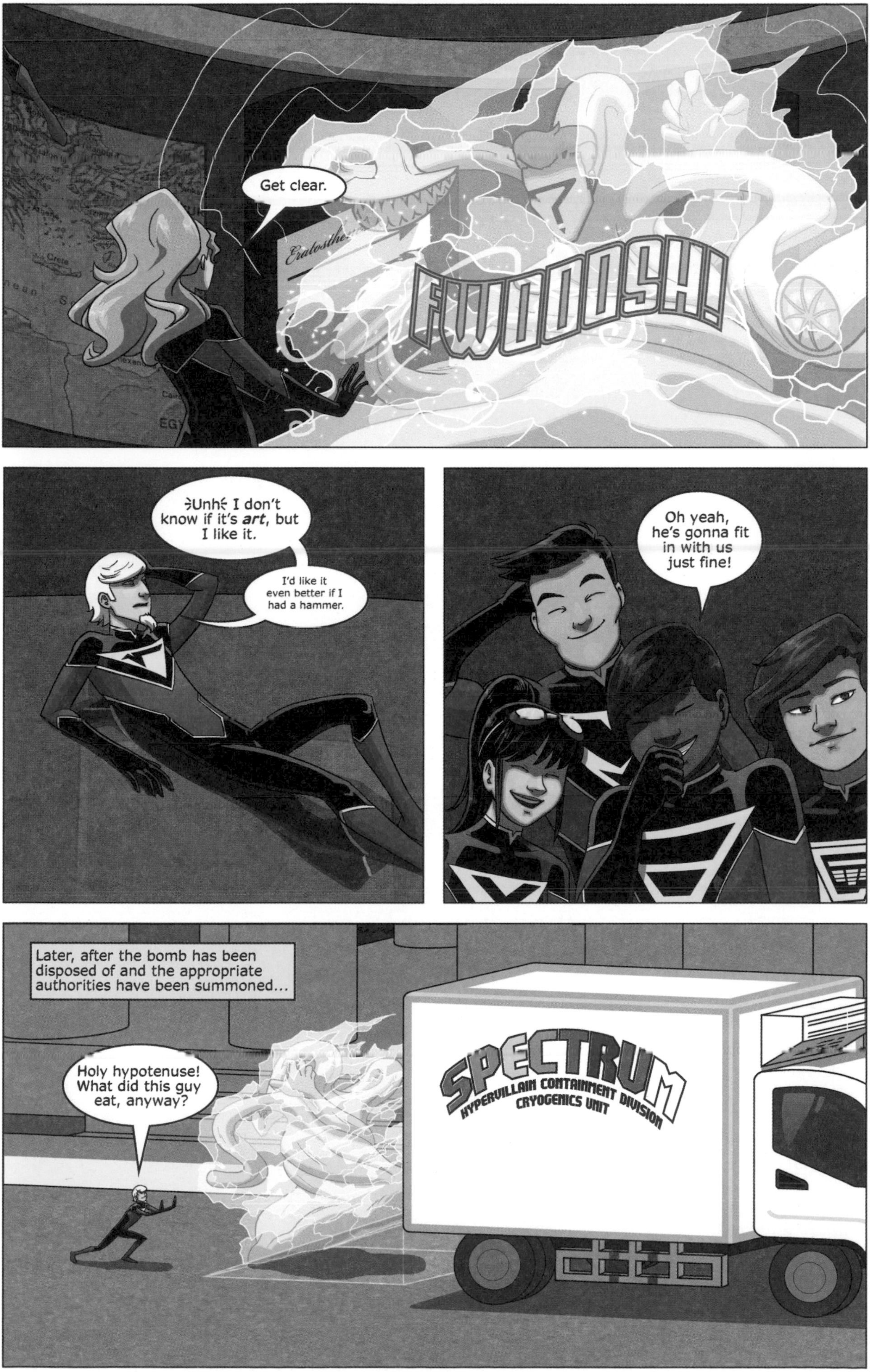

Get clear.
FWOOOSH!
Unh I don't know if it's *art*, but I like it.
I'd like it even better if I had a hammer.
Oh yeah, he's gonna fit in with us just fine!
Later, after the bomb has been disposed of and the appropriate authorities have been summoned...
Holy hypotenuse! What did this guy eat, anyway?
SPECTRUM
HYPERVILLAIN CONTAINMENT DIVISION
CRYOGENICS UNIT

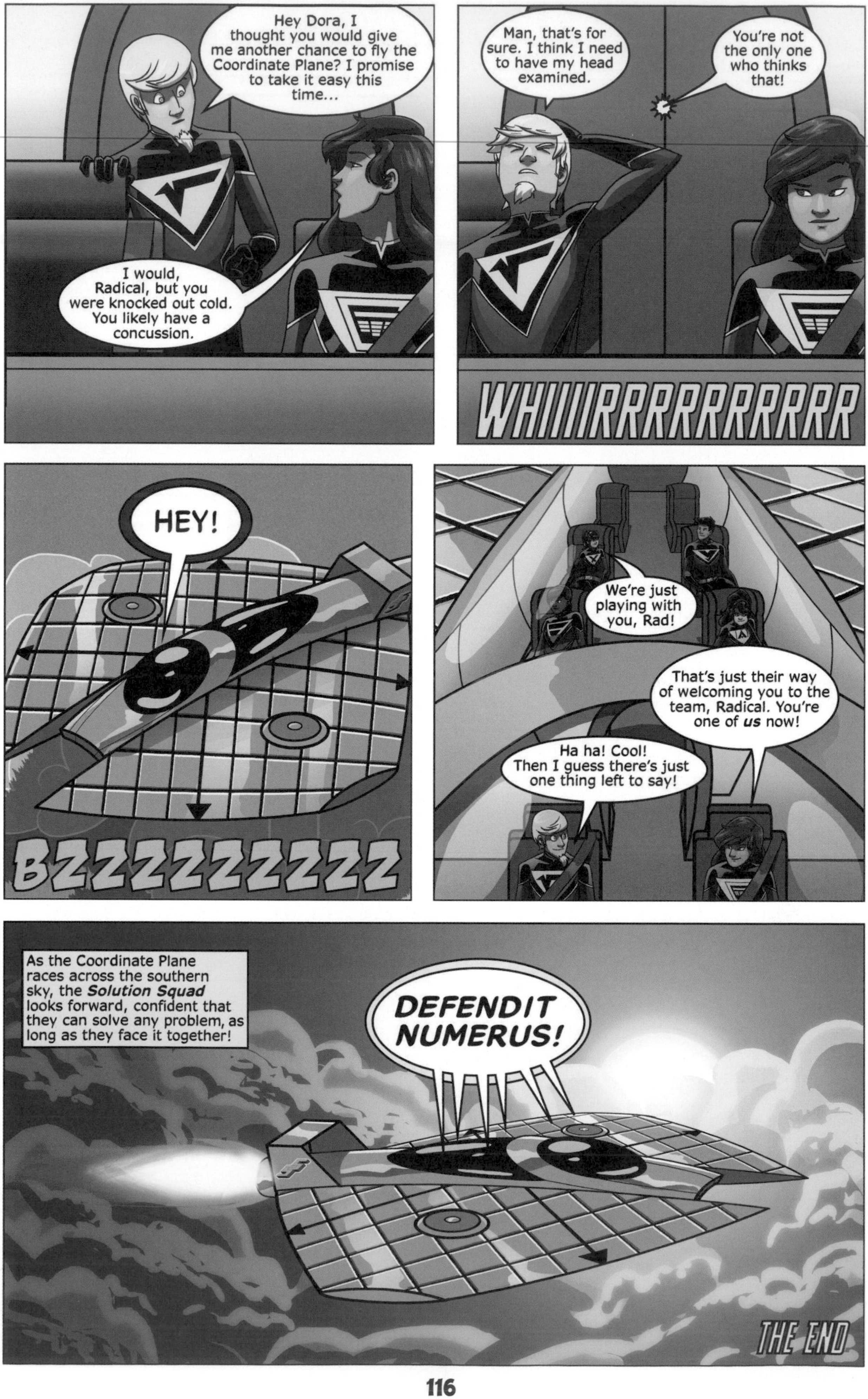
Hey Dora, I thought you would give me another chance to fly the Coordinate Plane? I promise to take it easy this time...
I would, Radical, but you were knocked out cold. You likely have a concussion.
Man, that's for sure. I think I need to have my head examined.
You're not the only one who thinks that!
WHIIIIRRRRRRRRRR
HEY!
BZZZZZZZZZZ
We're just playing with you, Rad!
That's just their way of welcoming you to the team, Radical. You're one of *us* now!
Ha ha! Cool! Then I guess there's just one thing left to say!
As the Coordinate Plane races across the southern sky, the ***Solution Squad*** looks forward, confident that they can solve any problem, as long as they face it together!
DEFENDIT NUMERUS!
THE END

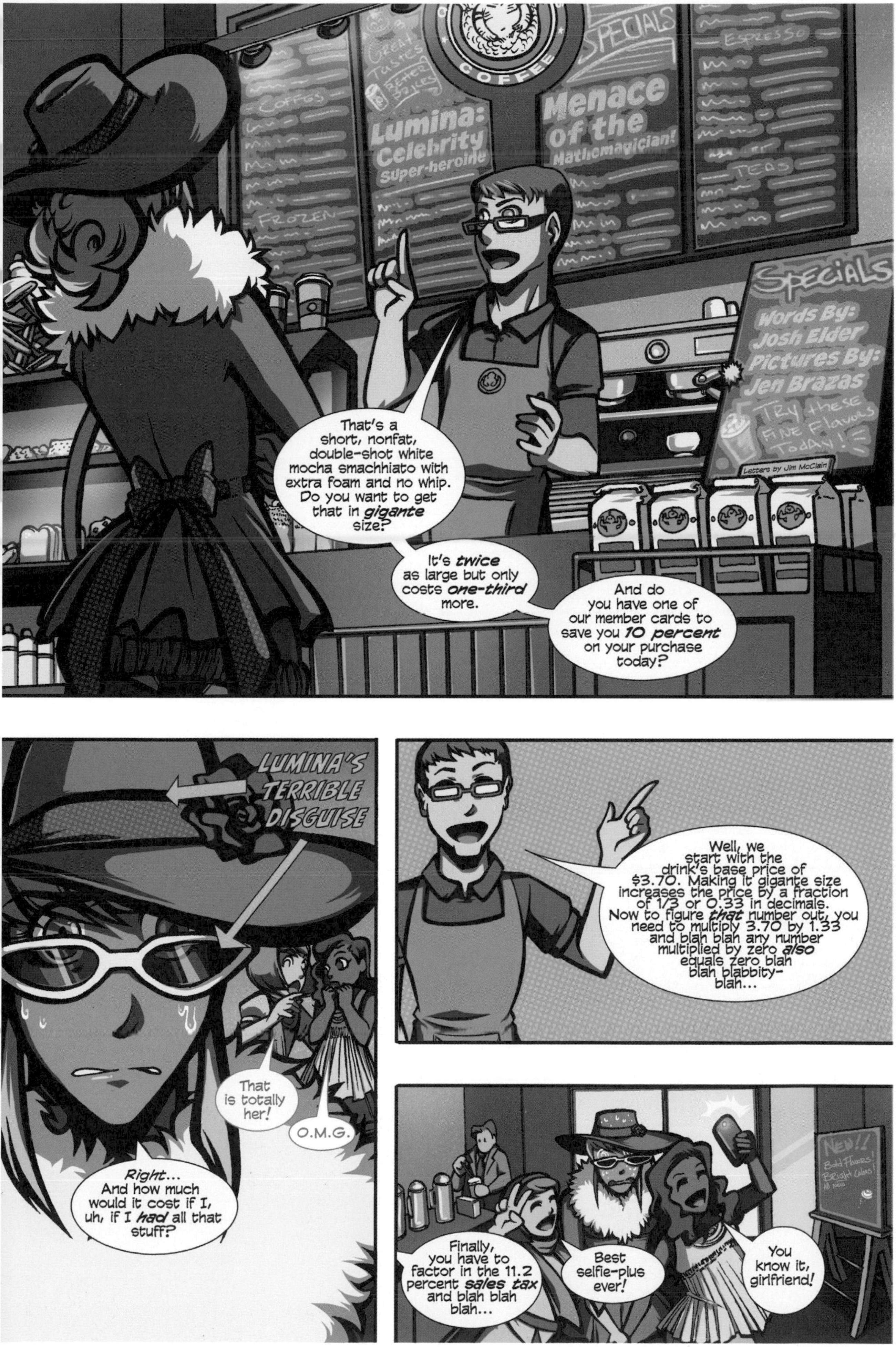

Lumina: Celebrity Super-heroine
Menace of the Mathmagician!
Specials
Words By: Josh Elder
Pictures By: Jen Brazas
Letters by Jim McClain
That's a short, nonfat, double-shot white mocha smachhiato with extra foam and no whip. Do you want to get that in *gigante* size?
It's *twice* as large but only costs *one-third* more.
And do you have one of our member cards to save you *10 percent* on your purchase today?
LUMINA'S TERRIBLE DISGUISE
Well, we start with the drink's base price of $3.70. Making it gigante size increases the price by a fraction of 1/3 or 0.33 in decimals. Now to figure *that* number out, you need to multiply 3.70 by 1.33 and blah blah any number multiplied by zero *also* equals zero blah blah blabbity-blah...
That is totally her!
O.M.G.
Right... And how much would it cost if I, uh, if I *had* all that stuff?
Finally, you have to factor in the 11.2 percent *sales tax* and blah blah blah...
Best selfie-plus ever!
You know it, girlfriend!

 **flutter** The social networking site for supers

Home Profile Find Heroes Settings Help Sign out

 # Lumina
@Luminahero

Name Lumina Perfect
Location New Apollon
Bio I'm just your typical teenage girl. I go to school, hang out with my friends, and save the world every other week or so.

168 following	31,168,094 followers	83 listed

Flaps 2,609

Favorites

Following

That's you!   ☰ Lists ▾

 Lumina @Luminahero
Late to the #AList team meeting, but I had to get my caffeine fix. You forgive me, right luminaries?

 Ma+hFr3ak @Ma+hFr3ak
@Luminahero Then let the countdown begin.

 HeroWatcher638 @HeroWatcher638
@Luminahero LOL! Can't save the world if u r falling asleep!

 Tamara Clearwater @LuminaFan4Life
@Luminahero We were totes there for reals!
w/ pics to prove it!!! =^^=

 BulkCoffeeDeals @BulkCoffeeDeals
@Luminahero Buy coffee, tea, and accessories in bulk 4 less! Get best deals!!!
www.bulkcoffeedeals.con/totallyfake...

 Savagesparrow @savagesparrow
@Luminahero When you get there, can you tell @AlphaMaleHero that he's my all-time-number-one favorite? Aside from you, of course! ;x

 MRLourdes-chan @MRLourdes-chan
@Luminahero Just this once, I suppose c:

Babetta @Babetta
@Luminahero Have fun with your meeting. Slug some bad guys for us!

@Luminahero: @LuminaFan4Life Uh oh! Guess I need to get a better disguise! #TimeToGoShopping #LikeINeededAnExcuse

@JoshElder: @LuminaHero When is the #AList going to throw down with @NerdcoreHimself again?

@JoshElder: @LuminaHero Cuz he's been talking all kinds of weapons-grade smack lately on Capebook.

@Ma+hFre3ak: @LuminaHero 5...

@LuminaHero: And the barista was super nice, but I just wanted some coffee, not a math lesson. #RewardCardsAreTheDevil

@LuminaFan4Life: @LuminaHero Totally! #DownWithMath

@Ma+hFr3ak: @LuminaHero 4...

118

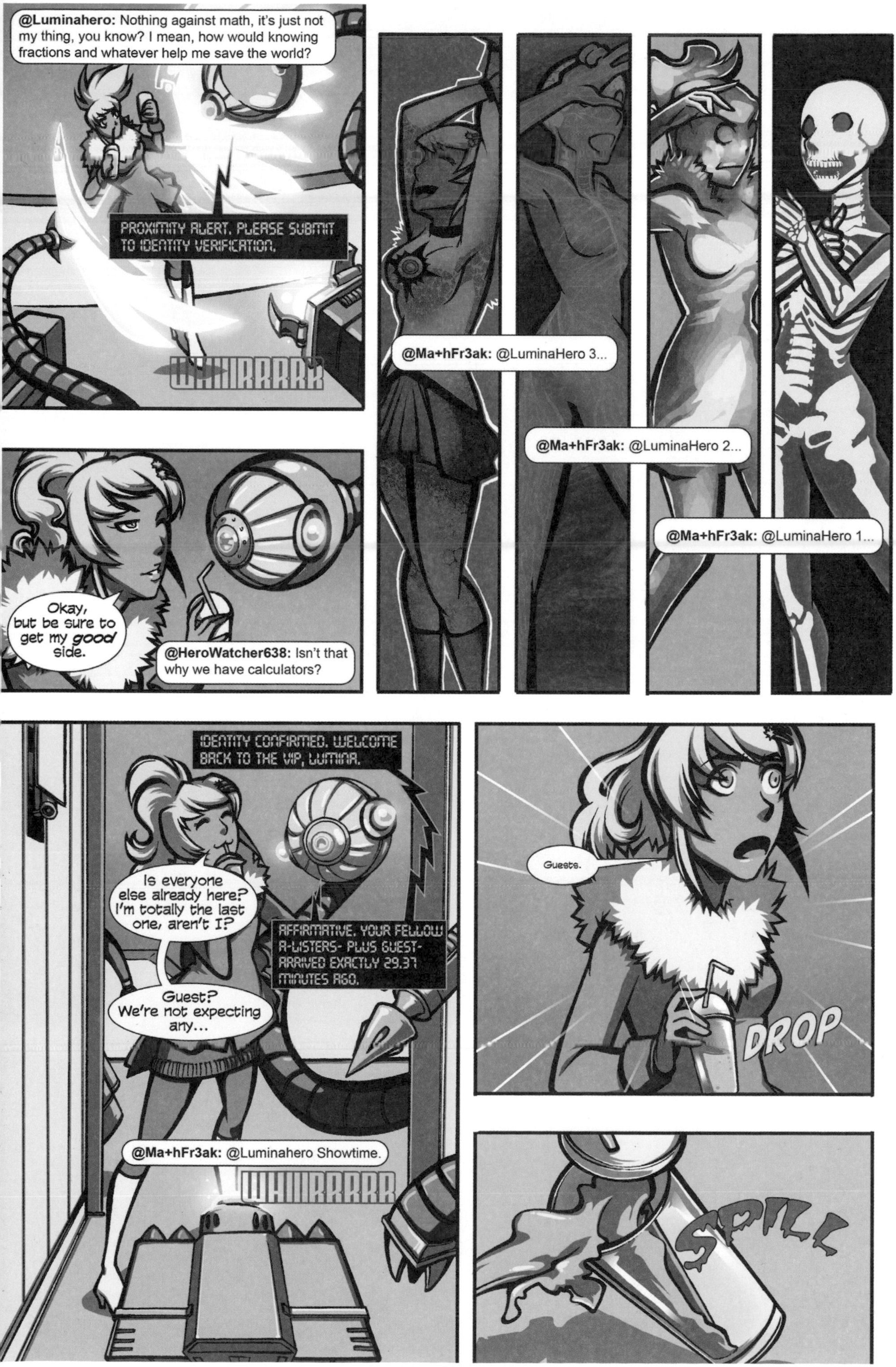

@Luminahero: Nothing against math, it's just not my thing, you know? I mean, how would knowing fractions and whatever help me save the world?
PROXIMITY ALERT. PLEASE SUBMIT TO IDENTITY VERIFICATION.
WHIIRRRRR
Okay, but be sure to get my *good* side.
@HeroWatcher638: Isn't that why we have calculators?
@Ma+hFr3ak: @LuminaHero 3...
@Ma+hFr3ak: @LuminaHero 2...
@Ma+hFr3ak: @LuminaHero 1...
IDENTITY CONFIRMED. WELCOME BACK TO THE VIP, LUMINA.
Is everyone else already here? I'm totally the last one, aren't I?
AFFIRMATIVE. YOUR FELLOW A-LISTERS- PLUS GUEST- ARRIVED EXACTLY 29.37 MINUTES AGO.
Guest? We're not expecting any...
@Ma+hFr3ak: @Luminahero Showtime.
WHIIRRRRR
Guests.
DROP
SPILL

Now I hope you don't mind, but we went ahead and got the show started without you.

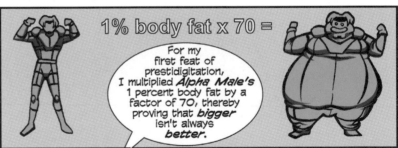

1% body fat x 70 =

For my first feat of prestidigitation, I multiplied *Alpha Male's* 1 percent body fat by a factor of 70, thereby proving that *bigger* isn't always *better*.

H/W: 5'10"/112lbs ÷ 2 = H/W: 2'11"/66lbs + 2'11"/66lbs

Second, I divided the lovely *Ingénova* in half, and a house divided against itself cannot stand.

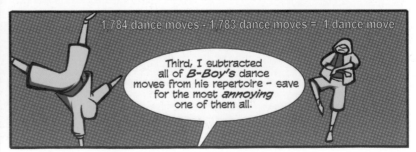

1,784 dance moves - 1,783 dance moves = 1 dance move

Third, I subtracted all of *B-Boy's* dance moves from his repertoire - save for the most *annoying* one of them all.

120

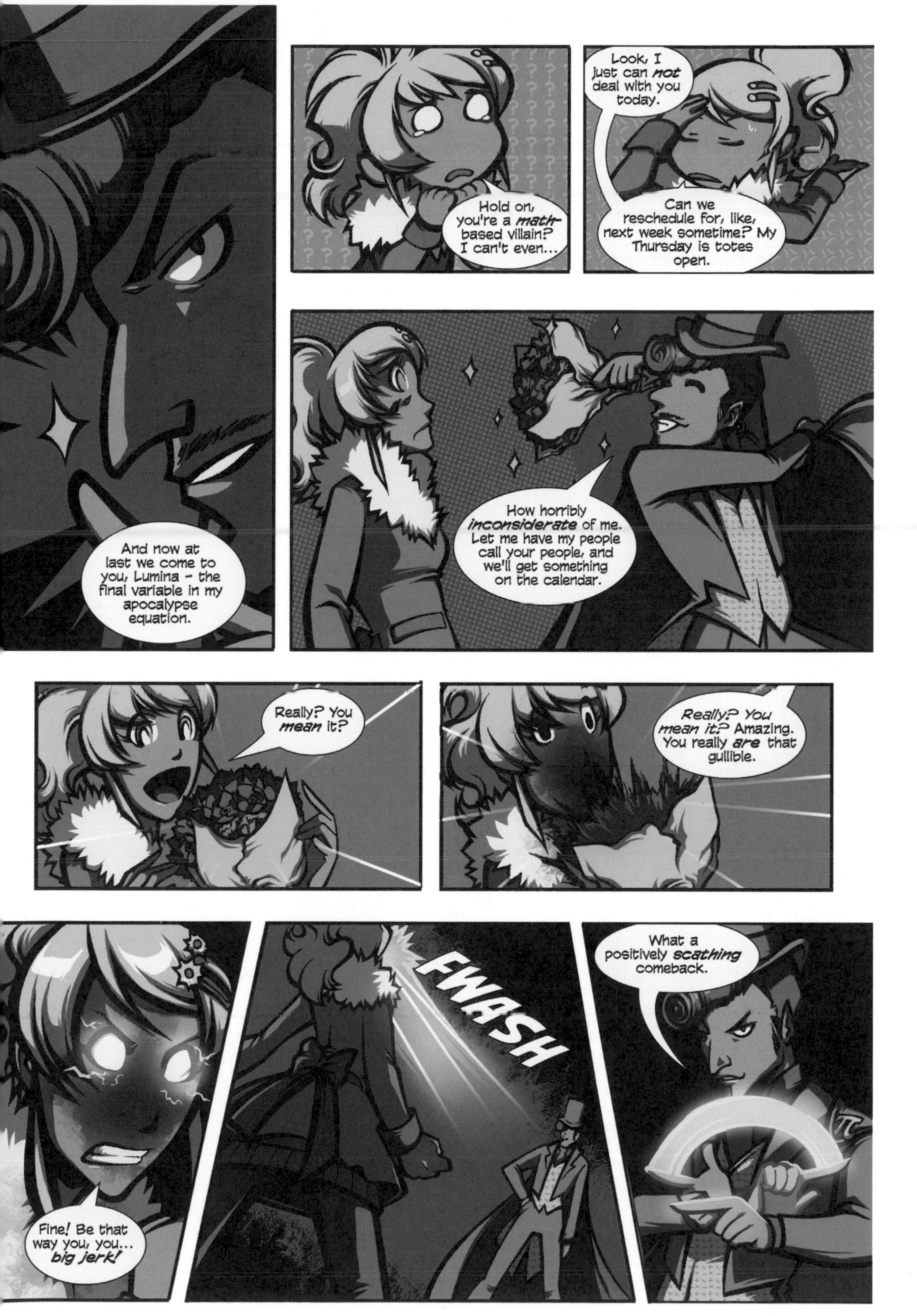
Hold on, you're a *math*-based villain? I can't even...
Look, I just can *not* deal with you today.
Can we reschedule for, like, next week sometime? My Thursday is totes open.
And now at last we come to you, Lumina - the final variable in my apocalypse equation.
How horribly *inconsiderate* of me. Let me have my people call your people, and we'll get something on the calendar.
Really? You *mean* it?
Really? You mean it? Amazing. You really *are* that gullible.
Fine! Be that way you, you... *big jerk!*
FWASH
What a positively *scathing* comeback.

Here's *mine.*

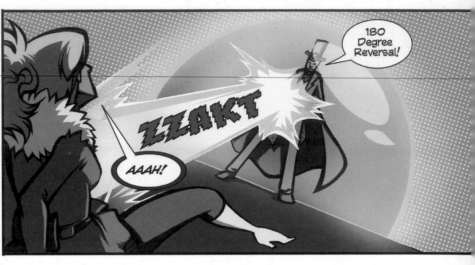

180 Degree Reversal!

AAAH!

ZZAKT

And I *just* bought that too...

And for my *next* trick... I avoided the VIP security system by *adding* my name to the guest list.

Let's see what happens when I *remove* yours.

Guest List Subtraction!

AAOOGAH

INTRUDER ALERT! INTRUDER ALERT!

This is *so* not my day.

USE OF MAXIMUM FORCE AUTHORIZED!

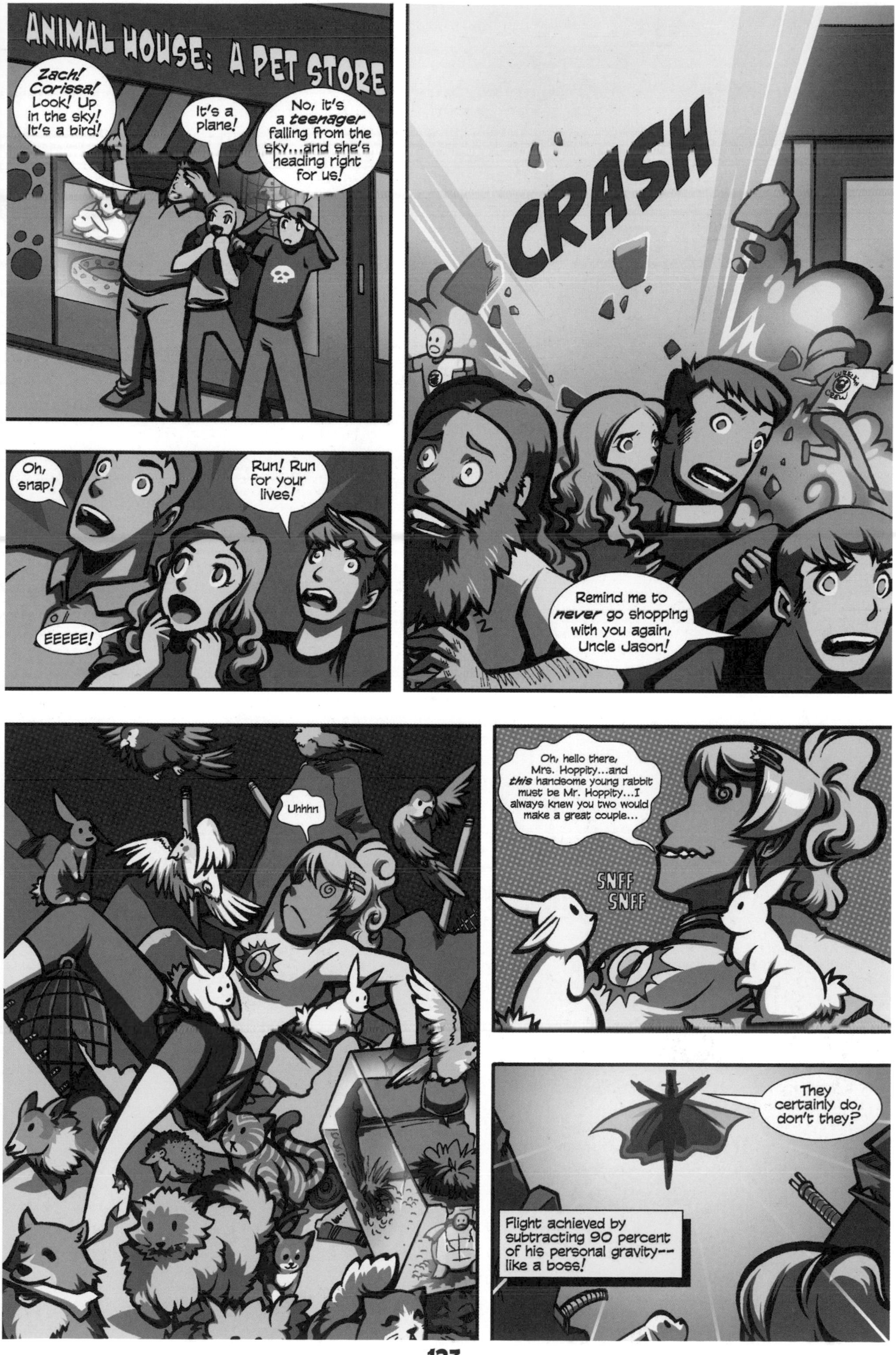
ANIMAL HOUSE: A PET STORE
Zach! Corissa! Look! Up in the sky! It's a bird!
It's a plane!
No, it's a *teenager* falling from the sky...and she's heading right for us!
CRASH
Oh, snap!
Run! Run for your lives!
EEEEE!
Remind me to *never* go shopping with you again, Uncle Jason!
Uhhhn
Oh, hello there, Mrs. Hoppity...and *this* handsome young rabbit must be Mr. Hoppity...I always knew you two would make a great couple...
SNFF SNFF
They certainly do, don't they?
Flight achieved by subtracting 90 percent of his personal gravity--like a boss!

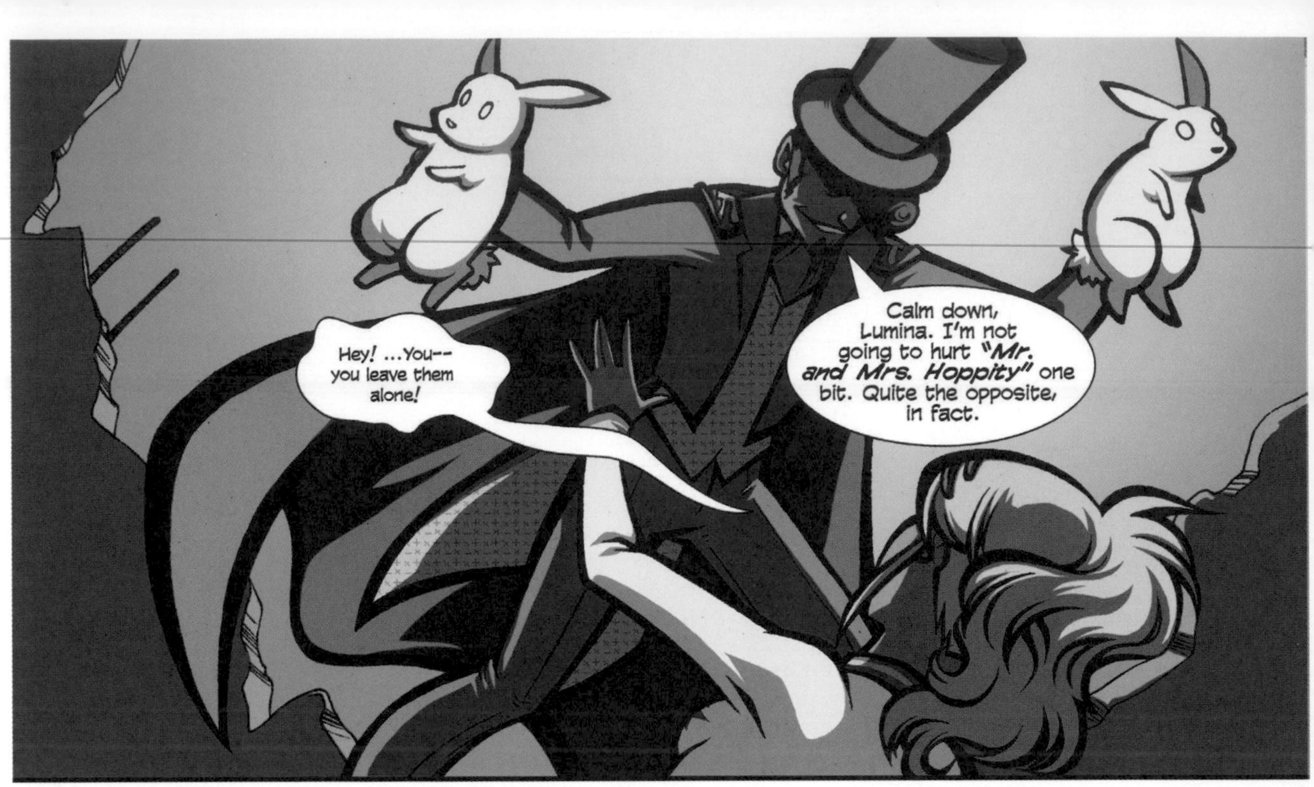
Hey! ...You--
you leave them
alone!
Calm down,
Lumina. I'm not
going to hurt "Mr.
and Mrs. Hoppity" one
bit. Quite the opposite,
in fact.

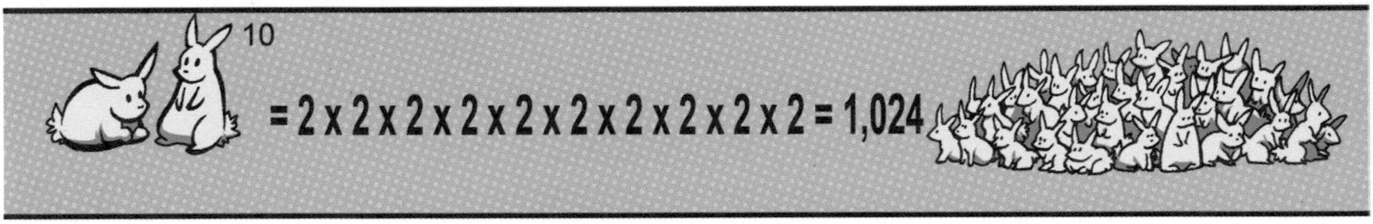
10
= 2 x 2 x 2 x 2 x 2 x 2 x 2 x 2 x 2 x 2 = 1,024

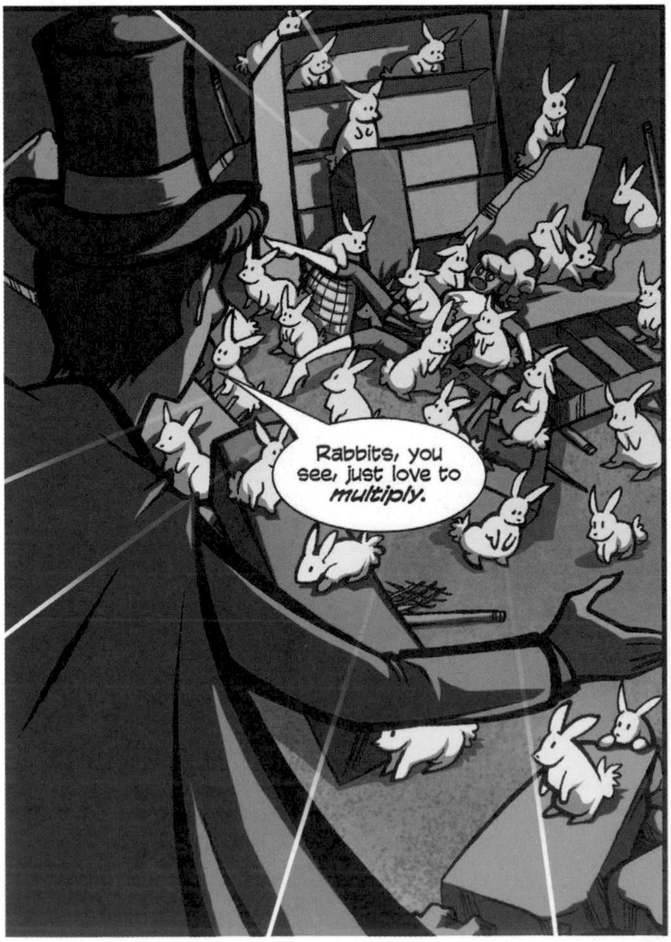
Rabbits, you
see, just love to
multiply.

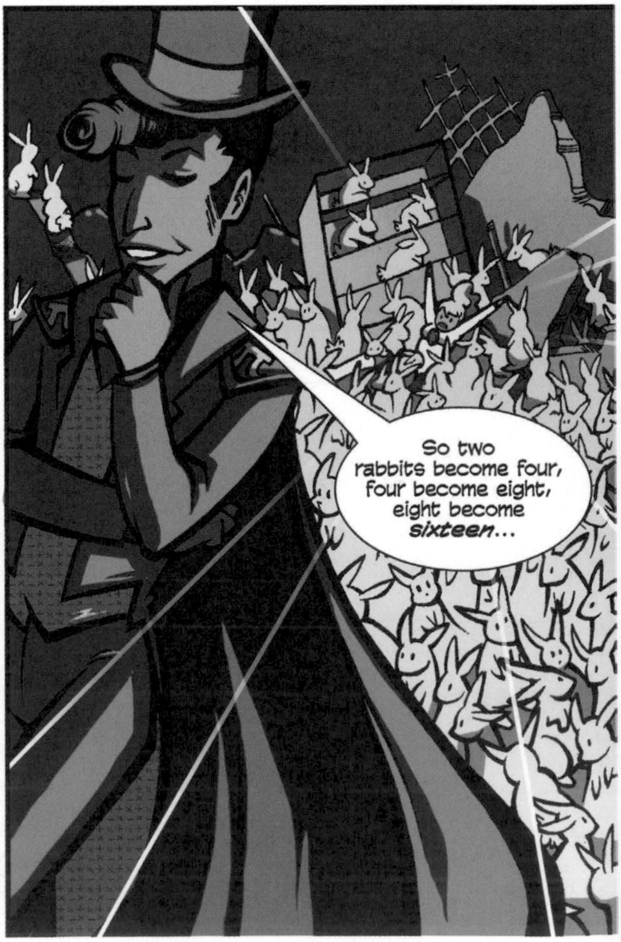
So two
rabbits become four,
four become eight,
eight become
sixteen...

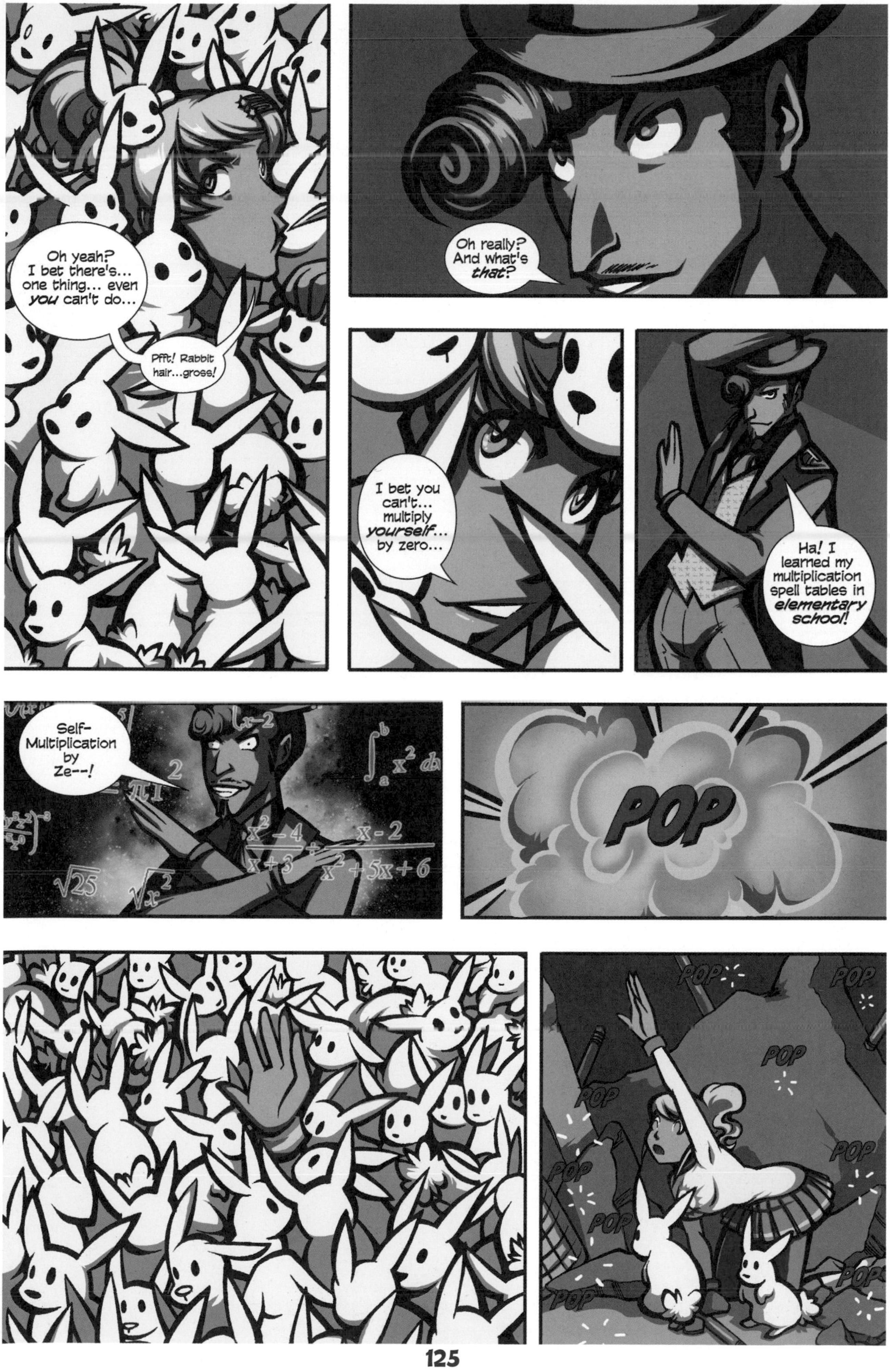
Oh yeah? I bet there's... one thing... even *you* can't do...
Pfft! Rabbit hair...gross!
Oh really? And what's *that*?
I bet you can't... multiply *yourself*... by zero...
Ha! I learned my multiplication spell tables in *elementary school!*
Self-Multiplication by Ze--!
POP
POP
POP
POP
POP
POP
POP
POP
POP

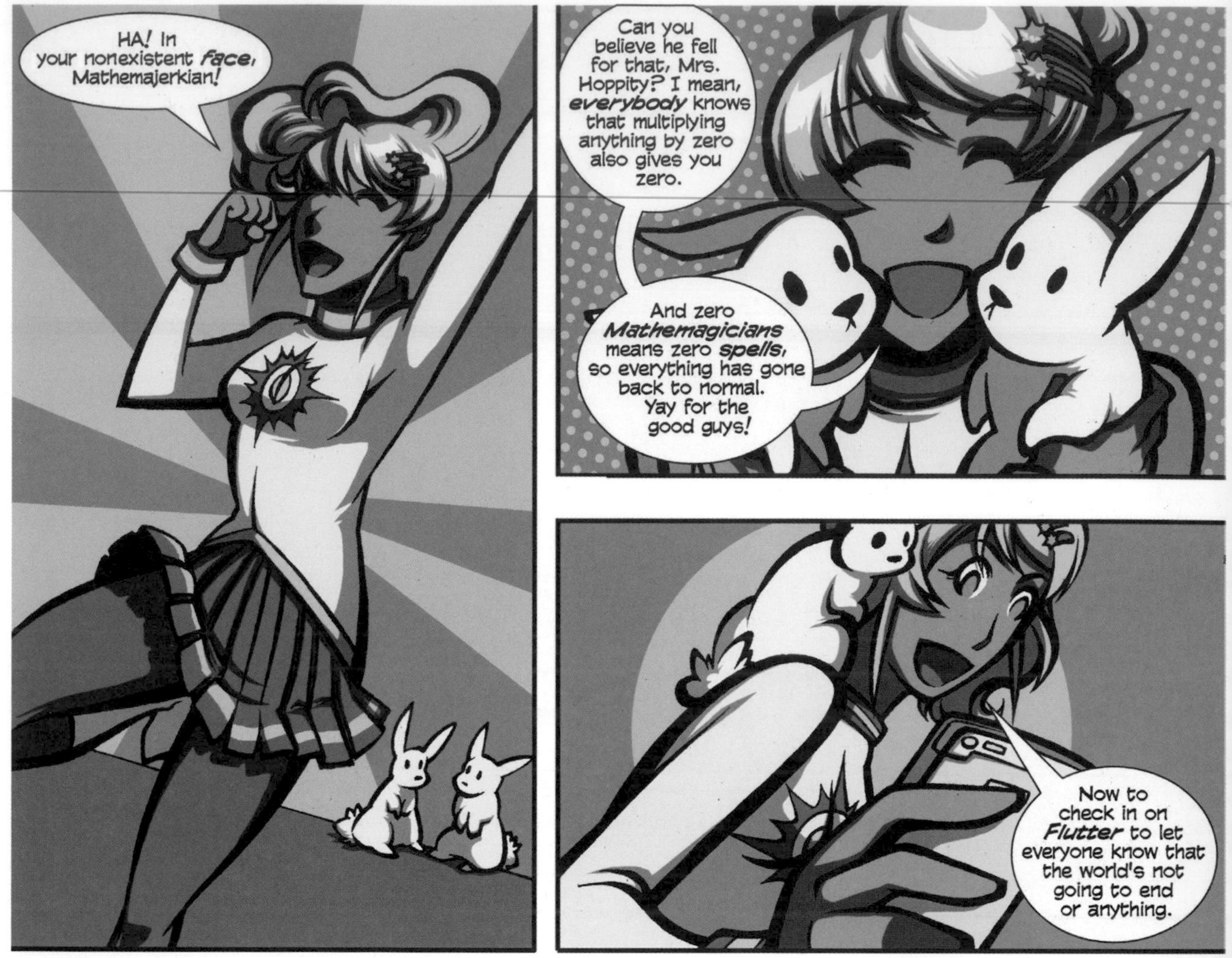
HA! In your nonexistent face, Mathemajerkian!
Can you believe he fell for that, Mrs. Hoppity? I mean, everybody knows that multiplying anything by zero also gives you zero.
And zero Mathemagicians means zero spells, so everything has gone back to normal. Yay for the good guys!
Now to check in on Flutter to let everyone know that the world's not going to end or anything.

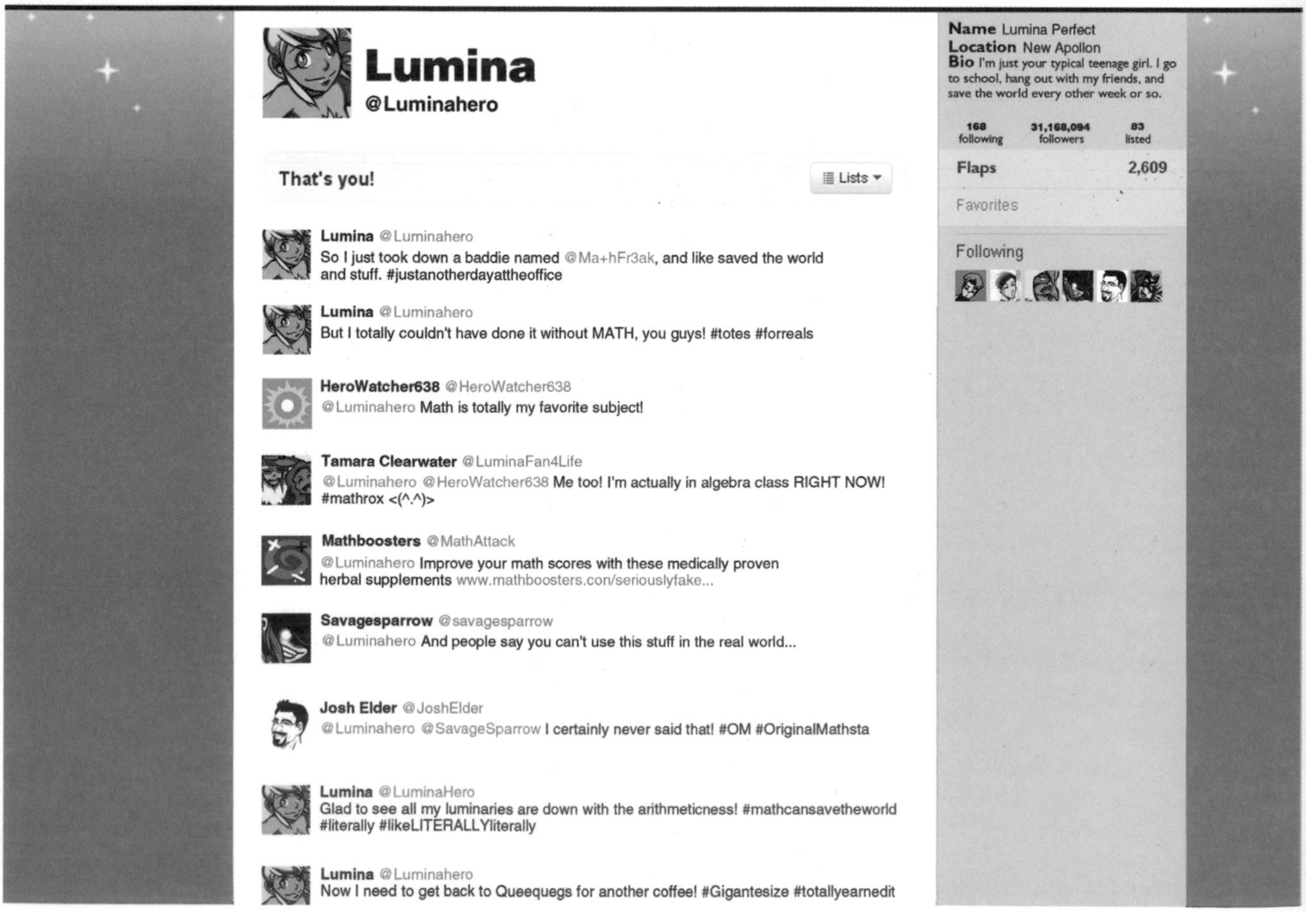
Lumina
@Luminahero
That's you!
Lists
Lumina @Luminahero
So I just took down a baddie named @Ma+hFr3ak, and like saved the world and stuff. #justanotherdayattheoffice
Lumina @Luminahero
But I totally couldn't have done it without MATH, you guys! #totes #forreals
HeroWatcher638 @HeroWatcher638
@Luminahero Math is totally my favorite subject!
Tamara Clearwater @LuminaFan4Life
@Luminahero @HeroWatcher638 Me too! I'm actually in algebra class RIGHT NOW! #mathrox <(^.^)>
Mathboosters @MathAttack
@Luminahero Improve your math scores with these medically proven herbal supplements www.mathboosters.com/seriouslyfake...
Savagesparrow @savagesparrow
@Luminahero And people say you can't use this stuff in the real world...
Josh Elder @JoshElder
@Luminahero @SavageSparrow I certainly never said that! #OM #OriginalMathsta
Lumina @LuminaHero
Glad to see all my luminaries are down with the arithmeticness! #mathcansavetheworld #literally #likeLITERALLYliterally
Lumina @Luminahero
Now I need to get back to Queequegs for another coffee! #Gigantesize #totallyearnedit
Name Lumina Perfect
Location New Apollon
Bio I'm just your typical teenage girl. I go to school, hang out with my friends, and save the world every other week or so.
168 following
31,168,094 followers
83 listed
Flaps 2,609
Favorites
Following

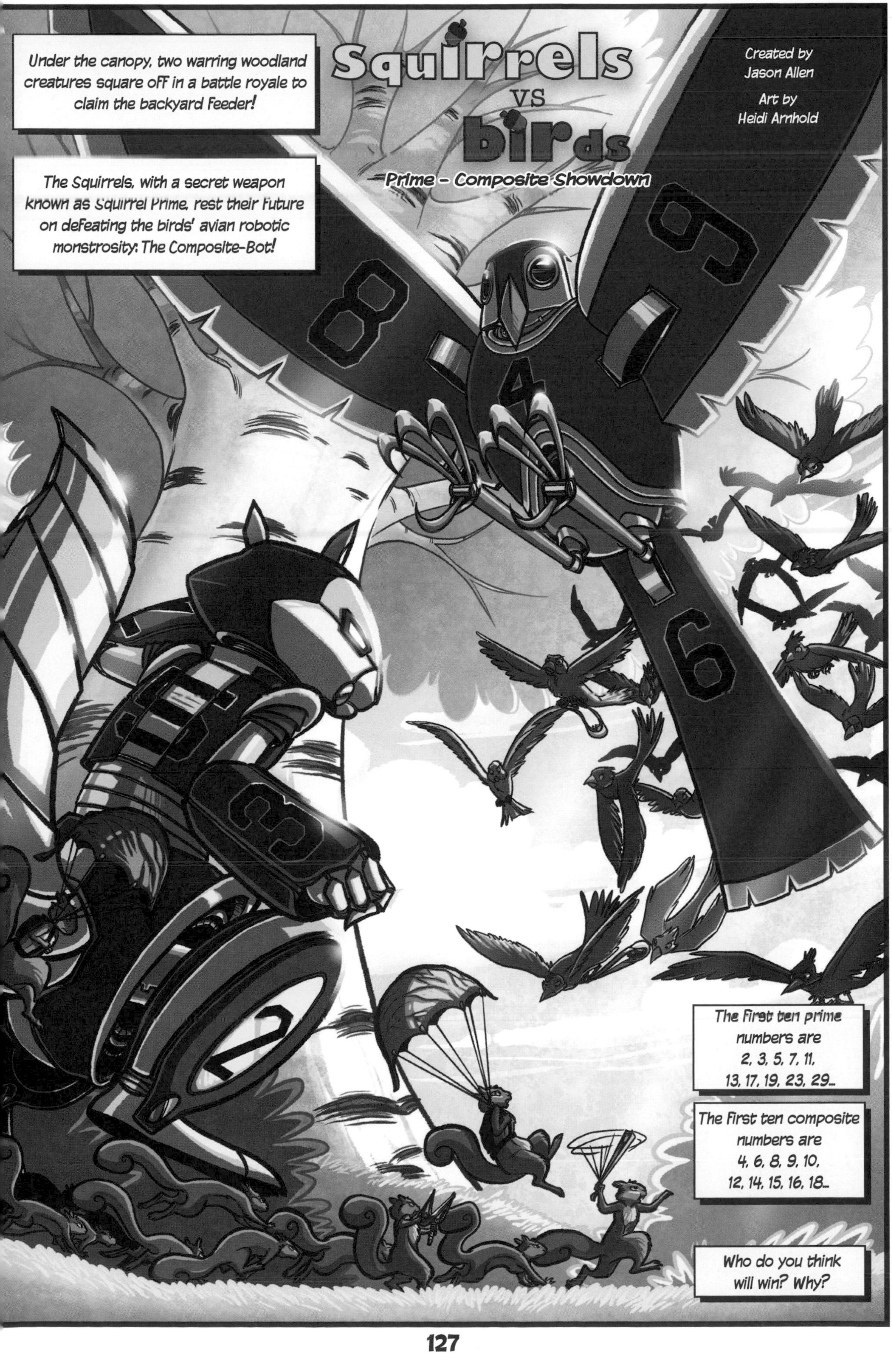
Under the canopy, two warring woodland creatures square off in a battle royale to claim the backyard feeder!
Squirrels vs birds
Prime - Composite Showdown
Created by Jason Allen
Art by Heidi Arnhold
The Squirrels, with a secret weapon known as Squirrel Prime, rest their future on defeating the birds' avian robotic monstrosity: The Composite-Bot!
8
9
4
6
3
2
The first ten prime numbers are 2, 3, 5, 7, 11, 13, 17, 19, 23, 29...
The first ten composite numbers are 4, 6, 8, 9, 10, 12, 14, 15, 16, 18...
Who do you think will win? Why?

SOCIAL STUDIES

"THE BLACK BRIGADE"

A 1779 CROGAN ADVENTURE BY CHRIS SCHWEIZER

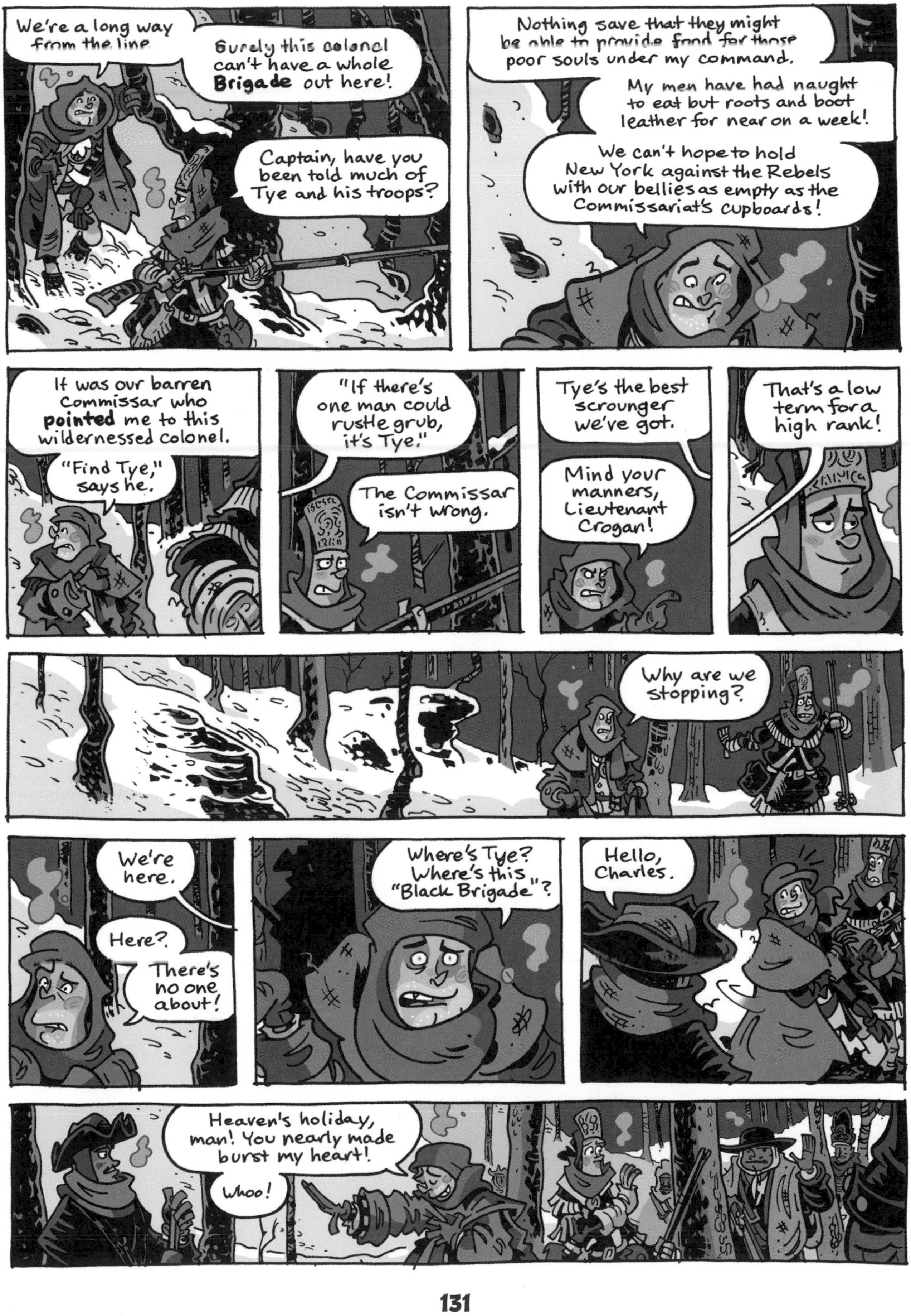

We're a long way from the line.
Surely this colonel can't have a whole **Brigade** out here!
Captain, have you been told much of Tye and his troops?
Nothing save that they might be able to provide food for those poor souls under my command.
My men have had naught to eat but roots and boot leather for near on a week!
We can't hope to hold New York against the Rebels with our bellies as empty as the Commissariat's cupboards!
It was our barren Commissar who **pointed** me to this wildernessed colonel.
"Find Tye," says he.
"If there's one man could rustle grub, it's Tye."
The Commissar isn't wrong.
Tye's the best scrounger we've got.
Mind your manners, Lieutenant Crogan!
That's a low term for a high rank!
Why are we stopping?
We're here.
Here?
There's no one about!
Where's Tye? Where's this "Black Brigade"?
Hello, Charles.
Heaven's holiday, man! You nearly made burst my heart!
Whoo!

My word. You're all Ethiopes. Remarkable!

Come now, young man. Take me to your camp. I've an urgent need to talk with Colonel Tye.

This **is** our camp.

But... Where's the **brigade**? Where's Colonel **Tye**?

Captain...

...this **is** Colonel Tye.

But... But you're **black**.

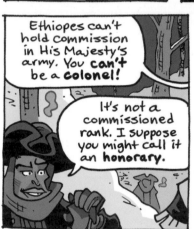
Ethiopes can't hold commission in His Majesty's army. You **can't** be a **colonel**!

It's not a commissioned rank. I suppose you might call it an **honorary**.

The other officers call him "Colonel" as a sign of **respect**, and an estimation of his **worth**.

Well! You can be proud of such high estimation, "Colonel." It's no mean thing.

Thank you, Captain...

Galt-Brown. Captain J. Galt-Brown of the 23rd.

Captain Galt-Brown, might I assume that you've come to beg **stores**? No one ventures this far out less'n they're short on provisions.

So you **do** have stores!

...

We **will**.

The 14th Continentals are taking food from Baker to Monmouth. We reckon thirty men, with cannon.

Only thirty men? Why, a **brigade** could—

"Brigade" is an honorary, too, isn't it?

I'm afraid so.

I haven't a **thousand** men at my command. I've got **twenty-four**.

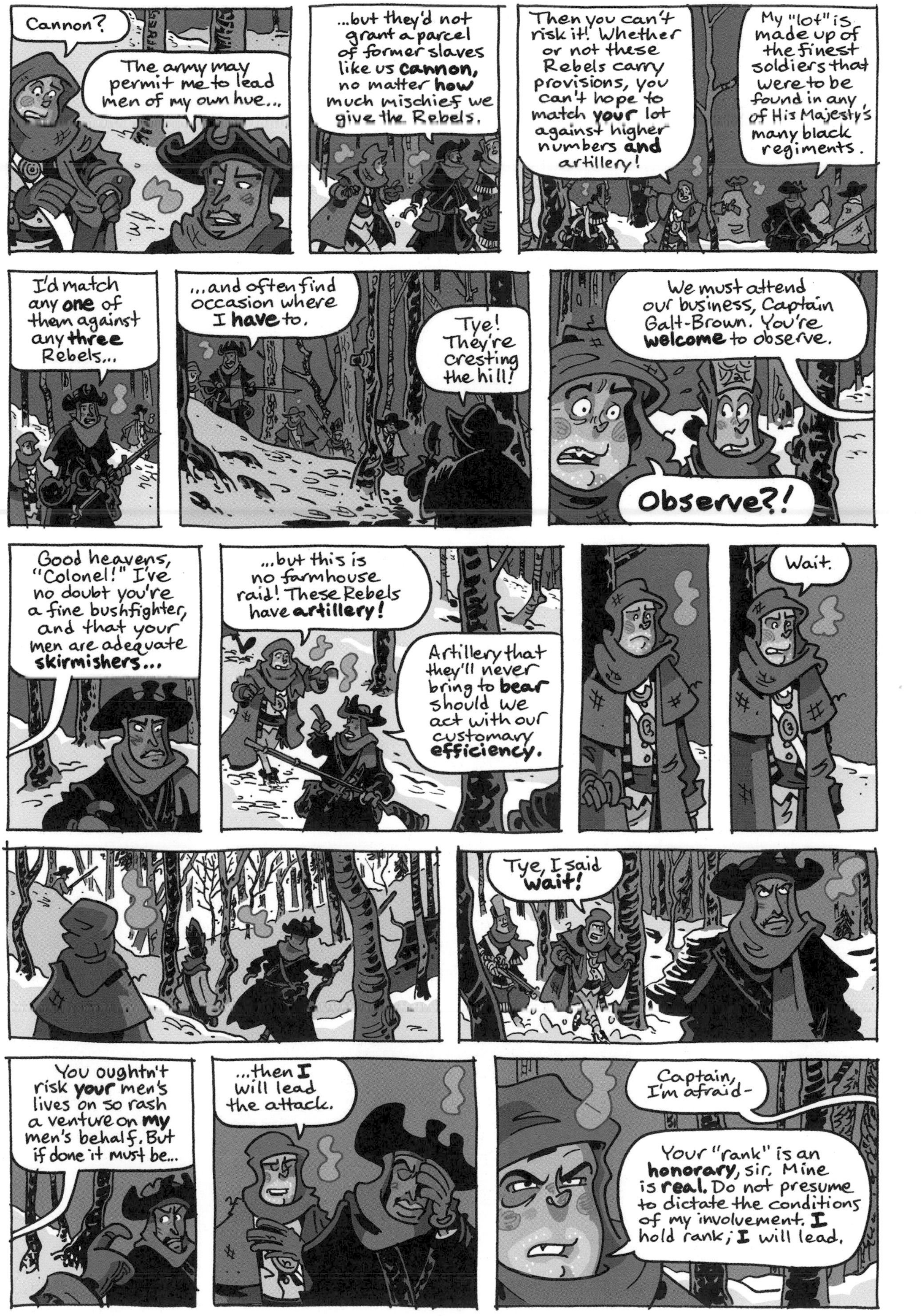
Cannon?
The army may permit me to lead men of my own hue...
...but they'd not grant a parcel of former slaves like us cannon, no matter how much mischief we give the Rebels.
Then you can't risk it! Whether or not these Rebels carry provisions, you can't hope to match your lot against higher numbers and artillery!
My "lot" is made up of the finest soldiers that were to be found in any of His Majesty's many black regiments.
I'd match any one of them against any three Rebels...
...and often find occasion where I have to.
Tye! They're cresting the hill!
We must attend our business, Captain Galt-Brown. You're welcome to observe.
Observe?!
Good heavens, "Colonel!" I've no doubt you're a fine bushfighter, and that your men are adequate skirmishers...
...but this is no farmhouse raid! These Rebels have artillery!
Artillery that they'll never bring to bear should we act with our customary efficiency.
Wait.
Tye, I said wait!
You oughtn't risk your men's lives on so rash a venture on my men's behalf. But if done it must be...
...then I will lead the attack.
Captain, I'm afraid-
Your "rank" is an honorary, sir. Mine is real. Do not presume to dictate the conditions of my involvement. I hold rank; I will lead.

Very well...
...Captain.

We are at your command.
The convoy will soon be past; if we are to act, it must be now.

Right.
Line your men up, "Colonel!" We'll step out and engage when they're alongside.

But firing from the trees—
We're not **bandits**, Tye, we're **soldiers**.

We'll face our enemies like King's men— in **line**.
There ain't men enough to make a proper volley, and we've no bayonet, anyway! It's a sure loss!

By my reckon, purposeless **risk** is like enough to **treason**.
We've no duty to **form** or **manner**. Our duty is to those who would depend on our **success**.

My men wouldn't thank you for craven acts on their behalf, **however** hungry they may be—
I ain't speaking of **your** men, sir.

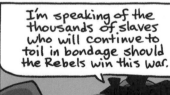

I'm speaking of the thousands of slaves who will continue to toil in bondage should the Rebels win this war.

Line up, Tye.

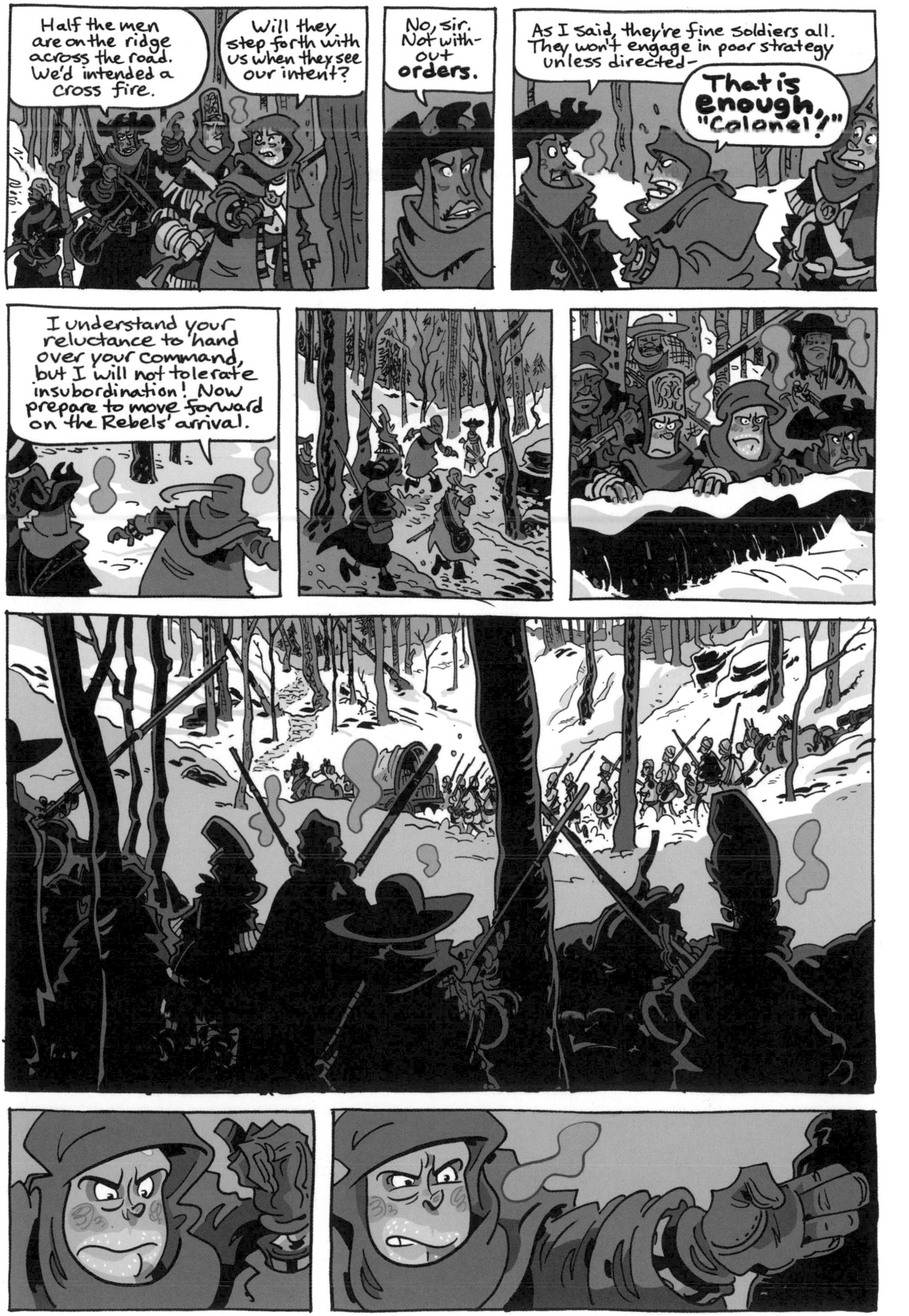
Half the men are on the ridge across the road. We'd intended a cross fire.
Will they step forth with us when they see our intent?
No, sir. Not with-out orders.
As I said, they're fine soldiers all. They won't engage in poor strategy unless directed-
That is enough, "Colonel!"
I understand your reluctance to hand over your command, but I will not tolerate insubordination! Now prepare to move forward on the Rebels' arrival.

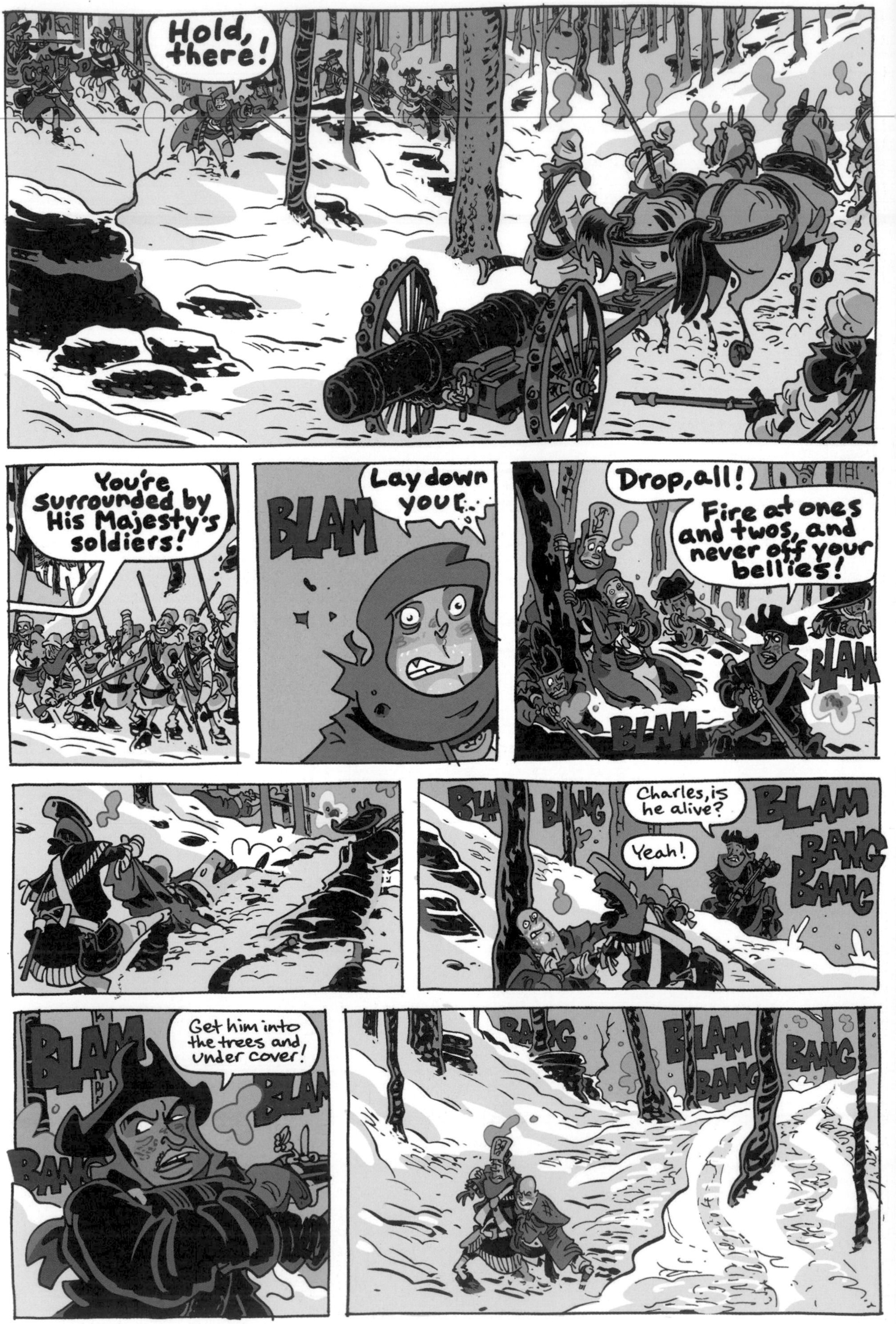
Hold, there!
You're surrounded by His Majesty's soldiers!
BLAM
Lay down your...
Drop, all!
Fire at ones and twos, and never off your bellies!
BLAM
BLAM
BLAM
BANG
Charles, is he alive?
Yeah!
BLAM
BANG
BANG
BLAM
Get him into the trees and under cover!
BANG
BANG
BLAM
BANG
BANG

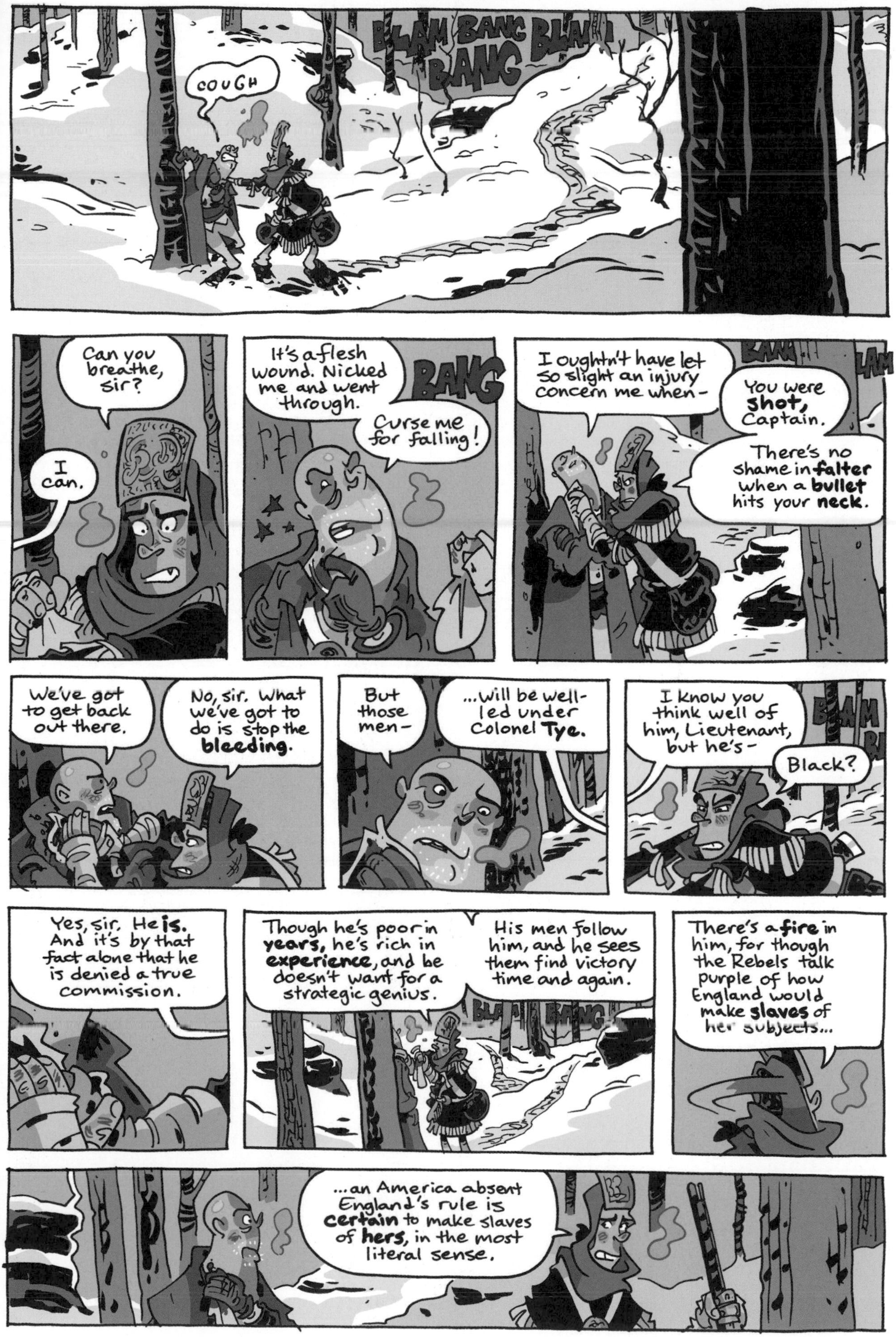
BLAM BANG BLAM
BANG
COUGH
Can you breathe, sir?
I can.
It's a flesh wound. Nicked me and went through.
BANG
Curse me for falling!
I oughtn't have let so slight an injury concern me when-
BANG
BLAM
You were **shot,** Captain.
There's no shame in **falter** when a **bullet** hits your **neck**.
We've got to get back out there.
No, sir. What we've got to do is stop the **bleeding**.
But those men-
...will be well-led under Colonel **Tye.**
I know you think well of him, Lieutenant, but he's-
Black?
Yes, sir. He **is.** And it's by that fact alone that he is denied a true commission.
Though he's poor in **years,** he's rich in **experience**, and he doesn't want for a strategic genius.
His men follow him, and he sees them find victory time and again.
BANG
There's a **fire** in him, for though the Rebels talk purple of how England would make **slaves** of her subjects...
...an America absent England's rule is **certain** to make slaves of **hers**, in the most literal sense.

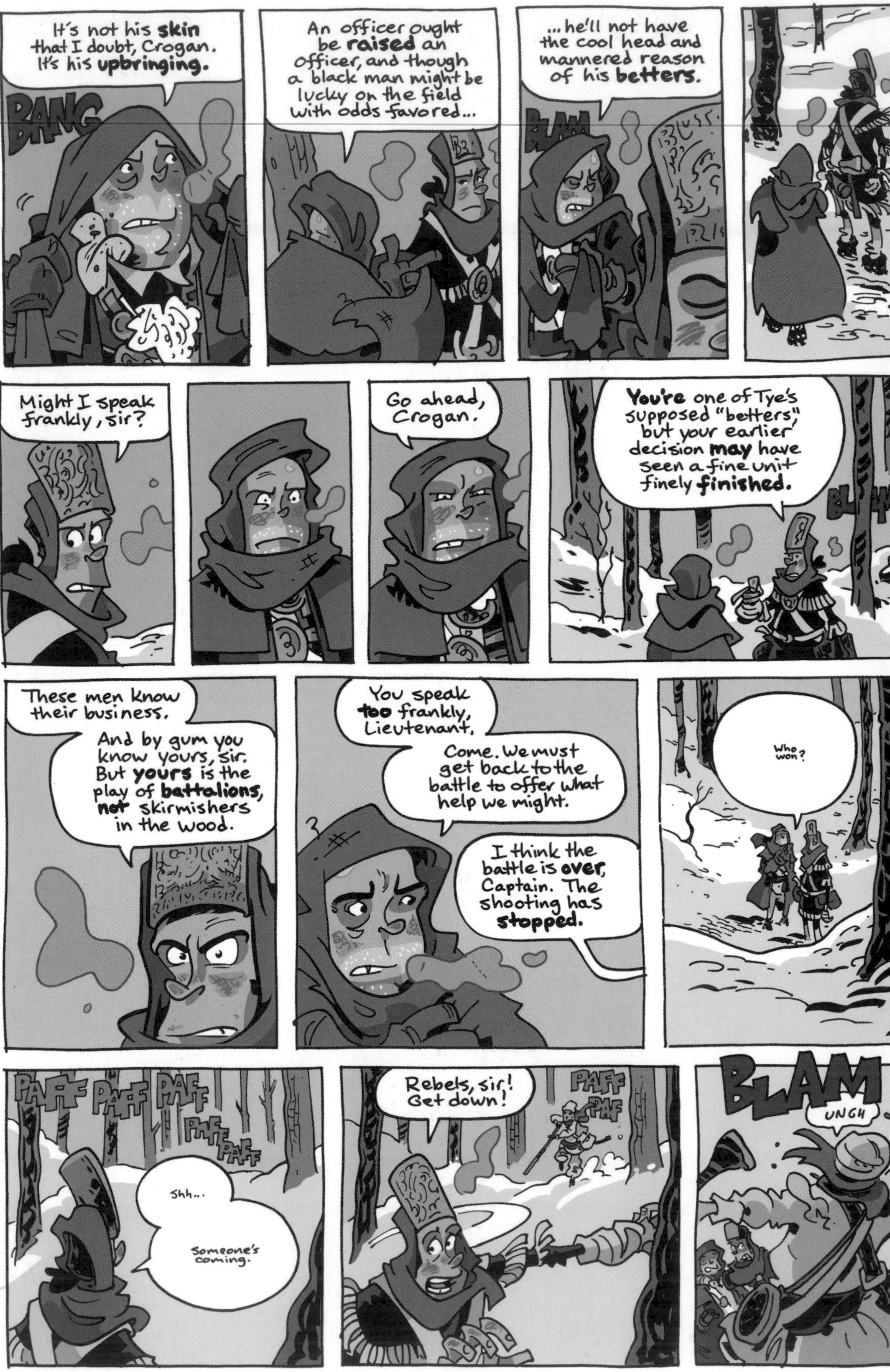
It's not his skin that I doubt, Crogan. It's his upbringing.
BANG
An officer ought be raised an officer, and though a black man might be lucky on the field with odds favored...
...he'll not have the cool head and mannered reason of his betters.
BLAM
Might I speak frankly, sir?
Go ahead, Crogan.
You're one of Tye's supposed "betters," but your earlier decision may have seen a fine unit finely finished.
BLAM
These men know their business.
And by gum you know yours, sir. But yours is the play of battalions, not skirmishers in the wood.
You speak too frankly, Lieutenant.
Come. We must get back to the battle to offer what help we might.
I think the battle is over, Captain. The shooting has stopped.
Who won?
PAFF PAFF PAFF PAFF PAFF
Shh...
Someone's coming.
Rebels, sir! Get down!
PAFF PAFF
BLAM
UNGH

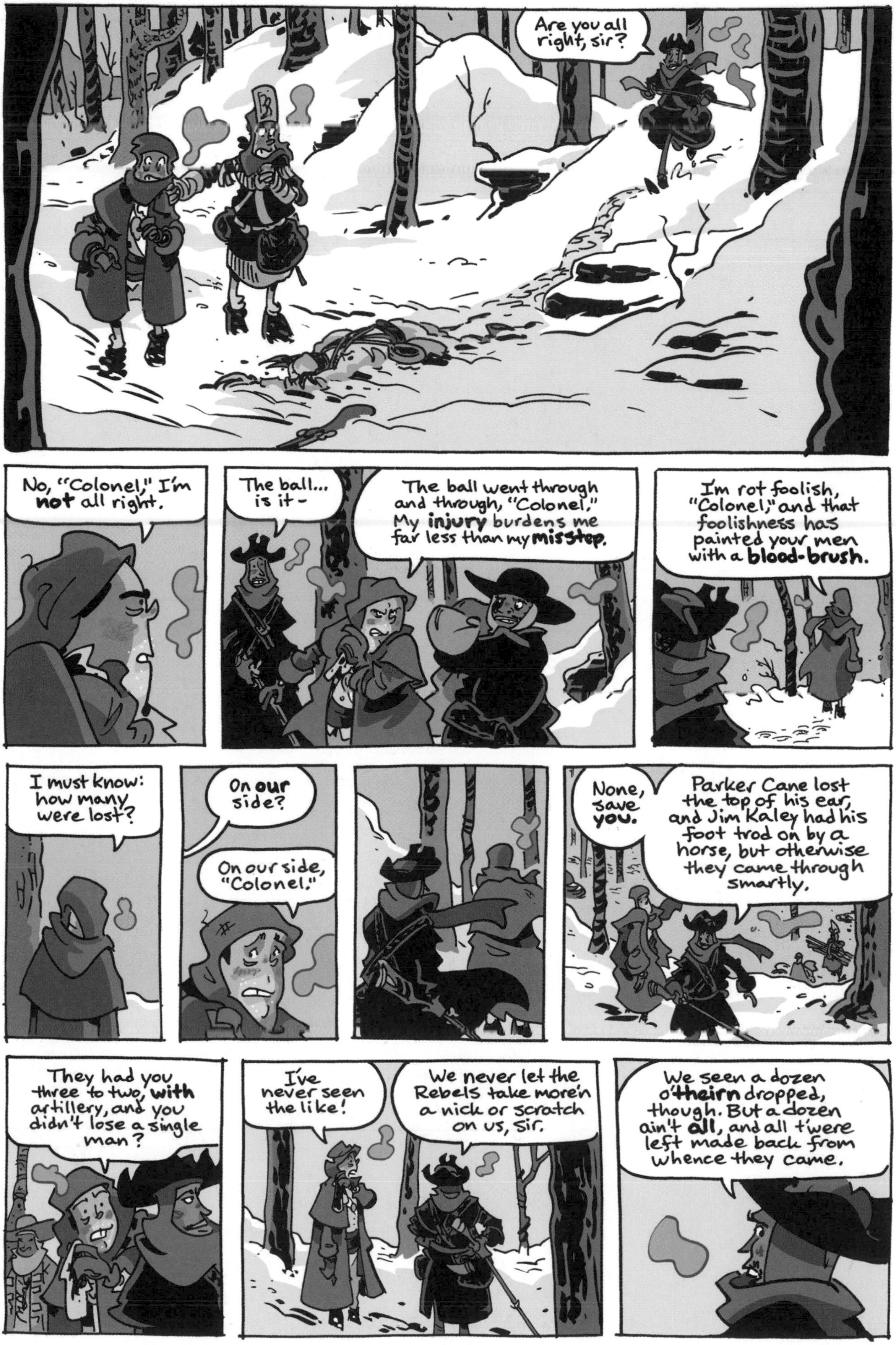

Are you all right, sir?
No, "Colonel," I'm **not** all right.
The ball... is it -
The ball went through and through, "Colonel." My **injury** burdens me far less than my **misstep**.
I'm rot foolish, "Colonel," and that foolishness has painted your men with a **blood-brush**.
I must know: how many were lost?
On **our** side?
On our side, "Colonel."
None, save **you**.
Parker Cane lost the top of his ear, and Jim Kaley had his foot trod on by a horse, but otherwise they came through smartly.
They had you three to two, **with** artillery, and you didn't lose a single man?
I've never seen the like!
We never let the Rebels take more'n a nick or scratch on us, sir.
We seen a dozen o'**theirn** dropped, though. But a dozen ain't **all**, and all t'were left made back from whence they came.

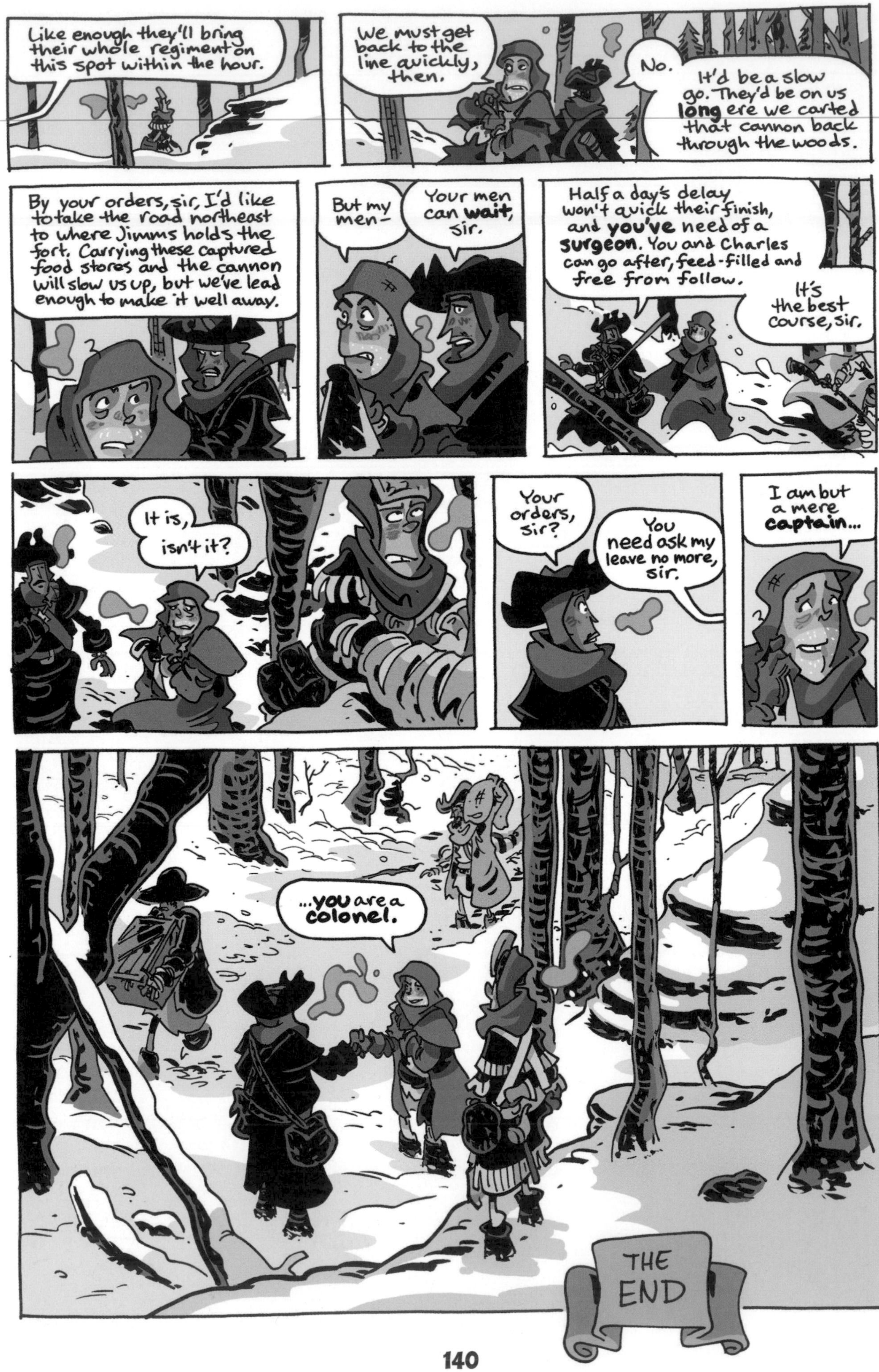
Like enough they'll bring their whole regiment on this spot within the hour.
We must get back to the line quickly, then.
No.
It'd be a slow go. They'd be on us long ere we carted that cannon back through the woods.
By your orders, sir, I'd like to take the road northeast to where Jimms holds the fort. Carrying these captured food stores and the cannon will slow us up, but we've lead enough to make it well away.
But my men-
Your men can wait, sir.
Half a day's delay won't quick their finish, and you've need of a surgeon. You and Charles can go after, feed-filled and free from follow.
It's the best course, sir.
It is, isn't it?
Your orders, sir?
You need ask my leave no more, sir.
I am but a mere captain...
...you are a colonel.
THE END

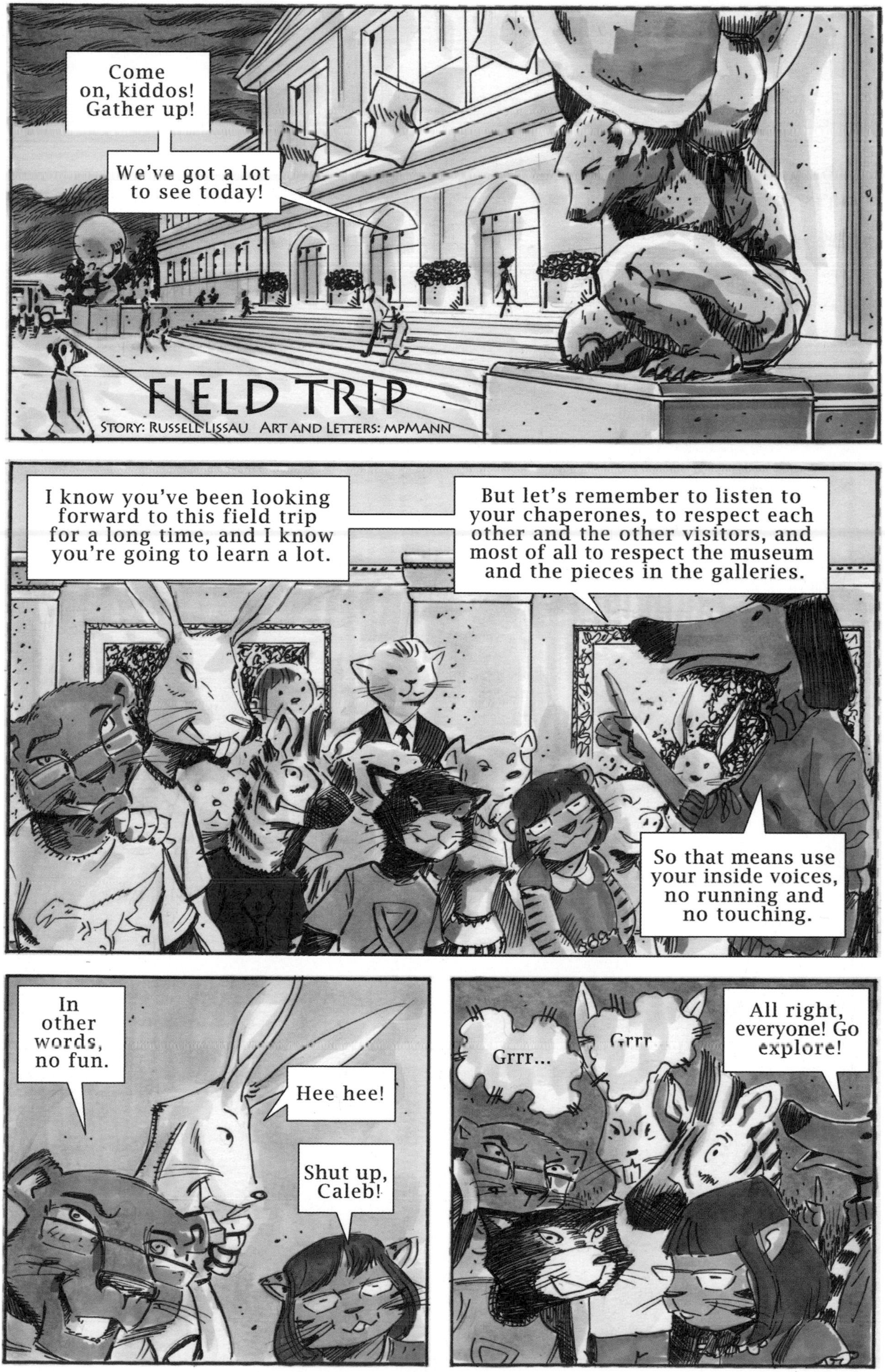
Come on, kiddos! Gather up!
We've got a lot to see today!
FIELD TRIP
Story: Russell Lissau Art and Letters: mpMann
I know you've been looking forward to this field trip for a long time, and I know you're going to learn a lot.
But let's remember to listen to your chaperones, to respect each other and the other visitors, and most of all to respect the museum and the pieces in the galleries.
So that means use your inside voices, no running and no touching.
In other words, no fun.
Hee hee!
Shut up, Caleb!
Grrr...
Grrr
All right, everyone! Go explore!

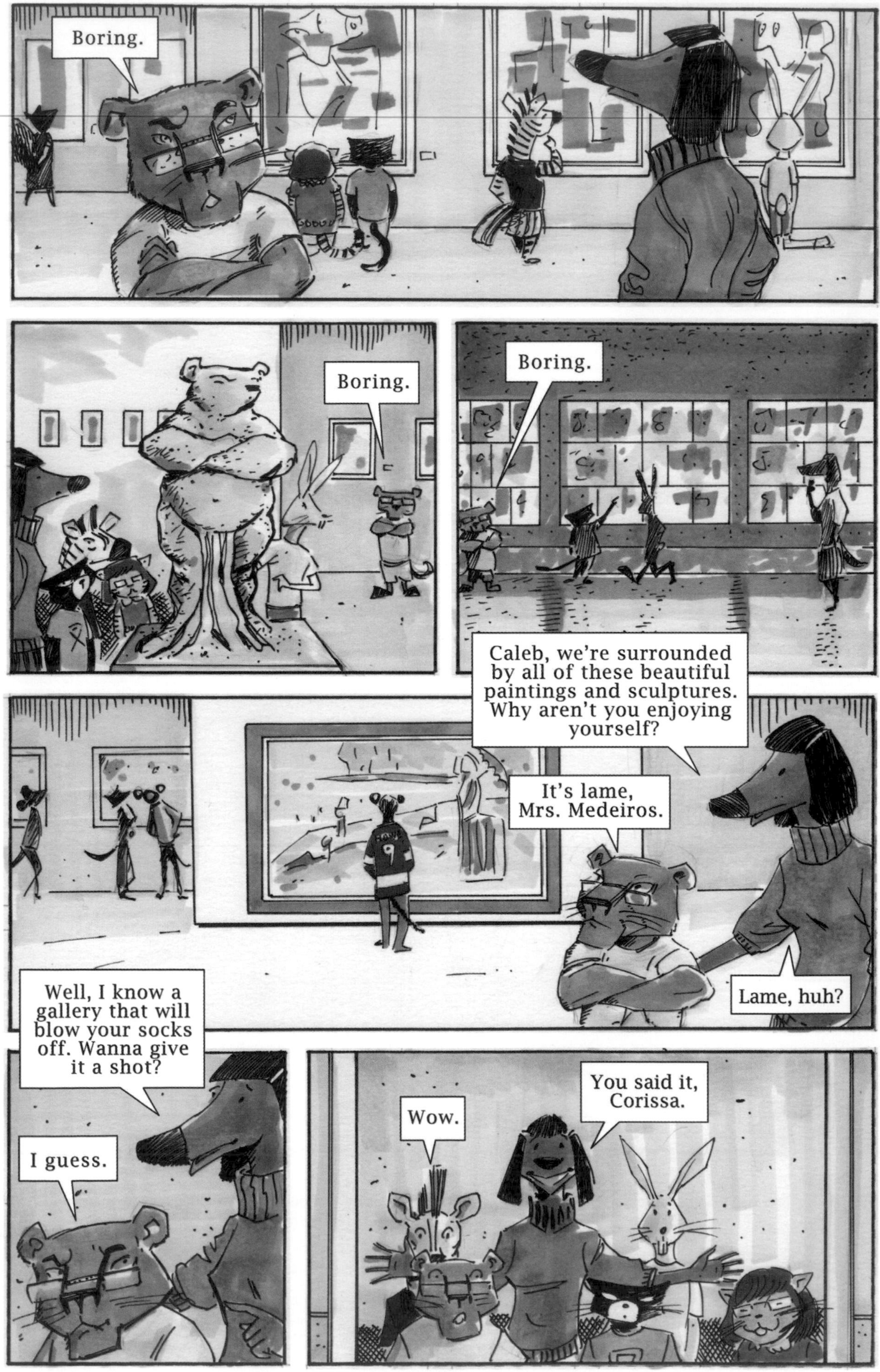
Boring.
Boring.
Boring.
Caleb, we're surrounded by all of these beautiful paintings and sculptures. Why aren't you enjoying yourself?
It's lame, Mrs. Medeiros.
Lame, huh?
Well, I know a gallery that will blow your socks off. Wanna give it a shot?
I guess.
Wow.
You said it, Corissa.

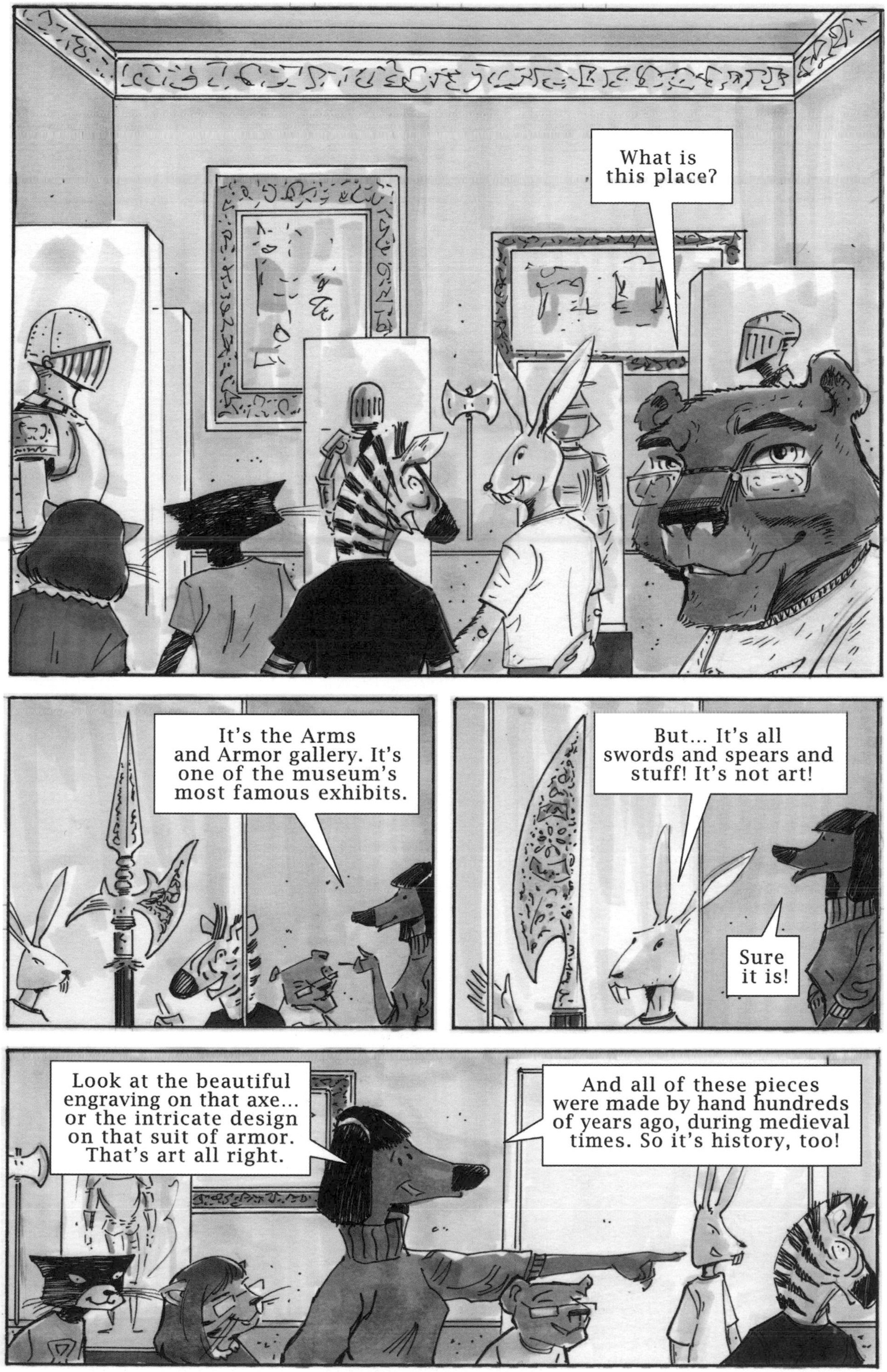
What is this place?
It's the Arms and Armor gallery. It's one of the museum's most famous exhibits.
But... It's all swords and spears and stuff! It's not art!
Sure it is!
Look at the beautiful engraving on that axe... or the intricate design on that suit of armor. That's art all right.
And all of these pieces were made by hand hundreds of years ago, during medieval times. So it's history, too!

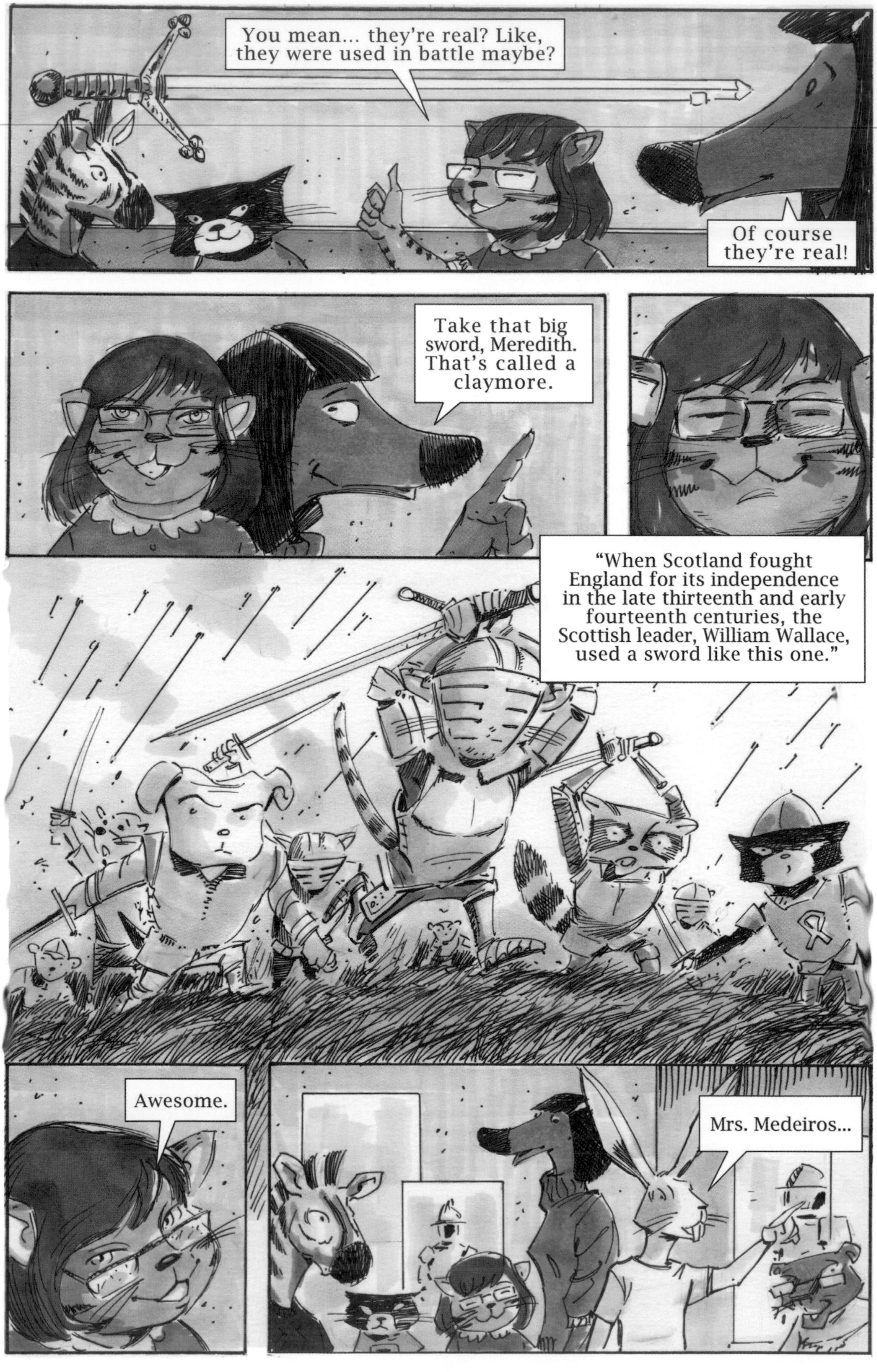

You mean... they're real? Like, they were used in battle maybe?
Of course they're real!
Take that big sword, Meredith. That's called a claymore.
"When Scotland fought England for its independence in the late thirteenth and early fourteenth centuries, the Scottish leader, William Wallace, used a sword like this one."
Awesome.
Mrs. Medeiros...

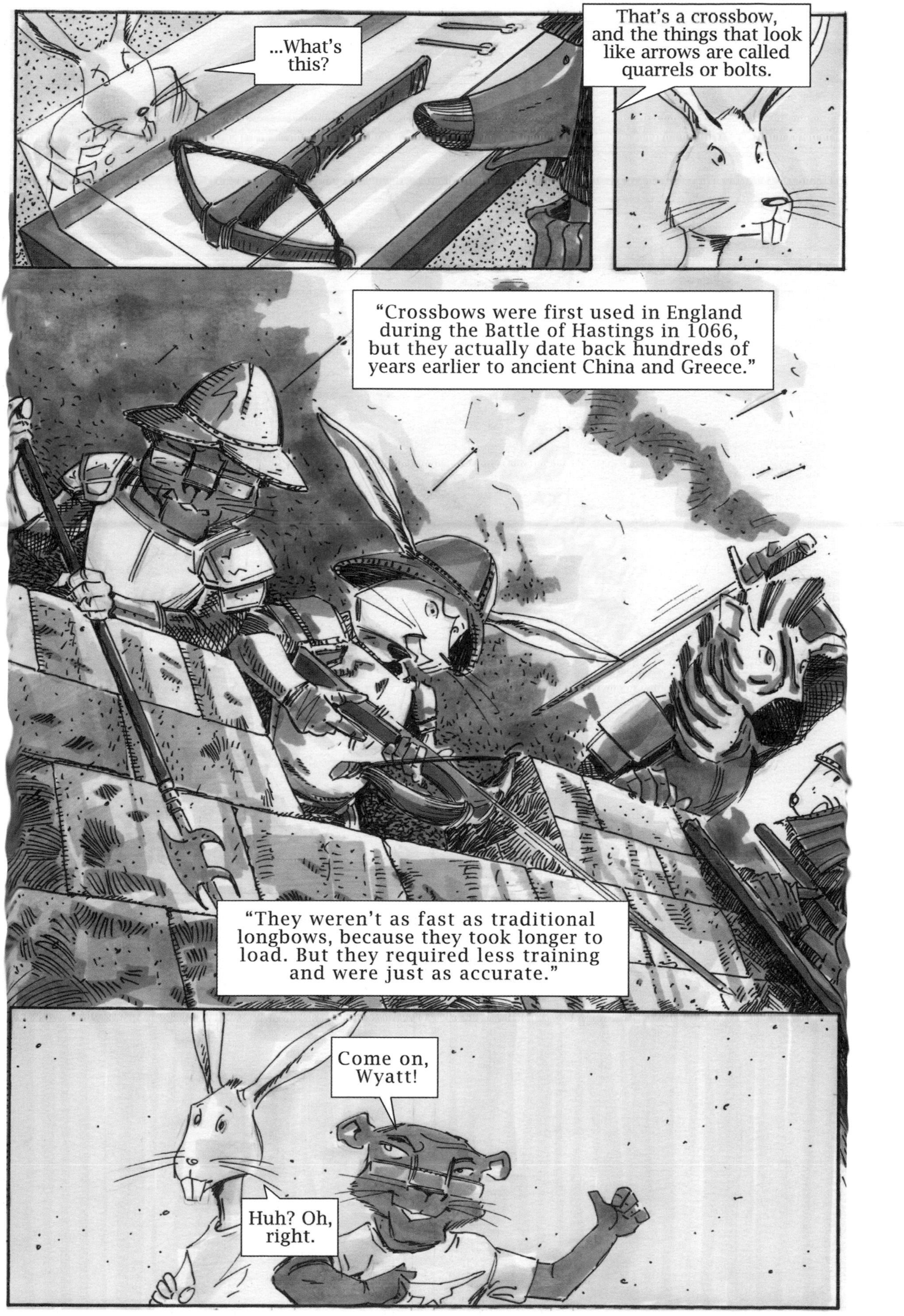
...What's this?
That's a crossbow, and the things that look like arrows are called quarrels or bolts.
"Crossbows were first used in England during the Battle of Hastings in 1066, but they actually date back hundreds of years earlier to ancient China and Greece."
"They weren't as fast as traditional longbows, because they took longer to load. But they required less training and were just as accurate."
Come on, Wyatt!
Huh? Oh, right.

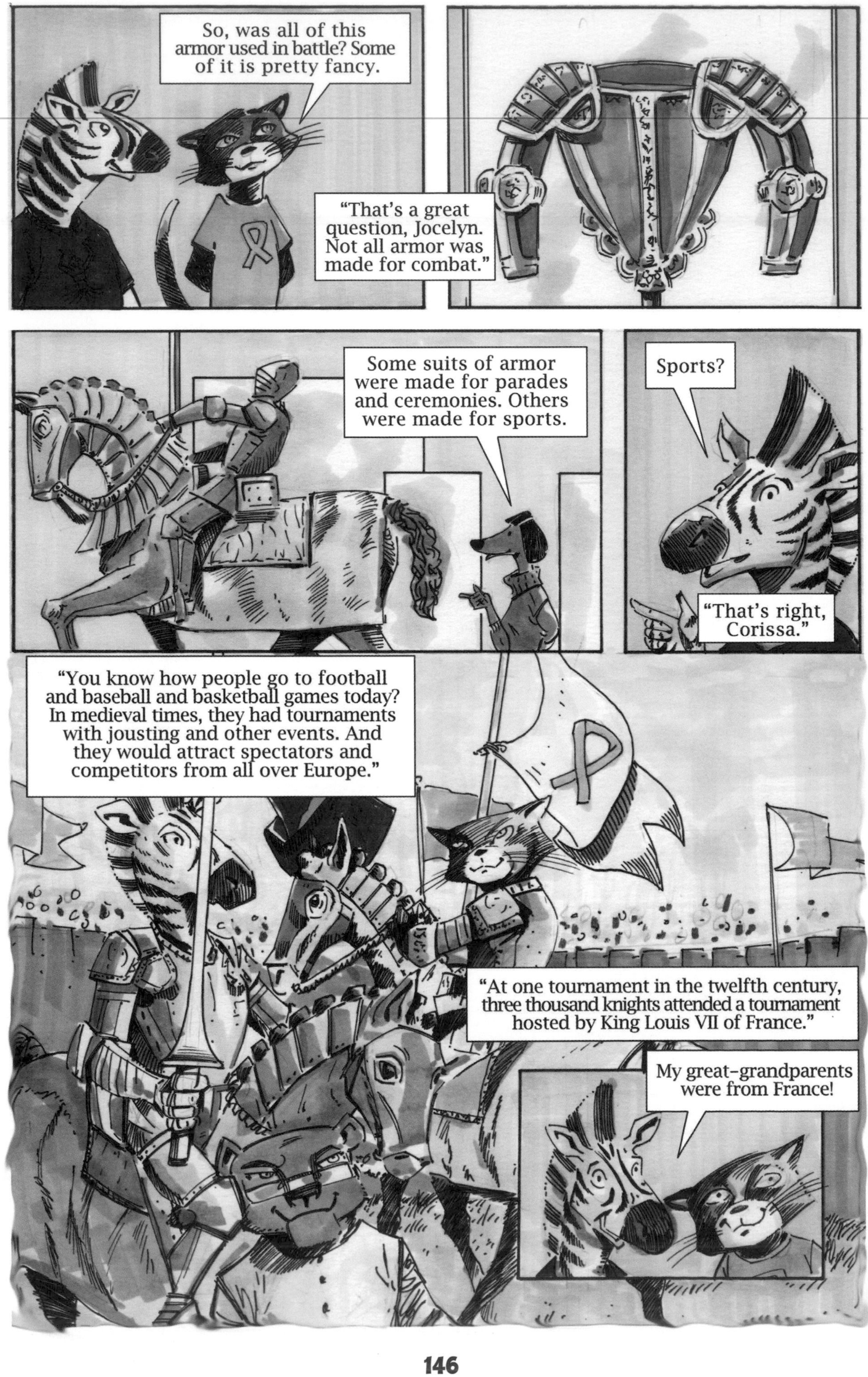
So, was all of this armor used in battle? Some of it is pretty fancy.
"That's a great question, Jocelyn. Not all armor was made for combat."
Some suits of armor were made for parades and ceremonies. Others were made for sports.
Sports?
"That's right, Corissa."
"You know how people go to football and baseball and basketball games today? In medieval times, they had tournaments with jousting and other events. And they would attract spectators and competitors from all over Europe."
"At one tournament in the twelfth century, three thousand knights attended a tournament hosted by King Louis VII of France."
My great-grandparents were from France!

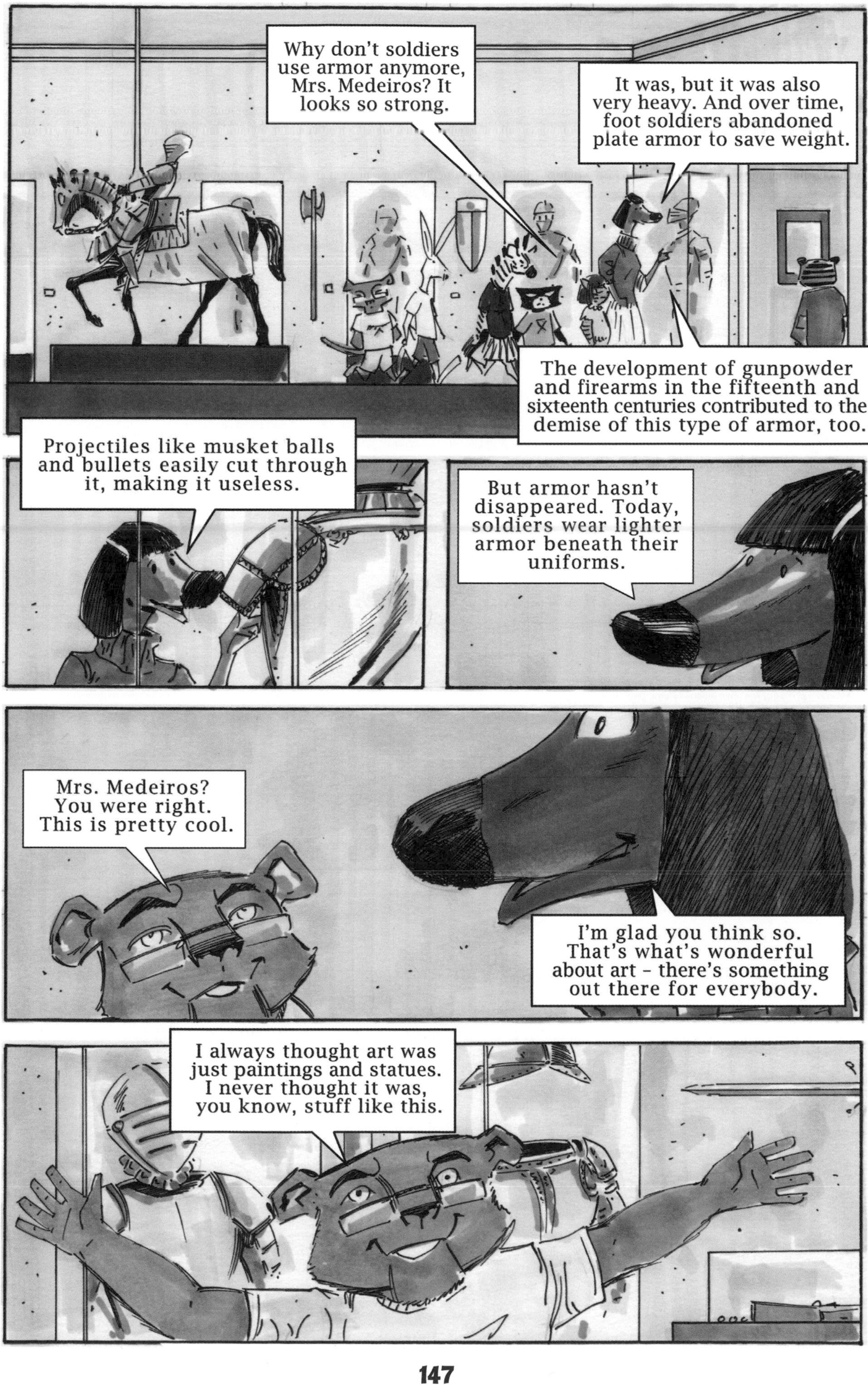

Why don't soldiers use armor anymore, Mrs. Medeiros? It looks so strong.
It was, but it was also very heavy. And over time, foot soldiers abandoned plate armor to save weight.
The development of gunpowder and firearms in the fifteenth and sixteenth centuries contributed to the demise of this type of armor, too.
Projectiles like musket balls and bullets easily cut through it, making it useless.
But armor hasn't disappeared. Today, soldiers wear lighter armor beneath their uniforms.
Mrs. Medeiros? You were right. This is pretty cool.
I'm glad you think so. That's what's wonderful about art – there's something out there for everybody.
I always thought art was just paintings and statues. I never thought it was, you know, stuff like this.

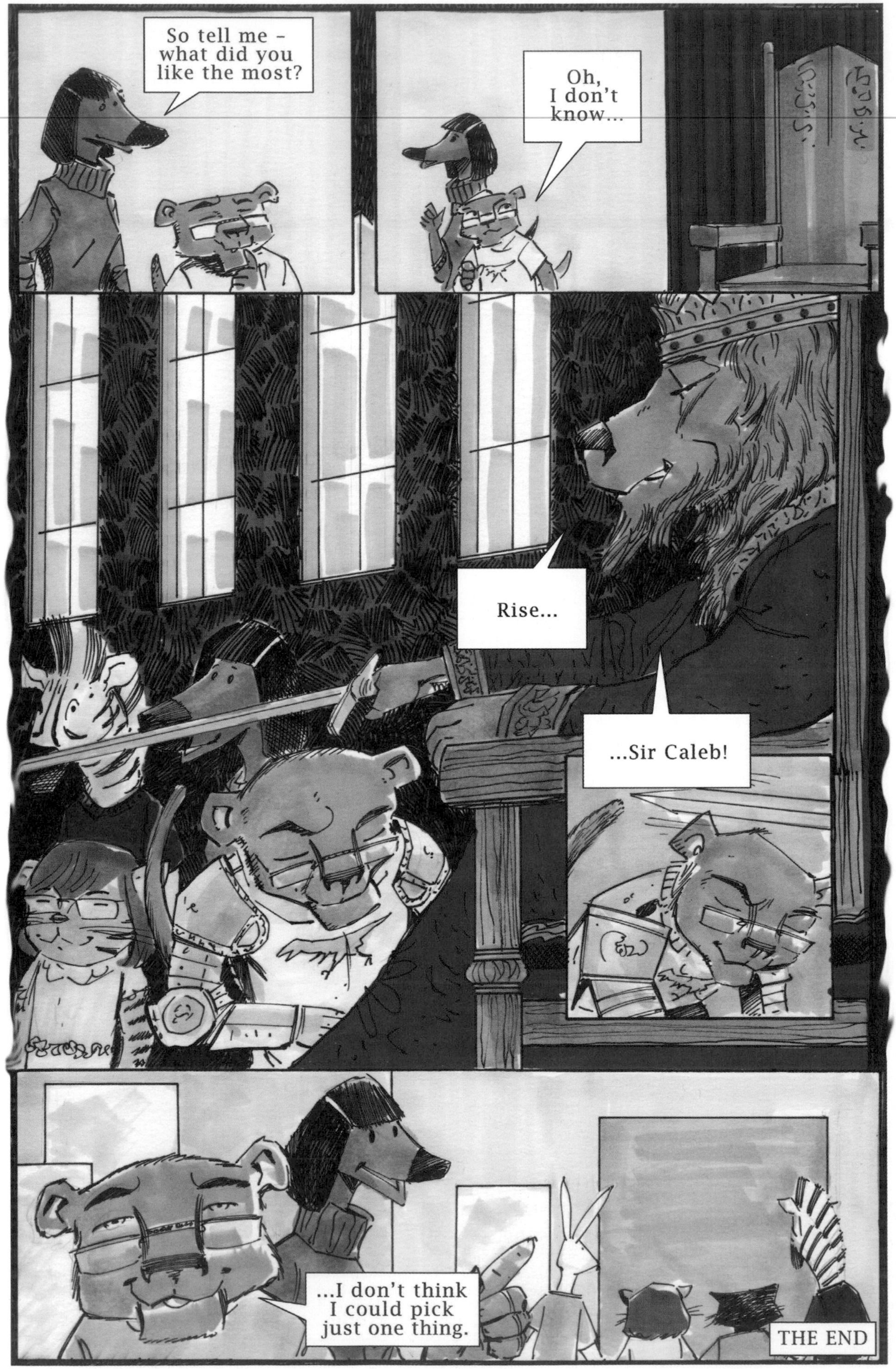
So tell me – what did you like the most?
Oh, I don't know...
Rise...
...Sir Caleb!
...I don't think I could pick just one thing.
THE END

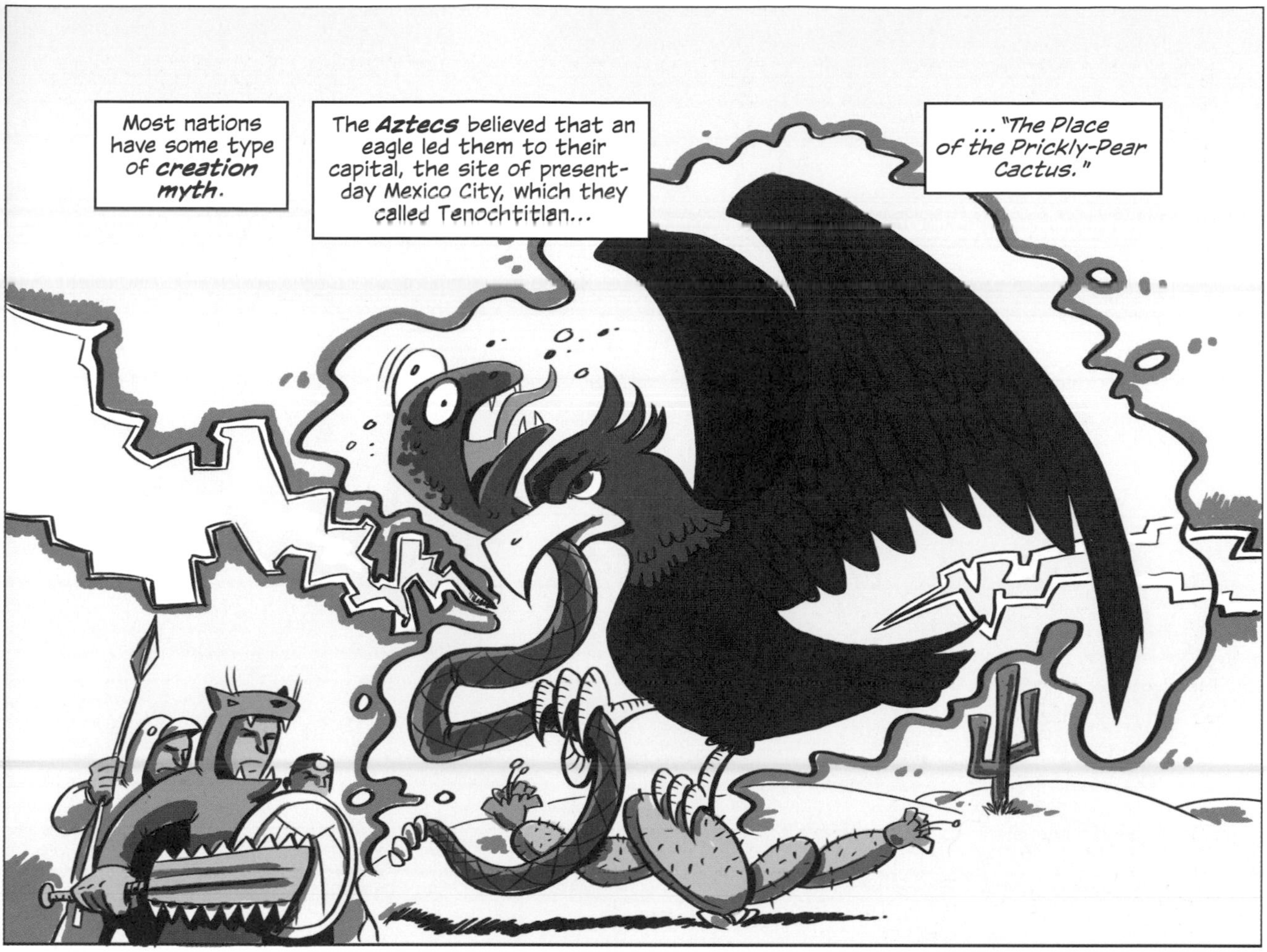
Most nations have some type of **creation myth**.
The **Aztecs** believed that an eagle led them to their capital, the site of present-day Mexico City, which they called Tenochtitlan...
..."*The Place of the Prickly-Pear Cactus.*"

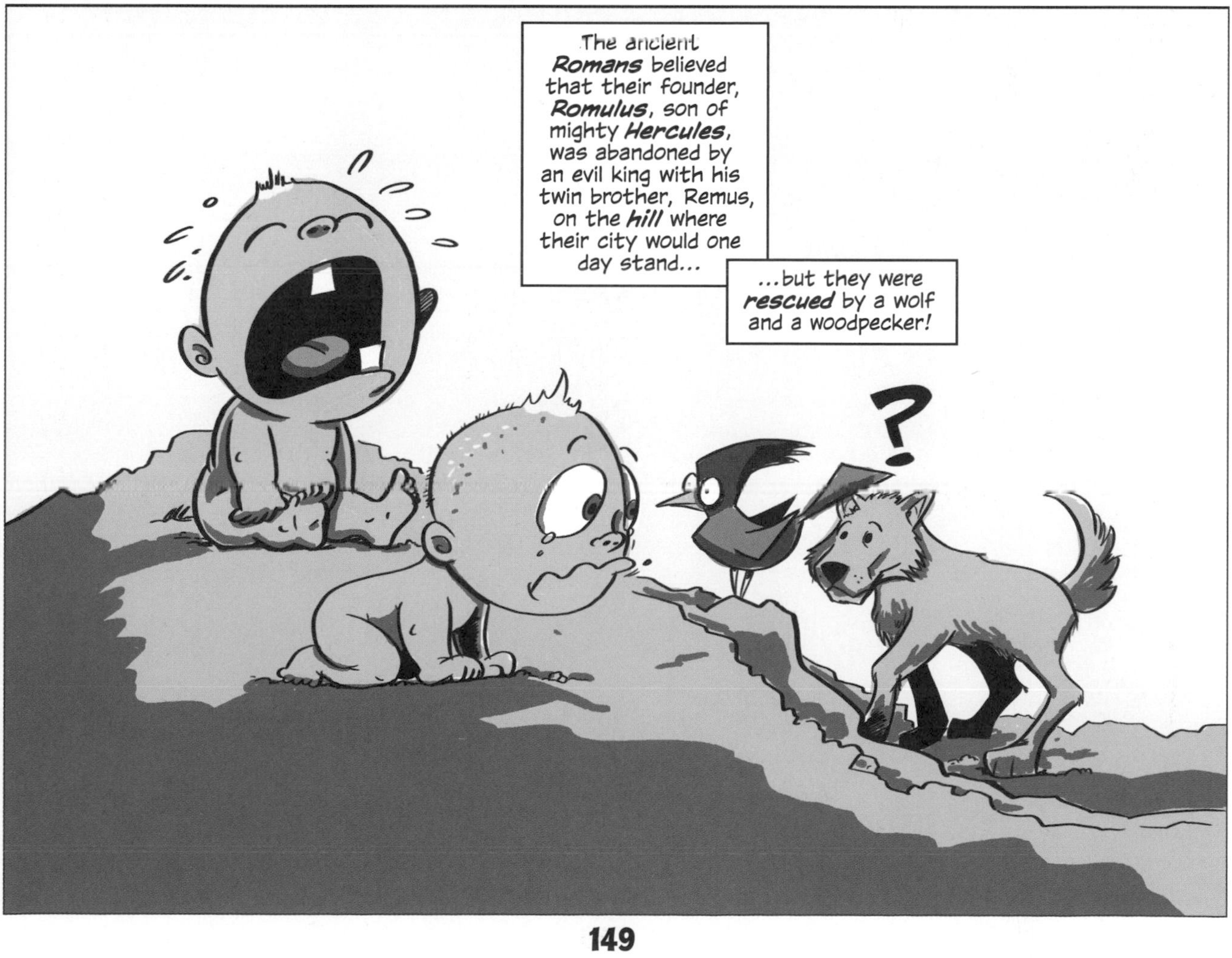
The ancient **Romans** believed that their founder, **Romulus**, son of mighty **Hercules**, was abandoned by an evil king with his twin brother, Remus, on the **hill** where their city would one day stand...
...but they were **rescued** by a wolf and a woodpecker!
?

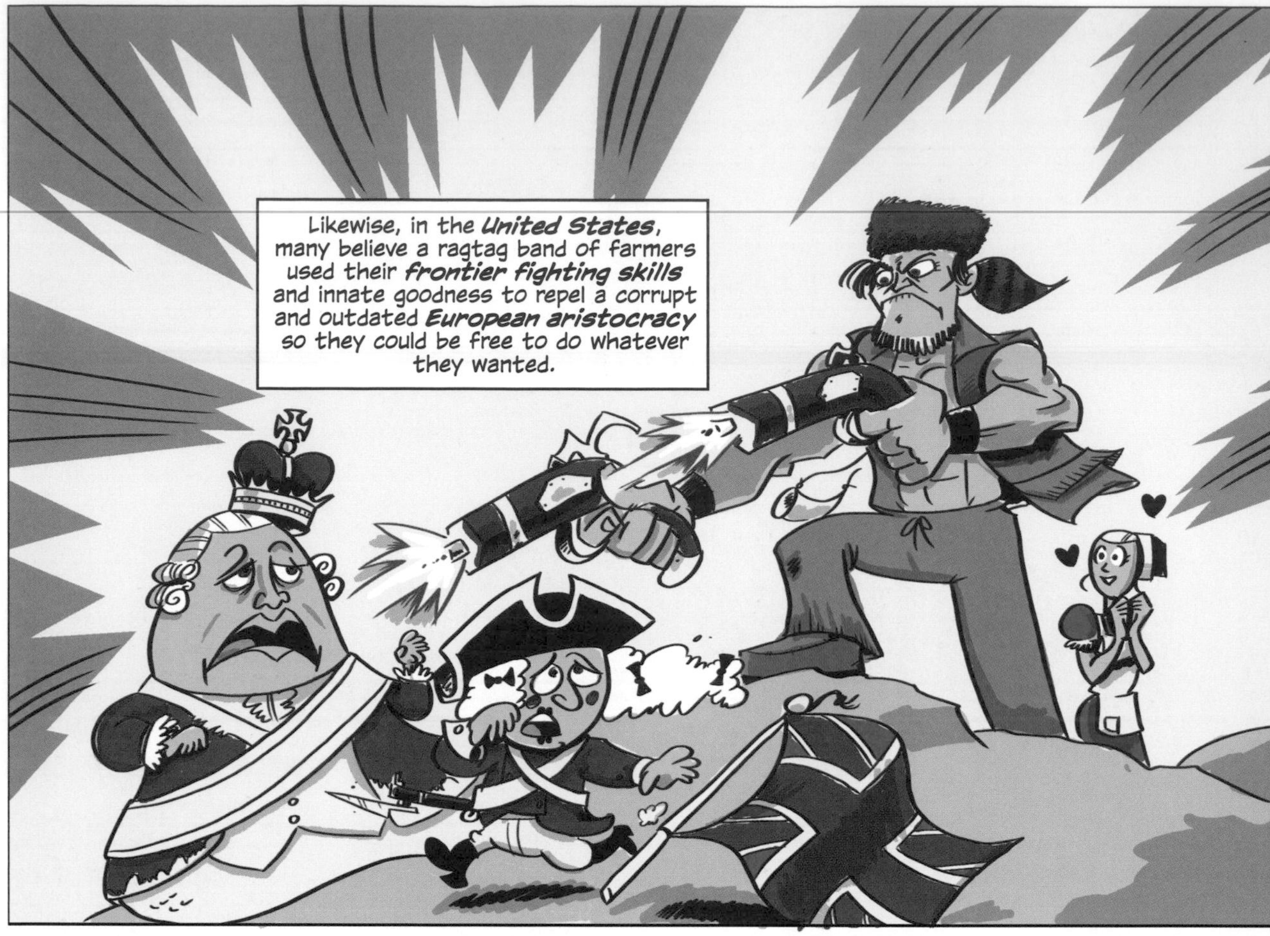
Likewise, in the United States, many believe a ragtag band of farmers used their frontier fighting skills and innate goodness to repel a corrupt and outdated European aristocracy so they could be free to do whatever they wanted.

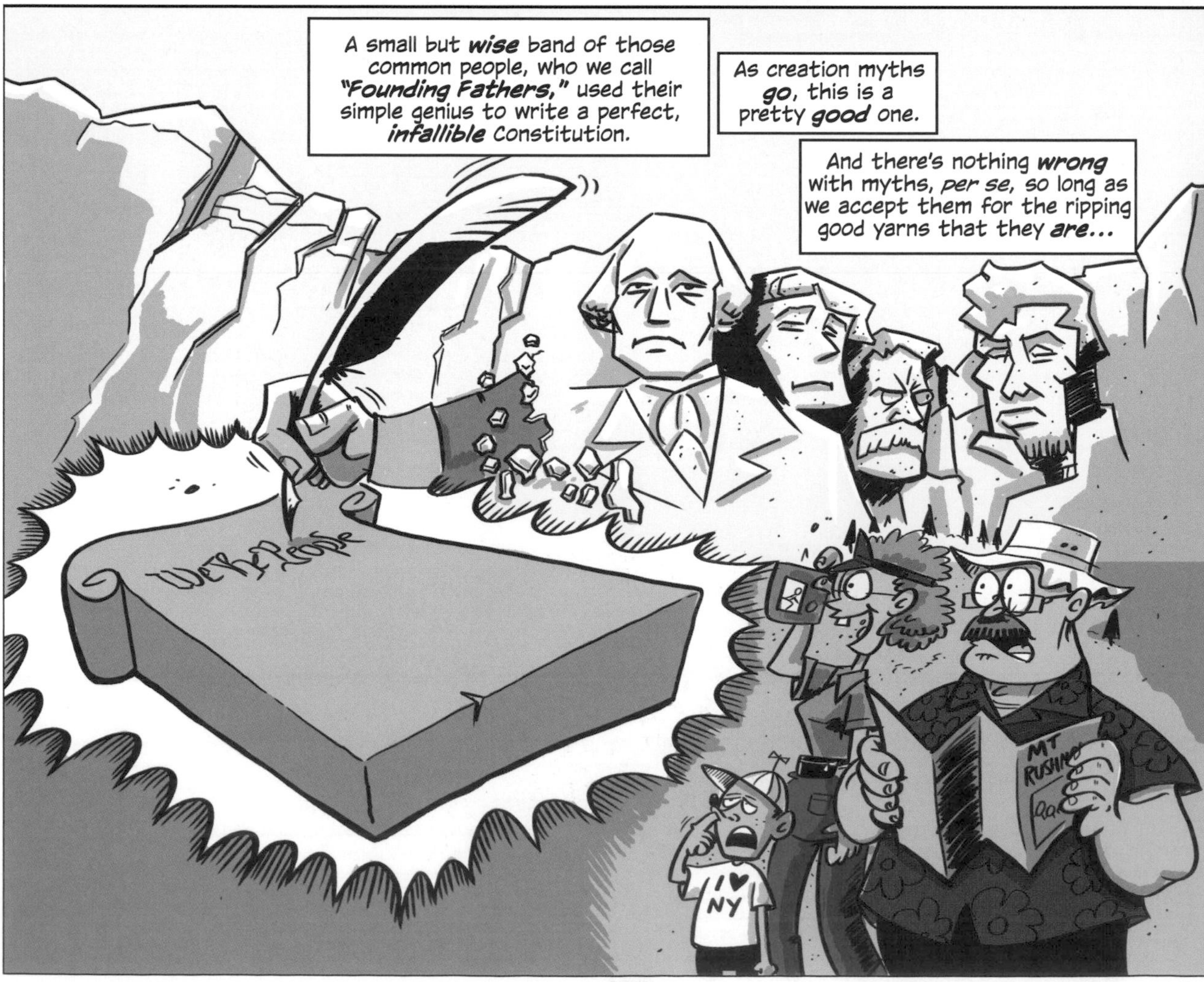
A small but wise band of those common people, who we call "Founding Fathers," used their simple genius to write a perfect, infallible Constitution.
As creation myths go, this is a pretty good one.
And there's nothing wrong with myths, per se, so long as we accept them for the ripping good yarns that they are...
MT RUSHMO
I ♥ NY

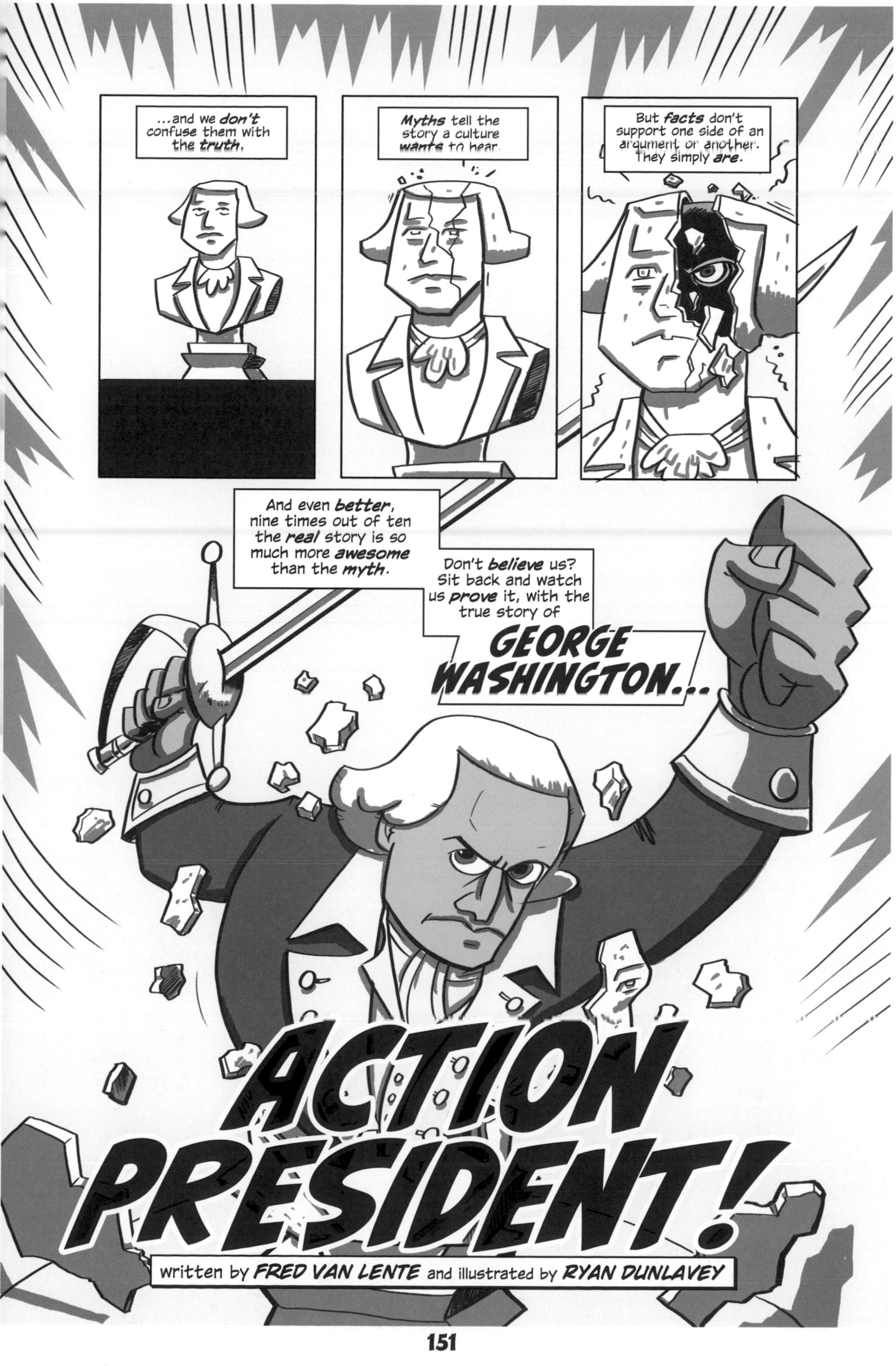

...and we don't confuse them with the truth.
Myths tell the story a culture wants to hear.
But facts don't support one side of an argument or another. They simply are.
And even better, nine times out of ten the real story is so much more awesome than the myth.
Don't believe us? Sit back and watch us prove it, with the true story of
GEORGE WASHINGTON...
ACTION PRESIDENT!
written by FRED VAN LENTE and illustrated by RYAN DUNLAVEY

The first thing you need to know about George was that *"common people"* he *ain't*.

In fact, he was as close as America gets to *royalty*.

He was born in 1732 to one of the tight-knit families of the *"Northern Neck"* of Virginia...

...whose vast tracts of land had been granted by King Charles II to those who stayed loyal to the Crown during the bloody *English Civil War* (1642-1651).

Despite his vast wealth, however, George grew accustomed to *loss* at an early age.

George's father died when he was eleven; his oldest brother *Lawrence* became a father figure to him, but *he* died before George turned 21.

He was expected to marry a fellow *Northern Necker*, which he did: Martha Custiss, in 1759.

By combining her lands with his inheritances, he became one of the *richest men* in the thirteen American colonies.

He also became one of Virginia's largest *slaveholders*, owning hundreds of men, women and children, who worked his estates.

A lot of people are puzzled by the fact that America was founded by, as comedian George Carlin put it, ***"slave owners** who wanted to be **free**."*

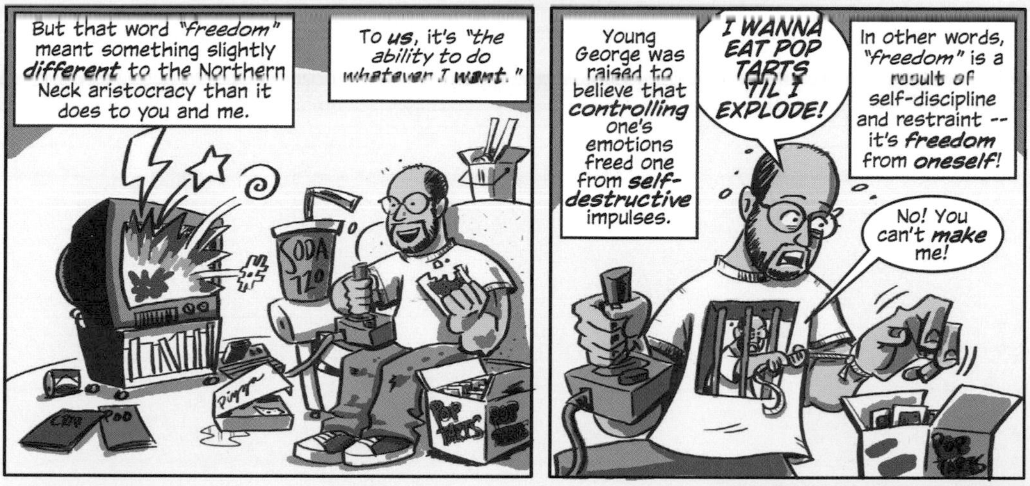
But that word *"freedom"* meant something slightly ***different*** to the Northern Neck aristocracy than it does to you and me.
To ***us***, it's *"the ability to do whatever I want."*
SODA 72 OZ
Pizza
POP TARTS
Young George was raised to believe that ***controlling*** one's emotions freed one from ***self-destructive*** impulses.
I WANNA EAT POP TARTS TIL I EXPLODE!
In other words, *"freedom"* is a result of self-discipline and restraint -- it's ***freedom*** from ***oneself***!
No! You can't ***make*** me!

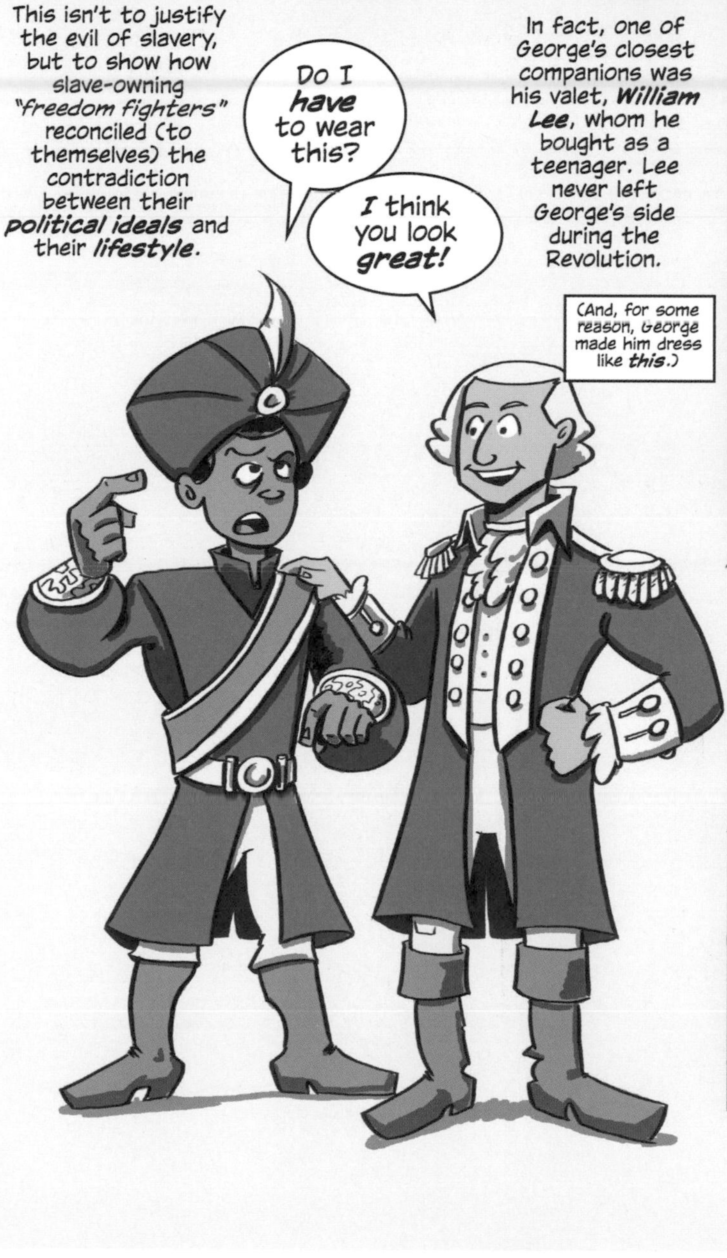
This isn't to justify the evil of slavery, but to show how slave-owning *"freedom fighters"* reconciled (to themselves) the contradiction between their ***political ideals*** and their ***lifestyle***.
Do I ***have*** to wear this?
I think you look ***great!***
In fact, one of George's closest companions was his valet, ***William Lee***, whom he bought as a teenager. Lee never left George's side during the Revolution.
(And, for some reason, George made him dress like ***this***.)

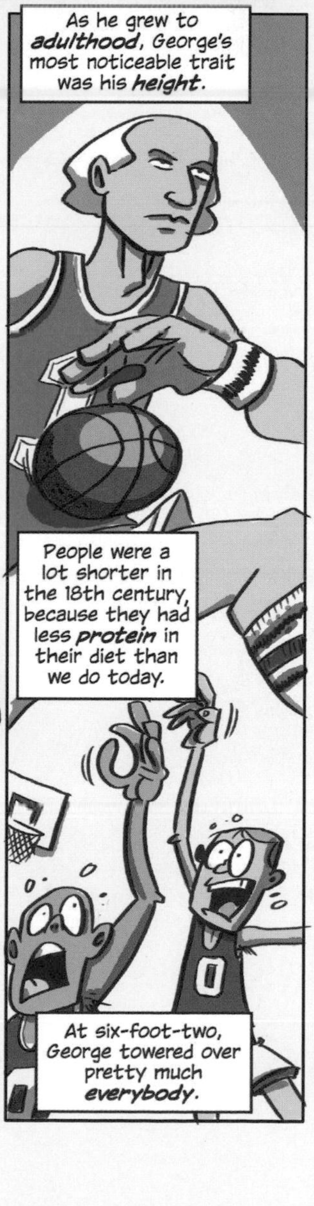
As he grew to ***adulthood***, George's most noticeable trait was his ***height***.
People were a lot shorter in the 18th century, because they had less ***protein*** in their diet than we do today.
At six-foot-two, George towered over pretty much ***everybody***.

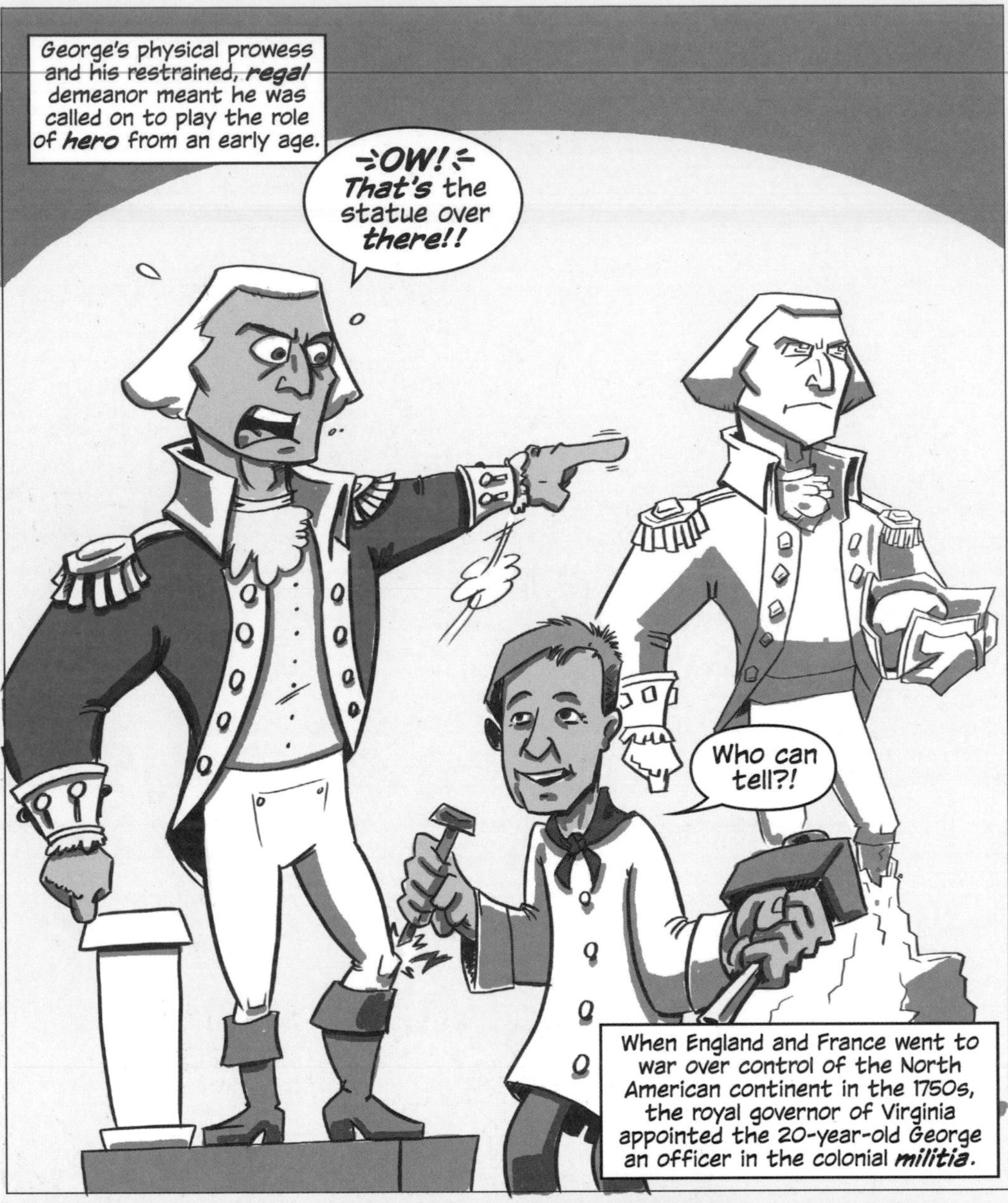
George's physical prowess and his restrained, *regal* demeanor meant he was called on to play the role of *hero* from an early age.
OW! *That's* the statue over *there!!*
Who can tell?!
When England and France went to war over control of the North American continent in the 1750s, the royal governor of Virginia appointed the 20-year-old George an officer in the colonial *militia*.

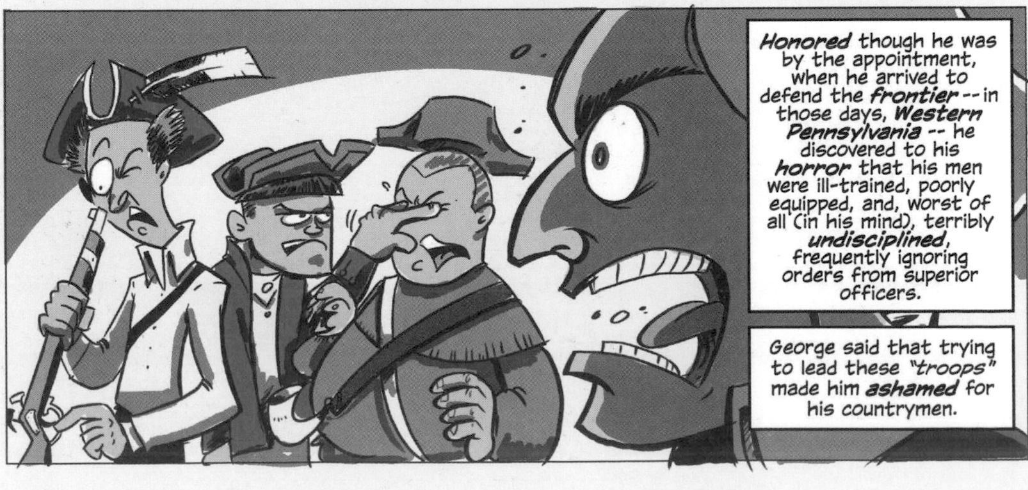
Honored though he was by the appointment, when he arrived to defend the *frontier* -- in those days, *Western Pennsylvania* -- he discovered to his *horror* that his men were ill-trained, poorly equipped, and, worst of all (in his mind), terribly *undisciplined*, frequently ignoring orders from superior officers.
George said that trying to lead these *"troops"* made him *ashamed* for his countrymen.

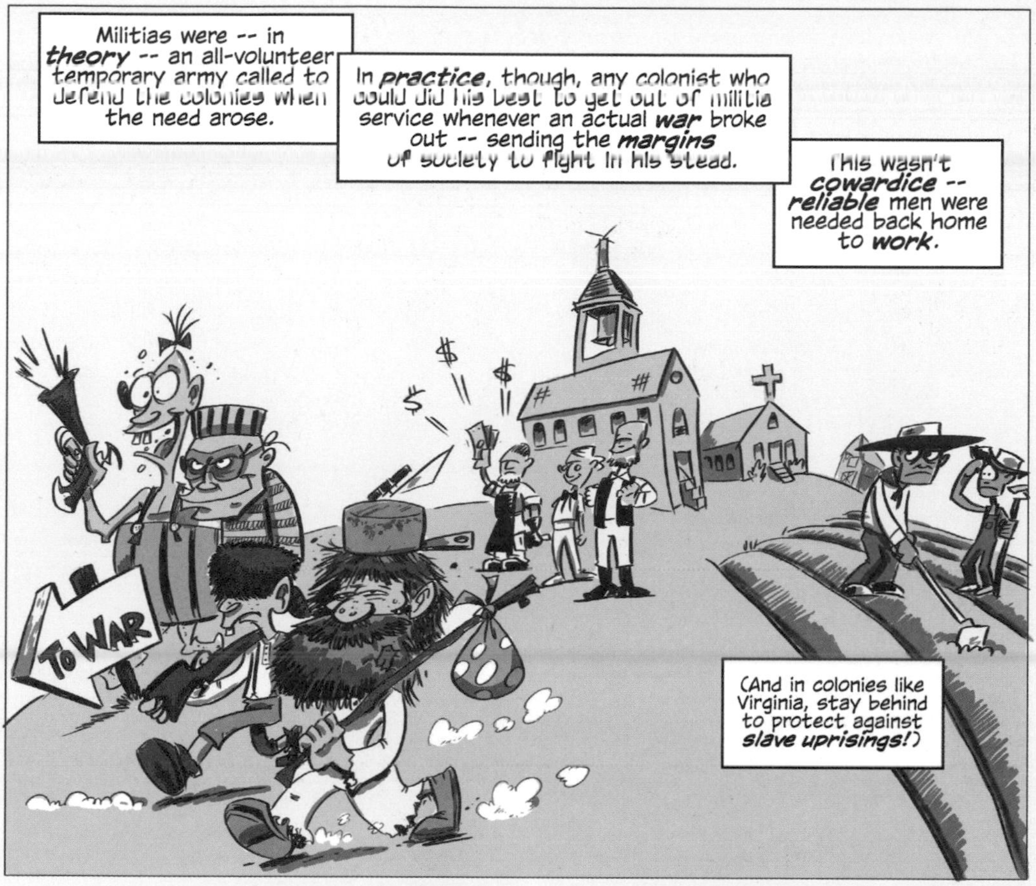
Militias were -- in *theory* -- an all-volunteer temporary army called to defend the colonies when the need arose.
In *practice*, though, any colonist who could did his best to get out of militia service whenever an actual *war* broke out -- sending the *margins* of society to fight in his stead.
This wasn't *cowardice* -- *reliable* men were needed back home to *work*.
TO WAR
(And in colonies like Virginia, stay behind to protect against *slave uprisings!*)

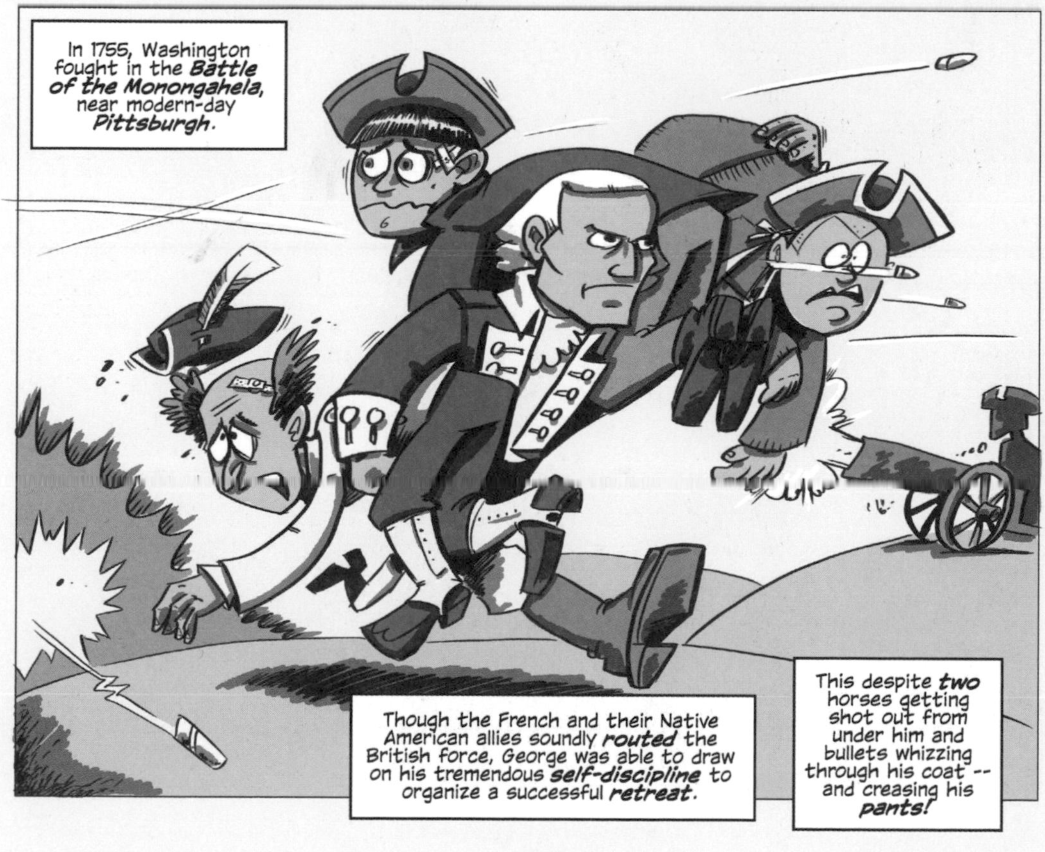
In 1755, Washington fought in the *Battle of the Monongahela*, near modern-day *Pittsburgh*.
Though the French and their Native American allies soundly *routed* the British force, George was able to draw on his tremendous *self-discipline* to organize a successful *retreat*.
This despite *two* horses getting shot out from under him and bullets whizzing through his coat -- and creasing his *pants!*

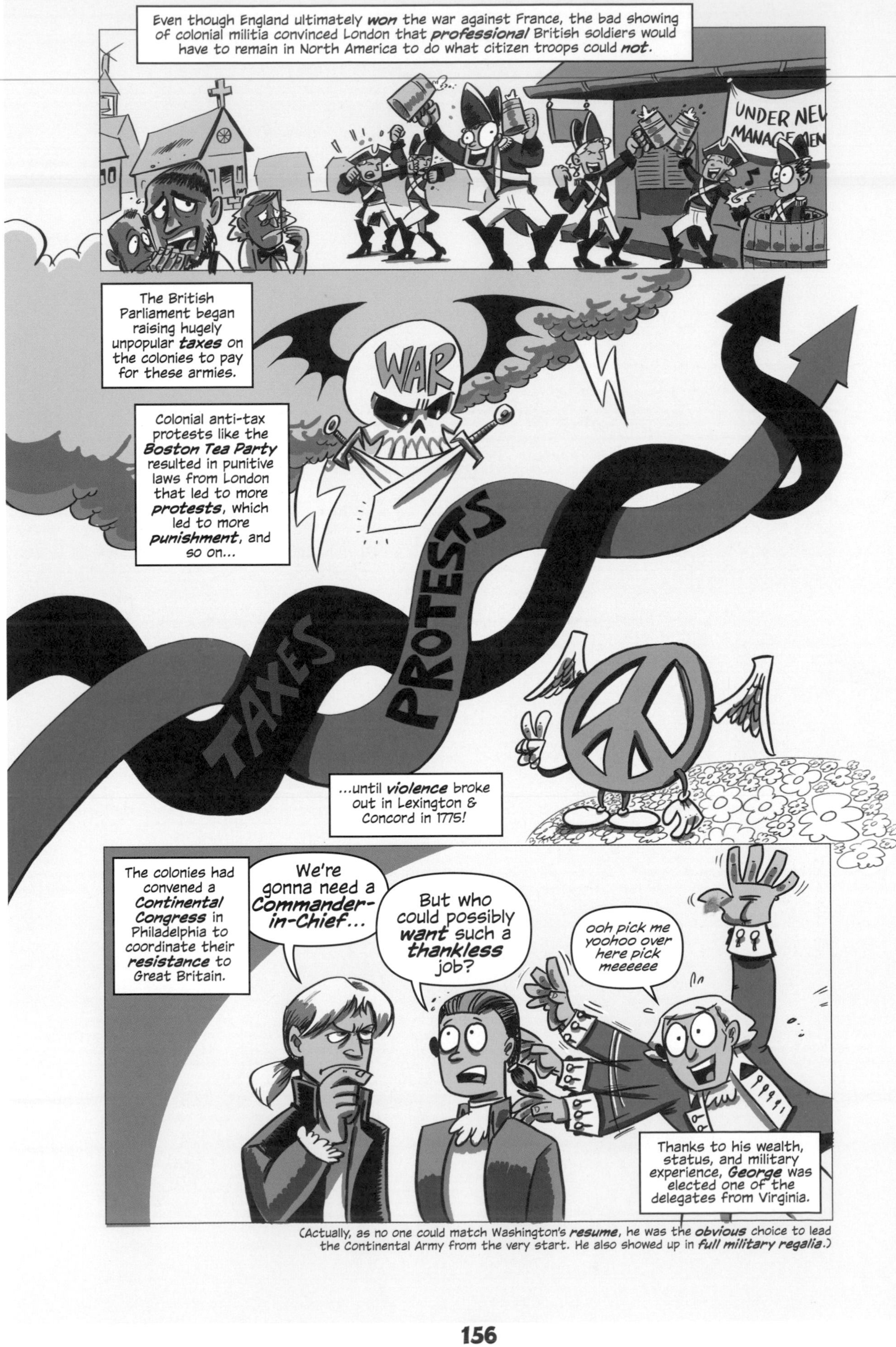
Even though England ultimately won the war against France, the bad showing of colonial militia convinced London that professional British soldiers would have to remain in North America to do what citizen troops could not.
UNDER NEW MANAGEMEN
The British Parliament began raising hugely unpopular taxes on the colonies to pay for these armies.
WAR
Colonial anti-tax protests like the Boston Tea Party resulted in punitive laws from London that led to more protests, which led to more punishment, and so on...
TAXES
PROTESTS
...until violence broke out in Lexington & Concord in 1775!
The colonies had convened a Continental Congress in Philadelphia to coordinate their resistance to Great Britain.
We're gonna need a Commander-in-Chief...
But who could possibly want such a thankless job?
ooh pick me yoohoo over here pick meeeeee
Thanks to his wealth, status, and military experience, George was elected one of the delegates from Virginia.
(Actually, as no one could match Washington's resume, he was the obvious choice to lead the Continental Army from the very start. He also showed up in full military regalia.)

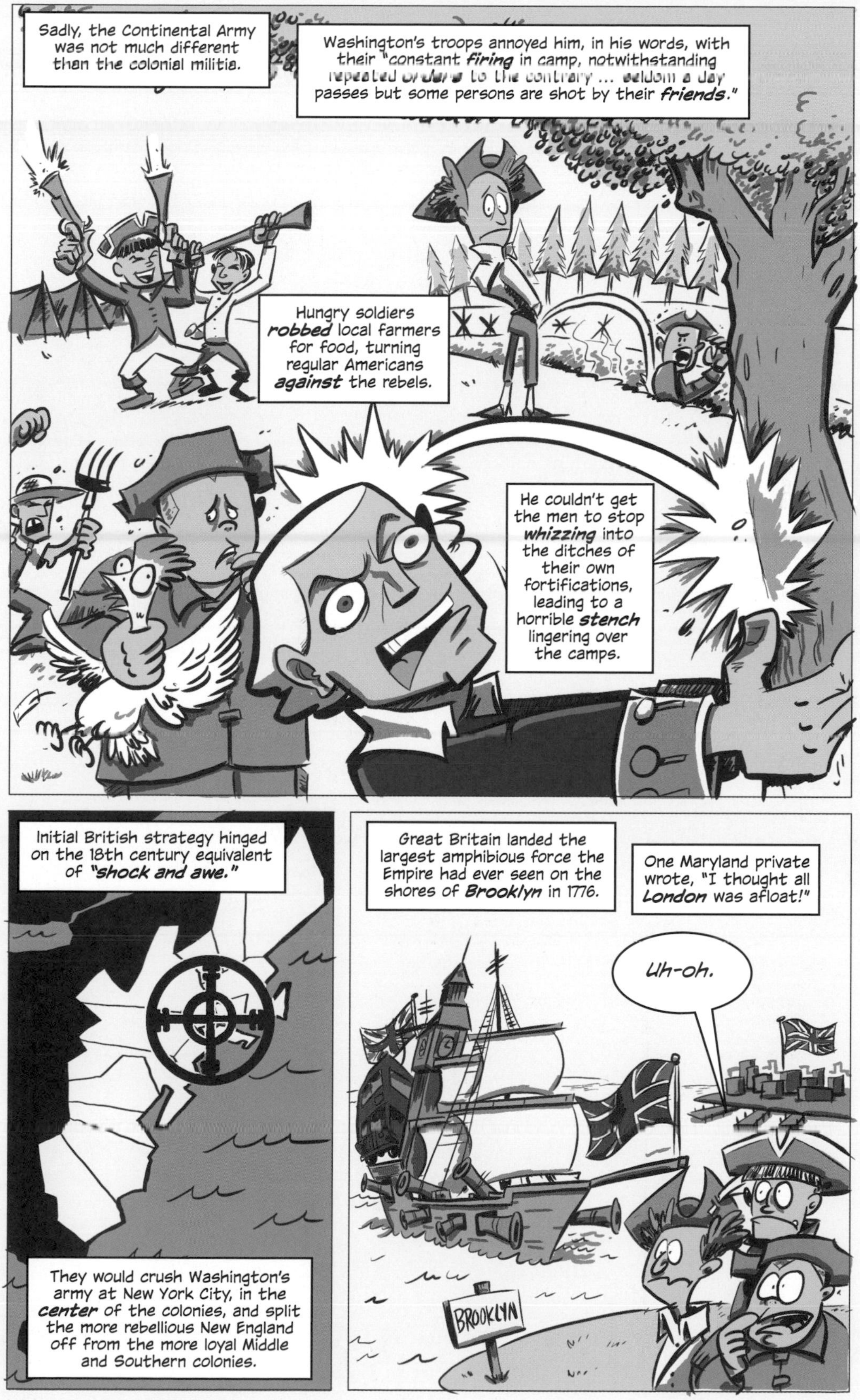

Sadly, the Continental Army was not much different than the colonial militia.
Washington's troops annoyed him, in his words, with their "constant ***firing*** in camp, notwithstanding repeated orders to the contrary ... seldom a day passes but some persons are shot by their ***friends***."
Hungry soldiers ***robbed*** local farmers for food, turning regular Americans ***against*** the rebels.
He couldn't get the men to stop ***whizzing*** into the ditches of their own fortifications, leading to a horrible ***stench*** lingering over the camps.
Initial British strategy hinged on the 18th century equivalent of ***"shock and awe."***
They would crush Washington's army at New York City, in the ***center*** of the colonies, and split the more rebellious New England off from the more loyal Middle and Southern colonies.
Great Britain landed the largest amphibious force the Empire had ever seen on the shores of ***Brooklyn*** in 1776.
One Maryland private wrote, "I thought all ***London*** was afloat!"
Uh-oh.
BROOKLYN

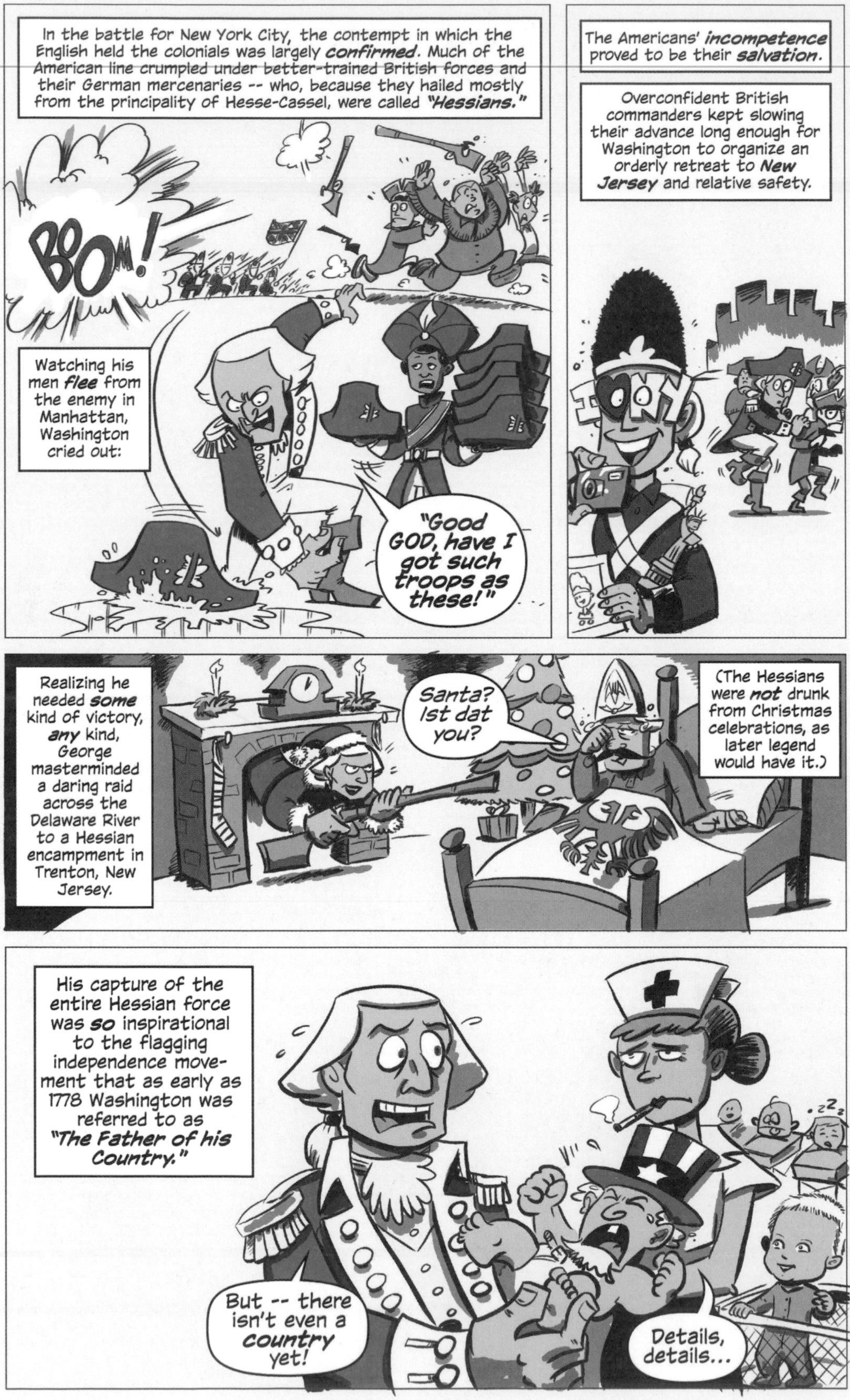
In the battle for New York City, the contempt in which the English held the colonials was largely *confirmed*. Much of the American line crumpled under better-trained British forces and their German mercenaries -- who, because they hailed mostly from the principality of Hesse-Cassel, were called *"Hessians."*
BOOM!
Watching his men *flee* from the enemy in Manhattan, Washington cried out:
"Good GOD, have I got such troops as these!"
The Americans' *incompetence* proved to be their *salvation*.
Overconfident British commanders kept slowing their advance long enough for Washington to organize an orderly retreat to *New Jersey* and relative safety.
Realizing he needed *some* kind of victory, *any* kind, George masterminded a daring raid across the Delaware River to a Hessian encampment in Trenton, New Jersey.
Santa? Ist dat you?
(The Hessians were *not* drunk from Christmas celebrations, as later legend would have it.)
His capture of the entire Hessian force was *so* inspirational to the flagging independence movement that as early as 1778 Washington was referred to as *"The Father of his Country."*
But -- there isn't even a *country* yet!
Details, details...

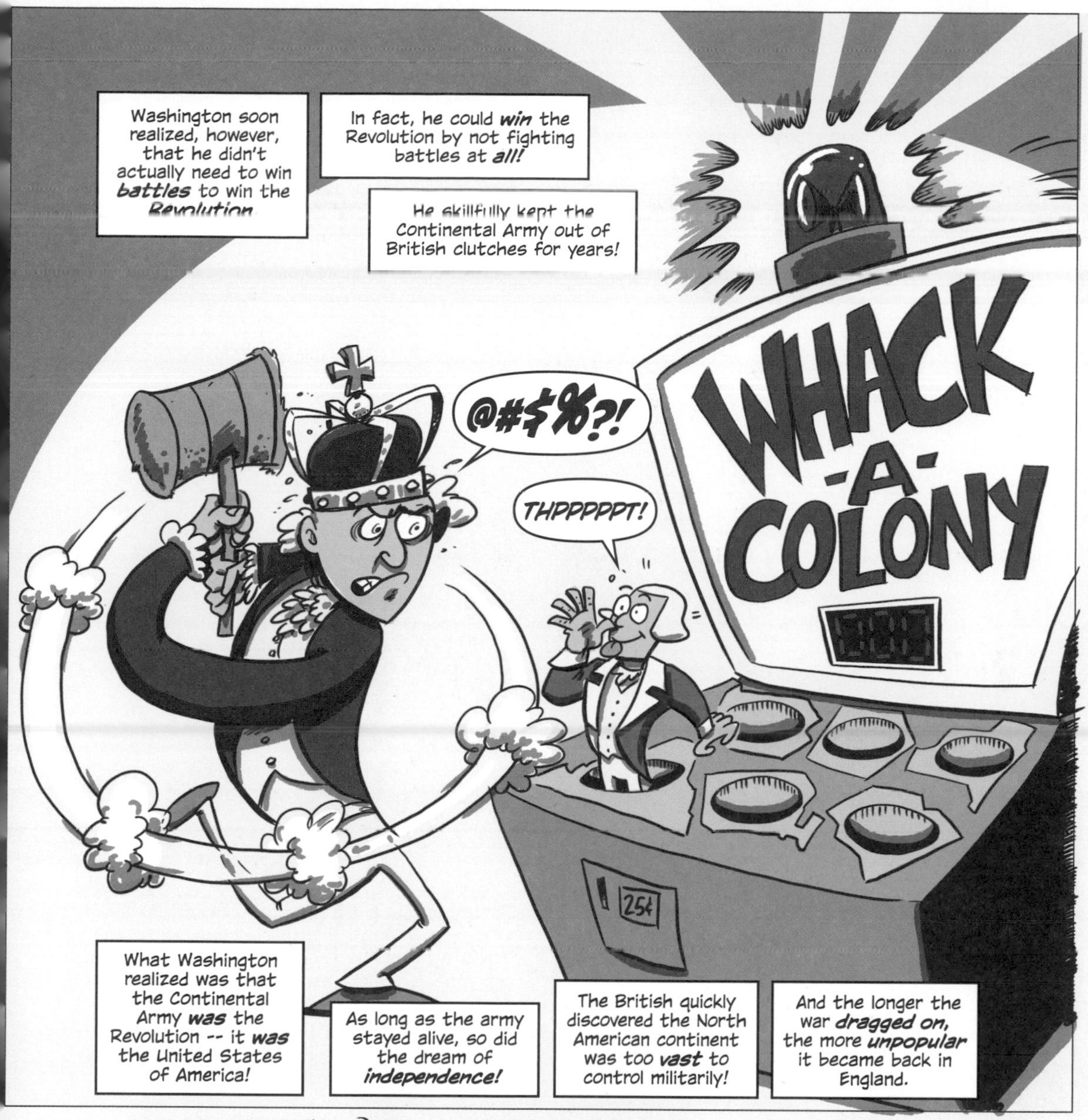
Washington soon realized, however, that he didn't actually need to win *battles* to win the *Revolution*.
In fact, he could *win* the Revolution by not fighting battles at *all!*
He skillfully kept the Continental Army out of British clutches for years!
WHACK -A- COLONY
@#$%?!
THPPPPPT!
25¢
What Washington realized was that the Continental Army *was* the Revolution -- it *was* the United States of America!
As long as the army stayed alive, so did the dream of *independence!*
The British quickly discovered the North American continent was too *vast* to control militarily!
And the longer the war *dragged on*, the more *unpopular* it became back in England.

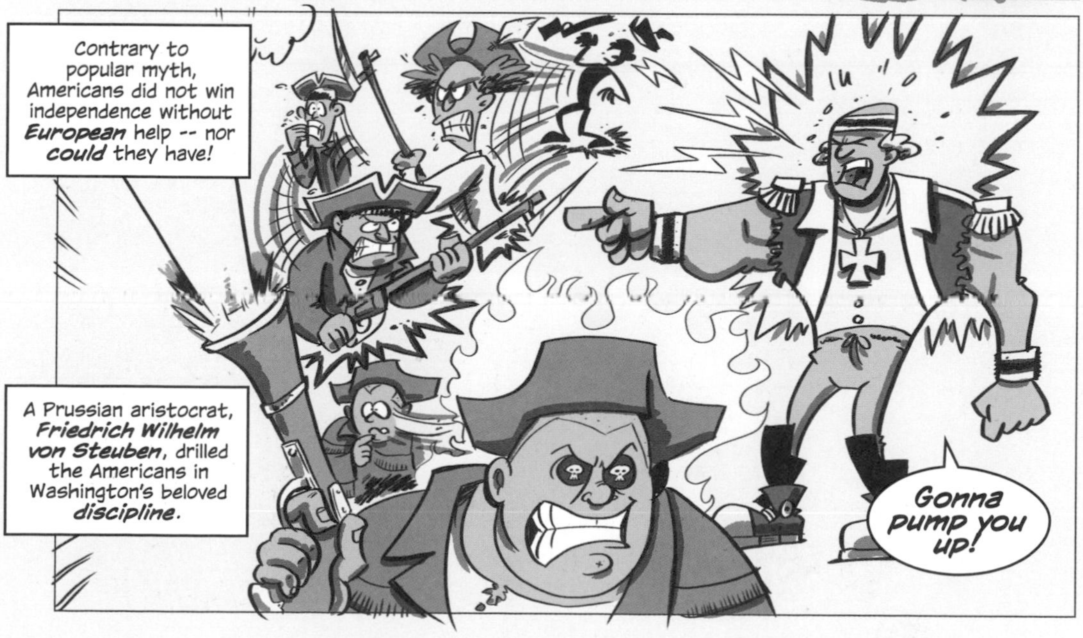
Contrary to popular myth, Americans did not win independence without *European* help -- nor *could* they have!
A Prussian aristocrat, *Friedrich Wilhelm von Steuben*, drilled the Americans in Washington's beloved *discipline*.
Gonna pump you up!

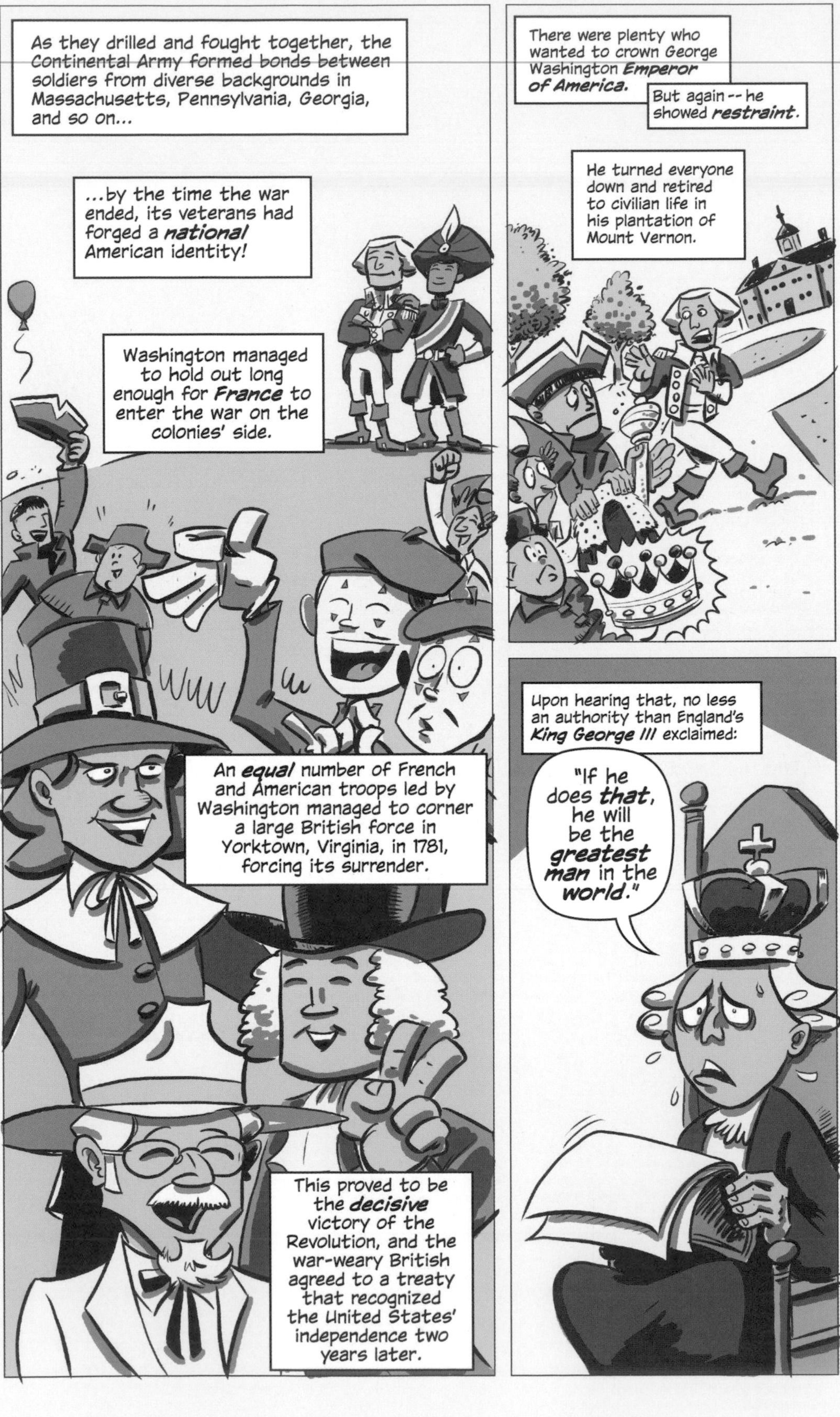

As they drilled and fought together, the Continental Army formed bonds between soldiers from diverse backgrounds in Massachusetts, Pennsylvania, Georgia, and so on...
...by the time the war ended, its veterans had forged a ***national*** American identity!
Washington managed to hold out long enough for ***France*** to enter the war on the colonies' side.
An ***equal*** number of French and American troops led by Washington managed to corner a large British force in Yorktown, Virginia, in 1781, forcing its surrender.
This proved to be the ***decisive*** victory of the Revolution, and the war-weary British agreed to a treaty that recognized the United States' independence two years later.
There were plenty who wanted to crown George Washington ***Emperor of America.***
But again -- he showed ***restraint***.
He turned everyone down and retired to civilian life in his plantation of Mount Vernon.
Upon hearing that, no less an authority than England's ***King George III*** exclaimed:
"If he does ***that***, he will be the ***greatest man*** in the ***world***."

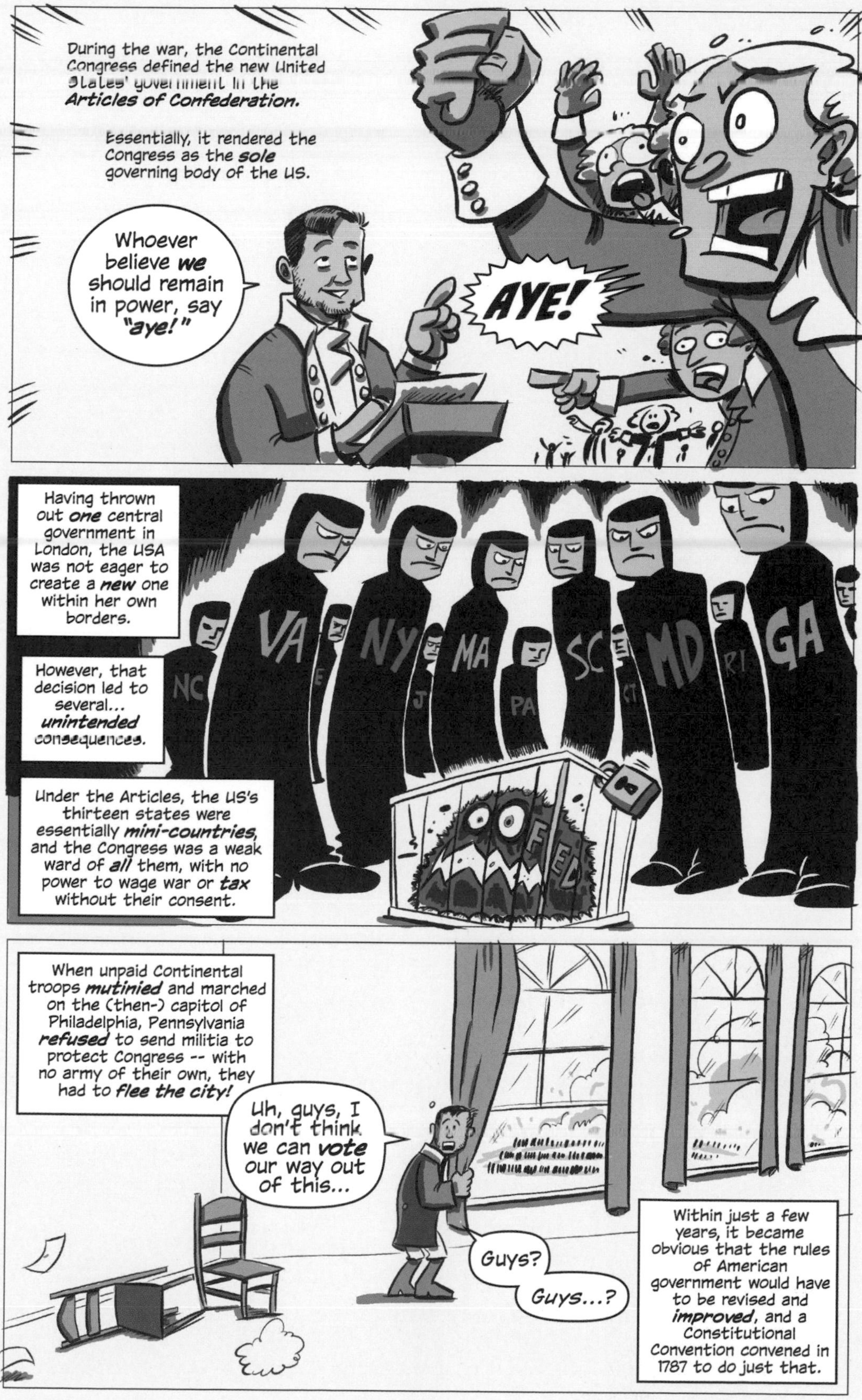
During the war, the Continental Congress defined the new United States' government in the *Articles of Confederation.*
Essentially, it rendered the Congress as the *sole* governing body of the US.
Whoever believe *we* should remain in power, say *"aye!"*
AYE!
Having thrown out *one* central government in London, the USA was not eager to create a *new* one within her own borders.
However, that decision led to several... *unintended* consequences.
Under the Articles, the US's thirteen states were essentially *mini-countries*, and the Congress was a weak ward of *all* them, with no power to wage war or *tax* without their consent.
NC
VA
NY
MA
PA
SC
MD
RI
GA
FED
When unpaid Continental troops *mutinied* and marched on the (then-) capitol of Philadelphia, Pennsylvania *refused* to send militia to protect Congress -- with no army of their own, they had to *flee the city!*
Uh, guys, I don't think we can *vote* our way out of this...
Guys?
Guys...?
Within just a few years, it became obvious that the rules of American government would have to be revised and *improved*, and a Constitutional Convention convened in 1787 to do just that.

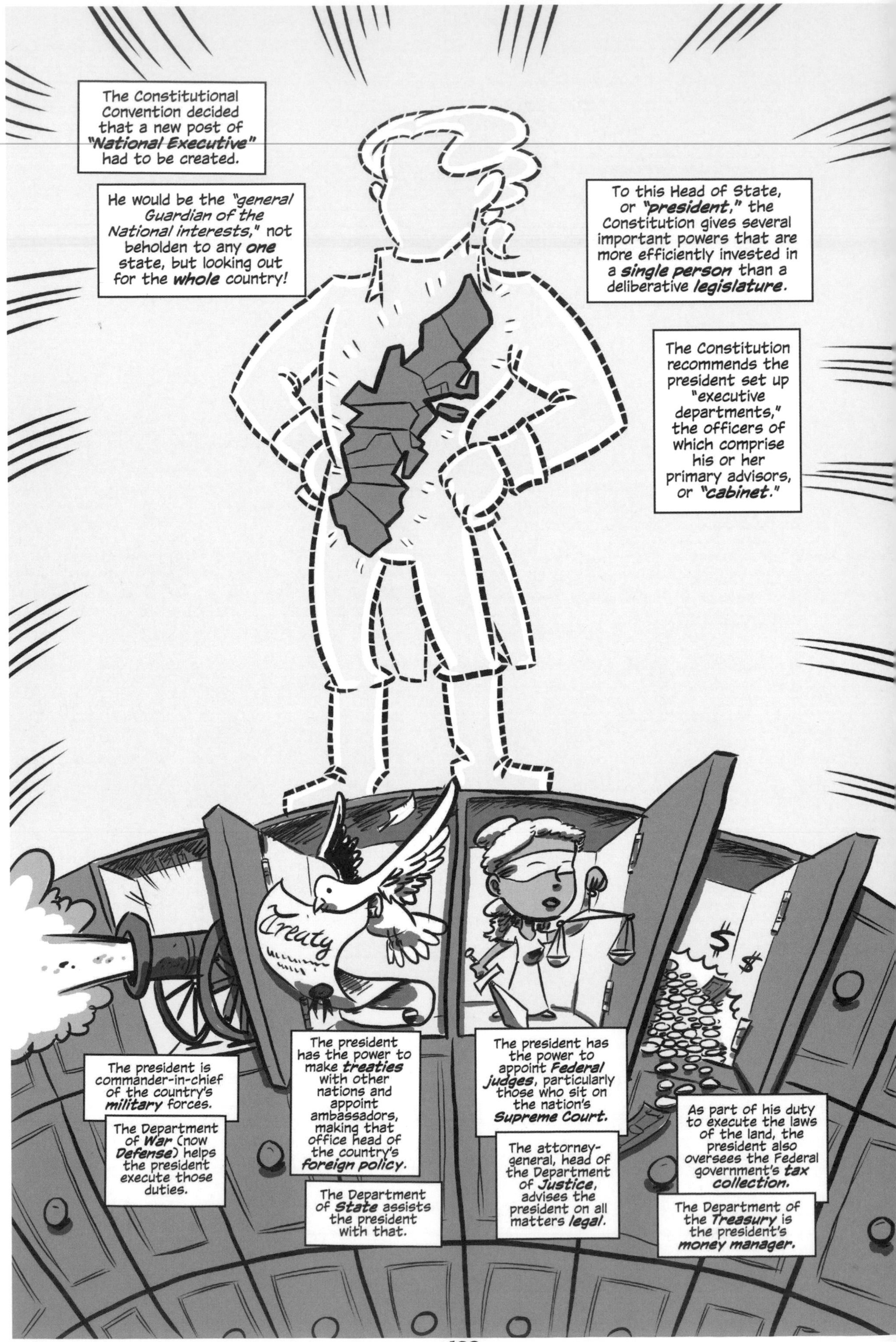

The Constitutional Convention decided that a new post of "National Executive" had to be created.
He would be the "general Guardian of the National interests," not beholden to any one state, but looking out for the whole country!
To this Head of State, or "president," the Constitution gives several important powers that are more efficiently invested in a single person than a deliberative legislature.
The Constitution recommends the president set up "executive departments," the officers of which comprise his or her primary advisors, or "cabinet."
Treaty
The president is commander-in-chief of the country's military forces.
The Department of War (now Defense) helps the president execute those duties.
The president has the power to make treaties with other nations and appoint ambassadors, making that office head of the country's foreign policy.
The Department of State assists the president with that.
The president has the power to appoint Federal judges, particularly those who sit on the nation's Supreme Court.
The attorney-general, head of the Department of Justice, advises the president on all matters legal.
As part of his duty to execute the laws of the land, the president also oversees the Federal government's tax collection.
The Department of the Treasury is the president's money manager.

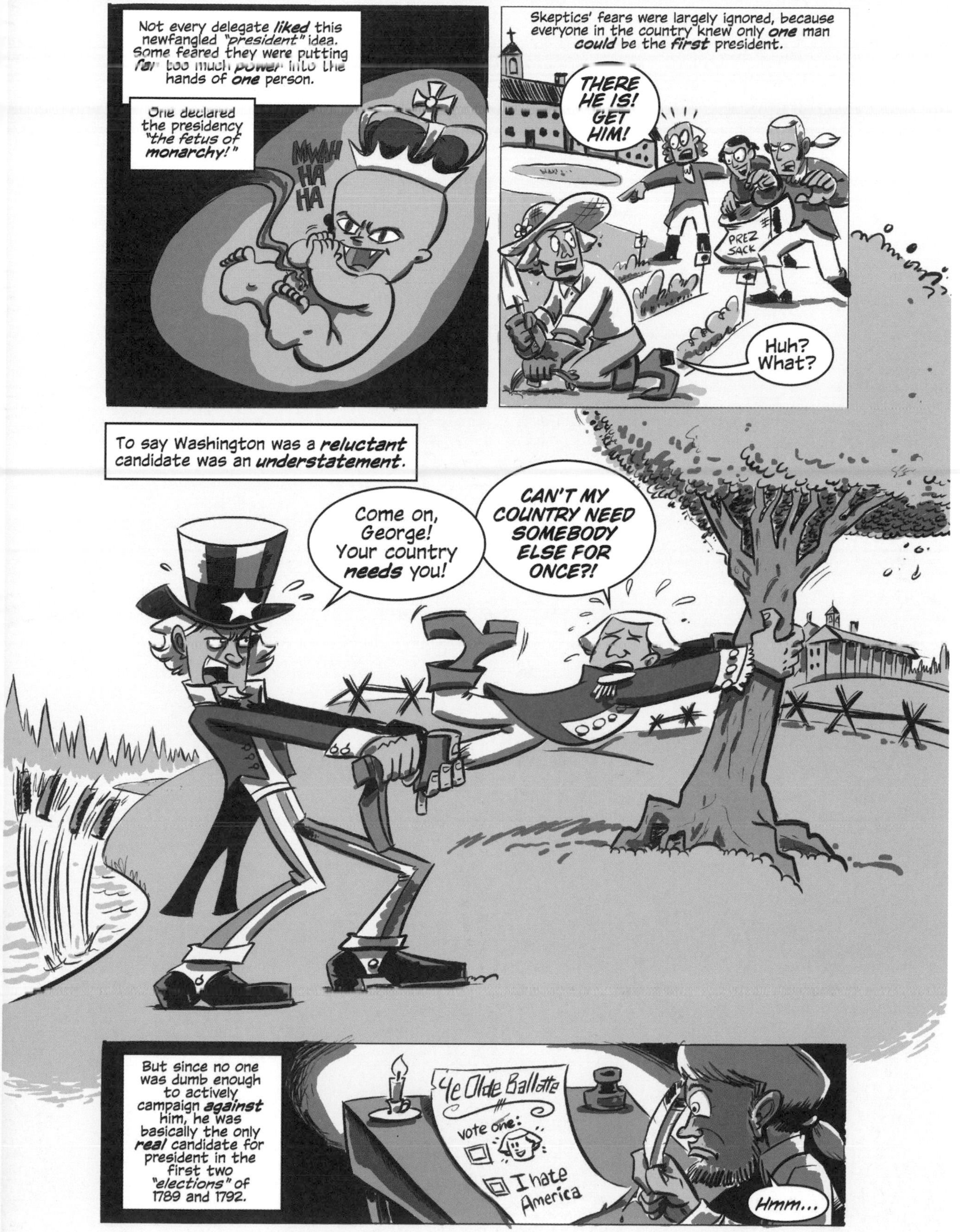

Not every delegate *liked* this newfangled *"president"* idea. Some feared they were putting *far* too much *power* into the hands of *one* person.
One declared the presidency *"the fetus of monarchy!"*
MWAH HA HA
Skeptics' fears were largely ignored, because everyone in the country knew only *one* man *could* be the *first* president.
THERE HE IS! GET HIM!
PREZ SACK
Huh? What?
To say Washington was a *reluctant* candidate was an *understatement*.
Come on, George! Your country *needs* you!
CAN'T MY COUNTRY NEED SOMEBODY ELSE FOR ONCE?!
But since no one was dumb enough to actively campaign *against* him, he was basically the only *real* candidate for president in the first two *"elections"* of 1789 and 1792.
Ye Olde Ballatte
vote one:
I hate America
Hmm...

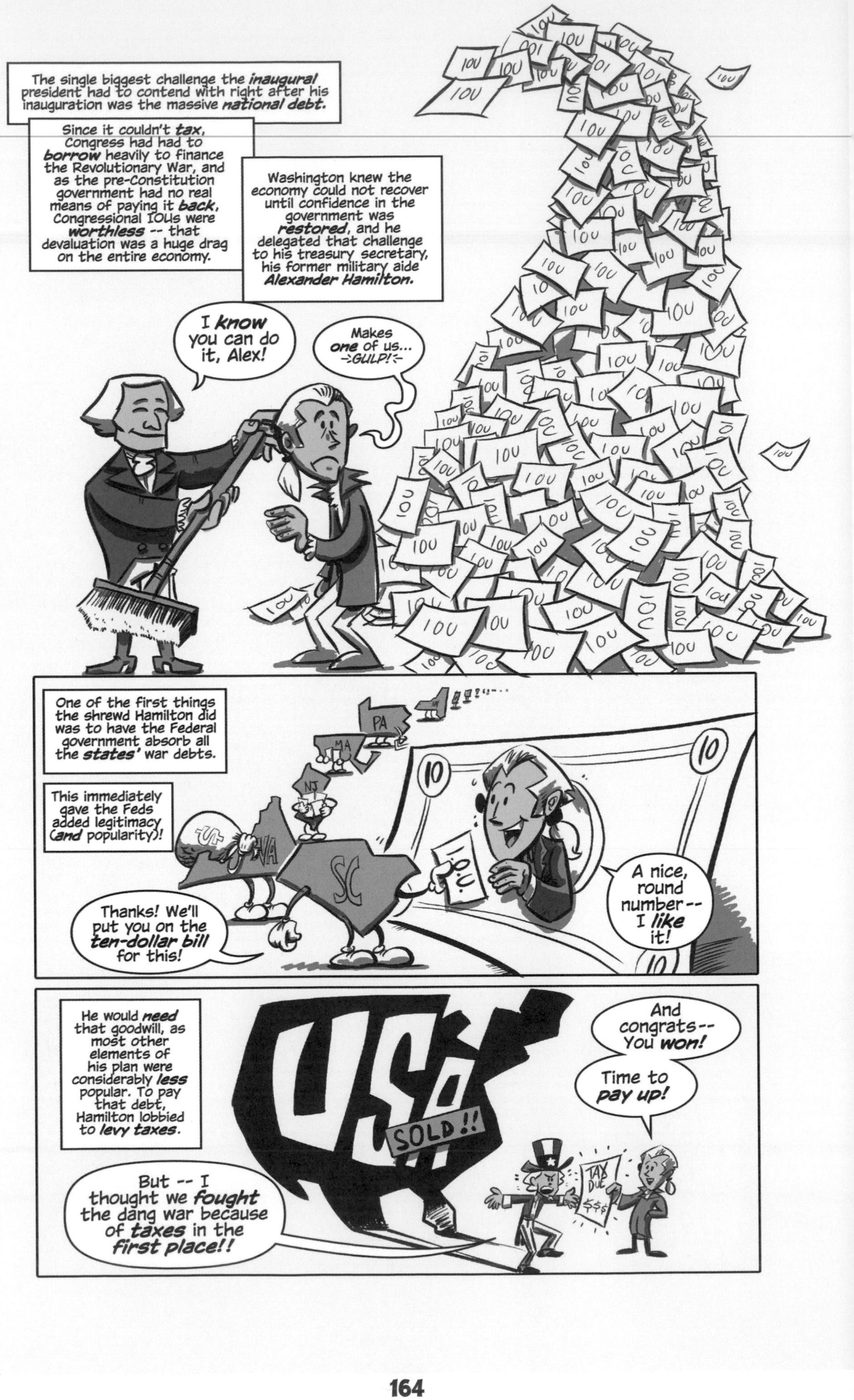

The single biggest challenge the *inaugural* president had to contend with right after his inauguration was the massive *national debt.*
Since it couldn't *tax*, Congress had had to *borrow* heavily to finance the Revolutionary War, and as the pre-Constitution government had no real means of paying it *back*, Congressional IOUs were *worthless* -- that devaluation was a huge drag on the entire economy.
Washington knew the economy could not recover until confidence in the government was *restored*, and he delegated that challenge to his treasury secretary, his former military aide *Alexander Hamilton.*
I *know* you can do it, Alex!
Makes *one* of us... *GULP!*
One of the first things the shrewd Hamilton did was to have the Federal government absorb all the *states'* war debts.
This immediately gave the Feds added legitimacy (*and* popularity)!
Thanks! We'll put you on the *ten-dollar bill* for this!
A nice, round number -- I *like* it!
He would *need* that goodwill, as most other elements of his plan were considerably *less* popular. To pay that debt, Hamilton lobbied to *levy taxes*.
SOLD!!
And congrats -- You *won!*
Time to *pay up!*
TAX DUE $$$
But -- I thought we *fought* the dang war because of *taxes* in the *first place!!*

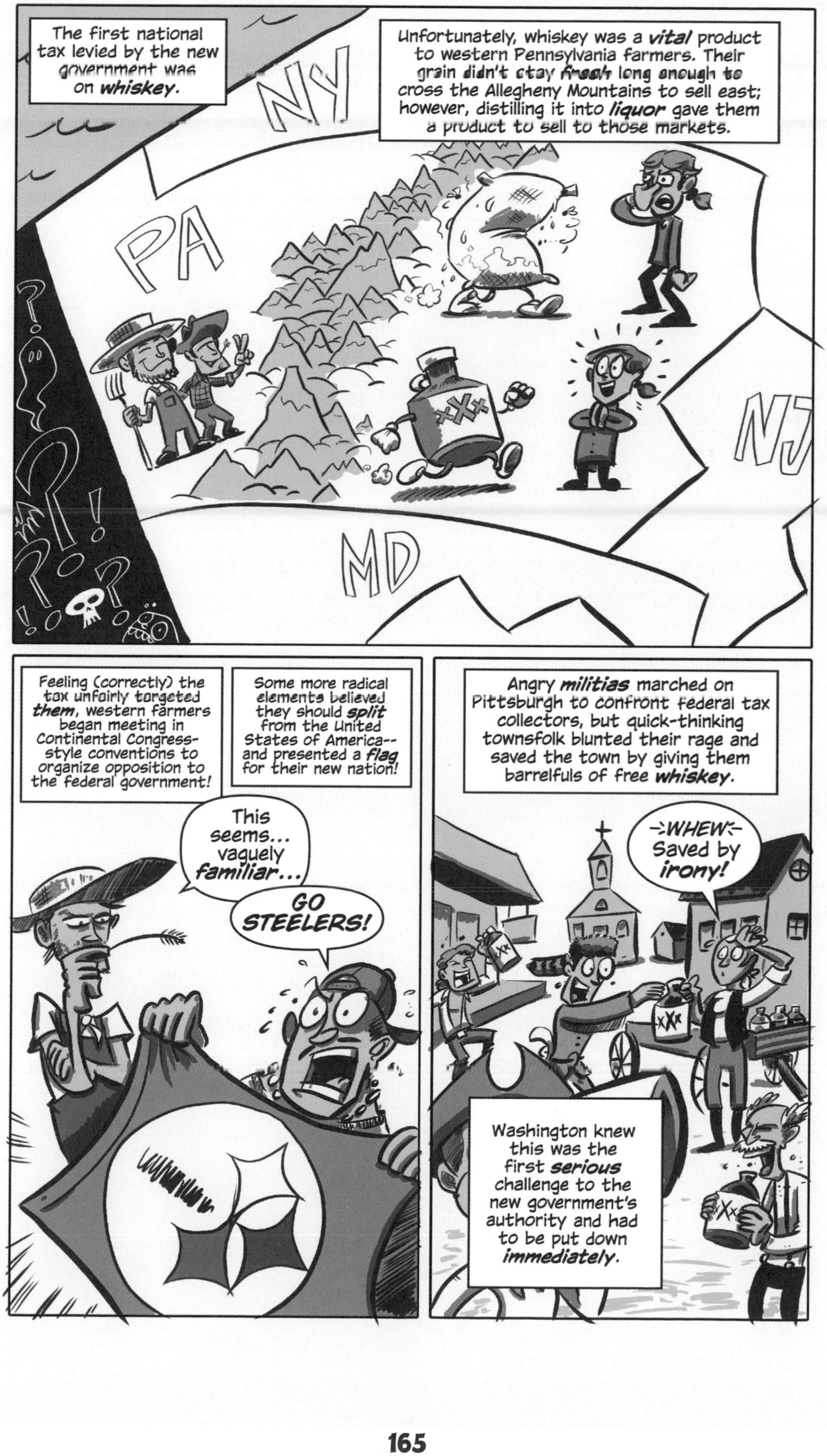
The first national tax levied by the new government was on *whiskey*.
Unfortunately, whiskey was a *vital* product to western Pennsylvania farmers. Their grain didn't stay fresh long enough to cross the Allegheny Mountains to sell east; however, distilling it into *liquor* gave them a product to sell to those markets.
NY
PA
NJ
MD
Feeling (correctly) the tax unfairly targeted *them*, western farmers began meeting in Continental Congress-style conventions to organize opposition to the federal government!
Some more radical elements believed they should *split* from the United States of America--and presented a *flag* for their new nation!
This seems... vaguely *familiar*...
GO STEELERS!
Angry *militias* marched on Pittsburgh to confront federal tax collectors, but quick-thinking townsfolk blunted their rage and saved the town by giving them barrelfuls of free *whiskey*.
WHEW Saved by *irony!*
Washington knew this was the first *serious* challenge to the new government's authority and had to be put down *immediately*.

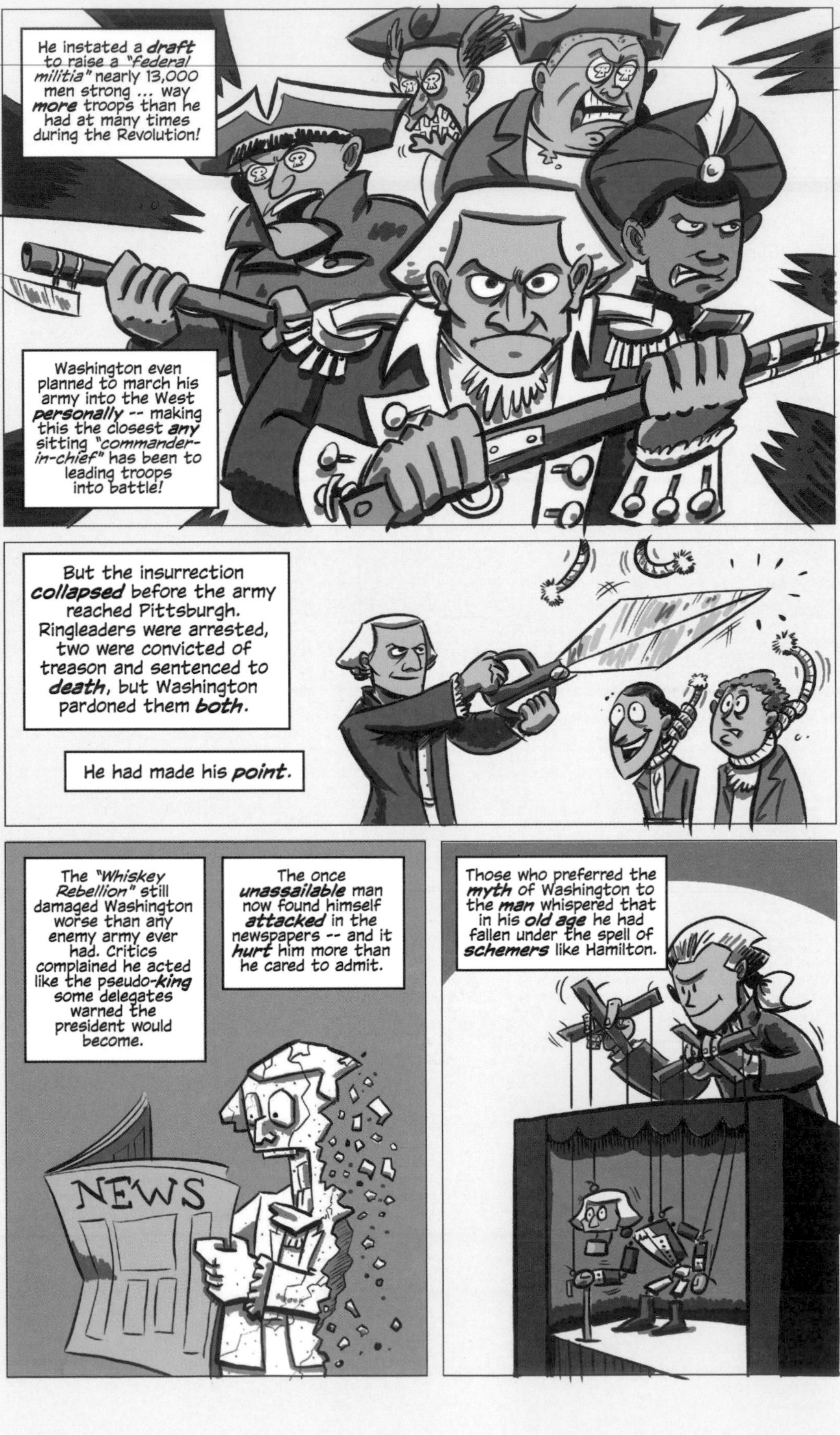
He instated a *draft* to raise a *"federal militia"* nearly 13,000 men strong ... way *more* troops than he had at many times during the Revolution!
Washington even planned to march his army into the West *personally* -- making this the closest *any* sitting *"commander-in-chief"* has been to leading troops into battle!
But the insurrection *collapsed* before the army reached Pittsburgh. Ringleaders were arrested, two were convicted of treason and sentenced to *death*, but Washington pardoned them *both*.
He had made his *point*.
The *"Whiskey Rebellion"* still damaged Washington worse than any enemy army ever had. Critics complained he acted like the pseudo-*king* some delegates warned the president would become.
The once *unassailable* man now found himself *attacked* in the newspapers -- and it *hurt* him more than he cared to admit.
NEWS
Those who preferred the *myth* of Washington to the *man* whispered that in his *old age* he had fallen under the spell of *schemers* like Hamilton.

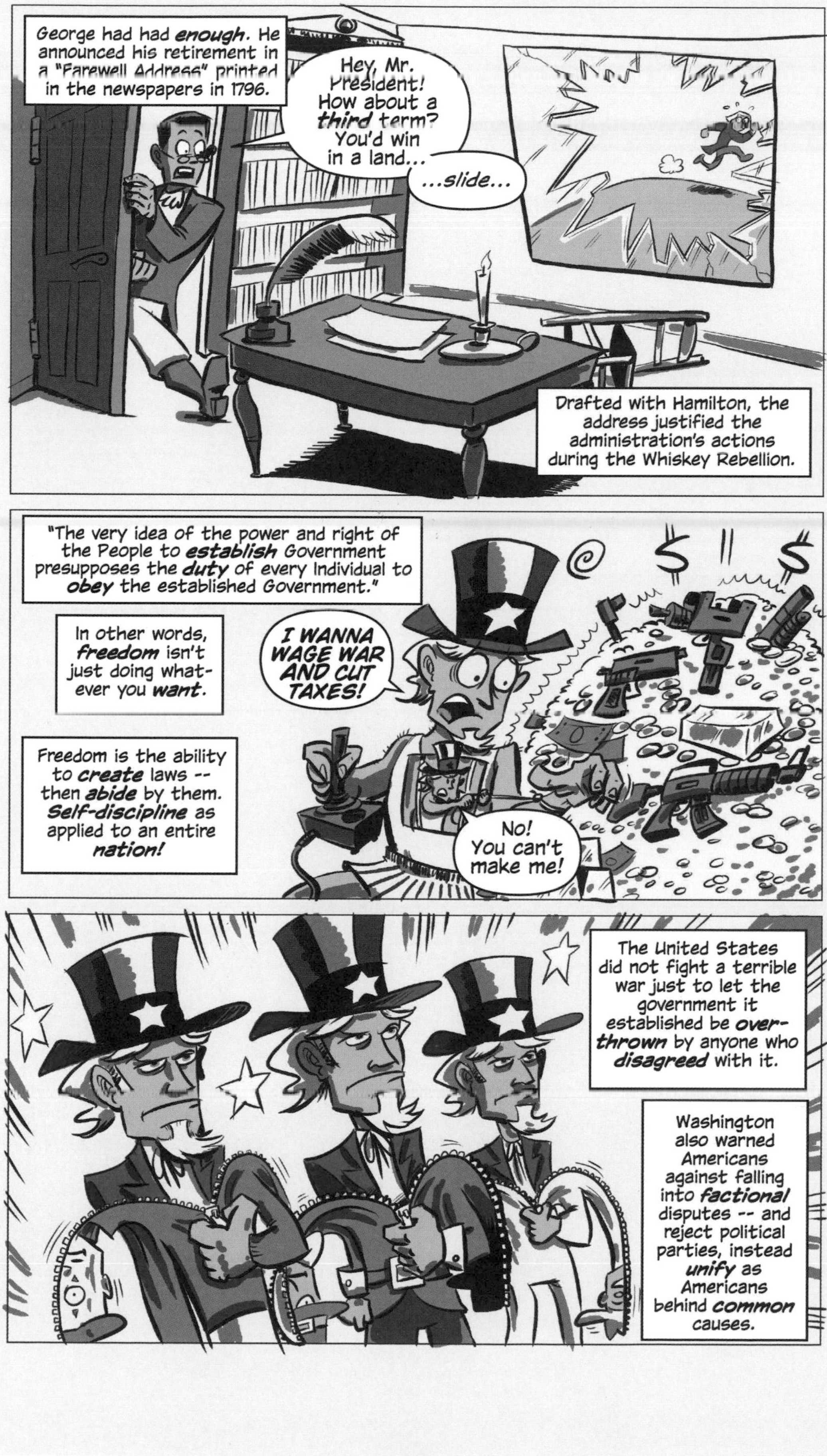
George had had **enough**. He announced his retirement in a "Farewell Address" printed in the newspapers in 1796.
Hey, Mr. President! How about a **third** term? You'd win in a land...
...slide...
Drafted with Hamilton, the address justified the administration's actions during the Whiskey Rebellion.
"The very idea of the power and right of the People to **establish** Government presupposes the **duty** of every Individual to **obey** the established Government."
In other words, **freedom** isn't just doing whatever you **want**.
I WANNA WAGE WAR AND CUT TAXES!
Freedom is the ability to **create** laws -- then **abide** by them. **Self-discipline** as applied to an entire **nation!**
No! You can't make me!
The United States did not fight a terrible war just to let the government it established be **overthrown** by anyone who **disagreed** with it.
Washington also warned Americans against falling into **factional** disputes -- and reject political parties, instead **unify** as Americans behind **common** causes.

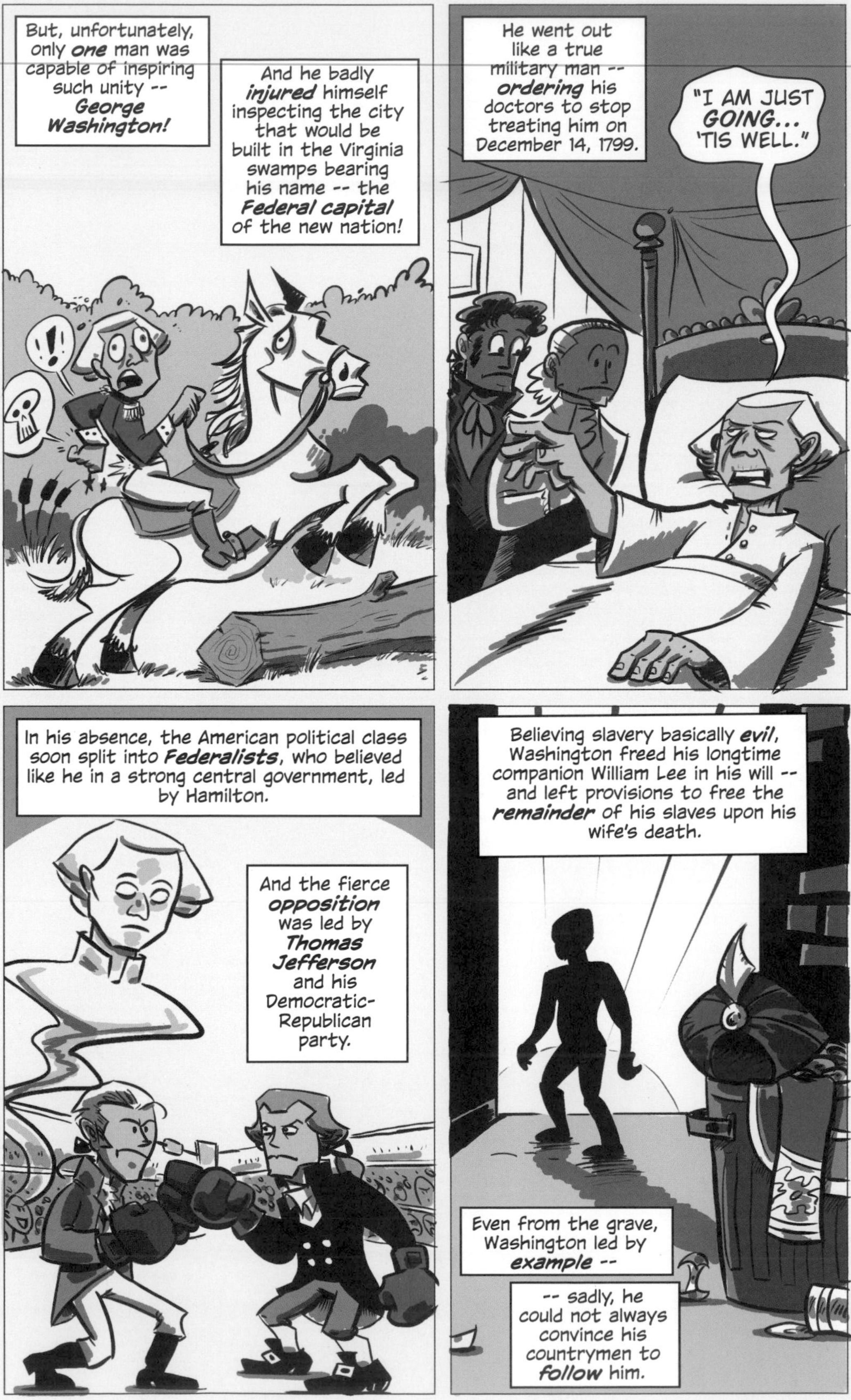
But, unfortunately, only one man was capable of inspiring such unity -- George Washington!
And he badly injured himself inspecting the city that would be built in the Virginia swamps bearing his name -- the Federal capital of the new nation!
!
He went out like a true military man -- ordering his doctors to stop treating him on December 14, 1799.
"I AM JUST GOING... 'TIS WELL."
In his absence, the American political class soon split into Federalists, who believed like he in a strong central government, led by Hamilton.
And the fierce opposition was led by Thomas Jefferson and his Democratic-Republican party.
Believing slavery basically evil, Washington freed his longtime companion William Lee in his will -- and left provisions to free the remainder of his slaves upon his wife's death.
Even from the grave, Washington led by example --
-- sadly, he could not always convince his countrymen to follow him.

CONTRIBUTORS

Jason Allen (Squirrels vs. Birds) is the creator of Squirrels vs. Birds "Prime–Composite Showdown." A corn-fed midwesterner, Jason relocated to the deep south in 2005. While adding "y'all" to his vernacular, he has illustrated characters and props on the television shows *Frisky Dingo* and *Archer*. He currently works in the action sports industry as a graphic designer, animator, and illustrator.

Heidi Arnhold (Squirrels vs. Birds) is a comic artist living in Atlanta, Georgia, who has worked on a multitude of projects involving such properties as *The Dark Crystal*, *Fraggle Rock*, and *Star Trek*. She has three rabbits, one husband, and a constant desire for doughnuts. Seek out more of her work by searching for "heidiarnhold" on most things, like deviantart, tumblr, and her own .com.

Gabriel Bautista (Albert the Alien) is a Chicago-based Eisner and Harvey Award–winning artist (*Comic Book Tattoo* by Image). He is the creator of comic competition website EnterVoid. com. In the event of a catastrophic world event, he will continue drawing comics and sell them out of his underground bunker. Until then, you can visit his website, YoGaboGabo.com to see his current projects.

Chris Beckett (Mail Order Ninja) is a comic colorist residing in Brooklyn. His favorite color is salmon, which also happens to be his third favorite freshwater fish. His least favorite color is camel, which weirdly enough is his favorite even-toed ungulate.

Michael Vincent Bramley (Finding Ivy) is a carbon-based lifeform. Its physical form has never left its home planet, but its imagination routinely drifts away to retrieve stories from other points in space and time. It originated in England, but now resides in New York, where it formed a permanent bond with a similar lifeform known as Alice Meichi Li.

Jen Brazas (Lumina) is the artist for Lumina and the creator of the webcomic Mystic Revolution (http://www.mysticrev.com). Jennifer spends her time jetting around the country attending anime conventions, drawing lots of pretty pictures, and playing way too much League of Legends.

Ben Caldwell (page 175) has worked in a variety of art and design fields over the past decade, including toy design, animation development, children's book illustration, and comic book illustration. His *Dare Detectives* comic was nominated for the Russ Manning Award for Most Promising Newcomer in Cartooning in 2005. His recent work includes the *All-Action Classics* comics, with *Dracula*, *Tom Sawyer*, *The Odyssey*, *The Wonderful Wizard of Oz*, and *The War of the Worlds*. Ben lives in New York with his wife, baby daughters, dog, and large collection of Chinese murder mysteries.

Katie Cook (The Power of Print) is an illustrator and comic book artist currently best known for her work on *Star Wars*, Jim Henson's *Fraggle Rock* and the Eisner Award–winning anthology *Mouse Guard: Legends of the Guard*.

Ryan Dunlavey (George Washington) is the artist of the *Comic Book History of Comics*, *Dirt Candy: A Cookbook*, the American Library Association award–winning *Action Philosophers* and the upcoming *Action Presidents*. Ryan's other credits include *G.I. Joe*, *M.O.D.O.K.: Reign Delay*, *Wolverine*, and *Tommy Atomic*, and artwork in *MAD*, *Wizard*, *ToyFare*, *Royal Flush*, and *Disney Adventures*.

Tracy Edmunds (Editor) is an educational author, editor, curriculum developer, and teacher who fervently believes in the power of comics as educational tools.

Josh Elder (Editor, Lumina, Mail Order Ninja) is the founder and President of Reading With Pictures. He is also co-creator of the award–winning graphic novel series and nationally syndicated comic strip *Mail Order Ninja* and writer of several series for DC Comics including *Scribblenauts Unmasked* and *Adventures of Superman*.

Chris Giarrusso (Cover Artist, G-Man: Reign of the Robo-Teachers) is best known for writing and drawing *G-MAN*, a series of graphic novels loved by all ages, featuring a young superhero who gains fantastic powers when he wears a magic cape. Chris currently lives and writes and draws in Queens, New York. Check out more of his art and animation at his official website, chrisgcomics.com.

Geoffrey Golden (Probamon!) writes humor for major studios and entertainment outlets, like Warner Bros, Fox, Capcom, National Lampoon, *Cracked Magazine*, Comedy.com, Lionsgate, and more. In 2010, Geoffrey successfully fund-raised to start *The Devastator*, "the quarterly comedy magazine for humans," which features writers and artists from *Conan*, *The Simpsons*, Onion News Network, Marvel, and DC Comics.

Roger Langridge (Doctor Sputnik) is probably best known for his work on the Harvey Award–winning *Muppet Show Comic Book*. He has worked for Marvel, DC, Dark Horse, and other publishers, as well as on many of his own creations, such as *Fred the Clown* and *Snarked!*, which won an Eisner Award in 2012.

Mike Lee (Special Delivery) is a novelist, game designer, and scriptwriter who never outgrew the wild adventures of his youth. When not battling space pirates or hunting rogue secret agents, he lives with his family in Nashville, Tennessee.

Janet Lee (Special Delivery) is an Eisner Award–winning illustrator of *Return of the Dapper Men* and two Marvel adaptations of Jane Austen novels. She lives in Nashville with her novelist husband, young son, a very sweet dog, and a very bad cat.

Alice Meichi Li (Finding Ivy) has been exhibited at Museum of Comic and Cartoon Art, Museum of Chinese in America, Artscape Baltimore, Galapagos Art Space, Bottleneck Gallery, and others. Her art has also appeared on Archie Comics's *Mega Man*, Dark Horse Comics's *Once Upon a Time Machine*, Image Comics's *Elephantmen*, *YRB Magazine*, and more. Fall down the rabbit hole: alicemeichi.com.

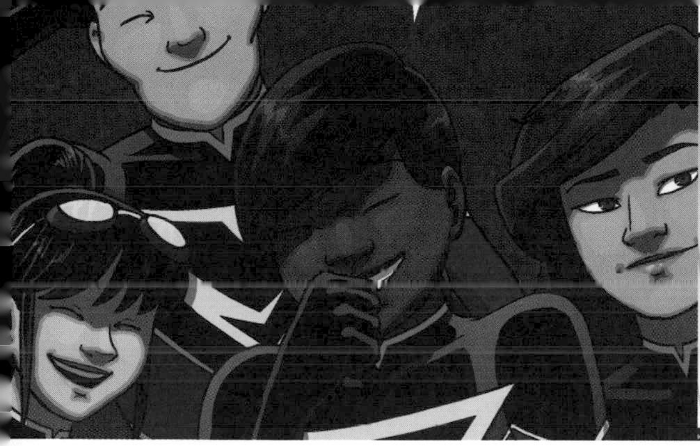

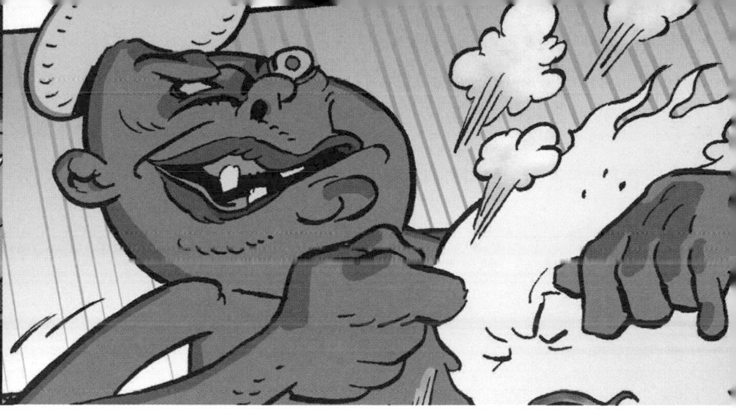

Russell Lissau (Field Trip) By day, Russell Lissau is a mild-mannered reporter in suburban Chicago. By night, he battles evil writing comic books, including *The Batman Strikes!*, *Strawberry Shortcake*, and the upcoming graphic novel *Old Wounds*. To learn more, check out www.facebook.com/russell.lissau.

Marvin Mann (Field Trip) has drawn and occasionally written webcomics, mini-comics, black-and-white and color pamphlets, comics using 3D modeling software, comics for the iPhone, and four graphic novels, *The Lone and Level Sands*, *Inanna's Tears*, *Some New Kind of Slaughter*, and *The Grave Doug Freshley* from Archaia.

Jim McClain (Solution Squad) is the creator, writer, and letterer of *Solution Squad* as well as the letterer for "Special Delivery to Shangri-La," "Lumina: Menace of the Mathemagician," and "Mail Order Ninja and the Silverback Horde." He is a 7th-grade math teacher at Pierre Moran Middle School in Elkhart, Indiana, and has been teaching for 27 years. *Solution Squad* is his first comic story. More at www.solutionsquad.net.

Rose McClain (Solution Squad) is the artist of *Solution Squad*. She is a freelance artist whose other works include *Scoundrels*, *Hench-Man*, and *Abigail Astoundo*. See more of her art on her deviantart site, rosemcclain.deviantart.com.

Brandon Montclare (Editor) has been a lifelong fan of comics and been employed in some part of the business since he was 12 years old. He's worked as an editor at TokyoPop (*Rising Stars of Manga*) and DC Comics (*All-Star Superman*, *Batman: Year 100*, *Hellblazer*). Nowadays, he's even started to write here and there (*Batman*, *Hulk*).

Paul Morrissey (Editor) is an Eisner Award–winning editor of several acclaimed comic books and graphic novels, including *The Muppet Show*, *Mouse Guard: Legends of the Guard*, and *Fraggle Rock*.

Trevor Mueller (Albert the Alien) is the writer/creator of *Albert the Alien* (digitally distributed by Thrillbent as well as at www.AlbertTheAlien.com), as well as several award-winning webcomic series (www.trevoramueller.com). Trevor has also contributed stories to several anthologies, including *Hope: The Hero Initiative* from Ronin Studios. Trevor gives lectures and presentations throughout the country at conventions, schools, and libraries.

Tintin Pantoja (Like Galileo...) was born in Manila and received a BFA in Illustration and Cartooning at the School of Visual Arts in New York, leading to a career in comics and commercial illustration. In 2005, she was nominated for the Friends of Lulu "Best Newcomer" award, and her published works include *Hamlet: The Manga Edition* for Wiley and three volumes of *Manga Math* for Graphic Universe. Check out her art at www.tintinpantoja.com.

James Peaty (Like Galileo...) A native of London, England, James has been working in American comics since 2005 on titles including *Green Arrow*, *JSA: Classified*, and *Supergirl*. Also an accomplished filmmaker, James's short thriller, "The Appraisal," was recently screened as part of London's Portobello Film Festival. A feature version of "The Appraisal" is due to go into production in early 2014.

Nate Pride (Probamon!) is a freelance artist and designer rooted in Michigan. He has also contributed art for the *Library of Wonder: Jules Verne Extraordinary Voyages* (Fall River Press) and was a featured artist in the Eisner Award–winning anthology *Mouse Guard: Legends of the Guard* (Archaia). More of his artwork can be seen at www.natepride.com.

Chris Schweizer (The Black Brigade) is the cartoonist behind *The Crogan Adventures*, a historical fiction series that follows the exploits of the fictitious Crogan family over the last three centuries. He lives in Nashville, Tennessee, where he makes history and horror comics. Sometimes he does animation design work, too. He has a daughter named Penny.

Tim Smith 3 (Mail Order Ninja) has done professional work for numerous high-profile entertainment companies over the years. Some of his more recent professional projects include *Spider-Man Unlimited* from Marvel Comics, *Sonic X* from Archie Comics, *Grim & Co.*, an original graphic novel from TokyoPop, *Tales from the Crypt* for Papercutz, and *Teen Titans Go* for DC Comics. Plus many more. To view more of TS3's work, please visit: www.timsmith3.com.

Fred Van Lente (George Washington) is the #1 *New York Times* bestselling author of *Marvel Zombies*, *Incredible Hercules* (with Greg Pak), *Odd Is On Our Side* (with Dean R. Koontz), as well as the American Library Association award-winning *Action Philosophers*. His original graphic novel *Cowboys & Aliens* (co-written with Andrew Foley) is the basis for the major motion picture starring Daniel Craig and Harrison Ford. Van Lente's other comics include *The Comic Book History of Comics*, *Taskmaster*, *Archer & Armstrong*, *Amazing Spider-Man* and *Hulk: Season One*. Fred loves hearing from readers at fred.vanlente@gmail.com.

Steve Wallace (Mail Order Ninja) is a writer/ illustrator/ letterer living in Little Rock, Arkansas. He spends most of his day in front of a computer; the other part he spends in front of a drawing table. You can read his mini-comics and get updates on his upcoming graphic novels at stevewallaceart.com.

Gene Luen Yang (Foreword: Comics & Education) began drawing comic books in the fifth grade. American-born Chinese, his first graphic novel from First Second was a National Book Award finalist, as well as the winner of the Michael L. Printz Award. In 2013, First Second released *Boxers & Saints*, his graphic novel diptych about the Boxer Rebellion.

THANK YOU FOR YOUR SUPPORT

A. David Lewis
Anke Wehner
Brett Anthony
Cheryl Trooskin-Zoller
Daniel Laloggia
Aaron Devrick
Anna Gaukel
Brett Jackson
Chris Buchheit
Daniel Lindsey
Adam Craik
Anna Gold
Brett Schenker
Chris Hammell
Daniel Loane
Adam Fotos
Anna Gonzales
Brian & Christa Fouhy
Chris Mills
Daniel Moore
Adam J. Monetta
Annette Kesterson
Brian Cooksey
Chris Norberg
Daniel Peretti
Adam Jones
Annette Martini
Brian Glass
Chris Ramsden
Daniel Southwick
Adam M Botsford
Apertome
Brian J. Crowley
Chris Robinson
Daniel Theodore
Adam Reyes
arcticwolfe
Brian Kolm
Chris Ryall
Danielle
Adam Robezzoli
Arlene Lipkewich
Brian Little
Chris Shields
Danny Dougherty
Adam Singer
Arleta Mann
Brian McNamara
Chris Wilson
Danny Pettry
Adam Wollet
Arthur Murakami
Brian Petkash
Christian Sager
Dara Naraghi
Addam Pool
Ash Fairless
Brian Sikkenga
Christie Caywood
Darcy Elliott
Adrian Betts
Ashleigh Popplewell
Brian Willis
Christine Beatty Mignola
Dare2Draw
Alan Robertson
Ashley Baltazar
Brian Wolter
Christopher
DarkGbz
Aldous Russell
Ashley Kiefer
Brontis Shane Orengo
Christopher Day
Darryal Ogle
Alex Forte
Ashley Rayner
Brotherwise Games
Christopher J. Foster
Darwyn & Marsha
Alex Greenwald

Audrey Watters
Bruce Nelson
Christopher Lawson
Dave Fallon
Alex Harrison
Aurelien Gaillard
Bryan Prindiville
Chuck Cottrell
Dave Maulding
Alex Wagner
Ava!
Bryce Hopkins
Chuck Suffel
Dave Roman
Alex Strife
Bad Mutha Booboosie
Bugeyedmonster2
Cindy Chu
Dave Wheeler
Alexis Fajardo
Barbara Bykowski
Byron Tanner
Citten
David Bednar
Alice Meichi Li
Beast
C.H.
Claire
David Burke
Alicia
Beau Gunderson
Caleb Benham
Clinton Diehl
David Catalano
Alicia Cordova
Beau Peep
Cameron Hays
Cody Peterson
David Crosslin
Allen Turner
Becky Conzett
Cameron Logue
Coll Wise
David Lugo
Amanda
Begyle Brewing
Camilla Zhang
Connie Elder
David Rapp
Amanda Meadows
Belinda Fernandez
Candice Reilly
Constantine Koutsoutis
Denis Legault
Amber Lanagan
Ben DeFeo
Carapace
CoolB
Derek Viramontes
Amy Durham Anderson
Ben Hall
Carl Antone
Corey Scott
Devil's Due Ent
Amy Fiori
Ben Peterson
Carl Kloster
Corin Dimopoulos
Dino Caruso
Amy Holland
Benjamin Bement
Carl Mageski
Cory Doctorow
Dipa Gandhi
Amy R
Benjamin Huang
Carl Witty
Courtney Riddles
DJ Francis
Amy Ratcliffe
Benjamin Towle

Carol McCullough
Craig Seasholes
Doctor Popular
Andra Kishimoto
Beth
Caroline Warmkessel
cwg.me
Don
Andrea Lipinski
Beth Denton
Carolyn Goodell
Cynthia Ho
Don Leibold
Andrea Manghiuc
Beth Williams
Carrie Easley
Dale Cusack
Doug Brown
Andres Avila
Bill Akunevicz Jr.
Carrie Stump
Dale Jacobs
Doug Steinhoff
Andrew & Valerie Grayson
Bill Williams
Casey Martin
Damian Niolet
Dr. Katie Monnin
Andrew Bavry
Bob Bretall
Cassidy
Damon
Drew
Andrew Ellison
Bobbie Kirby
Cate Hall
damon brodowski
Drew Scott
Andrew Farwig
Brad Denby
Caterina
Dan
Drew Tynan Robbins
Andrew Porwitzky
Brad Merritt
Catherine Lee
Dan Allison
drjekyll
Andrew Rostan
Bradley Diuguid
Cathy & Tim Heldman
Dan Mishkin
Dustin Ambler
Andrew Sanford
Brandon Baker
Chad Hershey
Dan Morris
Dylan Reed
Andrew Wilson
Brandon Eaker
Charis Loke
Dan Rivkin
Ed Erwin
Andy Capone
Brandon J. Carr
Charles Bullock
Dan Wu
Eddie Lehecka
Andy Diggle
Brandon Montclare
Charlie Von Eschen
Dana Sweeney
Edward Sizemore
Angela
Brandon Vessey
Charlotte Cheng
Dani
Elena Rakochy
Angela McLaughlin
Bree Smith
Cheryl Dahle

Daniel Burwen
Eli Edmunds
Anita M. King
Brendan Marcy
Cheryl Harris
Daniel Cassino
Eli Malone
Elisa Shoenberger
Garry Mac
Jack
Jenna Busch
John Anthony
Elizabeth Boyce
Gene Kelly
Jack Chiu
Jenna Cole
john avina
Elizabeth Corcoran
Gene Verley
Jacob
Jennifer Haines
John Chrastka
Elizabeth Meyer
George Clingerman
Jacob Canfield
Jennifer Luttrall
John Ervin
Elizabeth Shoemaker
Sampat
George Tramountanas
Jacob Lawrence
Jennifer Lynn Barnes
John H
ElleDee
Gerald F. Tyschper
Jacques E Nyemb
Jenny
John Hergenroeder
Ellen Miles
Gericke Cook
Jacqui Kennelly
Jenny Lee
John Hill
Ellen Myrick at Hamilton UMC
Gerolf Nikolay
Jaime Campbell
Jenny Piper
John Klump
Elliott Sawyer
GhettoManga Quarterly
Jake
Jeremy Bastian
John LaCount
Emily Olsen
Giacomo Santangelo
Jamal Collins
Jeremy Canceko
John Mennell
Emily Swan
Giao Phan
James Asmus
Jeremy Crawford
John O'Marra
Emota
Gill Hatcher
James Bucky Carter
Jeremy Larance
John Potten
EntropicInertia
Gillian Barlow Graham
James Kwak
Jeremy Melloul
John Roshell
Eric
Gina
James Post
Jeremy Mohler
John S. Troutman
Eric Agena
Gordon Dymowski

James Wright
Jeremy N. Fisher
John Shableski
Eric Conrad
Graham Williams
Jamie Gambell
Jeremy Wadhams
John Stratford
Eric Larnick
Grant Thomas
Jane Edith Wilson
Jeremy Wiggins
John Weidner
Eric Olson
Greg Moore
Jane Ponce
Jerzy Drozd
John Yap
Eric Palicki
Gregg Taylor
Janelle Asselin
Jesse Post
Jon Aegerter
Eric Wight
Gregory Norwood
Janet Lee
Jesse R Davis
Jon Buran
Erica Heflin
Gretrascis
Janet Weber
Jesse Richards
Jon Eadler
Erica Pelley Ziebarth
Greyson Fauchard
Jara Cervinka
Jessi
Jon Ionita
Eric Oassis
Gutem
Jared Polis
Jessica Daniel
Jon Leitheusser
Erik Evensen
Gwen Weinberger
Jarrett Roberts
Jessica Dawn
Jon Radoff
Erik Rinard
H. Jameel al Khafiz
Jasmin Kaw
Jessica Pease
Jonathan
Erik Saltwell
Hailey Ward
Jason
Jessica Reis
Jonathan H. Liu
Erik Taylor
Hawaiian Dave .
Jason A. Quest
Jill Bevington
Jonathan Martin
Erin Miles
Heather Disco
Jason Bane
Jill Thompson
Jonathan Prater
Erin Walker
Heather Peagler
Jason Bergman
Jillian Lerner
Jonathon Walters
Ernie Hacks
Heather Pritchett
Jason Franks
Jim
jonny kay
Ethan Decker
Herb Mumford
Jason Gavin

Jim Faber
Jordan Gibson
Evanthia Stavrou
Hillary Wolfe
Jason Horn
Jim Hirsch
Jorge Santiago Jr.
Eylene Parrish
Honor Gillies
Jason Nunley
Jim Kosmicki
José
fawn
Hooper Triplett
Jason Pfau
Jim McClain
Joseph
Featherae
HoppingFun
Jason Sacks
Jim Ottaviani
Joseph Trask
Felisha Dianne Lynch
Hunter Ardehali
Jason Urbanciz
jim ww
Josh Cruz
Ferrett Steinmetz
Hypocee
Jason W. Gavin
Jimmy Palmiotti
Josh Greathouse
flann
Ian
Jason Warzecha
Jo Walker-Smith
Josh Seven
Frank Boosman
Ian Aberle
Jason Y.
JoAnn DeSalvatore
Josh Taylor
Fred Niedermeyer
Ian Chipman
Jax
Jocelyn
Joshua Carmody
Fred Van Lente
Ian Mattingly
Jay Davidson
Jocelyn Paige Kelly
Joshua Hime
Frederick Yelk Woodruff
Infinity Merchants Com
Jay Miller
Jodi Garber-Simon
Joshua Stone
Freya
Inverse Press
Jay Peteranetz
Jodi Scaife
Joshua T. Aitkenhead
Gérard Kraus
Ivan
Jean-Daniel Lariviere
Joe Manley
Josiah Meints
gabrielgarzada7
J K
JediPanda
Joe Vecchio
Joy Maul
Gail de Vos
J Mitchell
Jeff
Joel Rothman & Stacey Ballis
Joyce Vivirski
Gail Kwak
J. Roche
Jeff Barbanell

Joey
Judy Ottenstroer
Galen Lim
J. Torres
Jeff Reid
Joey Esposito
Juliana Xavier
Gannon Beck
J.R. Deans
Jeff Stokely
Johannes Braun
Julie Holley
Garnet Edmunds55
JABenson
Jeffrey
John
Julie Vermeer Fowler
June Shieh
Kora Bongen
m1101
Meghan Augusta
Morgan Loomis
Justin Castaneda
Kristen H.
MacEpic
Mel Caylo
Mr. Brown
Justin Turner
Kristen Johansen
Madelaine Fischer
Melissa Bykowski
Muhammad Saleem
Justin Vaux
Kristie Bondy
Magnus
Mell Scalzi
Muneera Mak
K Miklusak
Kristine Roper
Marc
Menachem Cohen
myfish32
Kaia Gavere
Kristofor
Marc Fishman
Menachem Luchins
Myron McMillin
Kaitune
Kyle
Marc Wilhelm
Mica Hendricks
Nachie Castro
Kara Y. Frame
Kyle Gnepper
Marcel André Perret-Gentil
Micah Baldwin
Najela
Karen B Wehner
Kyle Lowry
Marcus
Michael "Waffles" Nguyen
nanaki
Karen Gavigan
Kyle Terrell
Marcus Ervin
Michael Alexander
  Giangrasso
Nancy
Karen Luk
kytyn
Marcus Eubanks
Michael Campbell
Nancy Gibney
Karen Romano Young
L. Parker Gibson
Margaret Richter
Michael Connolly
Nanette Fisher
Karen Simmons
Lance Conatser
Maria

Michael DeGrandis
Naomi Arram
Karl Heffernan
Lance Curran
Maria Dumont
Michael Farah
Nasreen Wahid
Kat Kan
Lar deSouza
Maria Frey Griffin
Michael Giba
Natasha Lewis
Kate Carleton
LastAndroid
Marion Bolds Gillins
Michael Gradin
Nathan Alderman
Katharine Le Busque
Laura Harper
Marisa Elana James
Michael Hoes
Nathan Herald
Kathe Andersen
Laura Kajpust
Mark Andrew Smith
Michael Husson
Nathan Hughes
Katherine Glick
Laura M. Jimenez
Mark Foo
Michael Judge Brislin
Nathan Lueth
Kathleen Markham
Laura Miello
Mark Geary
Michael Kinyon
Nathan McCurley
Kathryn
Laura Szumowski
Mark Geary
Michael Lapinski
Nathan Seabolt
Kathy Bugajsky
Lauren
Mark Schweikert
Michael LaRiccia
Neil Bryer
Katie Doyle
Lauren Sidle
Mark Stegbauer
Michael Litman
Neill Cameron
Katrina
Lea Hernandez
Martchela
Michael Moreci
Nick Boisson
Kay Lunkenheimer
Lee Hollman
Martha Cornog
Michael O'Connell
Nick Dazé
Kazu Kibuishi
Lee Meyer
Martial M.
Michael Rank
Nick Dragotta
KDumbleton
Leef Smith-Mission:
   Comics & Art
Martin Gregory
Michael Ring
Nick Fegley
Keith Robinson
Leigh Brodsky-Schubert
Martin Grider
Michael Silberman
Nick Sousanis
Keith Stanziola
Leigh Webb
Martina Rolli

Michael Takahara
Nicki Howe Workman
Keith Tyschper
Leo Antolini
Marvin Chevcallier
Michael Vuolo
Noah Miller
Kelly
leonard san pedro
Marvin Mann
Michael Weidenfelder
Noah Sachs
Kelly Farrow
Lesley Karpiuk
Mary Ellen Francis
michaelZ
Olivia Tien
Kelly Harrass
Lewiji
Mason Johnson
Michele Hong Herro
Onrie Kompan
Kelsey Rohwer
Lewis Shadoff
Mathieu Doublet
Michelle J. Yee
Pam Chipman
Kelvin
Linda Panszczyk
Matt Doering
Michelle Meyer
Parker Adair
Ken Marcus
Lisa
Matt Holland
Mike Eagan
Pat Quinn
Ken Rubin
Lisa Kwon-Brooks
Matt J
Mike Frantz
Patrick Curry
KentL
Liz Potsch
Matt Madden
Mike Hall
Patrick Hess
Kevan Chandler
Liz Rizzo
Matt Powers
Mike Kiley
Patrick McMullen
Kevin
Liza Murphy
Matt Riggsby
Mike Pawuk
Patrick Montero
Kevin Gilfether
Long Le
Matt Schlotte
Mike Rice
Patrick Rennie
Kevin Hodgson
Lonnie Millsap
Matt Upson
Mike Shiplack
Patrick Scullin
Kevin J. Maroney
Lori Taylor
Matt Zitron
Mikey Rollins
Patrick Scullin
Kevin Mines
Lucas Trerice
Matthew Bowers
Mikko K.
Paul
Kevin Temmer
Luke E.
Matthew Rex
Min Xiu Wu

Paul Fischer
Khaiya
Luke McCullough
mattlibrarian
Mister Hope
Paul H
Khalid Birdsong
Lys Fulda
mattolution
Molly
Paul Jenkins
Kim Riser
M. Sweeney Lawless
Maureen Bakis
Monica Bykowski
Paul Maes
Kohl Glass
M.H.
Max Cantor
Monique Pihl
Paul Tayloe
Komainu
M.K. Hobson
Megan Anne
Morgan Baumbach
Penny
peshk
Rosie Siman
Sharon Millyard
terry spurling
Yvonne Svae-Grotli
Pete Clark
Round Table Companies
Shaun Manning
Tesche
Zachary Pearson
Peter Bensley
Roxanne Smith
Shawn Granger
That Kids Book
Zack Rosenberg
Peter Hanneman
Roy Cowing
Shredded Angel
theArtsofLife
zahncr
Peter Hepburn
Roy Blumenthal
Sidney T Kan
thmazing
Zeke Abuhoff
Peter Ryan
Ruby Boiko
Simon Raoul
Thom Barthelmess
ZombieVittles
Phil
Rudy Hernandez
slycreations
Thom Dunn
Phil Gibson
Russ
Snow Wildsmith
Thom Wetzel
Philip Cahiwat
Russell Burlingame
Spiro
Thomas
Phillip Miles
Russell Lissau
Spyke Alexander
Thomas Denton
Pj Perez
Russell Willis
Stance & Speed
Thomas P. Heer
Poet Mase
Ryan Closs
stefano
Tim Miner
Poming Chu

Ryan J. Lucas
Stephanie
Tim Sarrantonio
PonSquared
Ryan K Lindsay
Paul H
Stephanie Phillips
Tim Gibson
Portal
Ryan McGrail
Stephanie Wooten
Timothy C Brown
Prax Jarvin
Ryan Schrodt
Stephen "Switt!" Wittmaak
Todd Carney
Ralph S
Ryan Wheaton
Stephen Hadden
Todd Nienkerk
ramuva
Ryan Worrell
Stephen Hancock
Tom B.
Randy Lander
Ryvre Hardrick
Stephen Mellor
Tom Burns
Rangaprabhu
   Parthasarathy
Ryvre Hardrick
Stephen R
Tom Ellison
ranti
S. Reblesky
Stergios Botzakis
Tom Leary
RCMason
SabrWolf
Steve
Tom Mayo
rcalrond
sallythetimid
Steve Conley
Tom Shortridge
Rebecca Taylor
Salma Chadha
Steve Higgins
Tom Smith
Reid Garrett Hoffman
Sam Finley
Steve Horton
Tom Stillwell
Rhel
Samantha
Steve Raiteri
Tomas Sanchez
Richard Bruning
Sampsa Virtanen
Steve Stark
Tope Oluwole
Richard Dansky
Samuel A. Rebelsky
Steve VanHorn
Tracy Edmunds
Richard Wolfe
Samuel Beckh
Steven Goldman
Tracy Williams
Rick Paula
Santiago
Steven Hager
Trapper Markelz
Rima M
Santiago Anglé
Stu_1977_SEmelb
Travis White-Schwoch
Risa Shire
Sarah
Sua Thov
Trevor
River Roberts

Sarah
Sue Christensen
Trevor Hirst
Rob Browning
Sarah Ohavis
Sue Mansell
Trey Alexander
Rob M. Worley
Sarah Schanze
Susan
Veronica Wasserman
Rob Valois
Sarah Stanley
Susan Goff
Vesna Jovanovic
Robert Burke
Sarah Stumpf
Suzie Q Sailaway
Victoria Bellisario
Robert Coker
Scryth
Suzy Maidens
Marcinkiewicz
Victoria Landau
Robert E. Stutts
Scott Fogg
Sylvie Juliet Shaffer
Virginia Verner
Robert Jarosinski
Scott Heinowski
T Dedman
Vivian Greene
Robert Young
Scott Wegener
Tawnly Pranger
Wayne Watrach
Robin Brenner
Sean Byrne
teacher_geek
WF
Robin Horman
Sean Hull
Ted Martin
William Diedrich
Robin Nyzio
Sean O'Shea
Ted Pollari
William Hodge
RobPeters
Seth Johnson
tegan zimmerman
William Morland
Robyn Hawk
Seth Thomson
Temoore
Win Bent
Roger Langridge
Shad Bolling
Terri Lindeman
Wong Kum Yew
Rolando Roman
Shahan Panth
Terry Bosky
worlddumbination
Rose Jermusyk
Shannan Starnes Rosa
Terry Hall
Xaak
Rose Mendoza
Shannon Segilola
Terry Kinzer
Yen Yen Woo

Book design by Tim Lynch
Cover Illustration by Chris Giarrusso

Andrews McMeel Publishing, LLC
an Andrews McMeel Universal company
1130 Walnut Street, Kansas City, Missouri 64106

www.andrewsmcmeel.com

www.readingwithpictures.org

14 15 16 17 18 SHO 10 9 8 7 6 5 4 3 2 1

ISBN: 978-1-4494-5878-2

Library of Congress Control Number: 2014932923

Made by:
Shanghai Offset Printing Products Ltd.
Address and place of production:
No. 1320, Xinwei, Liguang Community,
Guanlan Subdistrict, Bao'an District, Shenzhen,
Gaungdong Province, China 518110
1st Printing – 5/19/14

READING with PICTURES

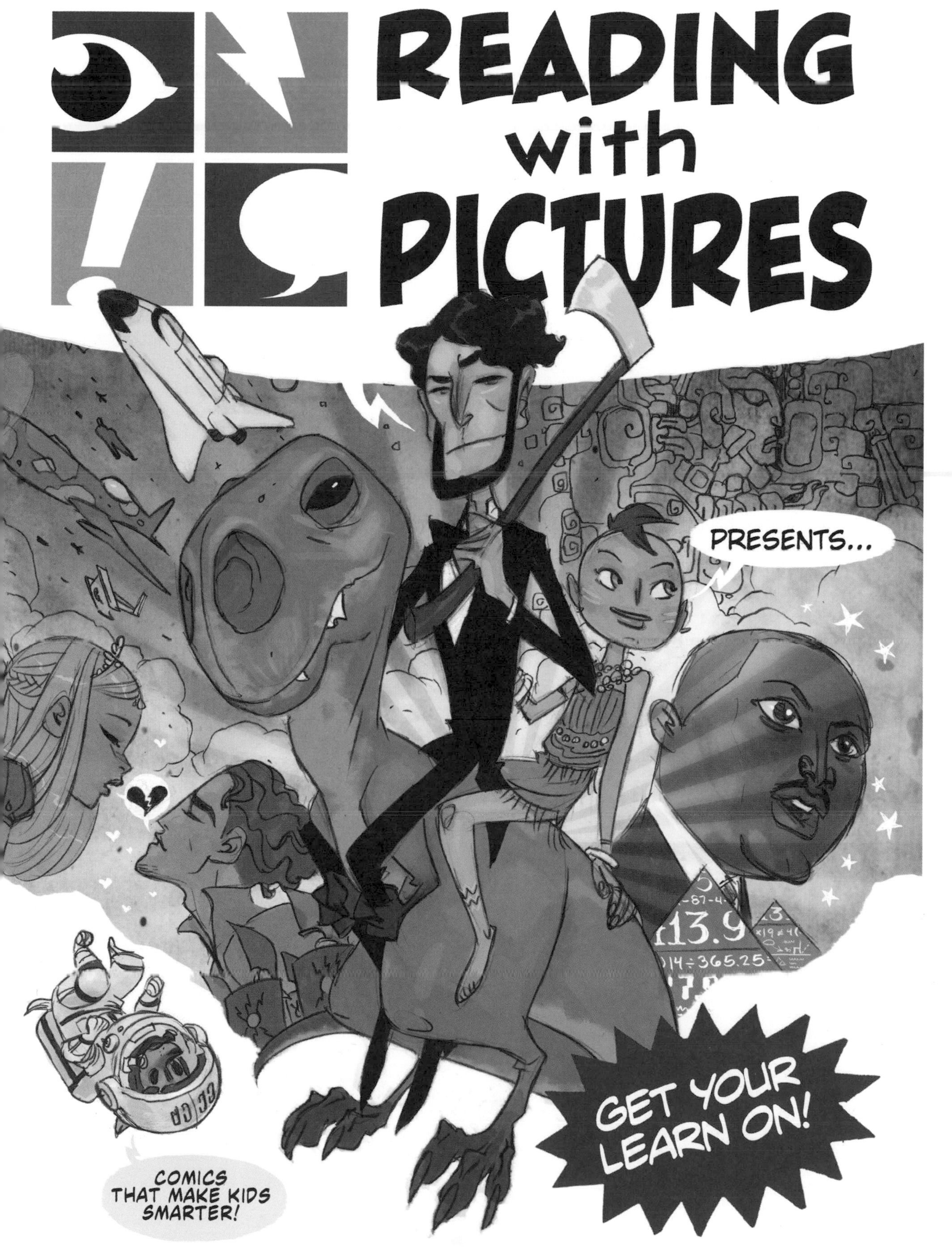
PRESENTS...
GET YOUR LEARN ON!
COMICS THAT MAKE KIDS SMARTER!

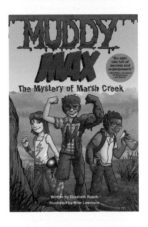
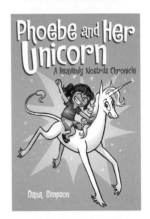
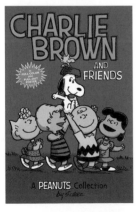